The SABR/LIBOR Market Model

The SABR/LIBOR Market Model
Pricing, Calibration and Hedging for Complex Interest-Rate Derivatives

Riccardo Rebonato
Kenneth McKay
and
Richard White

A John Wiley and Sons, Ltd., Publication

This edition first published 2009
© 2009 Riccardo Rebonato, Kenneth McKay and Richard White

Registered office
John Wiley & Sons Ltd, The Atrium, Southern Gate, Chichester, West Sussex, PO19 8SQ, United Kingdom

For details of our global editorial offices, for customer services and for information about how to apply for permission to reuse the copyright material in this book please see our website at www.wiley.com.

Wiley also publishes its books in a variety of electronic formats. Some content that appears in print may not be available in electronic books.

Designations used by companies to distinguish their products are often claimed as trademarks. All brand names and product names used in this book are trade names, service marks, trademarks or registered trademarks of their respective owners. The publisher is not associated with any product or vendor mentioned in this book. This publication is designed to provide accurate and authoritative information in regard to the subject matter covered. It is sold on the understanding that the publisher is not engaged in rendering professional services. If professional advice or other expert assistance is required, the services of a competent professional should be sought.

ISBN 978-0-470-74005-7(H/B)

A catalogue record for this book is available from the British Library.

Set in 10/12pt Times New Roman by Laserwords Private Ltd, Chennai, India.
Printed in England by CPI Antony Rowe, Chippenham, Wiltshire

Contents

Acknowledgements

It is a pleasure to acknowledge the help provided by many colleagues and friends. In particular, the advice and suggestions of Paul Doust, Andrei Pogudin, Jian Chen, Raphael Albrecht, Dhermider Kainth and Michael Dogwood have been of great help. This book is much the better thanks to them.

We are grateful to John Wiley for agreeing to publish this book, and for the enthusiasm they have shown for the project. Caitlin Cornish has been a most efficient and supportive commissioning editor.

Finally, two of us (RR and KM) cannot help feeling some pangs of envy towards our third co-author, Richard. Unfortunately for us, but probably wisely for him, a few months into the project Richard decided to take a year off to tour the world with his girlfriend. We suspect that the pleasures of proofreading and reference checking may have played a part in making trekking through Siberia appear more attractive than it is normally cracked up to be. Be that as it may, his contribution to this book has been so important that, proofreading or no proofreading, he has earned full authorship, and we feel proud to have him as third co-author. (Just don't do this again, Richard.)

Chapter 1

Introduction

All models are wrong, but some models are useful

We present in this book a financially motivated extension of the LIBOR market model that reproduces for all strikes and maturities the prices of the plain-vanilla hedging instruments (swaptions and caplets) produced by the SABR model. In other words, our extension of the LIBOR market model accurately recovers in a financially motivated manner the whole of the SABR smile surface.

As the SABR model has become the 'market standard' for European options, just the recovery of the smile surface by a dynamic model could be regarded as a useful achievement in itself. However, we have tried to do more. As we have stressed in the opening sentences, we have tried to accomplish this task in a way that we consider financially justifiable.

Our reason for insisting on financial reasonableness is not (just) an aesthetic one. We believe that the quality of a derivatives model should be judged not just on the basis of its ability to price today's hedging instruments, but also on the basis of the quality of the hedges it suggests. We believe that these hedges can be good only if the model is rooted in empirical financial reality. The 'empirical financial reality' of relevance for the pricing and hedging of complex derivatives is the dynamics of the smile surface. We explain below why we believe that this is the case.

We are therefore not just offering yet another model. We present a 'philosophy' of option pricing that takes into account the realities of the industry needs (e.g., the need to calibrate as accurately as possible to the plain-vanilla reference hedging instruments, the need to obtain prices and hedges in reasonable time) while reproducing a realistic future evolution of the smile surface (our 'financial reality').

Until recently choosing between fitting today's prices very accurately and being respectful of 'financial reality' (given our meaning of the term) entailed making hard choices. For instance, some approaches, such as local-volatility modelling (see, e.g., Dupire (1994), Derman and Kani (1994)), fulfilled (by construction) very well the first set of requirements (perfect fitting of today's smile). This made local volatility models very popular with some traders. Yet, the dynamics of the smile these models implied were completely wrong. Indeed, the SABR model, which constitutes the starting point for our extension, was introduced to remedy the wrong *dynamics* imposed by the local-volatility framework.

On the other hand, financially much more palatable models, such as the Variance Gamma model (see, e.g., Madan and Seneta (1990)) and its 'stochastic volatility' extensions (see, e.g., Madan and Carr (1998)), have failed to gain acceptance in the trading rooms because of their computational cost and, above all, the difficulties in achieving a quick and stable calibration to current market prices. These prices may be 'wrong' and the Variance Gamma models 'right', but this is not a discussion the complex derivatives trader is interested in entering into – and probably wisely so.

We believe that these hard choices no longer have to be made. The framework we present recovers almost exactly today's market prices of plain-vanilla options, and at the same time implies a reasonable future evolution for the smile surface. We say 'reasonable' and not 'optimal'. The evolution our model implies is not the 'best' from an econometric point of view. Two of us (RR and RW), for instance, believe that a two-state Markov-chain model for the instantaneous volatility does a much better job at describing how smile surfaces evolve, especially in times of market turmoil. We have published extensively in this area (see, e.g., Rebonato and Kainth (2004) and White and Rebonato (2008)), and our ideas have been well received in academic circles. Yet we are aware that the approach, even after all the numerical tricks we have discovered, remains too awkward for daily use on the trading floor. It is destined to remain 'another interesting model'. This is where the need for realism comes into play. We believe that the extension of the LMM that we present provides a plausible description of our financial reality while retaining tractability, computational speed and ease of calibration.

As we said, we take the SABR model (Hagan *et al.*) as the starting point for our extension of the LMM. This is not just because the SABR model has become the market standard to reproduce the price of European options. It is also because it is a good model for European options. Again, pragmatism certainly played a part in its specification as well. A log-normal choice for the volatility process is not ideal, both from a theoretical and (sometimes) from a computational point of view. However, the great advantages afforded by the ability to have an analytic approximation to the true prices, the ease of calibration and the stability of the fitted parameters have more than offset these drawbacks. The main strength of the SABR model, however, is that it is financially justifiable, not just a fitting exercise: the dynamics it implies for the smile evolution when the underlying changes are fundamentally correct – unlike the dynamics suggested by the even-better-fitting local-volatility model.

If the SABR model is so good, why do we need to tinker with it? The problem with the SABR model is that it treats each European option (caplet, swaption) in isolation – in its own measure. The processes for the various underlyings (the forward rates and swap rates) do not 'talk to each other'. It is not obvious how to link these processes together in a coherent dynamics for the whole yield curve. The situation is strongly reminiscent of the pre-LMM days. In those days market practitioners were using the Black (1976) formula for different caplets and swaptions (each with its own 'implied volatility'), but did not know how to link the processes together for the various forward rates to a coherent, arbitrage-free evolution for the whole yield curve. This is what the LMM achieved: it brought all the forward rates under a single measure, and specified dynamics that, thanks to the no-arbitrage 'drift adjustments', were simultaneously valid for all the underlyings. Complex instruments could then be priced (with a deterministic volatility).

We are trying to do something very similar. With our model we bring the dynamics of the various forward rates *and stochastic volatilities* under a single measure. To ensure absence of arbitrage we also derive 'drift adjustments'. Not surprisingly, these have to be applied both to the forward rates and to their volatilities. When this is done, complex derivatives, which depend on the joint realization of all the relevant forward rates, can now be priced.

All of this is not without a price: when the volatilities become stochastic, there is a whole new set of functions to specify (the volatilities of the volatilities). There is also a whole correlation structure to assign: forward-rate/forward-rate correlations, as in the LMM; but also the forward-rate/volatility and volatility/volatility correlations. For, say, a 10-year, quarterly deal, this could provide a fitting junky with hundreds of parameters to play with. Since implying process parameters from market prices is an inverse problem (which also has to rely on the informational efficiency of the market),[1] we are very wary of this approach. Instead, our philosophy can instead be summarized with the sound bite:

> Imply from market prices what you can (really) hedge, and estimate econometrically what you cannot.

This is for us so important that we must explain what we mean. Ultimately, it goes back to our desire to reproduce the dynamics of the smile surface as well as we (realistically) can.

One may say: 'If the price of an option is equal to the cost of the instruments required for hedging, and if a model, like the local volatility one, reproduces the prices of all of today's hedging options perfectly, what else should a trader worry about?' We agree with the first part of the statement ('the price of an option is equal to the cost of the instruments required for hedging'), but the bit about 'the cost of the instruments required for hedging' refers not just to today's hedging, but *to all the hedging costs incurred throughout the life of the complex deal*. This, after all, is what pricing by dynamic replication is all about. Since volatility (vega) hedging is essential in complex derivatives trading, future re-hedging costs mean future prices of plain-vanilla options (future caplets and swaptions). Future prices of caplets and swaptions means future implied volatilities. Future implied volatilities means future smiles. This is why a plausible evolution of the smile is essential to complex derivatives pricing: it determines the future re-hedging costs that, according to the model, will be incurred during the life of the deal. If a model implies an implausible level or shape for the future smile (as local-volatility models do), it also implies implausible future prices for caplets and swaptions and therefore implausible re-hedging costs.

One of us (RR) has discussed all of this at some length in a recent book (see Rebonato (2004a), Chapter 1 in particular). Since we want to keep this book as concise and to-the-point as possible, we shall not repeat the argument in detail – matters, indeed, are a bit more complex because in a diffusive setting the theoretical status of vega hedging is at the very least dubious. Even here, however, we must say that our argument, despite its plausibility, does not enjoy universal acceptance. There is a school of thought that believes in what we call a 'fully implied' approach. In a nutshell, this approach says something like: 'Fit *all* the plain-vanilla option prices today with your model, without worrying too much whether your chosen model may imply implausible dynamics for the smile; use *all* the plain-vanilla instruments you have fitted to for your hedging; future re-hedging costs may indeed be different from what your model believes; but you will make compensating errors in your complex instrument *and in the hedges*.'

---

[1] See the discussion in Rebonato (2006).

Again, one of us (RR) has argued at length against this view. In brief, the objections are that for the 'all-implied' approach to work option markets must either be perfectly informationally efficient or complete. The first requirement is appealing because it suggests that traders can be spared the hard task of carrying out complicated and painstaking econometric analyses, because the market has already done all this work for them: the information, according to this view, is already all in the prices, and we only have to extract it. While this optimistic view about the informational efficiency of the market may hold in the aggregate about very large, liquid and heavily scrutinized markets (such as the equity or bond markets), it is not obvious that it should be true in every corner of the investment landscape. In particular, it appears to me a bit too good to be true in the complex derivatives arena, as it implies, among other things, that supply and demand cannot affect the level of option prices – and hence of implied volatilities (an 'excess' supply of volatility by, say, investors should have no effect on the clearing levels of implied volatilities because, if it made options too 'cheap', it would entice pseudo-arbitrageurs to come in and restore price to fundamentals). Again, see the discussion by Rebonato (2004a) about this point.

The second line of defence for the 'all-implied' approach is somewhat less ambitious. It simply implies that 'wrong' prices can be 'locked in' by riskless trades – much as one can lock in a forward rate if one can trade in the underlying discount bonds: if one can trade in discount bonds of, say, six and nine months, one can lock in the future borrowing/lending rate without worrying whether this implied level is statistically plausible or not. This view, however, implies that the market in complex derivatives is complete, i.e., that one can notionally trade, or synthetically construct, a security with a unit payment in every single state of the world of relevance for the payoff of the complex security we want to price. But plain-vanilla instruments (caplets and European swaptions) emphatically do *not* span all the states of the world that affect the value of realistically complex derivatives products. The relevant question is therefore how much is left out by the completeness assumption. We believe that the answer is 'far too much'.

Our approach therefore is to calibrate our model as accurately as possible to those instruments we are really going to use in our hedging (this is the 'hedge what we really can' part of our sound bite). We then try to 'guesstimate' as accurately as possible using econometric analysis the remaining relevant features of the future smile (remember, this ultimately means 'of the future re-hedging costs') and to ensure that our calibrated model reflects the gross features of these empirical findings in the whole if not in the detail. This is why we give such great importance to the econometric estimation of the dynamic variables of our models as to devote a whole part of the book (Part III) to the topic.

But, if the future smile is unknown today, what hopes can we have of calibrating our model appropriately, and therefore of guessing correctly the future re-hedging costs? Our hopes lie in the fact that the future smile surface may well be stochastic, but certain regularities *are* readily identifiable. We may not be able to guess exactly which shape the smile surface will assume in the future, but we should make sure that these identifiable regularities are broadly recovered. An informed guess, we believe, is way better than nothing. If the goal seems too modest, let us not forget that the local-volatility model miserably fails even this entry-level test of statistical acceptability.

So, we do not peddle the snake-oil of the 'perfect model with the perfect hedge'. After all, if a substantial degree of uncertainty did not remain even after the best model was used, it would be difficult to explain why, in a competitive market, the margins enjoyed by complex derivatives traders are still so much wider than the wafer-thin margins available in less uncertain, or more readily hedgeable, asset classes. The name of the game therefore is not to hope that we can eliminate all uncertainty (perhaps by deluding ourselves that we can 'lock in' all the current market prices). A more realistic goal for a good model is to offer the ability to reduce the uncertainty to an acceptable minimum by making as judicious a use as possible of the econometric information available.

This is what we believe our modelling approach can offer. And this is why our book is different from most other books on derivatives pricing, which tend to be heavy on stochastic calculus but worryingly thin on empirical analysis.

Finally, we are well aware that there are conditions of market stress that our model 'does not know about'. We therefore propose in the last chapter of our book a pragmatic hedging approach, inspired by the work two of us (RR and RW) have done with the two-state Markov-chain approach mentioned above. This approach can ensure a reasonable hedging strategy even in those situations when the (essentially diffusive) assumptions of our model fail miserably. This will be an unashamedly 'outside-the-model' hedging methodology, whose strength relies on two essential components: the empirical regularities of the dynamics of the smile surface; and the robustness of the fits we propose. As these are two cornerstones of our approach, we believe that we have a chance of succeeding.

Part I

The Theoretical Set-Up

Chapter 2

The LIBOR Market Model

> ... When we have contracted a habitude and intimacy with any [pricing model]; tho' in [using it] we have not been able to discover any very valuable quality, of which [it] is posseess'd; yet we cannot forbear preferring [it] to [new models], of whose superior merit we are fully convinc'd ...
>
> Adapted from David Hume, *A Treatise on Human Nature*, 1740.[1]

In order to make our treatment self-consistent, we review in this chapter the 'standard' (i.e., deterministic-volatility) LIBOR market model (LMM). The most influential original papers published in refereed journals about the LMM were by Brace, Gatarek and Musiela (1997), Jamshidian (1997) and Rutkowski (1998). For a treatment of the topic conceptually aligned with our way of looking at things, see Rebonato (2002) and Rebonato (2004a). For a discussion of the historical development of interest-rate modelling leading to the LMM and beyond, see Rebonato (2004b). In order to set the LMM in the broader modelling context of term-structure models, a very good discussion and many references can be found in Hughston (2003) and Hughston and Brody (2000).

For the purposes of the following discussion, the most important thing to remember is that, despite the name, the LMM is not a *model*; rather, it is a set of no-arbitrage conditions among forward rates (or discount bonds). The precise form of these no-arbitrage conditions depends on the chosen 'unit of account' (the numeraire). As it turns out, these no-arbitrage conditions are purely a function of the volatilities of, and the correlations among, the state variables (in our case, the forward rates). This is because 'physically' the origin of the no-arbitrage condition is the covariance between the payoff and the discounting. In a nutshell the reasoning goes as follows. We can discount cashflows in several different ways (i.e., we can use several different *stochastic* numeraires to relate a future payoff to its values today). These different stochastic numeraires will in general co-vary (positively or negatively) with the same payoff in different ways. For instance, the stochastic discounting might be high just when the payoff is high, thereby reducing its value today, or *vice versa*. However,

---

[1]OK, we have cheated a bit. David Hume was not really talking about pricing models, and his original quote goes as follows: '... When we have contracted a habitude and intimacy with any person; tho' in frequenting his company we have not been able to discover any very valuable quality, of which he is posseess'd; yet we cannot forbear preferring him to strangers, of whose superior merit we are fully convinc'd ...' Still, we think the spirit of the quote remains valid.

the value today of a payoff must be independent of the arbitrary way we have chosen to discount it. It should therefore be intuitive that, in order to obtain a numeraire-independent price, we must somehow adjust the dynamics of the state variable in order to account and compensate for this co-variation. What is needed to go from this intuition to a specific form for the no-arbitrage conditions is just a moderate amount of stochastic-calculus plumbing. This is what we turn to in the following.

2.1   Definitions

We assume that in the economy a discrete set of default-free discount bonds, P_t^i, are traded. We denote the generic instantaneous forward rate at time t, resetting at time T and paying at time $T + \tau$ by $f(t, T, T + \tau)$. The N reset times are indexed and numbered from 1 to N: $T_1, T_2, \ldots, T_N$. If we work with spanning forward rates, the payment time for the ith forward rate coincides with the reset time for the $(i + 1)$th forward rate. The forward rates are then denoted by

$$f(t, T_i, T_{i+1}) = f_t^i, \quad i = 1, 2, \ldots, N \tag{2.1}$$

The instantaneous volatilities of the forward rates are denoted by

$$\sigma(t, T_i) = \sigma_t^i, \quad i = 1, 2, \ldots, N \tag{2.2}$$

The instantaneous correlation between forward rate i and forward rate j is denoted by

$$\rho(t, T_i, T_j) = \rho_{i,j}^t, \quad i, j = 1, 2, \ldots, N \tag{2.3}$$

For discounting a numeraire must be chosen. A valid numeraire must be strictly positive in all states of the world. To make life easier, it is much better if it does not pay dividends or coupons. A possible choice can be a discount bond, $P_t^i = P(t, T_i)$.

The link between the forward rates and the discount bonds introduced above is via the definition:

$$f_t^i = \left(\frac{P_t^i}{P_t^{i+1}} - 1 \right) \frac{1}{\tau_i} \tag{2.4}$$

with

$$\tau_i = T_{i+1} - T_i \tag{2.5}$$

We call τ_i the tenor of the forward rate, but note that this definition is not universal.

The description of the (discrete) yield curve is completed by providing the value of the spot rate, i.e., the rate for lending/borrowing from spot time to T_1, given by

$$r_0 = \left(\frac{1}{P_0^1} - 1 \right) \frac{1}{\tau_1} \tag{2.6}$$

We stress that this set-up provides a description of a *discrete* set of forward rates indexed by a *continuous* time index.

In the deterministic-volatility LMM the evolution of these forward rates is described by equations of the form

$$\frac{df_t^i}{f_t^i} = \mu^i \left(\{f_t\}, \{\sigma_t\}, \rho, t \right) dt + \sigma^i (t, T_i) dz_t^i \tag{2.7}$$

with

$$\mathbb{E}\left[dz_t^i dz_t^j \right] = \rho(t, T_i, T_j) \, dt \tag{2.8}$$

Here f_t is the vector of spanning forward rates that constitute the yield curve, σ_t the vector of the associated volatilities, and ρ the matrix of the associated correlations. Note that, in principle, the functions $\sigma^i(t, T_i)$ need not be the same for different forward rates; we have therefore used a superscript to identify the possibly different volatility functions. If these functions *are* the same for all the forward rates, and if the dependence on t and T_i of this common function (say, $\sigma(\cdot)$) is of the form

$$\sigma(t, T_i) = \sigma(T_i - t) \tag{2.9}$$

then the LMM is said to be time homogeneous. This is important, because, as explained at length in Rebonato (2002), in this case the future smile surface will exactly 'look like' today's smile surface. If this can be achieved, it is (most of the time) a very desirable feature, for the reasons explained in the Introduction.[2]

Finally, note that, with a slight abuse of notation, we will often denote these time-homogeneous functions as

$$\sigma(T_i - t) = \sigma_t^i \tag{2.10}$$

In this equation the superscript i or T_i now denotes the dependence on the expiry of the forward rate, T_i, of the *same* volatility function for all the forward rates. So, in the time-homogenous formulation, at a given time t, the volatilities of two forward rates differ only because they have different times to expiry – i.e., they are at different times of their otherwise identical 'life'. This is what makes the smile surface time invariant.

As for the drifts, $\mu^i \left(\{f_t\}, \{\sigma_t\}, \rho, t \right)$, which appear in Equation (2.7), these will be derived in a unified manner when dealing with the LMM-SABR model.

2.2   The Volatility Functions

There are, of course, many financially plausible functions that satisfy Equation (2.10) above. One of us (RR) has explained at length in Rebonato (2002) and Rebonato (2004a) why the

---

[2] See, however, the discussion in Chapter 15.

following specification provides a good choice:

$$\sigma_t^T = [a + b(T - t)]\exp[-c(T - t)] + d =$$

$$[a + b(\tau)]\exp[-c(\tau)] + d \qquad \tau = T - t \qquad\qquad (2.11)$$

A selction of possible shapes of this functional form is shown in Figure 2.1. Summarizing briefly, this functional form has the following properties.

- It allows for a monotonically decaying or for a humped volatility function. This is desirable because Rebonato (2002) and Rebonato (2004a) explain that a humped volatility should be appropriate for normal trading periods and a monotonically decaying one for excited periods. In a nutshell, the argument points to the fact that, in normal market times, the actions of the monetary authorities are such that the maximum uncertainty in the value of rates is found neither in immediately resetting forward rates, nor in forward rates with very long expiries. It is in the intermediate-maturity range that the uncertainty should be greatest. In Part III we present empirical evidence to buttress the claims made in the references above.

- It is, of course, square-integrable and allows for closed-form solutions of the integrals of its square. As we shall see, this is important because these integrals are linked to the pricing of plain-vanilla and complex instruments.

- Its parameters lend themselves to an easy interpretation. For instance, $a + d$ is the value of the instantaneous volatility of any forward rate as its expiry approaches zero; d is the value of the instantaneous volatility for very long maturities; the maximum of the hump, if the choice of parameters allows for one, is given by $\widetilde{\tau} = \frac{1}{c} - \frac{a}{b}$. If we believe in the 'financial story' presented in the references above, we can check whether our market-fitted parameters are consistent with it. Also, we can compare the position of the maximum obtained from these market fits with the econometric evidence presented in Part III of this book.

- When market fits are carried out for at-the-money swaptions or caplets, 'natural' fits are obtained, with parameters that lend themselves to the financial interpretation above.

- When coupled with a simple correlation function, the functional form (2.11) describes well and in a parsimonious manner the whole at-the-money swaption surface. See, for instance, the studies by Rebonato (2006) and White and Rebonato (2008).

    For these reasons, this is the particular functional form that we shall use, and expand upon, in this book. However, there is no loss of generality in doing so, and all of our treatment would still hold if any other form for the time-homogeneous function $g(\cdot)$ were used.

2.3   Separating the Correlation from the Volatility Term

Let us go back to Equation (2.7) and rewrite it as

$$\frac{df_t^i}{f_t^i} = \mu^i\left(\{f_t\}, \{\sigma_t\}, t\right)dt + \sum_{k=1}^{m} \sigma_{ik}dz_k \qquad\qquad (2.12)$$

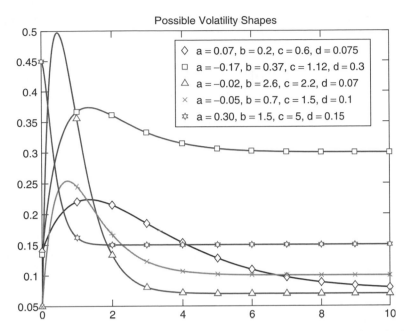

Figure 2.1 Possible shapes of the volatility function in Equation (2.11). Note how both 'excited' (series 5) and 'normal' states (series 1 to 4) can be obtained.

where we now assume that we are dealing with m ($m \leq N$) factors and that the Brownian increments are independent:

$$\mathbb{E}\left[dz_j dz_k\right] = \delta_{jk} dt \tag{2.13}$$

where δ_{ij} is the Kronecker delta ($\delta_{ij} = 1$ for $i = j$ and 0 otherwise). The quantities σ_{ik} can be interpreted as the loadings of the ith forward rate onto the kth factor. Clearly, because of this independence, the relationship between the volatility σ_i and the loadings σ_{ik} is given by

$$\sigma_i(t) = \sqrt{\sum_{k=1}^{m} \sigma_{ik}^2(t)} \tag{2.14}$$

If we have chosen the function in such a way that the relationship

$$\int_0^{T_i} \sigma_i(t)^2 dt = \widehat{\sigma}_i^2 T_i \tag{2.15}$$

holds true, then the market caplets will be correctly priced. (In the equation above, and everywhere in the book, the quantity $\widehat{\sigma}$ represents the Black implied volatility – recall that, for the moment, we are dealing with a world without smiles.) For this reason we call Equation (2.14) the caplet-pricing condition.

Let us now multiply and divide each loading σ_{ik} by the volatility, σ_i, of the ith forward rate:

$$\frac{df_t^i}{f_t^i} = \mu^i \left(\{\mathbf{f}_t\}, \{\sigma_t\}, t\right) dt + \sigma_i \sum_{k=1}^{m} \frac{\sigma_{ik}}{\sigma_i} dz_k \qquad (2.16)$$

Making use of the caplet-pricing condition, this can be rewritten as

$$\frac{df_t^i}{f_t^i} = \mu^i \left(\{\mathbf{f}_t\}, \{\sigma_t\}, t\right) dt + \sigma_i \sum_{k=1}^{m} \frac{\sigma_{ik}}{\sqrt{\sum_{k'=1}^{m} \sigma_{ik'}^2}} dz_k \qquad (2.17)$$

If we now define the quantity b_{ik} as

$$b_{ik} \equiv \frac{\sigma_{ik}}{\sqrt{\sum_{k'=1}^{m} \sigma_{ik'}^2}} \qquad (2.18)$$

Equation (2.17) can be expressed in a more compact way as

$$\frac{df^i}{f^i} = \mu^i \left(\{\mathbf{f}_t\}, \{\sigma_t\}, t\right) dt + \sigma_i \sum_{k=1}^{m} b_{ik} dz_k \qquad (2.19)$$

Let us now denote by $\mathbf{b}$ the $[N \times m]$ matrix of elements b_{jk}. It can be readily shown that the correlation matrix can be expressed as

$$\mathbf{b}\mathbf{b}^{\mathrm{T}} = \rho \qquad (2.20)$$

Expression (2.19) is very useful. It tells us that we can decompose the stochastic part of the evolution of the forward rate into a component, σ_i, that only depends on the volatility (and that we may want to hedge with caplets), and a component, the matrix $\mathbf{b}$, that only affects the correlation (and that we may want to use for historical fitting). The link between the loadings b_{ik} and the prices of caplets is shown below.

2.4   The Caplet-Pricing Condition Again

We have stated above that in a smile-less world the instantaneous and implied Black volatilities are linked by the relationship

$$\widehat{\sigma}_i^2 T_i = \int_0^{T_i} \sigma(u, T_i)^2 du \qquad (2.21)$$

If Equation (2.21) is satisfied, the Black price of the ith caplet is exactly recovered. If we have chosen the function $g(T_i - t)$ in such a way that its root-mean-square is equal to the

Black volatility, the caplet-pricing condition

$$\sum_{k=1,m} \sigma_{jk}^2 = \sigma_j^2 \qquad (2.22)$$

simply becomes

$$\sum_{k=1,m} b_{jk}^2 = 1 \qquad (2.23)$$

Suppose now that the function $g(\cdot)$ is parametrized by a set of coefficients, perhaps the parameters $\{a, b, c, d\}$ discussed above. For any given parametrization one can check, for each forward rate, whether the integral of the square of the instantaneous volatility out to the expiry of the forward rate does coincide with the total Black variance. For the functional form for $g(\cdot)$ specified above, this means checking whether the relationship[3]

$$\widehat{\sigma}_{T_i}^2 T_i = \int_0^{T_i} ([a + b(\tau)] \exp[-c(\tau)] + d)^2 \, d\tau \qquad (2.24)$$

holds true.

In general, a given set of parameters $\{a, b, c, d\}$ will not allow the exact fulfilment of condition (2.24) for more than four forward rates. Therefore, even in a world without smiles, the same set of parameters $\{a, b, c, d\}$ will not recover the Black caplet prices of all the forward rates. In order to achieve the exact recovery of the prices of all of today's caplet prices, we associate to each forward rate a different scaling factor, k_{T_i}, defined as

$$k_{T_i}^2 = \frac{\widehat{\sigma}_{T_i}^2 T_i}{\int_0^{T_i} ([a + b(\tau)] \exp[-c(\tau)] + d)^2 \, d\tau} \qquad (2.25)$$

and write for the forward-rate-specific instantaneous volatility function

$$\sigma_t^i = k_{T_i} [a + b(T_i - t)] \exp[-c(T_i - t)] + d \qquad (2.26)$$

By introducing this forward-rate-specific scaling factor the caplet condition is therefore fulfilled by construction everywhere along the curve.

We note that the introduction of the forward-rate-specific scaling factors $\{k_{T_i}\}$ makes the evolution of the term structure of volatilities no longer strictly time homogeneous – this is clear, because the scaling factors are not functions of the *residual*, but of the *initial* time to maturity. This will be an acceptable price to pay for a perfect (smile-less) fit only to the extent that all the quantities $\{k_{T_i}\}$ will turn out to be close to 1 (or, actually, to any constant). Indeed, in practice this works very well, and one of us (RR) has shown at length (see, e.g., Rebonato (2002) and Rebonato (2004a)) that imposing the condition that all the

---

[3] In Equation (2.24) the integration is over $\tau = T - t$, and the lower and upper limits of integration are therefore T and 0, respectively.

scaling terms $\{k_{T_i}\}$ should be as close as possible to 1 is a very good way to parametrize the function $g(\cdot)$.

Despite the fact that the scaling terms $\{k_{T_i}\}$ are unashamedly 'fudge factors' that, in a perfect world, we would gladly do without, these quantities will turn out to be crucial for the stochastic-volatility extension that we present in Chapter 4.

In sum: we have split the stochastic part of the evolution of the forward rates into a component, related to caplet prices, that purely depends on the volatility and a component that purely depends on the correlation. It is to this second part that we now turn.

2.5   The Forward-Rate/Forward-Rate Correlation

In the deterministic-volatility LMM the correlation matrix has always been the poor relation of the volatility function. When we move to the LMM-SABR model a lot more care must be given to the specification of the correlation surface. We therefore begin to look at it in more detail than is usually done with the standard LMM even if we are still in a deterministic-volatility setting.

2.5.1   The Simple Exponential Correlation

The simplest functional form for a correlation function is possibly the following:

$$\rho(t, T_i, T_j) = \exp[-\beta|T_i - T_j|] \qquad t \leq \min(T_i, T_j) \qquad (2.27)$$

with T_i, T_j the expiries of the ith and jth forward rates, and β a positive constant. By Equation (2.27) the farther apart two forward rates are, the more decorrelated they are. Furthermore, for any positive β one can rest assured that the corresponding matrix ρ will always be an admissible correlation matrix (i.e., a real, symmetric matrix with positive eigenvalues).

These two desirable features are naturally recovered by Equation (2.27). What expression (2.27) does not handle well is the fact that two forward rates, separated by the same 'distance', $T_i - T_j$, will decorrelate just as much irrespective of the expiry of the first. So, according to the parametrization (2.27), the decorrelation between the forward rates expiring in 1 and 2 years' time is the same as the decorrelation between the forward rates expiring in 29 and 30 years' time. As we show in Part III (Empirical results), this is empirically a very poor approximation.

Why has this functional form been used so often? The reason is that, despite this financial blemish, it has an important computational advantage: in the LIBOR market model the following quantities (covariance elements)

$$C(i, j, k) = \int_{T_k}^{T_{k+1}} \sigma_u^i \sigma_u^j \rho(u, T_i, T_j) du \qquad (2.28)$$

play an essential role, as they enter the drift for the forward rates and must be calculated, either implicitly or explicitly, to evaluate any complex payoff. Note, however, that if the correlation function ρ_{ij} is of the form (2.27), there is no explicit time dependence on the integration time variable in Equation (2.28): $\rho(t, T_i, T_k) = \rho(T_i, T_k) = \rho_{ij}$. Therefore one can write

$$C(i, j, k) = \rho_{ij} \int_{T_k}^{T_{k+1}} \sigma_u^i \sigma_u^j \, du \qquad (2.29)$$

If one chooses a sufficiently simple functional form for the instantaneous volatility (such as the one discussed above), the integral (2.29) can be pre-calculated analytically. This can lighten the computational burden considerably.

Whether the unpleasant financial features of the functional form (2.27) are important or not depends on the instrument being priced. Rebonato (2002) argues at length that for European swaptions the dependence of their price on the specific functional form of the correlation function is modest.[4] However, for products like CMS spread options a satisfactory description of the dependence of the decorrelation factor, β, on the expiry of the forward rates can be very important. See again the empirical data presented in Part III. For this reason we present an alternative functional form in the following section.

2.5.2   The Multiplicative Correlation

Several ways to improve on the simple specification (2.27) have been proposed. See, e.g., Schoenmakers and Coffey (2000). We have identified the problem with the simple correlation function to be the fact that the decorrelation (brought about by the exponential decay β) only depends on the distance between two forward rates. To overcome this problem the challenge is therefore to introduce a dependence of the decorrelation factor, β, on the expiries of the forward rates, $\beta = \beta(T_i, T_j)$, in such a way that the resulting correlation matrix remains real, symmetric and positive definite.

A simple way to achieve this goal is the following. Consider, for simplicity, a 5×5 real symmetric matrix. In general it could have 10 (i.e., $\frac{n^2 - n}{2}$) independent elements. If we assign these 10 elements as we wish (keeping them, of course, between -1 and 1) there is no guarantee that the resulting matrix will be positive definite, i.e., that it will be a valid correlation matrix. However, if we only specify $(5 - 1)$ quantities, a_1, a_2, a_3 and a_4 (keeping them, of course, again between -1 and 1) and these are linked as in the matrix below:

$$\begin{bmatrix} 1 & a_1 & a_1 a_2 & a_1 a_2 a_3 & a_1 a_2 a_3 a_4 \\ a_1 & 1 & a_2 & a_2 a_3 & a_2 a_3 a_4 \\ a_1 a_2 & a_2 & 1 & a_3 & a_3 a_4 \\ a_1 a_2 a_3 & a_2 a_3 & a_3 & 1 & a_4 \\ a_1 a_2 a_3 a_4 & a_2 a_3 a_4 & a_3 a_4 & a_4 & 1 \end{bmatrix} \qquad (2.30)$$

then it is easy to show (Doust, 2007) that the resulting real symmetric matrix *is* always positive definite, i.e., it is a possible correlation matrix. (We note in passing that this result is similar in spirit to the construction in Schoenmakers and Coffey (2000).) This is because

---

[4]That is why it is so difficult to extract information about the correlation function from the market prices of European swaptions.

the matrix (2.30) admits Cholesky decomposition

$$
\begin{bmatrix}
1 & 0 & 0 & 0 & 0 \\
a_1 & \sqrt{1-a_1^2} & 0 & 0 & 0 \\
a_1 a_2 & a_2\sqrt{1-a_1^2} & \sqrt{1-a_2^2} & 0 & 0 \\
a_1 a_2 a_3 & a_2 a_3 \sqrt{1-a_1^2} & a_3 \sqrt{1-a_2^2} & \sqrt{1-a_3^2} & 0 \\
a_1 a_2 a_3 a_4 & a_2 a_3 a_4 \sqrt{1-a_1^2} & a_3 a_4 \sqrt{1-a_2^2} & a_4 \sqrt{1-a_3^2} & \sqrt{1-a_4^2}
\end{bmatrix}
\tag{2.31}
$$

The condition such that this gives a valid correlation matrix is that all the elements along the main diagonal be real. This is always going to be the case, for instance, if the a_is are chosen so that

$$
-1 \le a_i \le 1 \quad \text{for any } i
\tag{2.32}
$$

This is a very simple condition to satisfy.[5]

In order to be sure that one is constructing a valid $[n \times n]$ correlation matrix one can therefore proceed as follows. First of all we fill in the elements on the diagonal:

$$
\rho_{ii} = 1
\tag{2.33}
$$

We then define the elements in the first row by the relationship

$$
\rho_{1,j} = \prod_{k=1}^{j-1} a_k = \rho_{j,1}, \quad j = 2, \ldots, n
\tag{2.34}
$$

By inspection (assuming $i > j$) we then note that

$$
\rho_{i,j} = \frac{\rho_{1,i}}{\rho_{j,1}} = \frac{\rho_{1,i}}{\rho_{1,j}} = \frac{\prod_{k=1}^{i-1} a_k}{\prod_{k=1}^{j-1} a_k} = \prod_{k=j}^{i-1} a_k
\tag{2.35}
$$

Finally, the elements in the upper triangle of the correlation matrix are determined by the symmetry relationship: $\rho_{ij} = \rho_{ji}$. So, given the $(n-1)$ quantities a_i, $i = 1, 2, \ldots, n-1$, we know how to build a valid $[n \times n]$ correlation matrix.

The question that remains outstanding is: how do we choose the quantities a_i? The answer depends on how smooth we want our resultant correlation matrix to be: too many parameters may well give a better fit, but we risk chasing unavoidable numerical noise.

---

[5]In general, the elements of the forward–forward correlation matrix are likely to be all positive and hence the condition in practice will often be $0 < a_i \le 1$ for all i.

When all the elements of the correlation matrix are positive (this is a plausible case for forward rates) the following is a systematic way to proceed.

Let us write

$$a_k = \exp[-\beta_k \Delta T] \tag{2.36}$$

where ΔT is the spacing between forward rates. Then

$$\rho_{i,j} = \prod_{k=j}^{i-1} a_k = \prod_{k=j}^{i-1} \exp[-\beta_k \Delta T] = \exp\left[-\sum_{k=j}^{i-1} \beta_k \Delta T\right] \tag{2.37}$$

This is nice because when $\beta_k = \beta_0$ for all ks the expression above becomes

$$\rho_{i,j}^0 = \exp\left[-(i-j)\beta_0 \Delta T\right] = \exp\left[-\beta_0 |T_i - T_j|\right] \tag{2.38}$$

i.e., the 'traditional' exponentially decaying correlation function (2.27). The 'physical' meaning of this choice is that every additional increment ΔT of distance from *any* forward rate brings about exactly the same degree of decorrelation, $\exp[-\beta_0 \Delta T]$. When all the β_ks are identical, it is easy to see that this corresponds exactly to the simple exponential correlation.

Then, as we give further flexibility to the dependence of the quantities β_k on k we gain the ability to specify that the degree of decorrelation between the jth and kth forward rates should depend on the expiry of the first of the two rates. For instance, if we believe that the decorrelation between, say, the ninth and tenth forward rates should be less pronounced than the decorrelation between the first and second, this will simply be reflected in the requirement that

$$\exp[-\beta_1 \Delta T] < \exp[-\beta_9 \Delta T] \quad \Rightarrow \beta_1 > \beta_9$$

We can systematically increase the flexibility of our model correlation function by requiring, for instance, that the dependence of the quantities β_k on k should progress to take on a wider range of functional forms. Note, however, that we do not only want β_k to be a (weakly) decreasing function in k. We must also require $\beta_k > 0$ for all k to ensure the conditions on a_i. A linear or quadratic function does not automatically guarantee this easily. However, if we choose $\beta_k = g_0 + g_1/k + g_2/k^2 + \ldots$ for positive g_i, then the β_k are both decreasing in k and always positive. Obviously, alternative forms are also possible with the maximum flexibility, of course, corresponding to the case when all the $(n-1)$ quantities $\beta_1, \beta_2, \ldots, \beta_{n-1}$ are allowed to be 'fitting parameters'.

We will discuss in Part III how well this functional form can describe real correlation matrices (the answer, as we shall see, is 'very well'–otherwise we would not have bothered presenting the approach...). For the moment, we present the types of correlation shapes that can be produced by the Doust formulation.

2.6 Possible Shapes of the Doust Correlation Function

We show in this section the shapes of the correlation surface that the Doust correlation function can naturally assume. Figure 2.2 displays the case when every a_i is set equal to

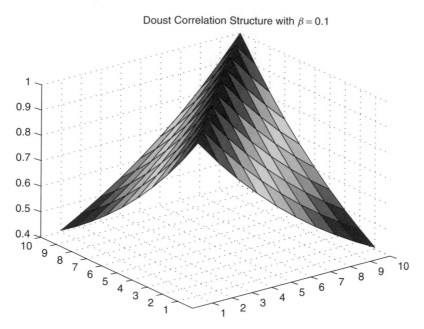

Figure 2.2   Doust correlation structure with $\beta_1 = 1$.

the same value:

$$a_i = \exp[-\beta_9 \Delta T] \qquad (2.39)$$

It is easy to see that, in this simple case, we indeed recover the exponentially decaying surface more traditionally described by the function

$$\rho(t, T_i, T_k) = \exp[-\beta |T_i - T_j|] \qquad t \leq \min(T_i, T_j) \qquad (2.40)$$

The interesting features of the Doust function are displayed in Figure 2.3, obtained with the $a_i = \exp[-\beta_i]$ in Table 2.1 (and an equal spacing of $\Delta T = 1$ year).

Here we clearly see that the shape of the correlation surface, when looked at down the main diagonal, changes from convex at the 'front', to concave at the 'back'. This is indeed what intuition and empirical evidence (see Chapter 10) tell us should happen.

Finally, a very simple and very useful generalization of the Doust correlation function can always be introduced at 'no extra cost'. In fact we can always impose that the long-term decorrelation among forward rates should not go asymptotically to zero with increasing 'distance', but to some finite level, *LongCorr*, simply by rewriting the original correlation function, $\widehat{\rho}_{ij}(t)$, in the form

$$\rho_{ij}(t) = LongCorr + (1 - LongCorr)\widehat{\rho}_{ij}(t) \qquad (2.41)$$

If the matrix $\widehat{\rho}_{ij}(t)$ is a valid correlation matrix, one can rest assured that so is the matrix $\rho_{ij}(t)$, at least as long as $LongCorr > 0$.

This extension is so simple and so useful that in the following we will implicitly assume that it is always carried out.

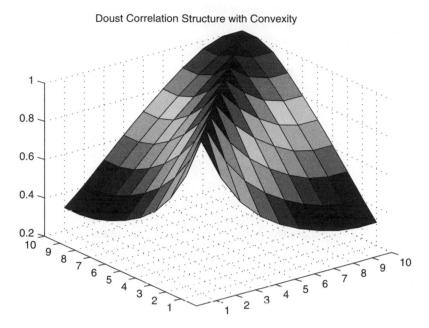

Doust Correlation Structure with Convexity

Figure 2.3 Doust correlation structure with convexity.

Table 2.1 The quantities β_i used to obtain Figure 2.3

β_i	$a_i = \exp[-\beta_i]$
0.250	0.7788
0.220	0.8025
0.180	0.8353
0.145	0.8650
0.120	0.8869
0.100	0.9048
0.080	0.9231
0.040	0.9608
0.001	0.9990

2.7 The Covariance Integral Again

Consider again integrals of the type

$$C(i, j, k) = \int_{T_k}^{T_{k+1}} \sigma_u^i \sigma_u^j \rho(u, T_i, T_j) du \equiv I_k \qquad (2.42)$$

As mentioned above, these integrals appear in the drifts of the forward rates in the LIBOR market model, and are the computational bottlenecks for the Monte Carlo evolution of the state variables (typically the forward rates). However, the ability to 'pull' the correlation out of the integral is lost as soon as any other functional form, other than linear, is chosen for the dependence of the correlation on the running time to maturity $T_i - s$. Even if one simply looks at time-homogeneous functions, for any correlation function expressed as a function of the difference of functions $g(\cdot)$ other than a linear function

$$\rho_{ij}(T_i - t, T_j - t) = f\left[g\left(T_i - t\right) - g\left(T_j - t\right)\right] \tag{2.43}$$

the dependence on t makes the integral unlikely to be analytically feasible. (Clearly, if $g(t, T_i) = \alpha + \beta(T_i - t)$, $g(T_i - t) - g(T_j - t) = \beta(T_i - T_j)$.)

Consider now Equation (2.37), which describes the Doust correlation between a forward rate *exactly* of maturity T_i and another forward rate *exactly* of maturity T_j. As real or simulation time goes by, the distance between the two forward rates remains the same, but, since in the Doust model (and in reality) the correlation does not purely depend on their distance, the correlation between the two rates will change. We therefore can no longer pull the correlation out of the integral.

We can see more clearly what happens as follows. First of all note that, as the clock moves from time T_0 to time T_1, the correlation matrix evolves from the correlation seen at time T_0 to the same correlation with the last row and column dropped. If we keep the labels for the forward rates the same as at time T_0, then at time T_1 the correlation between forward rates, say, 4 and 5, is the same as the correlation between forward rates 3 and 4 at time T_1. It is exactly because of this self-similarity that we can call the Doust correlation function time homogeneous. If our simulation uses steps as large as the spacing between the resets of forward rates (and we 'freeze all quantities at the start of their values at the start of the time step'), it is therefore easy to see that in the discrete-time Euler approximation calendar time does not enter the covariance integral.

With deterministic-volatility LMM it is easy to use computational 'tricks' (see, e.g., Hunter, Jaeckel and Joshi (2001) or Joshi and Stacey (2006)) that make such long-stepping numerically feasible. With a stochastic-volatility LMM, however, the step size cannot be too long, because it must be sufficiently fine to allow the forward rate to 'feel' the variation of the stochastic volatility. This being the case, one often has to take intermediate Monte Carlo steps in between reset times – the more so, the longer the tenor of the forward rate. This therefore raises the question of what happens to the correlation matrix at these 'in between' times.

To see matters clearly, let's now denote by $a_i^j(t)$ the decorrelation for times t between T_j and T_{j+1} between the forward rates labelled at time T_0 by $i - 1$ and i:

$$a_i^j(t) \quad \text{for } T_j \leq t \leq T_{j+1} \tag{2.44}$$

So, the quantities given by Equations (2.33) to (2.35) are given in the new notation by $a_i^0(T_0)$. If we then use the mapping from a_i to the β_i in Equation (2.36), the problem can be recast in terms of what happens to the decaying constants β_i as time moves in between reset times. We therefore similarly define

$$\beta_i^j(t) \quad \text{for } T_j \leq t \leq T_{j+1} \tag{2.45}$$

With this definition it is reasonable to require that, to first order,[6]

$$\beta_i^j(t) = \beta_{i-1-j}^0 \frac{t - T_j}{T_{j+1} - T_j} + \beta_{i-j}^0 \frac{T_{j+1} - t}{T_{j+1} - T_j} \quad \text{for } T_j \leq t \leq T_{j+1} \quad (2.46)$$

So, the decaying constant, $\beta_i^j(t)$, and hence the decorrelation factors, $a_i^j(t)$, and hence the whole correlation matrix, $\rho_{ij}(t)$, can all be expressed for any intermediate time between resets as a function of the initial decaying constants and calendar time (and, of course, the reset times). The expression is very simple and linear in the integration time t. Depending on the functional form chosen for the instantaneous volatility function, it may still allow analytic integration of the covariance integral. But even if this is not the case, not everything is lost. If one wanted to avoid the numerical integration of the covariance elements, one could store in memory (computer memory, that is) pre-calculated correlation matrices evaluated at the intermediate time steps. This is not as awful as it sounds because of the time homogeneity of the correlation matrix. One simply has to store as many correlation matrices as there are time steps per tenor (so, for a quarterly tenor and a monthly time step this would mean storage of three correlation matrices). After the first reset, everything will look exactly the same again, at least for evenly spaced forward rates.

---

[6]The linear approximation that we make here is the reason for working with the decaying constants, $\beta_i^j(t)$, rather than with the decorrelation factors, $a_i^j(t)$.

Chapter 3

The SABR Model

3.1 The SABR Model (and Why it is a Good Model)

The SABR model is very well explained in the paper by Hagan *et al.* (2002). This is an excellent and very clearly written paper, and we only report the main results here for completeness. Unlike much of the current literature, the approach by Hagan and colleagues does not just provide a clever approximation for an option pricing problem, but places the topic in a clear context of trading, hedging and modelling relevance. It explains clearly why, even for European options, 'just fitting' today's market prices (no matter how well) is not good enough. One can compare the SABR model with another all-fitting approach (the local-volatility model). Despite the fact that the latter fits (by construction) the market even better, Hagan and his coauthors explain clearly why it is nonetheless not a good idea to hedge even European options using a local-volatility approach. This is because the latter predicts that the smile will move when the underlying moves in ways that are not borne out in market reality. This is an empirical issue, not a theoretical one that can be settled by looking at the quality of *today's fit* to the market.

Let us expand on this point a bit, because we think it is a crucial one. The superiority of the SABR over the local-volatility model is not an *a priori* theoretical one. It could have been that the world was such that option prices change with the underlying as predicted by the local-volatility model. If this had been the case, there would be no value in the SABR model, and it would make sense to use the local-volatility approach. This is not a question that can be settled by looking at today's smile (that tells us about changes in option prices versus *strike*, as opposed to changes in option prices as the *underlying* moves). Hedging has everything to do with smile dynamics and very little to do with the risk-neutral density (which is predicted to be virtually the same by the local-volatility and the SABR models). Once again, the reader would benefit from reading the original work by Hagan *et al.* where these ideas are clearly discussed. See also Rebonato (2002) and (2004a, especially Chapter 12) where one of us (RR) expands on these concepts at greater length than we want to do here.

3.2   Description of the Model

In the SABR model the underlying (in our case, a forward rate, f_t^T, of expiry T) follows the dynamics[1]

$$df_t^T = \left(f_t^T\right)^{\beta^T} \sigma_t^T dz_t^T \tag{3.1}$$

$$\frac{d\sigma_t^T}{\sigma_t^T} = v^T dw_t^T \tag{3.2}$$

$$E^{\mathbb{Q}^T}\left[dz_t^T dw_t^T\right] = \rho^T \tag{3.3}$$

The model is fully specified once we add to the equations above the initial conditions f_0^T and σ_0^T. It is a CEV model augmented by stochastic volatility.

A few observations are in order.

1. We are working in the (terminal) measure, $\mathbb{Q}^T$, under which both the forward rate and its volatility are martingales (driftless). We can always do this if we work with one forward rate in isolation at a time. Under this same measure, however, the process for another forward rate and for its volatility would not be driftless. We will derive the appropriate drifts in Chapter 4.

2. All the parameters of the model, v^T, β^T and ρ^T, are just constants, not functions of time.

3. All the parameters of the model, v^T, β^T and ρ^T, are specific to a particular forward rate. To make this clear we have appended the superscript T.

4. We have indicated that the increments dz_t^T and dw_t^T are the increments of *standard* Brownian motions under the measure $\mathbb{Q}^T$ by appending the same superscript T. This should be understood as a shorthand notation for $dz_t^{\mathbb{Q}^T}$ and $dw_t^{\mathbb{Q}^T}$. Since each forward rate defines uniquely the terminal measure, $\mathbb{Q}^T$, under which its process is driftless, there is no ambiguity in using the lighter notation.

5. Within the SABR model there is no way for the various forward rates to interact with each other (for instance, we cannot use the SABR model to determine the payoff of a path-dependent option). Each forward rate lives in its own measure and does not know anything about the other forward rates. The SABR model as it stands cannot describe the dynamics of a yield curve.

6. There is no mean reversion in the process for the volatility. Again, since we are looking at one forward rate at a time, this is not necessarily a problem, as long as the

---

[1]A remark on notation. In the original paper, the symbol α was chosen for the volatility in order to create a catchy acronym – S is the typical symbol for the underlying, β is common enough for exponents and ρ is the near-universal choice for correlations. If you string them together – with the peculiar choice of symbol for the volatility – it (almost) reads SABR.

Now, we like a nice acronym as much as the next man – and one of us is guilty of calling his molecular dynamics optimization code ROSAMUND, an acronym not coincidentally identical to the name of his now-wife. However, almost nothing will convince us of the merit of changing the time-honoured convention of calling volatilities σ. So, *pace* Hagan and friends, in this book the SABR volatility will be called σ, not α. Sorry.

correct *terminal* distribution is obtained for the forward rate at hand. The existence of a 'term structure' of parameters, v^T, β^T and ρ^T, is not *a priori* an indication of model mis-specification, because, for each forward rate, the set $\{v^T \ \beta^T \ \rho^T\}$ could be regarded as providing a reduced-form description of a possibly more complex process. Again, as long as this reduced-form model parametrized by the parameters $\{v^T \ \beta^T \ \rho^T\}$ is capable of reproducing the correct terminal (time-T) distribution for the forward rate f_t^T, there are no conceptual flaws in the approach.

Points 2, 3, 5, are crucial to the development that we present in Chapter 4. This being the case, it is worthwhile expanding on this aspect a bit.

What do we mean by 'reduced form'? By this we mean that the *constant, forward-rate-specific* SABR parameters could be some average, integral or, in general, some more complex *functions* of forward-rate-*independent* latent variables. Perhaps the true description of how all the forward rates evolve entails a set of forward-rate-independent mean-reverting processes for the volatilities. If this were true, the forward-rate-specific volatility of volatility, v^T, would be just a function of, say, the same reversion speed and reversion level that apply to all the forward rates. Or, perhaps, the true volatility of the volatility is a time-homogeneous function of the time to expiry of the forward rate, and v^T is just, say, its root-mean-squared value. In either case the forward-rate-specific volatility of volatility, v^T, would simply represent the number to put into the simpler SABR process in order to get the same price that the more complex and 'fuller' model would obtain for a plain-vanilla option.

The situation is strongly reminiscent of expiry-dependent 'implied' Black volatilities in a deterministic-volatility, log-normal world. The fact that these volatilities are different for different forward rates points to the fact they are the root-mean-squares of the underlying time-dependent but forward-rate-independent instantaneous volatilities. See Chapter 2.

We cannot tell just by looking at the parameters v^T, β^T and ρ^T which true latent function is appropriate in our case. Their dependence on the forward-rate expiry can provide, however, a necessary condition to be satisfied if we want our explanation to be plausible. The expiry dependence of v^T, β^T and ρ^T, in other words, can tell us which explanation is wrong, but cannot, by itself, tell us which one is right. To make this decision we must also use the empirical analysis presented in Part III. This is one of the reasons why this analysis is so important.

Again, for the SABR model the more complex, 'true' underlying model does not matter, because it deals with European options. As long as the correct 'effective' parameters have been distilled, this can be perfectly fine. Using these effective parameters (v^T, β^T and ρ^T) is, however, no longer fine when we need the joint evolution of many forward rates. That is why we have written this book.

3.3 The Option Prices Given by the SABR Model

Hagan *et al.* (2002) use singular perturbation techniques to obtain the plain-vanilla option prices implied by the SABR model, and from these the associated implied volatilities. Recall that implied volatilities are just 'the wrong number to put in the wrong formula to get the right price' (Rebonato, 1999a, 2004a), so there is no great fundamental meaning in obtaining implied volatilities rather than prices. However, for very good reasons, these 'wrong numbers' have become the common metric in the market place to communicate the prices of options. In terms of Black implied volatilities, $\widehat{\sigma}(K, T)$, the call prices for strike K implied by a SABR model with initial conditions f_0^T and σ_0^T and parameters ν^T, β^T and ρ^T are given by

$$\widehat{\sigma}(K, f, T) = A \cdot \left(\frac{z}{\chi(z)} \right) \cdot B \tag{3.4}$$

with

$$A = \frac{\sigma_0^T}{(fK)^{\frac{1-\beta}{2}} \left[1 + \frac{(1-\beta)^2}{24} \ln^2 \frac{f}{K} + \frac{(1-\beta)^4}{1920} \ln^4 \frac{f}{K} + \dots \right]} \tag{3.5}$$

$$B = \left[1 + \left(\frac{(1-\beta)^2}{24} \frac{(\sigma_0^T)^2}{(fK)^{1-\beta}} + \frac{\rho\beta\nu\sigma_0^T}{4(fK)^{\frac{1-\beta}{2}}} + \frac{2 - 3\rho^2}{24} \nu^2 \right) \cdot T + \dots \right] \tag{3.6}$$

$$z = \frac{\nu}{\sigma_0^T} (fK)^{\frac{1-\beta}{2}} \ln \frac{f}{K} \tag{3.7}$$

$$\chi(z) = \ln \left(\frac{\sqrt{1 - 2\rho z + z^2} + z - \rho}{1 - \rho} \right) \tag{3.8}$$

This approximate expression is very accurate as long as one does not look at strikes that are too out-of-the-money or expiries that are too long. What 'too out-of-the-money' or 'too long' means depends on the volatility and the volatility of volatility.

3.4   Special Cases

In some cases the approximate expression above becomes much more accurate, or exact. We report the results for these cases below.

3.4.1   ATM Options

For at-the-money options, the expressions above simplify to

$$\widehat{\sigma}(f, f, T) = \frac{\sigma_0^T}{f^{(1-\beta)}} \left[1 + \left(\frac{(1-\beta)^2}{24} \frac{(\sigma_0^T)^2}{(f)^{2-2\beta}} + \frac{\rho\beta\nu\sigma_0^T}{4(f)^{1-\beta}} + \frac{2 - 3\rho^2}{24} \nu^2 \right) \cdot T \right] \tag{3.9}$$

3.4.2   The Normal Case ($\beta = 0$)

For the special but important case of a Gaussian diffusion with log-normal stochastic volatility the expressions (3.5) to (3.8) become

$$\widehat{\sigma}(K) = \alpha \frac{\ln f/K}{f - K} \cdot \left(\frac{z}{\chi(z)} \right) \cdot \left\{ 1 + \left[\frac{\alpha^2}{24 f K} + \frac{2 - 3\rho^2}{24} \nu^2 \right] T \right\}$$

$$z = \frac{\nu}{\alpha} \sqrt{fK} \ln \frac{f}{K}$$

3.4.3   The Log-Normal Case ($\beta = 1$)

Similarly, in the log-normal case one obtains

$$\widehat{\sigma}(K) = \alpha \cdot \left(\frac{z}{\chi(z)}\right) \cdot \left\{1 + \left[\frac{\rho\alpha v}{4} + \frac{2 - 3\rho^2}{24}v^2\right]T\right\}$$

$$z = \frac{v}{\alpha}\ln\frac{f}{K}$$

3.5   Qualitative Behaviour of the SABR Model

In order to investigate the qualitative behaviour of the SABR model we have taken real market fits to caplet prices of different maturities, and looked at the changes in implied volatilities as each of the driving parameters (v, β and ρ) and initial conditions (f_0^T and σ_0^T) were changed.

The reference point from which the parameters were shifted was given by a set of market inputs (US$, 6th April 2006) for a 'normal' day in our data set. These reference parameters and initial values for the state variables are reported in Table 3.1.

3.5.1   Dependence on σ_0^T

The main effect of an increase in the initial volatility, σ_0^T from 0.0295 to 0.0325, is to shift the smile upwards. In Figure 3.1 we plot the Black implied volatility smile for the 6m × 1y swaption parameters given in Table 3.1 with and without a small perturbation in the initial volatility.

As seen in Figure 3.1, a change in σ_0^T causes an almost parallel shift upwards in the Black implied volatility smile across strikes. The result is not too surprising if we recall that σ_0^T is just the expectation at time 0 of the future volatility for any time $t \le T$. Therefore a small perturbation of σ_0 upwards will result in higher average volatility.

Looking at small effects, one can see in Figure 3.2 that an increase in the initial volatility brings about a modest steepening of the smile (low strikes increase more than high strikes). In relative terms, however, Figure 3.3 shows that the most pronounced *percentage* changes occur near the at-the-money level.

Table 3.1   The values of the state variable and model parameters of the reference swaptions used to determine the sensitivities. The last row (labelled 'T') gives the time to swaption expiry.

	Swaption quotes for USD, 6th April 2006					
	6m → 1y	1y → 1y	2y → 1y	5y → 1y	7y → 1y	10y → 1y
f	0.05252	0.05234	0.05298	0.05523	0.05607	0.05715
β	0.5	0.5	0.5	0.5	0.5	0.5
σ_0	0.02952	0.03446	0.03792	0.03903	0.03709	0.03452
ρ	−0.25	−0.25	−0.29	−0.24	−0.24	−0.24
v	0.6100	0.4600	0.4000	0.3350	0.3130	0.280
T	0.50137	1.00000	2.00548	5.00274	7.01096	10.00822

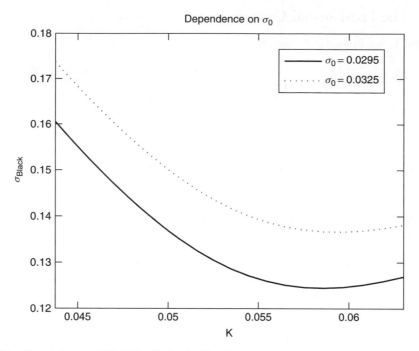

Figure 3.1 Dependence of Black implied volatility, $\hat{\sigma}$, on σ_0.

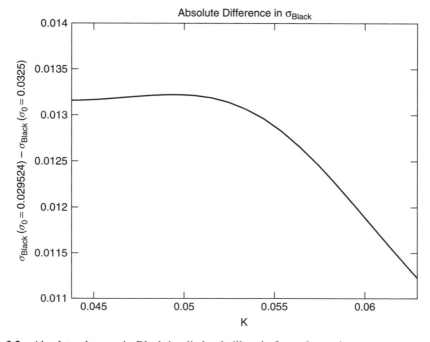

Figure 3.2 Absolute changes in Black implied volatility, $\hat{\sigma}$, for a change in σ_0.

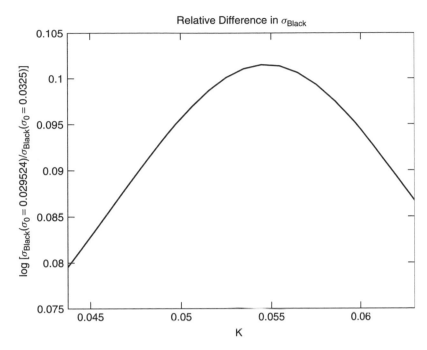

Figure 3.3   Logarithmic change in Black implied volatility, $\hat{\sigma}$, for a change in σ_0.

3.5.2   Dependence on β

The exponent β has three main effects on the smile:

- the first, and most commonly recognized one, is a progressive steepening of the smile as β goes from 1 to 0;

- the second is a lowering of the level of the smile as β increases;

- the third is the introduction of a curvature to the smile as β goes from 1 to 0.

First, let us comment on the decrease in level as β increases. This is not surprising because the 'total' volatility of the change in forward rate is given by $f^\beta \sigma(t)$. Everything else remaining the same, as β increases from 0 towards 1 the term f^β decreases in magnitude (it is equal to 1 for $\beta = 0$ and equal to the forward rate for $\beta = 1$), thereby reducing the total volatility seen by the change in forward rate. *Ceteris* are, however, never *paribus* with fitting. For a given market smile, changing β changes both slope and level (and, to a lesser extent, curvature) of the smile; the initial value of the volatility changes (to first order) just the level. Therefore, in the plots below that refer to the sensitivity to changes in β, we adjust the σ_0 parameter to maintain the level of total volatility: $\sigma_0 f^\beta = \sigma_0' f^{\beta'}$.

The plots in Figure 3.4 show the Black implied volatility smiles using the first column of f, σ_0, ρ, ν and T from the table of swaptions, i.e., the 6-month option expiring into a 1-year swap from 6th April 2006. The beta has been changed from $\beta = 0.5$ to $\beta = 0$

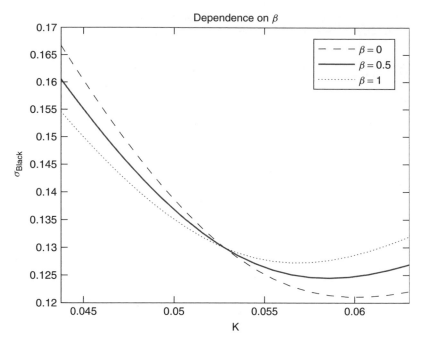

Figure 3.4 Black implied volatility smile as a function of β.

and to $\beta = 1$ and σ_0 adjusted to maintain the same level of total volatility. Looking at the steepening effect first, we see from the plots that the steepness of the smile decreases as $\beta = 0 \rightarrow 1$. This change is more pronounced in the out-of-the-money options. In Figure 3.5 we observe that the Black implied volatility decreases much more at -2 standard deviations from the at-the-money level than it increases at $+2$ standard deviations; this shows a clear decrease in the steepness.

As we shall show below, the steepening effect is similar to what a decrease in the (negative) correlation ρ produces. So very similar-quality smile fits can be obtained with different combinations of β and ρ. This is undesirable. To 'fix' this problem, it is market practice to fix either of the two parameters, and optimize over the other. At the time of writing, it appears that a market consensus has crystallized around a value for β of 0.5. See Section 3.9 for a discussion of why we think that this is the case.

The curvature effect is discussed below. It is rather insidious, because it can affect the vega hedging significantly. For the moment we can simply notice that an increase in β not only decreases the steepness but also decreases the curvature. This is evident by noticing that the implied volatility at low strikes (especially at longer maturities) falls much more rapidly than the high strike increase.

Therefore, when carrying out fit to market implied volatilities, β (together with ρ – see below) mainly picks up the burden of recovering the slope, ν accounts for most of the curvature (but β also plays a role – see below) and σ_0^T 'mops up' the level error that this introduces. Matters are not quite as neat and clean, however, because, as we have seen, σ_0^T also affects (albeit to a small degree) the steepness of the smile.

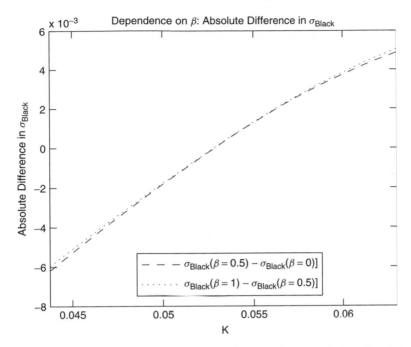

Figure 3.5 Change in the Black implied volatility smile for a change in β from $0 \to 0.5$ and from $0.5 \to 1$.

3.5.3 Dependence on ρ

As we said, as one moves ρ from 0 to -0.5 the smile becomes more and more negatively sloped. The plot in Figure 3.6 shows principally a pronounced change in the steepness of the curve as ρ decreases, with the secondary effect of a small decrease in its curvature. When we compare this effect with changes in β we see how the two play against each other. How the market resolves this issue is discussed in Sections 3.8 and 3.9.

3.5.4 Dependence on v

Finally, we see that increasing v increases the curvature of the smile. It becomes clear here how 'curvature' is different from 'slope'. Increases in β and ρ induce (primarily) a decrease in out-of-the-money Black implied volatility and an increase in in-the-money Black implied volatility, i.e., a change in the slope of the smile. Figure 3.7 shows how increasing v causes the Black implied volatility of both in- and out-of-the-money options to increase, i.e., for the smile to take on more curvature.

Note, however, the changes are not entirely symmetric across the smile. Parameters β and ρ have a secondary effect on curvature just as v has a secondary effect on steepness. This is apparent in the fact that the changes at in- and out-of-the-money strikes are not symmetric in their magnitude. The interaction of these three parameters on slope and curvature allows this model to capture subtle differences in the shape of the implied volatility smile.

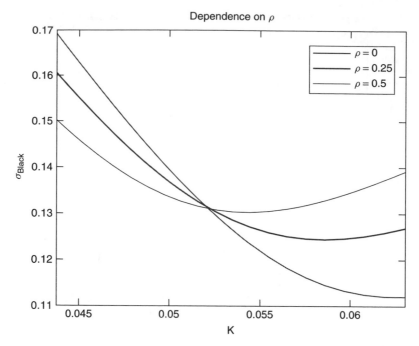

Figure 3.6   Black implied volatility smile for $\rho \in \{0, -0.25, -0.50\}$.

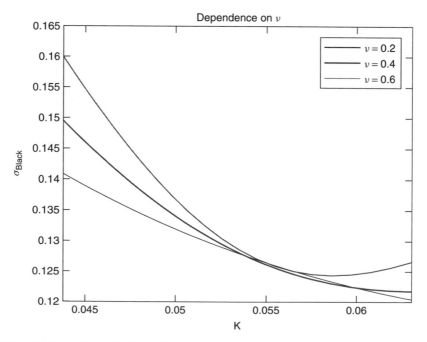

Figure 3.7   Black implied volatility smile for $\nu \in \{0.2, 0.4, 0.6\}$.

3.6   The Link Between the Exponent, β, and the Volatility of Volatility, ν

We look in this section at one important potential problem with the SABR model, linked to the 'overloading' of the smile curvature on the exponent, β, and on the volatility of volatility, ν. To understand the nature of the problem, let's assume for the moment that in reality forward rates do not follow a SABR process, or, rather, that they follow a degenerate one, with $\beta = 0$ and no volatility of volatility:

$$df_t = \sigma dz_t \tag{3.10}$$

The call prices are therefore exactly given by the Gaussian call formula (see Hagan *et al.* (2002) Equation (A.54a))

$$C(t, f) = (f - K) N\left(\frac{f - K}{\sigma_N \sqrt{T}}\right) + \sigma_N \sqrt{T} G\left(\frac{f - K}{\sigma_N \sqrt{T}}\right)$$

where $G(q) = \left(1/\sqrt{2\pi}\right) \exp\left(-\frac{1}{2}q^2\right)$. As an experiment, we produce prices for several strikes and an option expiry of 1 year, and we turn these prices into implied volatilities. We then 'forget' how we obtain these implied volatilities, and fit to these the SABR parameters, imposing the condition $\beta = 0$. We obtain, as we should, no volatility of volatility, $\nu = 0$. So far, so good.

Let's suppose now that a trader erroneously believes that the true process is a square-root CEV with SABR-like stochastic volatility:

$$df_t = \sigma_t f_t^{\frac{1}{2}} dz_t \tag{3.11}$$

$$\frac{d\sigma_t}{\sigma_t} = \nu dw_t \tag{3.12}$$

$$\mathbb{E}[dz_t dw_t] = \rho dt \tag{3.13}$$

where, with a mild abuse of notation, we have employed the same symbol (σ) for the deterministic Gaussian volatility and the stochastic square-root volatility.

Now, the trader does not know what the true correlation and volatility of volatility is, and therefore fits the observed prices to the erroneous model. Note from Figure 3.8 that the fit obtained with the wrong β is every bit as good as the fit we obtained using the true process (with $\beta = 0$ and no volatility of volatility). From the discussion above, however, we expect that the correlation between the forward rate and the volatility will be wrong: as the Gaussian process produces a steeper smile, the wrong stochastic square-root process will generate a negative correlation that is not really there. This is indeed what we find. But the more surprising result is that the fit to the wrong model also 'invents' a considerable amount of volatility of volatility that was absent in the true model. For a 1-year option with an initial forward-rate value of 5% the 'fake' volatility of volatility that the fit with $\beta = 1/2$ 'invents' is about 18% for $\beta = 1/2$ and about 29% for $\beta = 1$.

What is happening is that, as we pointed out above, the exponent β is not only responsible for the steepness of the smile (as is well known), but also for the fatness of the (left) tail

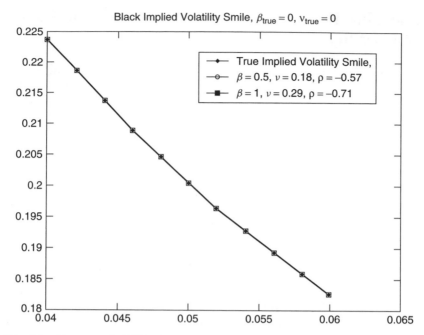

Figure 3.8 The Hagan *et al.* (2002) formula can recover virtually identical smiles under different σ_0, β, v, ρ assumptions. Here $\beta_{\text{true}} = 0$ and $v_{\text{true}} = 0$ is nearly identical to the alternative smiles $\beta = 0.5, v = 0.18, \rho = -0.57$ and $\beta = 1, v = 0.29, \rho = -0.71$.

of the risk-neutral distribution: for instance, $\beta = 0$ will assign more probability to very low (and indeed negative!) values of the forward rate than $\beta = 1/2$ or $\beta = 1$. A fit with the wrong beta will interpret this fat left tail as being due to a stochastic volatility (and, of course, a negative correlation between the forward rate and the volatility).

This is a worrying feature, because such an important feature as the presence or absence of stochasticity in the volatility – a feature that, in our example, can be conjured up or made to disappear by a suitable choice of β – will considerably change the hedging.

What *can* be said with confidence is that, if the $\beta = 0$ SABR fit produces a non-zero volatility of volatility, then this feature is 'robust': the exact 'amount of' volatility of volatility may be different for different exponents, but the trader is certainly exposed to stochasticity in volatility.

So, is stochastic volatility a reality or an artefact of fitting a wrong model? This is a topic we shall tackle in Part III (devoted to empirical findings). We can give a sketch of one possible line of attack. If we choose the type of process (absolute, percentage, square-root, etc.) and look at the returns in forward rates in the light of the chosen process, we can obtain the distribution of implied standard deviations associated with the observed moves. This distribution will be conditional on the model chosen. So, for instance, suppose that we wanted to test the hypothesis that the true process is a normal process with zero volatility of volatility. What we may find is that, under this assumption, there are too many exceptionally large (positive or negative) changes in forward rates. These changes in forward rates would cease to be exceptional, however, if they had been drawn from distributions with different volatilities. Our empirical findings would lead us to reject the hypothesis of zero volatility of volatility and to suggest that stochastic volatility *is* there. How much, and relating to which type of process (normal, square-root, log-normal, etc.), is a much tougher question.

We can make this analysis more systematic along these lines, and indeed we carry out these tests in Part III. This is important if we want to be able to hedge properly.

3.7   Volatility Clustering in the (LMM)-SABR Model

Volatility clustering describes the stylized market fact that realizations of high volatility tend to come in clusters. It is often claimed that in order to obtain volatility clusters one needs GARCH-type models, which explicitly model serial autocorrelation (of a special type) in volatility. Whatever the merits or the shortcomings of GARCH-type models, we do not need them to produce the important stylized fact of volatility clustering. This is because the diffusion equation for the stochastic volatility may well have independent *increments*, but the *level* of volatility at time t is certainly not independent of the level at time $t - dt$. The point is obvious, but it is worth repeating because the claim has often been made that the independence of the increments of SABR-like diffusive equations for the volatility cannot produce volatility clustering.

Admittedly, a SABR-like process may not be the best mechanism to produce volatility clustering, but the SABR equations *can* produce this effect. To illustrate the point Figure 3.9 shows a particular simulated SABR volatility path ($\beta = 0.5$, $v = 40\%$) and Figure 3.10 the percentage changes in the theoretical (SABR) forward rate. The clustering of high volatility realizations when the volatility is higher is clearly evident. The volatility clustering observed for a real forward rate (the 1-year USD forward rates, f^1, which is discussed in more detail in Part III) is also shown in Figure 3.11 for a qualitative visual comparison.

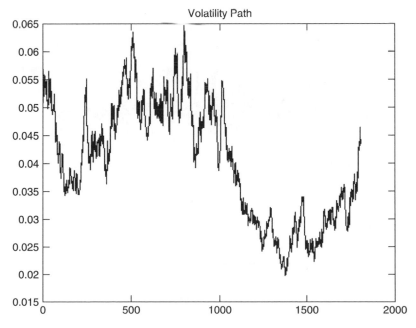

Figure 3.9   A particular simulated SABR volatility path ($\beta = 0.5$, $v = 40\%$).

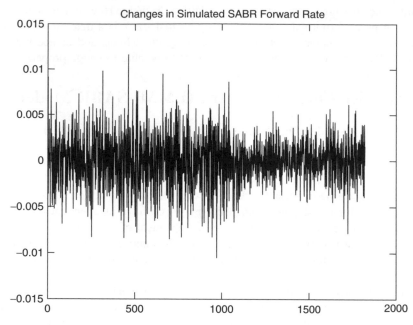

Figure 3.10   The percentage changes in the theoretical (SABR) forward rate obtained with the volatility path in Figure 3.9.

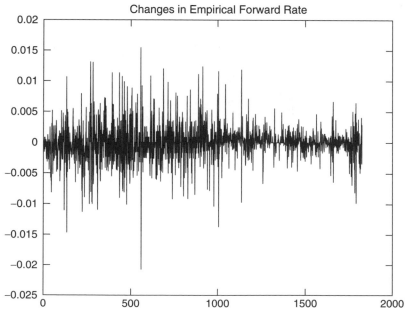

Figure 3.11   The volatility clustering observed for a real forward rate (the 1-year USD forward rate, f^1).

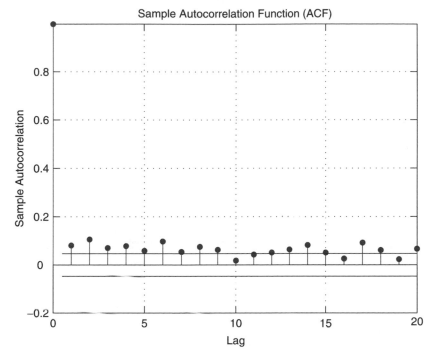

Figure 3.12 Autocorrelation of the squared changes in the simulated forward-rate series.

What *does* appear somewhat different, at least from a casual inspection, is the autocorrelation of the squared changes. See Figure 3.12. The non-zero autocorrelation for lags greater than zero, when one looks at the absolute value of the changes in the underlying variable, is a well-documented phenomenon (see, e.g., Campbell *et al.* (1996)). It reflects the fact that, conditional on a given move in the forward rate being large, the next move (of the same or of opposite sign) is also likely to be large. Notice that the autocorrelation for the SABR simulation in this example appears to have longer persistence as a function of lag than the empirical autocorrelation in the particular observed forward rate.

If any conclusion can be drawn from such limited data, it is perhaps that the bursts of high volatility are more localized (mean-reverting?) and less persistent in reality than in the SABR model. This is a subtle effect, and we do not pursue the analysis further here.

Also, Rebonato and Gaspari (2006) and Rebonato and Chen (2008) point out that when US$ rates are in an excited state the nature of the serial co-dependence may radically change. This is another subtle effect. The SABR model, which does not 'know' about different states, cannot capture this feature. We show how to deal with periods of market excitations (albeit in an approximate manner) in Section 4.8 and in Chapter 15.

These *caveats* notwithstanding, the (LMM)-SABR model can capture the most important serial features of the volatility process, i.e., volatility clustering and the positive serial autocorrelation for absolute changes.

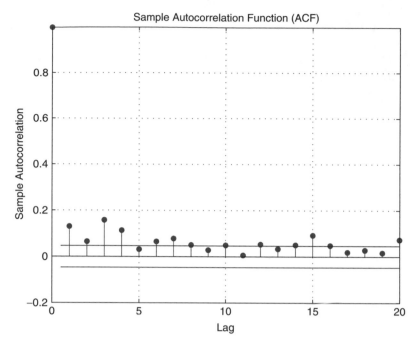

Figure 3.13   Autocorrelation of the squared changes in the USD 1-year forward-rate time series.

3.8   The Market

In this section we discuss the nature of fits to market prices using the SABR model. Typically, one finds that the fits are over-determined, i.e., fits of similar (and very good) quality can be obtained with very different couples $\{\beta, \rho\}$. The discussion in the previous sections helps to understand why this is the case. So, in order to avoid solutions 'bouncing' back and forth between apparently very local minima, it is common practice to fix the exponent β to a pre-chosen value (often 0.5), and to let ρ do the fitting work related to the slope (and, as we have seen, let ν do part of the fitting work related to the curvature). We follow in the next sections a similar approach, but we would like not to rule out the choice of $\beta = 0$. This has computational and other advantages (see the discussion below). For instance, we explain in Part III that, despite some obvious negative features (i.e., the possibility of negative rates), this choice has some nice statistical features. In any case, what we discuss in this section does not depend in a material way on this choice.

We present in the following the salient features of the time series of σ_0^T, ν^T and ρ^T as fitted over 733 business days (from 15th December 2004 to 5th October 2007).

3.8.1   Analysis of σ_0^T ($\beta = 0.5$)

Starting from the initial and expected value of the volatility (with the expectation taken on the fitting date) for options on 1-year caplets of expiry from 6 months to 10 years one observes an overall decline of the level of the volatility until the beginning of August 2007. Then the period of market turmoil of the late summer of 2007 becomes clearly visible. As

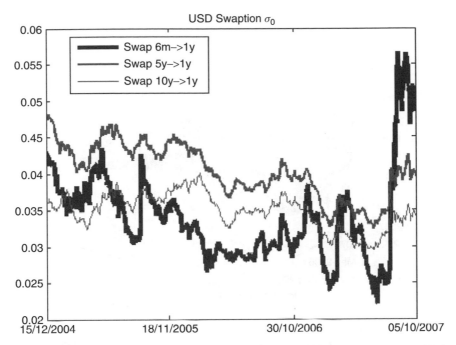

Figure 3.14 SABR parameter σ_0 from USD swaptions between 15th December 2004 and 5th October 2007 for the 6m, 5y, and 10y into 1y swaptions.

is to be expected from the discussion in the previous section, the value of σ_0^T is therefore closely linked to the overall 'excitation' (volatility level) of the market. See Figure 3.14.

Let us then look at the quantity σ_0^T on several trading days as a function of the time to expiry. See Figures 3.15 and 3.16. The overall decline in the level of volatility is again clearly visible – no surprises here. The more interesting feature is that on 'normal' days the function σ_0^T presents a humped shape, but during 'excited' periods (e.g., 17th August 2007) it becomes monotonically declining. This observation should be compared with the discussion in Section 2.2. When we introduce our LMM-SABR model, this observation will be an important ingredient in the financial justification for the function $g(\cdot)$ that we use.

3.8.2 Analysis of v^T ($\beta = 0.5$)

Looking at the time series of v^T we observe a similar qualitative behaviour: the volatility of volatility first declines until August 2007, and then increases significantly during market turmoil. Again, the increase is more marked for short expiries. See Figure 3.17. As the volatility of volatility controls the curvature of the smile, this behaviour is clearly related to the fact that, when markets become more excited, the left and right tails of the distribution become fatter, and the smile correspondingly more curved.

Overall, it appears that the market tends to retain the same value v^T (given the choice of $\beta = 0.5$) for extended periods of time, and then to shift to a different level. Compare the fundamental difference between the time series of changes in σ_0^T (Figure 3.14) and of changes in v^T. This is important for the choices we make in Chapter 4.

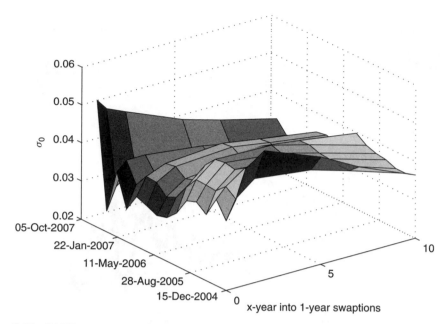

Figure 3.15   SABR parameter σ_0 from USD swaptions between 15th December 2004 and 5th October 2007 for the 6m, 1y, 2y, 5y, 7y, and 10y into 1y, 2y, 3y, 4y, 5y, 7y, and 10y swaptions.

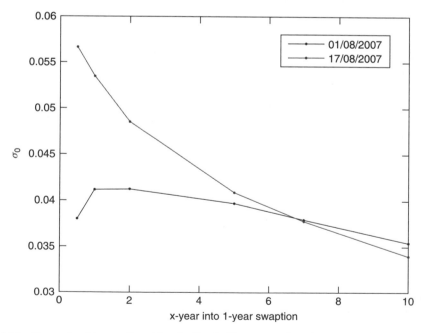

Figure 3.16   Example of 'normal' and 'excited' volatility. n-year into 1-year swaptions on 1st August 2007 and 17th August 2007.

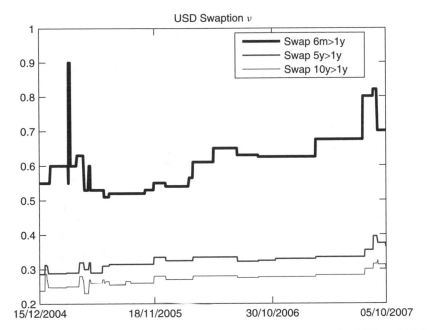

Figure 3.17   SABR parameter ν from USD swaptions between 15th December 2004 and 5th October 2007 for the 6m, 5y, and 10y into 1y swaptions.

Finally, we note that for all dates the graph of ν^T as a function of caplet expiry displays a monotonic shape. For many trading days the curves lie almost on top of each other, but during market turmoil there is a visible steepening of the curve.

3.8.3   Analysis of ρ^T ($\beta = 0.5$)

Finally, we consider the time series of ρ^T. See Figure 3.18. It is more difficult in this case to identify the precise onset of market turmoil, because the data show an overall decline in the SABR correlation over time for all expiries, with the maximum 'tilt' occurring for short expiries. Recall, however, that a more negative correlation ρ means a steepening of the smile, greater value for out-of-the-money receivers and an increase in risk reversals. These *are* all features associated with turbulent times.

3.9   How Do We Know that the Market has Chosen $\beta = 0.5$?

We have repeatedly mentioned above that 'the market seems to endorse the choice of $\beta = 0.5$ for the SABR model'. Apart from anecdotal evidence (which in practice means, apart from talking to traders), how do we know that this is the case?

To answer this question, we have refitted the market prices of swaptions assuming that the true exponent was $\beta = 0$ and looked at the time series of the fitted parameters, exactly as we did above for $\beta = 0.5$. What we observe now is that there is a much greater variation from

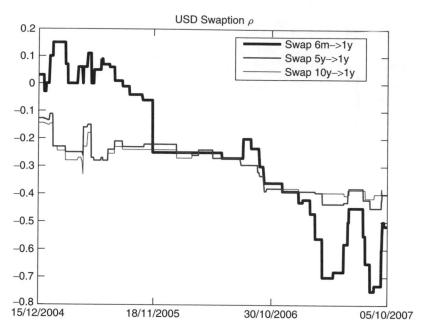

Figure 3.18   SABR parameter ρ from USD swaptions between 15th December 2004 and 5th October 2007 for the 6m, 5y, and 10y into 1y swaptions.

one day to the next of many of the supposedly constant fitted parameters. See Figures 3.19 and 3.20. This makes us believe that, as a by-product of using a 'wrong' exponent, we are giving spurious variability to quantities that should in reality be constant over time.

Needless to say, quantities such as the volatility of volatility (ν) or the correlation (ρ) should never change for a well-specified model. The need to recalibrate the model too frequently and too radically is a sign of trouble. One of us (RR) has discussed these topics at great length in Rebonato (2002) and Rebonato (2004a). So, it is a good idea to settle for the choice of the exponent β that makes the theoretically constant parameters as truly constant as possible.

Apart from aesthetic considerations, it is quite plausible to surmise that, once traders have 'locked onto' a model such as SABR, they will update daily the quantities, such as the level of volatility, that change rapidly as a function of the information flow, but that they will only change more 'structural' features when major market events warrant it.

In short, we believe that the choice of $\beta = 0.5$ has more of a 'sociological' or game-theoretical explanation (self-reinforcing coordination of traders' behaviour) than a fundamental one (in terms of market informational efficiency). It is, however, at least a regularity that can give some guidance in an otherwise rather murky area.

Be that as it may, the upshot of all this is that a good criterion for reverse-engineering the market β is to see which choice of the exponent makes parameters such as the volatility of volatility or the correlation most stable on most days. When we do this we find that the market has, either wisely or conventionally, chosen $\beta = 0.5$ as the current choice.

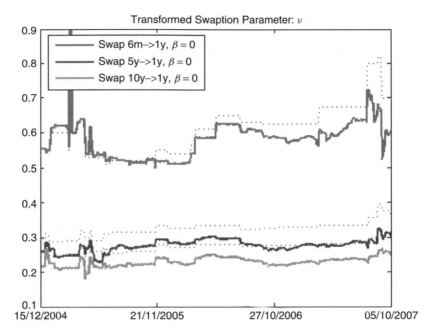

Figure 3.19   SABR parameter ν transformed from the market $\beta = 0.5$ to $\beta = 0$.

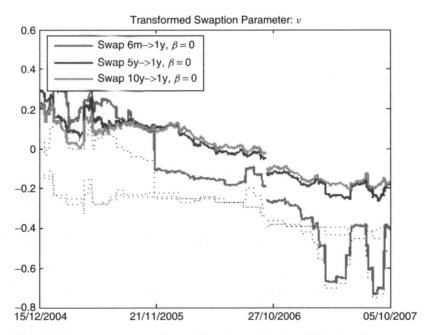

Figure 3.20   SABR parameter ρ transformed from the market $\beta = 0.5$ to $\beta = 0$.

3.10   The Problems with the SABR Model

3.10.1   Log-Normality of the Volatility Process

We said that we like the SABR model. This does not mean that we believe it is perfect (and we think that the authors would agree with us), but, looking back again at the aphorism 'All models are wrong, but some models are useful', we feel that it definitely falls in the category of useful models.

We should distinguish between problems with the SABR model (meant as a set of coupled stochastic differential equations) and problems with the asymptotic approximation to the model (what is normally used in the market place).

Let us start from the former (i.e., the 'true-model' problems). The first problem is that, for reasons of tractability, the process for the volatility is assumed to be a pure geometric diffusion. This is tractable, but not nice. Continuous-time log-normal processes display unpleasant features, such as divergence to infinity with probability 1 in finite time (see, e.g., Karatzas and Shreve (1991)). From a more mundane angle, given a Wiener process of the type

$$\frac{dx_t}{x_t} = \sigma \, dz_t \tag{3.14}$$

its solution is of the form

$$x_t = x_0 \exp\left[-\frac{1}{2}\sigma^2 t + \sigma\sqrt{t}Z\right] \tag{3.15}$$

with $Z \sim \mathcal{N}(0.1)$. The expectation of x_T at a generic time T, given its value, x_t, at an earlier time t, is given by

$$\mathbb{E}_t(x_T) = x_t \tag{3.16}$$

because

$$\mathbb{E}_t\left(\exp\left[-\frac{1}{2}\sigma^2 t + \sigma\sqrt{t}Z\right]\right) = 1. \tag{3.17}$$

This is, of course, very well known. What is less commonly appreciated is that the expectation in Equation (3.17) tends to be made up of very many 'low' paths, and a few very high ('close-to-explosive') paths. Again, this does not say anything more profound than the fact that for a log-normal process the median is different from the mean. But when the volatility of volatility is 'high' (and, after parametrization of the SABR model to market prices, this is often the case), the median can become *very* different from the mean – which means that a very small number of high paths must compensate for a very large number of low realizations. This can give rise to problems of numerical convergence and, sometimes, of stability.[2]

---

[2]Whenever the most commonly sampled value, x_{mp}, is significantly different from the mean, the first few samples are by definition likely to be in the neighbourhood of x_{mp}. An average computed from these values will be biased, the more so the more x_{mp} differs from the true average value $<x>$. See Sornette (2003) and Redner (1990) for a clear discussion in the context of random multiplicative processes.

3.10.2 Problems with the (Stochastic) CEV Process

> You can check in any time you want
> but you can never leave.
>
> *Hotel California* by The Eagles (1976)[3] – a veiled reference to the absorbing
> properties at zero of CEV processes.

The second problem with the SABR model is that it is a stochastic-volatility enrichment of a CEV model. It therefore pays to look at the properties of the simpler CEV processes in some detail.

Much is made of the ability of CEV processes to avoid negative rates. This is true, but the price to pay for this feature is high. To see what the problems are, we follow Andersen and Andreasen (1998) and consider a process, x_t, with an SDE of the form

$$dx_t = \phi(x_t)\sigma(t)dz_t \tag{3.18}$$

and such that $x(0) > 0$ (i.e., such that its value *today* is strictly positive). By Equation (3.18) the total volatility of x, i.e., the quantity $\phi(x_t)\sigma(t)$, is assumed to be separable into a purely time-dependent part, $\sigma(t)$, and a stochastic component, $\phi(x_t)$, which is perfectly functionally dependent on the process itself. We would like to impose, for reasons explained below, that, if the forward process were ever to attain zero, its total volatility should collapse to zero. Since the term $\sigma(t)$ is deterministic and purely time-dependent (in particular, it does not depend on x), if we want to achieve this goal we must require that $\phi(0) = 0$.

It is easy enough to write an SDE such as (3.18). However, if we want to make sure that to this SDE there should correspond well-behaved solutions we have to impose some conditions on $\phi(x_t)$. To this effect, let us require that the function ϕ should satisfy the local Lipschitz continuity condition and the linear growth condition. The linear growth condition need not concern us too much, at least for the range of exponents $(0 < \beta \leq 1)$ we are interested in. The local Lipschitz condition, however, *is* of interest to us: it requires that, for any $\epsilon > 0$, one can always find a constant, C_ϵ, dependent on ϵ, such that, for x and y positive but smaller than ϵ,

$$|\phi(x) - \phi(y)| \leq C_\epsilon |x - y| \tag{3.19}$$

If both the linear growth condition and the local Lipschitz condition are satisfied, one can show that there always exist well-behaved (non-explosive), pathwise unique solutions for the arbitrage-free SDE (3.18) of the process x. More precisely, the growth condition ensures that the solution does not explode, and the Lipschitz condition ensures that it is unique. Furthermore, if, as we requested, $x(0) > 0$, the process remains positive at all times.

This all sounds encouraging. However, the CEV process (Equation (3.18)) we are interested in, i.e., a process where the function $\phi(x_t)$ has the form

$$\phi(x_t) = x(t)^\beta \tag{3.20}$$

---

[3]Lyrics by Don Felder, Don Henley and Glenn Frey.

will not satisfy the local Lipschitz condition at zero[4] for

$$0 < \beta < 1 \tag{3.21}$$

However, the following properties still hold. Given a process as in (3.18), with $0 < \beta < 1$:

1. all its solutions are non-explosive;

2. for $\beta \geq 1/2$ the SDE (3.18) has a *unique* solution;

3. for $\beta = 1$, $x = 0$ is an unattainable barrier (the forward process always remains *strictly* positive);

4. for $0 < \beta < 1$, $x = 0$ is an attainable barrier;

5. for $0 < \beta < 1/2$ the solution is not unique, unless one assigns a separate boundary condition for $x = 0$.

If $1/2 < \beta < 1$, the uniqueness of the solution (Property 2), the attainability of zero (Property 3) and the requirement $\phi(0) = 0$ ensure that zero is an absorbing barrier. Property 5, however, states that for $0 < \beta < 1/2$ the solution is in general not unique. This can be remedied by adding a financial requirement. What can this financial requirement be? Let us assume that the forward rate (or the asset price) has reached zero. We know that, for $\beta > 0$, it cannot become negative. Could it perhaps be 'reflected back' into positive territory? Conditional on the price process, x, being at zero, if any positive value were accessible, the associated relative price could not possibly be a martingale (there is no way that its expectation taken at the time when the zero level has been reached could be equal to zero). In more financial terms, we should certainly buy this asset (for \$0) at the boundary, because in the future it will be worth either zero, or something positive. This is just the definition of an arbitrage. Therefore we must add the financial requirement that zero should be an *absorbing* barrier: if the rate or price ever reaches it, it must remain there forever.

The solution seems both elegant and 'innocuous'. In reality it can be financially rather unpleasant, especially in those regimes (of very low rates) where this feature can make a difference. Let's see why this is the case.

To begin with, let's remind ourselves that when rates become as low as those found in the JPY yield curve in the late 1990s, or in US\$ in the early 2000s, percentage volatilities tend to be very high – when in 2002 US\$ rates were around 1.00%, for instance, the associated percentage volatilities were around 60%. What does this mean for CEV processes? It is well known how to find a CEV volatility, σ_β, so as to match closely, at-the-money, the market caplet prices produced by a given percentage volatility, σ – see, e.g., Rebonato (2004a). To first order this approximate equivalent CEV volatility is given by

$$\sigma_\beta f^\beta = \sigma f \tag{3.22}$$

---

[4]This can be seen as follows. Recall first the average value theorem, which states that, given a differentiable function, $\phi(.)$, and two points in its domain, x and y, it is always possible to write $\frac{\phi(x)-\phi(y)}{x-y} = \phi'(\eta)$, for some $\eta \in [x, y]$. Given our choice for the function ϕ, i.e., $\phi(x) = x^\beta$, its derivative, ϕ', is $\phi'(x) = \beta x^{\beta-1}$. Therefore $\phi'(0)$ is not bounded for $0 < \beta < 1$, and the local Lipschitz condition (3.19) cannot be satisfied.

where σ is the percentage volatility. Using this equivalence, we can study the absorbing properties of CEV processes with the levels of rates and volatilities observed in the US$ swaption market in the early 2000s: we can take the market percentage volatilities (of the order of 60%), convert them into CEV volatilities, start the forward rate process from a value of around 1%, impose the absorbing-barrier condition, and see what happens. When simple numerical experiments are carried out, the 'exact' CEV process for a forward rate starting at around 1% gives a probability of approximately 50% of it being absorbed at zero over five years. Therefore, in the low-rate, high-volatility regime of interest the choice we made for the behaviour of the process upon reaching the zero barrier is not just an innocuous tinkering at the edges of a probability distribution, but has very important pricing consequences. In other terms, by requiring zero to become an absorbing barrier, we have eliminated all possibilities of arbitrage, but we may not be happy with the financial implications of our choice.

The concern is not a 'philosophical' one about 'what truly happens' at zero, but is the very concrete observation that, because of absorption at zero, the density in the strictly positive region becomes progressively depleted: given a fixed horizon T, as more and more paths reach zero and remain absorbed there forever, the probability density of non-zero terminal values becomes smaller and smaller. The overall density, as time goes by, becomes the sum of an infinitely sharp delta distribution at the origin, plus a diffuse but smaller and smaller distribution for the remaining values of the forward rate. Furthermore, any diffusive path sooner or later will reach the x-axis. Therefore, in the limit as T goes to infinity all the probability mass becomes concentrated at the origin. The zero level therefore effectively acts as a 'black hole': every path will eventually fall into it, and none will escape.

If you think that this is 'just a mathematical oddity' and that we should not worry about it, consider the following: with the rates and the volatility mentioned above, *and even neglecting discounting*, the forward price of a European digital call struck at zero (i.e., the price of a contract that pays $1 if rates in five years' time are strictly positive) is about 50 cents! Would *you* like to sell the European digital at this level?

When looked at in this light, the choice of an exponent $\beta = 0$ looks perhaps more desirable. Admittedly, the dreaded negative rates cannot be avoided, but paths that stray into negative territory can 'come back from the dead' and become positive again, thereby avoiding the 'black hole' (or, Hotel California-like) behaviour of the CEV absorbing barrier at 0. The resulting Gaussian distribution is, of course, much better behaved, and its shortcomings (the possibility of negative rates) are out in the open for everybody to see. Computationally, the simulations required to price complex products are simpler, and the SABR approximations for the implied volatility are more accurate. Finally, the drift corrections for forward rate and volatilities are simpler.

What can we say empirically? We will address this question in Part III, but we can already anticipate that, in reality, the scant available evidence suggests that no single exponent is correct for all levels of rates. And if simple (and not-so-simple) statistical tests are run against different values of a single exponent, the value of $\beta = 0$ cannot be rejected (at least over an extended range of forward rate levels).

For all these reasons, we would not like to discard the choice of $\beta = 0$ for the LMM-SABR approach. We acknowledge that the market currently appears to have settled around a value of $\beta = 1/2$, i.e., to have chosen a square-root process for the forward rate. Fits to market data with either exponent are, however, almost indistinguishable. If the reader disagrees with our choice, our treatment remains still valid.

   Whatever the choice, the fundamental problem does not go away: when rates are high, it barely matters what happens close to zero, and choosing between a displaced diffusion, a CEV process or a Gaussian process is a bit of a metaphysical issue. When it does matter, i.e., when rates are really low, then no choice is entirely satisfactory, and the prudent trader who has to price a product with very low strikes or barriers will do well to check the sensitivity of his results to different modelling assumptions.

Chapter 4

The LMM-SABR Model

Student: [...] I'll study everything with skill,
I've got some cash, lots of good will;
My mother told me: stay at home.
But I'm keen to learn; that's why I've come.
Mephistopheles: Well, well, you've arrived at the right college.[1]

Mephistopheles enrolling a new student on his LMM-SABR course.

In the previous two chapters we have briefly presented the standard (i.e., deterministic-volatility) LIBOR market model and the SABR model and we have explained why we like both these approaches. In Parts III and IV we will also point out that the SABR model describes surprisingly well how the smile moves in reality when the underlying moves.[2] This feature is at the root of successful delta hedging and these positive results reinforce our belief that the SABR model is a good place to start. What we need is a dynamic extension of the static SABR model. This can be provided by the SABR-LIBOR market model.

The LIBOR market model was the standard for pricing complex products before smiles appeared in the interest-rate markets. Monotonically declining smiles can, to some extent, be shoe-horned within the framework of the LIBOR market model. 'Hockey-stick' smiles, however, require more radical surgery.

There are many ways to obtain non-monotonic smiles in interest rates. Two of us (RR and RW) have done work (see, e.g., Rebonato and Kainth (2004), White and Rebonato (2008)) with two-state Markov-chain volatility models. Glasserman and Kou (2003) and others have worked with jump-diffusion processes. Levy Market Models (that can be seen as generalizations of jump-diffusion models) have been suggested by Kluge (2005) and made somewhat more tractable by Eberlein and Ozkan (2005). All these have remained, however, somewhat 'fringe' developments. Most of the work has in fact been done in the direction of stochastic-volatility extensions of the LIBOR market model. Without attempting to be complete, we should mention in this large strand the papers by Andersen and Andreasen (2000), Joshi and Rebonato (2003), Rebonato and Joshi (2002), Piterbarg (2003), Piterbarg (2005).

---

[1]*Faust – Part One*. Act One, Scene 7, 1776–1880. J.W. Goethe, David Luke translation.
[2]See the discussion in Rebonato *et al.* (2008) and in Part III.

The differences among most of these stochastic-volatility models are not great. The precise distributional assumptions for the volatility process are sometimes different; displaced diffusion sometimes replaces the CEV process; the numerical implementation can be more or less cumbersome. However, since volatility is a latent variable, determining what its 'true' distribution should be inhabits a murky area between heroic econometric analysis and an act of faith. As for the 'correct' exponent for the CEV process of the forward rates, empirical analysis seems to suggest that no single exponent works well for all levels of forward rates. See Section 8.5. For these 'fine details' of the stochastic-volatility models, we therefore believe that practicality and tractability should win the day.

What all the stochastic-volatility models mentioned above *do* share, however, is an inability to fit accurately the market smile surface in a manner which is simple, quick, robust and financially justifiable (i.e., without too many time-dependent 'fudge factors').

If this is the case, why not take the market-standard SABR model as the blue-print for the required stochastic-volatility extension of the LIBOR market model? We do not know whether the distributional assumptions for the volatility or for the CEV process for the forward rates implied by the SABR model are, statistically speaking, the 'best' possible modelling choices. But, in such an uncertain landscape, the more the dynamic extension of the LIBOR market model 'looks and feels' like the SABR model, the better our hopes will be to recover the smile surface, again, in a manner which is simple, quick, robust and financially justifiable.

This is the route taken by Henry-Labordere (2007) and Rebonato (2007b). We believe that the second approach is simpler, both to understand and to use. For this reason, the rest of the book is devoted to showing how to turn a promising idea into a complete pricing framework – by which we mean not just deriving the no-arbitrage 'equations of motion', but also the calibration, the empirical evidence to implement it, and the hedging.

4.1   The Equations of Motion

Recalling the discussion in Chapter 2, we start directly from a formulation that allows for a natural decomposition of the stochastic part of the dynamics into a component that only depends on the volatilities and one that only depends on the correlations.

Therefore, for $i = 1, 2, \ldots, N$ let the joint dynamics of the N forward rates and their instantaneous volatilities be defined by

$$df_t^i = \mu_t^i(\{f\}, \{s\}, \rho)dt + \left(f_t^i\right)^{\beta_i} s_t^i \sum_{j=1}^{N_F} b_{ij} d\hat{z}_j \tag{4.1}$$

$$ds_t^i = g(t, T_i)dk_t^i \tag{4.2}$$

$$\frac{dk_t^i}{k_t^i} = \mu_t^{k_i}(\{f\}, \{s\})dt + h_t^i \sum_{j=1}^{N_V} c_{ij} d\hat{w}_j \tag{4.3}$$

where N_F and N_V are the number of factors driving the forward-rate and volatility processes, respectively, and with $N_F \leq N$, $N_V \leq N$. The notation $\mu_t^i(\{f\}, \{s\})$ and $\mu_t^{k_i}(\{f\}, \{s\})$ indicates that, in general, the no-arbitrage drifts of the forward rates and of the volatilities depend on all the forward rates and volatilities.

If one sets

$$\sum_{j=1}^{N_F} b_{ij}^2 = 1 \tag{4.4}$$

$$\sum_{j=1}^{N_V} c_{ij}^2 = 1$$

and

$$\mathbb{E}\left[d\hat{z}_j d\hat{z}_k\right] = \delta_{jk} dt \tag{4.5}$$

$$\mathbb{E}\left[d\hat{w}_j d\hat{w}_k\right] = \delta_{jk} dt \tag{4.6}$$

$$\mathbb{E}\left[d\hat{z}_j d\hat{w}_k\right] = x_{jk} dt \tag{4.7}$$

where δ_{ij} is the Kronecker delta and x_{ij} is defined later, then each forward rate f_t^i and each factor k_t^i will have a CEV or log-normal instantaneous volatility s_t^i and h_t^i, respectively.

4.2 The Nature of the Stochasticity Introduced by Our Model

A few observations are in order. We have introduced stochasticity in the volatility by implicitly defining a quantity, say, p_t, defined as

$$p_t = \left(\frac{s_t^i}{g(t, T_i)}\right) \tag{4.8}$$

This can be regarded as the ratio of the total volatility to its deterministic part (or, as we shall see, to the time-t_0 expectation of the stochastic volatility). If, at time t_0, the functional dependence on expiry, T_i, of the expectations of the volatilities for all the forward rates, f^i, is perfectly captured by the function $g(t, T_i)$, then the initial values of the processes k_t^i would be identically equal to 1 (or, for that matter, to the same constant):

$$k_0^i = 1, \quad i = 1, 2, \ldots, N \tag{4.9}$$

If this is not the case the initial values k_0^i will not all be identical. In this case, we show below how to choose the $g(t, T_i)$ in such a way that these non-constant initial values for the scaling factors are in some sense optimal. For the moment, we simply note that, with a slight abuse of notation, we have used the same symbol for the scaling factors introduced in Chapter 2 and the stochastic process in Equation (4.3). This is not a coincidence. We pointed out there that, if all the $\{k^i\}$ had been chosen to be exactly equal to 1, the evolution of the smile surface would have been exactly self-similar. In the present formulation the factors $\{k^i\}$ have become stochastic processes, and therefore the future smile surface will display stochasticity. This is obviously desirable. Indeed, it is the whole point behind introducing a stochastic-volatility model. However, from the discussion in the Introduction, in general we still want that today's *expectation* of the future smile surface should not display a deterministic change – unless, of course, we believe that the smile *should* undergo a deterministic transformation. The formulation above ensures that this is the case. It also says something about future conditional expectations of the smile surface. If all the future stochastic values of the terms $\{k^i\}$ evolved to have the same value, this would roughly correspond to a shift upward or downward of future expectation of the whole conditional smile surface. This is desirable, because indeed we observe that the dominant mode of deformation of the smile surface is a quasi-parallel shift. To the extent that the future values $\{k^i\}$ are different, however, the future expectation of the conditional smile surface implies a change in its shape. If we want to limit the degree of these deformations, we therefore would like to impose a high degree of correlation among the processes $\{k^i\}$.

As far as the function $g(t, T_i)$ is concerned, we will require in the following that it should be time homogeneous:

$$g(t, T_i) = g(T_i - t) \tag{4.10}$$

We will use the functional form discussed in Chapter 2, but nothing hangs on this. The reader could even decide to dispense with time homogeneity. The equations that follow would still remain valid, but, in normal market conditions, the 'physics' would be poorer – the more so, the stronger the dependence on calendar time.[3]

4.3   A Simple Correlation Structure

The correlation, ρ_{ij}, between two forward rates (say, i and j) is given by

$$\rho_{ij} = \sum_{k=1}^{N_F} b_{ik} b_{jk} \tag{4.11}$$

The correlation, r_{ij}, between two instantaneous volatilities (say, i and j) is given by

$$r_{ij} = \sum_{k=1}^{N_V} c_{ik} c_{jk} \tag{4.12}$$

Define the matrix $b = \{b_{ij}, i = 1, \ldots, N, j = 1, \ldots, N_F\}$. Then

$$\rho = bb^T \tag{4.13}$$

where the superscript T denotes transpose. Similarly, define the matrix $c = \{c_{ij}, i = 1, \ldots, N, j = 1, \ldots, N_V\}$. Then

$$r = cc^T \tag{4.14}$$

---

[3]See, however, the discussion in Section 4.8 as to what to do in situations of market stress.

For exogenously assigned matrices ρ and r, the exact recovery of all their elements will in general not be possible unless $N_V = N_F = N$. If $N_V = N_F = N$ the matrices b and c are given by the eigenvectors of the matrices ρ and r, respectively.

Consider now the correlation between forward rate i and volatility q, R_{iq}. This is given by

$$R_{iq} = \sum_{k=1}^{N_F} \sum_{s=1}^{N_V} b_{ik} c_{qs} x_{ks} \tag{4.15}$$

The quantities $\{b_{ik}\}$ and $\{c_{qs}\}$ are already fixed from the requirement to match the exogenous matrices ρ and r. For an exogenous $N \times N$ matrix R we are then left with $N_V \times N_F$ quantities (the x_{sk}) to fix the N^2 quantities R. An exact solution will in general not be possible unless $N_V = N_F = N$.

4.4 A More General Correlation Structure

We present in this section a more symmetric correlation structure that sometimes can make the book-keeping and the implementation simpler and neater. The main advantage is that now the Brownian increments (i.e., the increments that we denoted $\{d\hat{z}_i\}$ and $\{d\hat{w}_j\}$ above) are *all* assumed to be independent, and are therefore treated on the same footing.

The joint dynamics of the forward rates and their instantaneous volatilities can now be written as

$$df_t^i = \mu_t^i dt + \left(f_t^i\right)^{\beta_i} s_t^i \sum_{j=1}^{M} e_{ij} dy_j, \quad i = 1, \ldots, N \tag{4.16}$$

$$ds_t^i = g(t, T_i) dk_t^i \tag{4.17}$$

$$\frac{dk_t^i}{k_t^i} = \mu_t^{k_i} dt + h_t^i \sum_{j=1}^{M} e_{N+i,j} dy_j, \quad i = 1, \ldots, N \tag{4.18}$$

for dy, an M-dimensional Brownian increment, with

$$\mathbb{E}\left[dy_j dy_k\right] = \delta_{jk} dt \tag{4.19}$$

$$M = N_V + N_F \tag{4.20}$$

$$\sum_{j=1}^{M} e_{ij}^2 = 1 \tag{4.21}$$

The associated super-correlation matrices, P, all fall under the general structure

$$P = \begin{bmatrix} \rho & R \\ R^T & r \end{bmatrix} \tag{4.22}$$

with $\rho = [N_F \times N_F]$, $r = [N_V \times N_V]$, $R = [N_F \times N_V]$. The elements of P are given by

$$P_{ik} = \sum_{m=1}^{M} e_{im} e_{km} \tag{4.23}$$

or, in matrix notation,

$$P = ee^T \tag{4.24}$$

If $N_V = N_F = N$ then $M = 2N$, the matrix P is of full rank M and the vectors e_i are the eigenvectors of the correlation matrix P.

This more general correlation structure has the benefit that we can define the innovations in the forward rate and volatility by

$$dz_t^k \equiv \sum_{j=1}^{M} e_{kj} dy_j, \text{ for } k = 1, \ldots, N$$

$$dw_t^k \equiv \sum_{j=1}^{M} e_{kj} dy_j, \text{ for } k = N+1, \ldots, 2N$$

where

$$\mathbb{E}\left[dz_t^j dz_t^k \right] = \rho_{jk} dt \tag{4.25}$$

$$\mathbb{E}\left[dw_t^j dw_t^k \right] = r_{jk} dt \tag{4.26}$$

$$\mathbb{E}\left[dz_t^j dw_t^k \right] = R_{jk} dt \tag{4.27}$$

We can therefore alternatively write the joint dynamics of the forward rates and their volatilities as

$$df_t^i = \mu_i dt + \left(f_t^i \right)^{\beta_i} s_t^i dz_t^i, \quad i = 1, \ldots, N \tag{4.28}$$

$$ds_t^i = g(t, T_i) dk_t^i \tag{4.29}$$

$$\frac{dk_t^i}{k_t^i} = \mu_t^{k_i} dt + h_t^i dw_t^i, \quad i = 1, \ldots, N \tag{4.30}$$

Note that all the eigenvalues of the overall matrix P must be positive for P to be a proper correlation matrix. This poses constraint on R (if the sub-matrix R is exogenously assigned). These and related issues are dealt with below.

4.5 Observations on the Correlation Structure

Specifying an input correlation structure for the LMM-SABR model is more important (and challenging) than for the deterministic-volatility LMM. This is because in order to recover the SABR caplet prices with our dynamic model we will have to impose requirements on the diagonal elements of the sub-matrix R, R_{ii}. More precisely, R_{ii} should be exactly equal to the SABR forward-rate/volatility correlation for the ith forward rate, ρ^i_{SABR} :

$$R_{ii} = \rho^i_{SABR} \tag{4.31}$$

We shall show formally that this is the case in Part III, Chapter 5, but it should already be plausible at this stage.

As the N quantities ρ^i_{SABR} are exogenously defined from the market fits, this imposes a serious constraint on the overall matrix P if we want to make sure that it remains a valid correlation matrix (i.e., positive definite). We will show in Chapter 7 how this can be accomplished, but we wanted to point out this non-trivial feature at this early stage in the presentation. Specifying the correlation matrix in the traditional LIBOR market model has always been the 'poor relation' in the calibration procedure. This is emphatically no longer the case in the extended LMM-SABR model.

Note also that R is not a symmetric sub-matrix (but ρ and r are). Also, speaking of a 'one-volatility factor' model implies that all the elements of r are equal to 1. This choice can pose heavy constraints on the positive definiteness of the matrix P for a sub-matrix R whose diagonal elements have been exogenously assigned with reference to the quantities ρ^i_{SABR}. For instance, suppose that two forward rates are strongly correlated with each other. If we impose that their volatilities should be perfectly correlated with each other, then it would be very difficult to have a correlation between the first forward rate and its volatility very different from the correlation between the second forward rate and its own volatility.

Finally, a comparison between the more symmetric and 'elegant' specification of the correlation matrix afforded by Equations (4.16) to (4.24) and the simpler specification presented in Equations (4.1) to (4.6) is in order. Treating the forward rates and their volatilities on the same footing as M stochastic variables linked by a complex correlation matrix allows a more compact notation, makes all the M Brownian increments independent and lends itself well to the calibration strategies presented in Chapter 7. It has, however, one potential drawback. If fewer factors than variables are used, it is not easy to specify how the chosen number of factors should be allocated among the factors. For instance, we may want to use six factors, and to 'use' four for the forward rates and only two for the volatilities (perhaps on the grounds that the volatilities should be highly correlated anyhow). However, once we reduce the number of factors, there is no perfect way to tell the model how to carry out this allocation of its resources. The 'uglier' formulation of Equations (4.1) to (4.7), on the other hand, naturally allows for any partition of the factors that we may like. The price to pay is that the Brownian draws are no longer independent, and the calibration to the correlation matrix becomes more cumbersome. The problem *can* be fixed and we will tackle this topic in Chapter 7.

4.6   The Volatility Structure

Let the instantaneous volatilities of the forward rates, $\sigma_i(t, T_i)$, be given by the product of a function, say, $g(\cdot)$, of the residual time to maturity, $T_i - t$, of the associated forward rate times and forward-rate-specific function k_t^i:

$$\sigma_t^i = k_t^i g(T_i - t) \tag{4.32}$$

For concreteness, the choice for $g(T_i - t)$ that we shall use in the following is the one introduced in Chapter 2:

$$g(\tau_i) = (a + b\tau_i) \exp(-c\tau_i) + d \tag{4.33}$$

with $\tau_i = T_i - t$. The quantities k^i follow the process

$$\frac{dk_t^i}{k_t^i} = \mu_t^{k_i} dt + h_t^T \sum_{j=1}^{M} e_{ij} dy_j^t \tag{4.34}$$

The function h_t^T has the form

$$h_t^T = h(T - t) \tag{4.35}$$

and is parametrized by a set of parameters $[l, m, n, \ldots]$. A possible parametrization is

$$h_{\tau_i} = \xi_i \left[(\alpha + \beta\tau_i) \exp(-\gamma\tau_i) + \delta \right] \tag{4.36}$$

With these choices

$$k_s^i = k_0^i \exp\left[\int_0^s -\frac{1}{2}\xi_i^2 h^2 (T_i - u) du + \xi_i h(T_i - u) \sum_{j=1}^{M} e_{ij} dy_j(u) \right] \tag{4.37}$$

We have chosen the functions introduced to describe the volatility and the volatility of volatility to be time homogeneous. The terminology is sloppy (and we therefore refine it in the next section), but the concept is essential, at least in conditions of market self-similarity – roughly speaking, in 'normal' market conditions. Our preference for time homogeneity translates our belief that, with the same proviso about normality of the market, the only relevant time variable is linked to the residual time to expiry of the various forward rates in the problem. With the important exception of the conditions discussed in Section 4.8, introducing an explicit time or expiry dependence is a 'fudge' to be avoided as much as possible. Time-dependent reversion levels, reversion speeds, displacement coefficients or volatilities, etc., make for good fitting but poor physics.

As this is one of our central beliefs, we make the term 'time homogeneous' a bit more precise in the next section.

4.7 What We Mean by Time Homogeneity

A stochastic process is *strictly stationary* if its probability density function is invariant under a time shift. This definition is too demanding for our purposes – just looking at the drift term will convince us of this.

A concept closer to what we need is that of a *wide-sense stationary stochastic process* (see Mantegna and Stanley (1999)). This has many incarnations, of which *covariance stationarity* is one of the most common. For a stochastic variable $x(t)$, this requires, *inter alia*, that

$$R(t_1, t_2) = \mathbb{E}\left[x(t_1)x(t_2)\right] \tag{4.38}$$

should only be a function of $t_2 - t_1$: $R(t_1, t_2) = R(t_2 - t_1)$.

This is clearly what we require for the deterministic-volatility LIBOR market model. But for the LMM-SABR model the covariance structure is stochastic, so condition (4.38) will not in general apply. We therefore require something even weaker, which reflects the fact that the covariance (and other statistics) *can* be stochastic, but in a 'self-similar' manner.

For our purposes we therefore define as *time homogeneous* a set of stochastic processes, $x_1(t), x_2(t), \ldots, x_n(t)$, whose second-order moments, $R_{jk}(t_1, t_2)$, defined as

$$R_{jk}(t_1, t_2) = \mathbb{E}\left[x_j(t_1)x_k(t_2)\right] \tag{4.39}$$

can be stochastic, but with distributions that are in turn covariance stationary.

The definition could be refined, but for our purposes will serve us well enough.

4.8 The Volatility Structure in Periods of Market Stress

The SABR and LMM-SABR models assume that one (stochastic) volatility regime prevails at all times. In reality a large body of work suggests that markets move, often rapidly, among different states, commonly described as 'normal' and 'excited'. For studies about regime switches in the interest-rate domain which is of greatest interest to us see, e.g., Rebonato (2006), White and Rebonato (2008), Rebonato and Gaspari (2006), Rebonato and Chen (2008). (Incidentally, the work by Rebonato and Chen (2008) suggests that *three* states – quiet, normal and excited – may better describe the dynamics of interest rates. We do not pursue this avenue here.)

This has great relevance for the simultaneous pricing of options of different expiry. To see why this is the case, consider the situation where we are in an excited state. The market 'knows' this, but also knows that in a matter of weeks or, at most, months, trading conditions will revert to normal. If this is the case, the market will take this information into account, by pricing short-dated options with a high volatility, medium-dated options with a volatility somewhat elevated with respect to normal times, and long-dated options with a volatility barely unchanged from their typical long-dated values – the more so, the longer-dated the option.

This is when time-homogeneous pricing models, which by and large we like, get into trouble. By construction they assume that calendar time is irrelevant, and that the only variable that matters to determine volatilities, correlations and volatilities of volatilities is the residual time to maturity of the forward rate(s). For time-homogeneous models a one-year

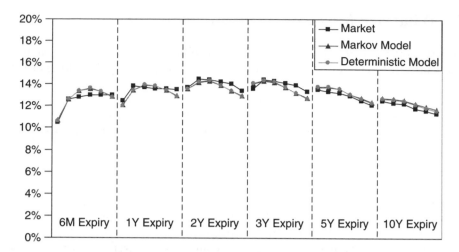

Figure 4.1 Fit to market data (US$) on 21st July 1998 in normal market conditions using a deterministic-volatility time-homogeneous implementation of the LMM. It is apparent that a small number of parameters (five, in this particular case) recover well the at-the-money volatility swaption matrix in its entirety. See White and Rebonato (2008) for further details.

option seen as of today will pretty much 'look' and behave like a one-year option in five or ten years' time. But if today we are in an excited state, this means that a time-homogeneous model fitted to short-dated options will propagate the current state of excitation *ad infinitum*. As a consequence the one-year option in ten years' time will be priced as if the current state of turmoil will still be present, say, ten years from now. What in normal times is a virtue, in excited periods therefore becomes a serious shortcoming. This 'curse of time homogeneity' is displayed in Figures 4.1 and 4.2, which clearly show that time-homogeneous models become, during excited periods, like a short blanket: either long-dated options are well priced, in which case short-dated ones are underpriced, or *vice versa*. There is no way to cover both the head and the feet of the swaption matrix (or, for other asset classes, of the smile surface) with a time-homogeneous model.

Two of us (RR and RW) have shown that an effective way to fix this problem in a financially justifiable manner is to posit a two-state Markov-chain process for the volatility. This means that at each point in time the volatility can be either in a normal or in an excited state. Given that the volatility is in a given state, it can either migrate to the other state with a transition probability p, or stay in the same state with probability $(1 - p)$. The normal and excited volatility functions can then be chosen to have the humped or exponentially decaying shapes discussed in Chapter 2. Rebonato and Kainth (2004) and White and Rebonato (2008) have shown that even such a conceptually simple model can give a very satisfactory and parsimonious description of the observed prices not only in normal market conditions, but also during periods of market excitation.

The problem is that these Markov-chain models may well be conceptually intuitive, but they are far from simple in terms of getting analytic or numerical approximations. With a lot of acrobatics one can obtain accurate approximations for European swaptions (see White and Rebonato (2008)), making calibration to the swaption matrix feasible, if not simple. When one moves to pricing and, above all, hedging complex options, for which Monte

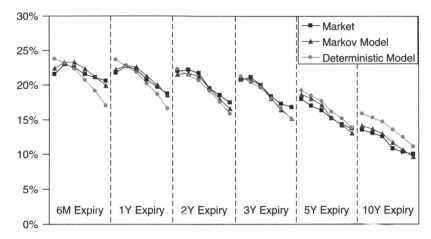

Figure 4.2 Fit to market data (US$) as in Figure 4.1 carried out four months later. The market is now excited, and the volatility at the short end (6 month into 1 year) is ~22% while that at the long end (10 years into 1 year) is 10%. The deterministic time-homogeneous volatility model attempts to fit this market by having an instantaneous volatility of the forward rates that is much higher close to maturity than far from it. However, this results in significant mispricing of options in common expiry blocks. One could, of course, improve the fits to the short-dated options, but this would systematically misprice the longer-dated ones, and *vice versa*. See White and Rebonato (2008) for further details.

Carlo techniques are needed, the numerical problems become too heavy to deal with for realistic pricing and hedging applications.[4]

What one needs is a deterministic-volatility approximation to the true two-state Markov-chain problem capable of producing *in nuce* the gist of the 'true' results. It must do so without peeking ahead (i.e., without knowing when the excited state will occur, or when the market will revert to the normal state). The only piece of information it can avail itself of from the 'true' Markov model is the probability of the market being in an excited or a normal state today. Chapter 15 in Part IV shows the effectiveness of the hedges that this reduced-form approach suggests. In this section we focus on the pricing implications of this reduced-form approach.

Let's assume for the moment that we believe that the probability today of being in an excited state is p. We would recognize this, either using a formal Bayesian estimation technique (see, e.g., Rabiner (1989)), or, by fitting the 'proper' two-state Markov-chain model described in White and Rebonato (2008). A good sanity check of our estimation of today's state as excited is that the best fit of the LMM-SABR model *to short-expiry options* should yield a monotonically decaying volatility function $g\,(\cdot)$ (and perhaps $h\,(\cdot)$ as well). As with the full Markov model we assume that there are two time-homogeneous volatility curves, *normal* and *excited*, given by

$$\sigma_{n,x}(t, T) = \left[a_{n,x} + b_{n,x}(T - t)\right] e^{-c_{n,x}(T-t)} + d_{n,x} \qquad (4.40)$$

---

[4]Here is a taste of the problems: suppose, for instance, that I perturb by a small amount a small transition probability. How many Monte Carlo paths do I have to run in order to be able to detect a stable difference with respect to the underperturbed case?

To approximate starting in an excited state and decaying to an (absorbing) normal state, we specify the Markov-approximation deterministic volatility as

$$\sigma(t, T; a_n, b_n, c_n, d_n, a_x, b_x, c_x, d_x, \lambda) =$$

$$(1 - pe^{-\lambda t})\sigma(t, T; a_n, b_n, c_n, d_n) + pe^{-\lambda t}\sigma(t, T; a_x, b_x, c_x, d_x) \qquad (4.41)$$

Note that function (4.41) is no longer time homogeneous, because of the presence of the unashamedly time-dependent term $e^{-\lambda t}$. This term does bring in a dependence on calendar time (something we generally argue against), but not as a fitting parameter with no financial justification. Yes, our model says that the future does not look like the present, but, in a situation of transitory market excitation, this is a virtue, not a sin. We have not sold our souls (yet) to the Mephistopheles of overfitting.

The parameter λ is of course related to how long we believe the volatility will remain in the excited state, given that it is in the excited state today. Since we are presenting a 'reduced-form' *Markov*-chain model, the permanence in the excited state does not depend on how long the system has already been excited. This may or may not be a shortcoming of the approach, depending on one's views about the market's informational efficiency. It is also clear that the parameter λ is in principle linked to the transition matrix of the 'true' two-state Markov chain. In practice it can be used (within reason!) as a fitting parameter, as discussed below.

As for the parameter p, we will show that it is natural to give it the interpretation of probability of being today in the excited state, but we can also simply regard Equation

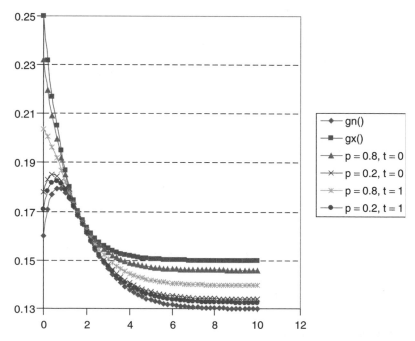

Figure 4.3   Volatility curves under normal and excited periods ($gn()$ and $gx()$), uncertainty in today's state (curve's probability of being in the excited state of $p = 0.8$ and 0.2 with $t = 0$), and evolution of the curve as time increases (to $t = 1$).

(4.41) as specifying a more complex, but still perfectly deterministic, form for the volatility function $g\,(\cdot)$. Figure 4.3 shows what this function may look like for various values of p and $t = 0$. If we pursue the probabilistic interpretation of p, for $p = 0$ we know for certain that we are in a normal state today. With this reduced-form model for $p = 0$ 'nothing happens' and we are back to the LMM-SABR treatment that we have presented so far. If $p = 1$ we know for certain that we are in an excited state today ($t = 0$) and we price very short-dated options almost exclusively with an excited volatility.

More interesting is what happens as calendar time increases. See, for instance, Figure 4.3 for the behaviour of function (4.41) when $t = 1$. We see that as time goes by the excited state begins to disappear, and that a short-dated option priced in one year's time experiences a different (less excited) volatility than a short-dated option priced today. How much less excited will depend on the value of λ. This is just what we wanted to achieve.

Before we go any further we should stress that *we should use a function like Equation (4.41) whenever we know with reasonable certainty that we are in an excited state*. We should do so irrespective of whether we want to follow the 'survival hedging' suggested in Chapter 15, Part IV. Using function (4.41) won't buy us very much in normal times (when p is close to zero), but will make a world of difference when p is close to 1.

4.9 A More General Stochastic Volatility Dynamics

We now have the ingredients of the LMM-SABR in place. As in the case of the LMM model, the no-arbitrage drifts are purely a function of volatilities and correlations. We are therefore in a position to use these inputs to calculate these no-arbitrage conditions.

Since in the literature there are a number of stochastic-volatility LMM models, but their drift adjustments are rarely derived or reported, we generalize slightly our notation, so that the reader can use our results for any stochastic-volatility model she may choose. Also, the more general notation in this brief section will be of use for estimation problems in Part III.

Let therefore the forward rate dynamics in a measure, $\mathbb{Q}$, other than its own terminal measure, be given by

$$df_t = \mu(f_t, t)dt + \sigma(f_t, t)k_t dz_t \qquad (4.42)$$

$$dk_t = \eta(k_t, t)dt + v(k_t, t)dw_t \qquad (4.43)$$

(We are being sloppy and not indicating the measure-$\mathbb{Q}$ dependence of the increments dz_t and dw_t – for once, we let the context suggest the appropriate measure.) Note that in this formulation σ is a deterministic function of f_t and t, and that k_t now takes the role of stochastic volatility. This framework of course includes both the SABR and our own SABR-LMM dynamics as special cases. We therefore obtain:

$$f_T = f_0 + \int_0^T \mu(f_t, t)dt + \int_0^T \sigma(f_t, t)k_t dz_t$$

$$= f_0 + \int_0^T \mu(f_t, t)dt + \int_0^T \sigma(f_t, t)\left(k_0 + \int_0^t \eta(k_s, s)ds + \int_0^t v(k_s, s)dw_s\right)dz_t$$

$$= f_0 + \int_0^T \mu(f_t, t)dt + \int_0^T \left\{ \sigma(f_t, t) \left(k_0 + \int_0^t \eta(k_s, s)ds \right) \right.$$

$$\left. + \sigma(f_t, t) \int_0^t v(k_s, s)dw_s \right\} dz_t$$

$$= f_0 + \int_0^T \mu(f_t, t)dt + \int_0^T \left\{ \alpha_t + \beta_t \int_0^t \gamma_s dw_s \right\} dz_t \tag{4.44}$$

with

$$\alpha_t = \sigma(f_t, t) \left(k_0 + \int_0^t \eta(k_s, s)ds \right) \tag{4.45}$$

$$\beta_t = \sigma(f_t, t) \tag{4.46}$$

$$\gamma_t = v(k_t, t) \tag{4.47}$$

We have written the formal solution in this form with a view to the treatment in Chapter 8. Of course we cannot directly evaluate any of these integrals – they are all stochastic because of the dependence on f_t and k_t in μ, σ and η. In Chapter 8 we use some approximations in order to estimate the moments of f^T.

Now that we have somewhat generalized our notation, we derive the no-arbitrage drifts for this more general stochastic-volatility framework, and then specialize the results to our particular LMM-SABR setting.

4.10   Calculating the No-Arbitrage Drifts

4.10.1   Preliminaries

The reader familiar with the change-of-numeraire technique can skip this section. For the reader who may like a refresher we present a simple derivation of the results we need.

We begin by giving some definitions and stating what is for our purposes the fundamental theorem of no-arbitrage. As always in this book, we make no attempt at mathematical rigour and always assume that all technical conditions are satisfied.

Definition 4.1 *Any traded asset with strictly positive value in every state of the world and that pays no dividends can be used as a numeraire. We shall denote it by N_t.*

Definition 4.2 *For any tradeable assets S_t, the ratio $A_t = \frac{S_t}{N_t}$ is called a relative price. It expresses the value of S in units of N.*

Definition 4.3 *We denote by $\mathcal{F}_t$ the natural filtration generated by the process S_t.*

With these definitions we can introduce one of the fundamental theorems of no-arbitrage.

Theorem 4.4 *For any tradeable asset (or portfolio of tradeable assets), S_t, and for any numeraire, N_t, a necessary and sufficient condition for the absence of arbitrage is that there should exist a risk-neutral measure, $\mathbb{N}$, associated with the numeraire, N_t, such that*

$$\mathbb{E}^{\mathbb{N}}\left[\frac{S_t}{N_t}|\mathcal{F}_s\right] = \frac{S_s}{N_s} \quad for\ t > s \tag{4.48}$$

In other words, to avoid arbitrage we must find a measure, $\mathbb{N}$, induced by our choice or numeraire, such that the relative price, $A_t = \frac{S_t}{N_t}$, is an $\mathbb{N}$-martingale.

We will not prove this theorem. The sufficient part of the theorem (i.e., if the risk-neutral measure exists then there is no arbitrage) is easy to prove. Going the other way (i.e., from absence of arbitrage to the existence of a pricing measure) is harder work, and the standard proof is financially not very illuminating. Working in discrete time and with a finite number of assets as usual makes life easier. The typical line of attack makes use of the separating hyperplane theorem and can be found in Duffie (2001), Harrison and Kreps (1979) or Dybvig and Ross (1992). Etheridge (2002) provides a step-by-step proof along these lines. Her treatment is about as simple and illuminating as it gets. A more intuitive sketch of the same proof (that does not explicitly mention the separating hyperplane theorem, but makes use of the same intuition) is given by Lengwiler (2006). Finally, Ross (2004) provides a different outline of the same proof using a somewhat less general, but financially more transparent and 'constructive', condition, i.e., the maximization of utility of a representative agent. For the reader who wants to understand the standard proof, I recommend starting from Lengwiler (2006) to capture the basic intuition, then moving to Etheridge (2002) for a step-by-step approach and finally progressing to Harrison and Kreps (1979) in order to cross and dot, respectively, all the mathematical ts and is.

In addition to this financial theorem (the 'physics' part of the problem), we need some stochastic calculus results, namely, the Radon–Nikodym derivative, the martingale representation theorem and the Cameron–Girsanov theorem. Taken together, these three tools will allow us to use the 'change-of-numeraire technique', i.e., to find in a systematic manner the no-arbitrage drifts under different choices of numeraires. We rely heavily on the approach by Baxter and Rennie (1996) in the following.

Starting with the martingale representation theorem, we start from the usual filtered probability space $\{\Omega, \mathbb{P}, \mathcal{F}\}$, and we let

- X be a strictly positive martingale with respect to the filtration generated by a $\mathbb{P}$-Wiener process,

- $z(t)$ be a standard Wiener process under $\mathbb{P}$, and

- $q(t)$ a real-valued (not necessarily deterministic!) previsible process, integrable with respect to $z(t)$.

Then, if some technical conditions are satisfied, the following theorem holds:

Theorem 4.5 *Given X, q and $z(t)$ as above, it is always possible to represent the martingale $X(t)$ in the form*

$$dX_t = X_t q(t) dz(t) \tag{4.49}$$

Two points are worth making. First, the requirement that X should be a martingale with respect to the filtration generated by a $\mathbb{P}$-Wiener process is essential to the proof, and reflects the fact that the Wiener process should be the only source of randomness in X. Second, despite the notation $(q(t))$, we are *not* saying that the distribution of X_t is log-normal. The 'volatility' $q(t)$ can be relatively horrible, and can certainly depend on X_t itself, and hence be stochastic.

We are now ready to move to Cameron–Girsanov's theorem. We place ourselves again in the usual filtered probability space $\{\Omega, \mathbb{P}, \mathcal{F}\}$, and we let

- $z(t)$ be a standard Brownian motion under a measure $\mathbb{P}$,

- $\mathcal{F}_t$ be the associated Brownian filtration,

- q^5 be an $\mathcal{F}_t$-adapted process which satisfies the Novikov regularity condition $\mathbb{E}^{\mathbb{P}}\left[\exp\left[\int_0^t q(u)^2 du\right]\right] < \infty$, and

- $z_q(t)$ be defined by

$$z_q(t) = z(t) + qt \tag{4.50}$$

If these conditions hold, then (see, e.g., Mikosch (1998)) Cameron–Girsanov's theorem actually makes three distinct, but related, statements.

Theorem 4.6

1. *The process* $\zeta(t) = \exp[-qz(t) - \frac{1}{2}q^2 t]$ *is a* $\mathbb{P}$-*martingale.*

2. *The process* $\zeta(t)$ *can be used to define a new probability measure* $\mathbb{Q}$, *equivalent to* $\mathbb{P}$, *via the relationship* $\mathbb{Q}(A) = \int_A \zeta_t(\omega) d\mathbb{P}(\omega)$.

3. *Under* $\mathbb{Q}$, *the process* $z_q(t)$ *is a standard Brownian motion.*

See, e.g., Neftci (1996, Chapter 14, page 291) and *passim* for a nice sketch of the proof of the first part of the theorem, i.e., of the fact that $\zeta(t)$ is a $\mathbb{P}$-martingale.

To get some intuition about Cameron–Girsanov's theorem, consider the expression $\mathbb{Q}(A) = \int_A \zeta(\omega) d\mathbb{P}(\omega)$ in the simpler discrete case, where A is now a subset of the sample space Ω containing a finite number of elementary events. To make matters even simpler, let's also consider the single-horizon case, when all the uncertainty will be revealed at a single time, T. In this case the expression $\mathbb{Q}(A) = \int_A \zeta_t(\omega) d\mathbb{P}(\omega)$ becomes

$$\mathbb{Q}(A) = \sum_{\omega_i \in A} \zeta(\omega_i^T) \mathbb{P}(\omega_i^T) \tag{4.51}$$

The transformation $\zeta(\omega_i^T) = \exp[-qz(\omega_i^T) - \frac{1}{2}q^2 T]$ changes the original probability of each event $\mathbb{P}(\omega_i^T)$ into a new probability $\mathbb{Q}(\omega_i^T)$. Under this new measure $\mathbb{Q}$ the probability of

---

[5]With a slight abuse of notation we have used the symbol q both for the 'volatility' of the martingale representation theorem and for the process that transforms the $\mathbb{P}$-Brownian motion into z_q. As we shall see, there is a good reason for this choice.

event A (that will be revealed at time T) is given by

$$\mathbb{Q}(A) = \sum_{\omega_i \in A} \mathbb{Q}(\omega_i^T)$$

In this expression $\zeta(\omega_i^T)$ is the realization of the $\mathbb{P}$-Brownian motion when event ω_i^T is realized at time T. The transformation is such that every 'new' probability is greater[6] than zero and smaller than or equal to one, and the sum, $\sum_{\omega_i \in A}$, over any $A \subseteq \Omega$ is strictly positive and smaller than or equal to one. In other terms, in the discrete, single-step case Cameron–Girsanov's theorem tells us that, as long as the transformation is carried out using the quantity $\zeta_T(\omega_i^T) = \exp[-qz(\omega_i^T) - \frac{1}{2}q^2 T]$ with the properties above, we can rest assured that the transformation changes a good probability measure into another *bona fide* probability measure.

After the stretching of the probability space carried out by $\zeta(T)$, what was in the original measure $\mathbb{P}$ a good standard Brownian motion will have been 'disrupted' in such a way that it is no longer a Brownian motion under $\mathbb{Q}$. But Cameron–Girsanov's theorem tells us that it doesn't take much to recreate a standard Brownian motion under $\mathbb{Q}$: just add to the original $\mathbb{P}$-Brownian motion a 'drift' term qt, and we are dealing again with a standard Brownian motion under $\mathbb{Q}$.

Clearly, for an 'atomic' set A containing the single discrete event $\omega(A = \omega)$, one can write

$$\frac{\mathbb{Q}(\omega)}{\mathbb{P}(\omega)} = \zeta_T(\omega) \tag{4.52}$$

If instead of dealing with discrete probabilities we are using probability densities, Equation (4.52) becomes

$$\frac{\mathbb{Q}(\omega)}{\mathbb{P}(\omega)} \Rightarrow \frac{d\mathbb{Q}(\omega)}{d\mathbb{P}(\omega)} \tag{4.53}$$

where, on the RHS, we now interpret the integration region A to have shrunk to encompass an infinitesimal neighbourhood of ω.

We have considered so far how probability measures (and Brownian motion defined over them) are transformed by the quantity $\zeta_T(\omega)$. But what about expectations? More precisely, what about expectations of quantities that are fully known if the realization of the Brownian motion is known?

To tackle this question, let's consider again the single-horizon problem and consider the unconditional expectation of a Brownian-motion-related random variable. More precisely, consider the payoff, X_T, of a security or derivative contract. Each realization of X_T (discrete or continuous as it may be), constitutes a random event whose value will be revealed at time T. The only really important thing about this random variable is that its value at time T must be perfectly knowable if one knows the realization at time T of the $\mathbb{P}$-Brownian motion, $z(\omega_i^T)$.

Now, to each realization of X_T we can assign a probability $\mathbb{P}(X_T)$ under the measure $\mathbb{P}$. Thanks to the discussion above, we can write under $\mathbb{Q}$ the expression for the probability,

---

[6]$\zeta(\omega_i^T)$ must be strictly positive because we are dealing with *equivalent* probability measures.

$\mathbb{Q}(A)$ (generated by the process $\zeta(T) = \exp[-qz(T) - \frac{1}{2}q^2T]$) of some set A of realizations of X_T (say, the positive realizations of X_T), as

$$\mathbb{Q}(A) = \int_A \zeta(X_T)d\mathbb{P}(X_T) \tag{4.54}$$

From this expression we can see that the expectation will be given by

$$E^{\mathbb{Q}}[X_T|\mathcal{F}_0] = E^{\mathbb{P}}\left[\frac{d\mathbb{Q}_T}{d\mathbb{P}_T}X_T|\mathcal{F}_0\right] \tag{4.55}$$

where the filtration has been denoted by $\mathcal{F}_0$ because we are dealing with a single-step problem. So, in this simplest of cases, the quantity $\frac{d\mathbb{Q}_T}{d\mathbb{P}_T}$ tells us by how much we have to change the measure $\mathbb{Q}$ so that the (unconditional) expectation taken at time 0 of X_T under $\mathbb{P}$ gives us the same value.

If we are looking at a single horizon (T in this case) the Radon–Nikodym derivative $\zeta(X_T)$ defines a random variable. This would be all we need if we were dealing with a European option. But what about a derivative whose value depends on the realization of the Brownian motion that drives our uncertainty at times $t_1, t_2, \ldots, t_n = T$? What we would like to do is to turn the random variable, $\zeta_0(X_T)$, into a process, $\zeta_t(X_T)$, i.e., roughly speaking, a random variable indexed by time. Let's try to do so by considering the *conditional* expectation taken at time t of the Radon–Nikodym derivative $\frac{d\mathbb{Q}(\omega_T)}{d\mathbb{P}(\omega_T)}$ out to a generic horizon T, with $0 \leq t \leq T$. (We continue to follow here the treatment of Baxter and Rennie (1996).)

The process ζ_t we have just constructed defines a strictly positive martingale:

$$\zeta_t = E^{\mathbb{P}}\left[\frac{d\mathbb{Q}(\omega_T)}{d\mathbb{P}(\omega_T)}|\mathcal{F}_t\right] = E^{\mathbb{P}}[\zeta_T|\mathcal{F}_t] \qquad \text{for } T \geqq t \tag{4.56}$$

So, the expectation taken at time t of the payoff X_T for any time $t \leq T$ before its value is known with certainty is given by

$$E^{\mathbb{Q}}[\zeta_t X_T|\mathcal{F}_t] = E^{\mathbb{P}}[\zeta_T X_T|\mathcal{F}_t] \tag{4.57}$$

$$E^{\mathbb{Q}}[X_T|\mathcal{F}_t] = \frac{1}{\zeta_t}E^{\mathbb{P}}[\zeta_T X_T|\mathcal{F}_t] \tag{4.58}$$

where we have 'taken out' of the expectation sign quantities (ζ_t) known at time t. Note that the Radon–Nikodym derivative process takes out exactly what we already know up to time t of the driving Brownian process that, with its full path to T, determines the value of X_T. We can check that expression (4.57) coincides with Equation (4.55) when $t = 0$:

$$E^{\mathbb{Q}}[\zeta_0 X_T|\mathcal{F}_0] = E^{\mathbb{Q}}[X_T|\mathcal{F}_0] = E^{\mathbb{P}}[\zeta_T X_T|\mathcal{F}_0] \tag{4.59}$$

where the middle term follows because $\zeta_0 = 1$.

We have got as much as we need from the mathematical part of the Cameron–Girsanov theorem. We need to inject some financial information into the problem to proceed further. The result that we want to obtain is that the Radon–Nikodym derivative is given by the ratio of the two numeraires that identify the equivalent measures $\mathbb{P}$ and $\mathbb{Q}$. To do this, we mirror again the treatment in Baxter and Rennie (1996), and suppose that in our economy we have $N+2$ securities, $S_t^1, S_t^2, \ldots, S_t^N$, B_t and C_t. Let's assume that both B_t and C_t satisfy the conditions (see above) for being possible numeraires. Either choice would implicitly define a measure, $\mathbb{Q}^B$ or $\mathbb{Q}^C$, under which relative prices are martingales (again, see above): so, under $\mathbb{Q}^B$, $\frac{S_t^1}{B_t}, \frac{S_t^2}{B_t}, \ldots, \frac{S_t^N}{B_t}$ and $\frac{C_t}{B_t}$ are martingales; under $\mathbb{Q}^c$, $\frac{S_t^1}{C_t}, \frac{S_t^2}{C_t}, \ldots, \frac{S_t^N}{C_t}$ and $\frac{B_t}{C_t}$ are martingales.

Given these choices the price at time t, V_t, of a payoff X_T at time T is equivalently given by

$$V_t^B = B_t \mathbb{E}^{\mathbb{Q}^B}\left[\frac{X_T}{B_T}|\mathcal{F}_t\right] \tag{4.60}$$

or by

$$V_t^C = C_t \mathbb{E}^{\mathbb{Q}^C}\left[\frac{X_T}{C_T}|\mathcal{F}_t\right] \tag{4.61}$$

We can now ask: how are these two measures related? We can answer this question thanks to the properties of the Radon–Nikodym process presented above. Namely, we can write

$$\mathbb{E}^{\mathbb{Q}^C}\left[X_\tau|\mathcal{F}_t\right] = \frac{1}{\zeta_t}\mathbb{E}^{\mathbb{Q}^B}\left[\zeta_t X_\tau|\mathcal{F}_t\right] \tag{4.62}$$

or

$$\zeta_t \mathbb{E}^{\mathbb{Q}^C}\left[X_\tau|\mathcal{F}_t\right] = \mathbb{E}^{\mathbb{Q}^B}\left[\zeta_\tau X_\tau|\mathcal{F}_t\right] \tag{4.63}$$

If the process X_t is a $\mathbb{Q}^C$-martingale, we have

$$\mathbb{E}^{\mathbb{Q}^C}\left[X_\tau|\mathcal{F}_t\right] = X_t \tag{4.64}$$

and therefore

$$\zeta_t X_t = \mathbb{E}^{\mathbb{Q}^B}\left[\zeta_\tau X_\tau|\mathcal{F}_t\right] \tag{4.65}$$

i.e., under $\mathbb{Q}^B$, it is the process $\zeta_t X_t$ that is a $\mathbb{Q}^B$-martingale. But we also know that, under $\mathbb{Q}^B$, $\frac{S_t^1}{B_t}, \frac{S_t^2}{B_t}, \ldots, \frac{S_t^N}{B_t}$ and $\frac{C_t}{B_t}$ are all martingales (the no-arbitrage condition). So, both $\frac{S_t^1}{B_t}$ and $\zeta_t \frac{S_t^1}{C_t}$ are $\mathbb{Q}^B$-martingales – and the same applies, of course, to the other securities. *But, if this is the case, we have a very simple and important result: the Radon–Nikodym process is just given by the ratio of the numeraires*:

$$\zeta_t = \frac{C_t}{B_t} \tag{4.66}$$

As we have seen, ζ_t is a strictly positive martingale. The martingale representation theorem therefore applies and we have

$$d\zeta_t = \zeta_t q_t dz_t \tag{4.67}$$

and

$$\zeta(t) = \exp\left[\int_0^t q_s dz_s - \frac{1}{2}q_s^2 ds\right] \tag{4.68}$$

Equation (4.68) immediately tells us that the process starts at $\zeta(0) = 1$. The only thing we still need in order to pin down uniquely the measure transformation is the 'volatility' process q_t. In order to obtain this we need to specify a process for C_t and B_t, use Ito's lemma for the ratio $\zeta_t = \frac{C_t}{B_t}$, look at the coefficient of the stochastic part, and we are done. This is exactly how we will apply below the change-of-numeraire technique to derive the drifts we need.

Given the initial condition ($\zeta(0) = 1$) and the 'volatility' of ζ_t, we know everything there is to know about the ratio ζ_t. Therefore, if we know the drift under one measure, we can immediately find the drift under another measure using Equation (4.63).

We apply this blue-print to two simple applications in the following subsection.

4.10.2   Standard LIBOR and LIBOR in Arrears

For a forward rate f_t^i that expires at time T_i and pays at time $T_i + \tau = T_{i+1}$, the discount bond, $P(t, T_{i+1})$, is a possible numeraire. The associated risk-neutral measure, $\mathbb{T}_i$, is known as the terminal measure. The numeraire is called the 'natural numeraire' (or the 'natural payoff' – see Doust (1995)).

The forward rate spanning T_i to T_{i+1} can be written in terms of discount bonds as

$$f_t^i \equiv f(t; T_i, T_{i+1}) \equiv \frac{P(t, T_i) - P(t, T_{i+1})}{\tau P(t, T_{i+1})} \tag{4.69}$$

Under the terminal measure we have

$$\mathbb{E}^{\mathbb{T}_i}\left[f(t; T_i, T_{i+1})|\mathcal{F}_s\right] = \frac{1}{\tau}\mathbb{E}^{\mathbb{T}_i}\left[\frac{P(t, T_i) - P(t, T_{i+1})}{P(t, T_{i+1})}|\mathcal{F}_s\right] \tag{4.70}$$

If we consider the quantity $P(t, T_i) - P(t, T_{i+1})$ as a (portfolio of) assets, we can write $P(t, T_i) - P(t, T_{i+1}) = S_t^i$. We can then apply the fundamental theorem above, and impose that $\frac{S_t^i}{N_t^i}$, which is the ratio of tradeable assets, must be a martingale. But since

$$\frac{S_t^i}{N_t^i} = \frac{P(t, T_i) - P(t, T_{i+1})}{P(t, T_{i+1})} = \tau f_t^i \tag{4.71}$$

it follows that the forward rate f_t^i itself, under its own terminal measure, must be a martingale

$$\mathbb{E}^{\mathbb{T}_i}\left[f_t^i | \mathcal{F}_s\right] = f_s^i \tag{4.72}$$

This is easy enough for the natural numeraire. In general, however, we want to calculate the no-arbitrage drifts that arise when the numeraire is *not* the natural numeraire. We present in this section the argument in detail in the LIBOR-in-arrears case, i.e., for the special case when the forward rate f_t^i resets and pays *at the same time*, T_i. For this problem, using the Radon–Nikodym weaponry to obtain the drift adjustment is a bit like using a cannon to swat a fly; still, we will pursue not only the simpler, *ad hoc* treatment, but also the more general treatment to serve us as a guide in the more complex settings we are interested in.

In the LIBOR-in-arrears case it is natural to discount the payoffs using the discount bond $P(t, T_i)$. This, however, is not the natural numeraire for the forward rate f_t^i. For the LIBOR-in-arrears case we therefore need the dynamics, and, in particular, the no-arbitrage drifts, of f_t^i under the measure $\mathbb{T}_{i-1}$ induced by the numeraire $P(t, T_i)$. As we said, to obtain these we proceed along two distinct routes: the first we call the 'brute-force' approach, and the second the 'change-of-numeraire' route.

LIBOR in Arrears: Brute-Force Approach

We first note that, by itself, f_t^i is not a traded asset. However, if multiplied by its own natural numeraire, $P(t, T_{i+1})$, it becomes a portfolio of traded assets:

$$\tau_i f_t^i P(t, T_{i+1}) = P(t, T_i) - P(t, T_{i+1})$$

To this portfolio of traded assets we can apply the fundamental theorem of asset pricing, this time under the measure, $\mathbb{T}_{i-1}$, associated with numeraire $P(t, T_i)$.[7] To apply the theorem we write the fundamental theorem as

$$\mathbb{E}_0^{\mathbb{T}_{i-1}}\left[\frac{\tau_i f_t^i P(t, T_{i+1})}{P(t, T_i)}\right] = \mathbb{E}_0^{\mathbb{T}_{i-1}}\left[\frac{P(t, T_i) - P(t, T_{i+1})}{P(t, T_i)}\right] = \frac{\tau f_0^i P(0, T_{i+1})}{P(0, T_i)} \tag{4.73}$$

and we define

$$X_t = \frac{P(t, T_{i+1})}{P(t, T_i)} = \frac{1}{1 + \tau f_t^i} \tag{4.74}$$

Note now that both X_t and $f_t^i X_t$ are relative prices (because they are assets, or portfolios of assets, divided by our chosen numeraire). By the fundamental theorem of asset pricing they must therefore be martingales under $\mathbb{T}_{i-1}$:

$$\mathbb{E}_0^{\mathbb{T}_{i-1}}\left[f_t^i X_t\right] = f_0^i X_0 \tag{4.75}$$

$$\mathbb{E}_0^{\mathbb{T}_{i-1}}[X_t] = X_0 \tag{4.76}$$

---

[7]Why do we call $\mathbb{T}_{i-1}$ the measure associated with numeraire $P(t, T_i)$? Because it is the measure under which the forward rate f_{i-1} is driftless!

Under the dynamics specified by Equation (4.42), we can use Ito's lemma to write down the equations of motion for X_t:

$$dX_t = \frac{\partial X_t}{\partial f_t} df_t^i + \frac{1}{2} \frac{\partial^2 X_t}{\partial f_t^2} \langle df_t^i, df_t^i \rangle \tag{4.77}$$

$$= -\tau X_t^2 \left(\mu^{i, \mathbb{T}_{i-1}} \left(f_t^i, t \right) dt + \sigma^i \left(f_t^i, t \right) k_t^i dz_t^{i, \mathbb{T}_{i-1}} \right) + \tau^2 X_t^3 \sigma^i \left(f_t^i, t \right)^2 \left(k_t^i \right)^2 dt$$

$$= \tau X_t^2 \left(\tau X_t \sigma^i \left(f_t, t \right)^2 \left(k_t^i \right)^2 - \mu^{i, \mathbb{T}_{i-1}} \left(f_t^i, t \right) \right) dt - \tau X_t^2 \sigma^i \left(f_t^i, t \right) k_t^i dz_t^{i, \mathbb{T}_{i-1}} \tag{4.78}$$

The drift of X_t is

$$\frac{\mathbb{E}^{\mathbb{T}_{i-1}} [dX_t]}{dt} = \tau X_t^2 \left(\tau X_t \sigma^i \left(f_t^i, t \right)^2 \left(k_t^i \right)^2 - \mu^{i, \mathbb{T}_{i-1}} \left(f_t^i, t \right) \right) \tag{4.79}$$

However, since X_t is a martingale under $\mathbb{T}_{i-1}$, this drift must be zero. This gives the drift of f_t^i under measure $\mathbb{T}_{i-1}$:

$$\mu^{i, \mathbb{T}_{i-1}}(f_t^i, t) = \tau \left(k_t^i \right)^2 \frac{\sigma^i \left(f_t^i, t \right)^2}{1 + \tau f_t^i} \tag{4.80}$$

This is the drift correction to be applied to the forward rate, f_t^i, in order to avoid arbitrage under the simplified 'stochastic volatility' model specified by Equation (4.42). This result closely resembles the drift obtained in the well-known deterministic-volatility case, which can be obtained if we set $k_t^i = 1$ and absorb it in the function $\sigma^i (f_t^i, t)^2$:

$$\mu^{i, \mathbb{T}_{i-1}}(f_t^i, t) = \frac{\tau \sigma^i (t)^2}{1 + \tau f_t^i} \tag{4.81}$$

Despite the formal similarity note that, in our stochastic-volatility result, the factor k_t^i is a full stochastic process.

The same no-arbitrage drift would have been obtained if we had considered the dynamics of $f_t^i X_t$ (which is just as well!). Indeed, this is exactly the line of attack typically used to obtain the no-arbitrage drifts in the deterministic-volatility case. See, e.g., Rebonato (2002). However, the approach we have followed does not give us much of a hint as to how we can find the no-arbitrage drift on the volatility, $\eta^i (k_t^i, t)$. To get this drift we must follow a different, more general, line of attack.

LIBOR in Arrears: The Change-of-Numeraire Approach

Recall the condition

$$\zeta_t X_t = \mathbb{E}^{\mathbb{T}_i} \left[\zeta_\tau X_\tau | \mathcal{F}_t \right] \tag{4.82}$$

which holds whenever X_t is a martingale under the measure $\mathbb{T}_i$. First, we apply this condition to $X_t = f_t^i$ which is a $\mathbb{T}_i$-martingale associated with its natural numeraire $P(t, T_{i+1})$. The dynamics of $\zeta_t^i f_t^i$ under the measure we are interested in (the $\mathbb{T}_{i-1}$-measure) are given by

$$
\begin{aligned}
d\left(f_t^i \zeta_t^i\right) &= \zeta_t^i df_t^i + f_t^i d\zeta_t^i + df_t^i d\zeta_t^i \\
&= \zeta_t^i \left[\mu^{i,\mathbb{T}_{i-1}}\left(f_t^i, t\right) dt + \sigma^i(f_t^i, t)k_t^i dz_t^{i,\mathbb{T}_{i-1}}\right] + \zeta_t^i f_t^i q_t^i dz_t^{i,\mathbb{T}_{i-1}} \\
&\quad + \sigma^i(f_t^i, t)k_t^i \zeta_t^i q_t^i dt \\
&= \zeta_t^i \left[\mu^{i,\mathbb{T}_{i-1}}(f_t^i, t) + \sigma^i(f_t^i, t)k_t^i q_t^i\right] dt \\
&\quad + \zeta_t^i \left[\sigma^i(f_t^i, t)k_t^i + f_t^i q_t^i\right] dz_t^{i,\mathbb{T}_{i-1}}
\end{aligned}
\tag{4.83}
$$

where the last term in the second equality $(\sigma^i\left(f_t^i, t\right) k_t^i \zeta_i_t q_t^i dt)$ follows because in this particular case we know that there is a perfect functional dependence between the forward rate, f_t^i, and the Radon–Nikodym derivative (which is just the ratio of the numeraires):

$$
\zeta_t^i = \frac{P(t, T_{i+1})}{P(t, T_i)} = \frac{1}{1 + \tau f_t^i}
\tag{4.84}
$$

The martingale condition means that we can write

$$
\mu^{i,\mathbb{T}_i \; 1}(f_t^i, t) + \sigma(f_t^i, t)k_t^i q_t^i = 0 \Rightarrow \mu^{i,\mathbb{T}_{i-1}}(f_t^i, t) = -\sigma(f_t^i, t)k_t^i q_t^i
\tag{4.85}
$$

We just need the volatility, q_t^i, of the Radon–Nikodym derivative. This can be obtained from a quick application of Itо's lemma to Equation (4.84):

$$
q_t^i = -\frac{\tau k_t^i \sigma^i(f_t^i, t)}{1 + \tau f_t^i}
\tag{4.86}
$$

and so Equation (4.85) becomes

$$
\mu^{i,\mathbb{T}_{i-1}}(f_t^i, t) = -\sigma^i(f_t^i, t)k_t^i q_t^i = \frac{\left[k_t^i \sigma^i(f_t^i, t)\right]^2 \tau}{1 + \tau f_t^i}
\tag{4.87}
$$

which is reassuringly identical to the result obtained above using the brute-force approach.

The beauty of this approach is that, following exactly the same blue-print, we can now also obtain at virtually no extra cost the no-arbitrage drift for the volatility. This is how it is done.

4.10.3 LIBOR in Arrears: The Volatility Drift

We now let $X_t = k_t^i$ be a martingale process under $\mathbb{T}_i$. The dynamics of $k_t^i \zeta_t^i$ under $\mathbb{T}_{i-1}$ are

$$
\begin{aligned}
d(k_t^i \zeta_t^i) &= \zeta_t^i dk_t^i + k_t^i d\zeta_t^i + dk_t^i d\zeta_t^i \\
&= \zeta_t^i \left[\eta(k_t, t)dt + v(k_t, t)dw_t^{\mathbb{T}_{i-1}}\right] + k_t \zeta_t q_t dz_t^{\mathbb{T}_{i-1}} + \rho \zeta_t q_t v(k_t, t)dt \\
&= \zeta_t \left[\eta(k_t, t) + \rho q_t v(k_t, t)\right] dt + k_t \zeta_t q_t dz_t^{i,\mathbb{T}_{i-1}} + \zeta_t v(k_t, t)dw_t^{i,\mathbb{T}_{i-1}}
\end{aligned}
\tag{4.88}
$$

where $dz_t^{i,\mathbb{T}_{i-1}}$ and $dw_t^{i,\mathbb{T}_{i-1}}$ are two standard Brownian motions under $\mathbb{T}_{i-1}$, which shock the forward rate, f_t^i, and the process, k_t^i, respectively. But again we know (from the definition of the dynamics) that $k_t^i \varsigma_t^i$ is a martingale under $\mathbb{T}_{i-1}$. It follows that

$$\eta^i(k_t^i, t) = -\rho_i q_t^i v^i(k_t^i, t)$$

$$= \rho_i \tau k_t^i \frac{\sigma^i(f_t^i, t)v^i(k_t^i, t)}{1 + \tau f_t^i} \tag{4.89}$$

In particular, under the SABR dynamics

$$df_t = \sigma_t (f_t)^\beta dz_t^{\mathbb{T}}$$

$$d\sigma_t = v\sigma_t dw_t^{\mathbb{T}}$$

$$\rho dt = \mathbb{E}\left[dz_t^{\mathbb{T}}, dw_t^{\mathbb{T}}\right]$$

where df_t and $d\sigma_t$ are driftless under their terminal measure $\mathbb{T}$, the volatility drift under measure $\mathbb{T}_{-1}$ becomes

$$\rho\tau (\sigma_t)^2 \frac{(f_t)^\beta v}{1 + \tau f_t} \tag{4.90}$$

where we have restored the usual SABR notation.

4.10.4   The Drifts in the General Case of Several Forward Rates

Obtaining the drift corrections for different numeraires is algebraically a bit messier, but conceptually no different. The tool of the Vailliant brackets presented in Rebonato (2002) can help with the algebraic manipulations. So, for forward rates spanning the periods $t_1, t_2, \ldots, t_i, t_{i+1}, \ldots$, the general dynamics are

$$df_t^i = \mu_i(f_t, k_t, t)dt + \sigma_i(f_t, t)k_t^i dz_t^i$$

$$dk_t^i = \eta_i(f_t, k_t, t)dt + v_i(k_t, t)dw_t^i$$

$$\left\langle dz_t^i dz_t^j \right\rangle = \rho_{ij} dt$$

$$\left\langle dw_t^i dw_t^j \right\rangle = r_{ij} dt$$

$$\left\langle dz_t^i dw_t^j \right\rangle = R_{ij} dt \tag{4.91}$$

where f_t is the vector $\{f_t^1, f_t^2, \ldots\}$ and $k_t = \{k_t^1, k_t^2, \ldots, \}$. Using the above procedure it is algebraically tedious, but conceptually straightforward, to show that under the $\mathbb{T}_j$-measure (i.e., the measure induced by the numeraire $P(t, T_{j+1})$) the drifts are

$$
\mu_i^{\mathbb{T}_j}(f_t, k_t, t) =
\begin{cases}
\sigma_i(f_t, t) k_t^i \sum\limits_{\alpha=j+1}^{i} \dfrac{\rho_{i\alpha}\sigma_\alpha(f_\alpha, t) k_t^\alpha \tau_\alpha}{1+\tau_\alpha f_t^\alpha} & i > j \\[2ex]
0 & i = j \\[2ex]
-\sigma_i(f_t, t) k_t^i \sum\limits_{\alpha=i+1}^{j} \dfrac{\rho_{i\alpha}\sigma_\alpha(f_\alpha, t) k_t^\alpha \tau_\alpha}{1+\tau_\alpha f_t^\alpha} & i < j
\end{cases}
\tag{4.92}
$$

$$
\eta_i^{\mathbb{T}_j}(f_t, k_t, t) =
\begin{cases}
R_{ii} v_i(k_t, t) \sum\limits_{\alpha=j+1}^{i} \dfrac{\rho_{i\alpha}\sigma_\alpha(f_\alpha, t) k_t^\alpha \tau_\alpha}{1+\tau_\alpha f_t^\alpha} & i > j \\[2ex]
0 & i = j \\[2ex]
-R_{ii} v_i(k_t, t) \sum\limits_{\alpha=i+1}^{j} \dfrac{\rho_{i\alpha}\sigma_\alpha(f_\alpha, t) k_t^\alpha \tau_\alpha}{1+\tau_\alpha f_t^\alpha} & i < j
\end{cases}
\tag{4.93}
$$

A very important observation is in order. Comparing the no-arbitrage drifts for the forward rates (Equation (4.92)) and for the volatilities (Equation (4.93)), *we note that the computationally expensive summation terms have exactly the same structure in the two cases.* It is therefore truly a case of two for the price of one! Once the no-arbitrage drifts for the forward rates have been calculated, the drifts for the volatilities come at virtually zero additional computational cost. This is one of the important reasons why the LMM-SABR approach is not only financially appealing, but also computationally realistic.

4.10.5 Volatility Drifts in the Swap Measure

The results in this subsection were first presented, to our knowledge, by Henry Labordere (2007), but without derivation. We show below how to derive them.

For a set of reset times $T_1, T_2, \ldots, T_i, T_{i+1}, \ldots, T_N$, with spacing $\tau_i \equiv T_{i+1} - T_i$, we introduce the definition of the following quantities:

- $S^{\alpha\beta}(t)$ for the swap rate for a swap starting at time T_α with final payment at T_β;
- $A^{\alpha\beta}(t)$ for the annuity of the swap fixed payments;
- $\mathbb{Q}^{\alpha\beta}$ for the measure induced by the choice of the swap annuity $A^{\alpha\beta}(t)$ as numeraire (i.e., the measure under which the swap rate $S^{\alpha\beta}(t)$ is a martingale).

With these definitions we have

$$
S^{\alpha\beta}(t) = \frac{P(t, T_\alpha) - P(t, T_\beta)}{A^{\alpha\beta}(t)}
\tag{4.94}
$$

with

$$A^{\alpha\beta}(t) = \sum_{i=\alpha}^{\beta-1} \tau_i P(t, T_{i+1})$$

The swap rate can be written in terms of the forwards as

$$S^{\alpha\beta}(t) = \sum_{i=\alpha}^{\beta-1} \omega_i(t) f_t^i \tag{4.95}$$

$$\text{where } \omega_i(t) = \frac{\tau_i P(t, T_{i+1})}{A^{\alpha\beta}(t)}$$

So the weights[8] themselves are stochastic and depend on all the forwards underlying the swap. However, in the swap measure, $\mathbb{Q}^{\alpha\beta}$, the weights are all martingales, i.e.

$$\mathbb{E}^{\mathbb{Q}^{\alpha\beta}}[\omega_i(t)|\mathcal{F}_s] = \omega_i(s) \ \forall i \text{ and } t \geq s \tag{4.96}$$

This is because, as Equation (4.95) shows, the weights are relative prices (ratios of asset prices to the chosen numeraire). Of course the swap rate is also a martingale under the swap measure.

We now specify general stochastic volatility dynamics for the forward rates as

$$df_t^i = \mu_i(f_t, t)dt + \sigma_i(f_t, t)k_t^i dz_t^i$$
$$dk_t^i = \eta_i(k_t, t)dt + v_i(k_t, t)d\hat{z}_t^i \tag{4.97}$$
$$\left\langle dz_t^i dz_t^j \right\rangle = \rho_{ij} dt$$
$$\left\langle d\hat{z}_t^i d\hat{z}_t^j \right\rangle = r_{ij} dt$$
$$\left\langle dz_t^i d\hat{z}_t^j \right\rangle = R_{ij} dt$$

where the notation $\mu_i(f_t, t)$ means the drift on the ith forward is some function of (potentially) all the forward rates and time (and similarly for the other symbols). To lighten the notation we drop the function arguments and time dependence (e.g., f_t^i becomes just f^i). Using Equation (4.95) we can write down the dynamics of $S^{\alpha\beta}$ as

$$dS^{\alpha\beta} = \sum_{i=\alpha}^{\beta-1} \{\omega_i df^i + f^i d\omega_i + df^i d\omega_i\}$$

$$= \sum_{i=\alpha}^{\beta-1} \{\omega_i \mu_i dt + \omega_i \sigma_i k^i dZ^i + f^i d\omega_i + \sigma_i k^i dZ^i d\omega_i\} \tag{4.98}$$

---

[8]From the definition of $A_{\alpha\beta}(t)$ it is clear that $\sum_{i=\alpha}^{\beta-1} \omega_i(t) = 1$ and that $\omega_i(t) > 0$, i.e., they have the property of positive weights.

$$= \sum_{i=\alpha}^{\beta-1} \left\{ \omega_i \mu_i dt + \sigma_i k^i dz^i d\omega_i \right\} + \sum_{i=\alpha}^{\beta-1} \left\{ f^i d\omega_i + \omega_i \sigma_i k^i dz^i \right\} \qquad (4.99)$$

Note that the second term is purely stochastic (i.e., it has no term in dt, since ω_i is a martingale). So, with a slight abuse of notation, we have

$$\mu_i = -\frac{1}{\omega_i} \frac{\sigma_i k^i \langle dz^i d\omega_i \rangle}{dt} \qquad (4.100)$$

and we are left with calculating the stochastic part of $d\omega_i$. We rewrite the weights as

$$\omega_i = \left(\sum_{j=\alpha}^{\beta-1} \frac{\tau_j P\left(t, T_{j+1}\right)}{\tau_i P\left(t, T_{i+1}\right)} \right)^{-1}$$

$$= \left(\sum_{j=\alpha}^{\beta-1} X_{ij} \right)^{-1} \quad \text{where } X_{ij} \equiv \frac{\tau_j P\left(t, T_{j+1}\right)}{\tau_i P\left(t, T_{i+1}\right)} \qquad (4.101)$$

Taking partial derivatives with respect to X_{ik} we get

$$\frac{\partial \omega_i}{\partial X_{ik}} = -\omega_i^2 \qquad (4.102)$$

$$\frac{\partial_i^2 \omega}{\partial X_{ik} \partial X_{ik'}} - 2\omega_i \frac{\partial \omega_i}{\partial X_{ik'}} = 2\omega_i^3 \qquad (4.103)$$

so

$$d\omega_i = -\omega_i^2 \sum_{j=\alpha}^{\beta-1} dX_{ij} + \omega_i^3 \sum_{j=\alpha}^{\beta-1} \sum_{k=\alpha}^{\beta-1} dX_{ij} dX_{ik} \qquad (4.104)$$

Now let us consider the dynamics of X_{ij}. This can then be written in terms of the forward rates

$$X_{ij}(t) \equiv \begin{cases} \frac{\tau_j}{\tau_i} \prod_{k=i+1}^{j} (1 + \tau_k f^k)^{-1} & i < j \\ \frac{\tau_j}{\tau_i} \prod_{k=j+1}^{i} (1 + \tau_k f^k) & i > j \end{cases} \qquad (4.105)$$

Taking partial derivatives with respect to f_t^k we get

$$\frac{\partial X_{ij}}{\partial f^k} = (2\mathbb{I}_{i>j} - 1) \frac{\tau_k X_{ij}}{1 + \tau_k f^k} \qquad (4.106)$$

where $\mathbb{I}_{i>j}$ is the indicator function that assumes a value of 1 when $i > j$ and 0 otherwise. The dynamics of X_{ij} are

$$\frac{dX_{ij}}{X_{ij}} = (2\mathbb{I}_{i>j} - 1) \sum_{k=\min(i,j)+1}^{\max(i,j)} \frac{\tau_k}{1+\tau_k f^k} df^k + \mathcal{O}(\langle df^k, df^k \rangle) \tag{4.107}$$

Finally the dynamics of $d\omega_i$ are

$$d\omega_i = -\omega_i^2 \sum_{j=\alpha}^{\beta-1} \left\{ (2\mathbb{I}_{i>j} - 1) X_{ij} \sum_{k=\min(i,j)+1}^{\max(i,j)} \frac{\tau_k}{1+\tau_k f^k} \sigma_k k^k dz^k \right\} \tag{4.108}$$

and the drift on the ith forward rate is

$$\mu_i(\mathbf{f},t) = -\frac{1}{\omega_i} \frac{\sigma_i \kappa^i \langle dz^i d\omega_i \rangle}{dt} \tag{4.109}$$

$$= \omega_i \sigma_i \kappa^i \sum_{j=\alpha}^{\beta-1} \left\{ (2\mathbb{I}_{i<j} - 1) X_{ij} \sum_{k=\min(i,j)+1}^{\max(i,j)} \frac{\tau_k}{1+\tau_k f^k} \sigma_k k^k i \rho_{ik} \right\} \tag{4.110}$$

$$= \sigma_i \kappa^i \sum_{j=\alpha}^{\beta-1} \left\{ (2\mathbb{I}_{i>j} - 1) \omega_j \sum_{k=\min(i,j)+1}^{\max(i,j)} \frac{\tau_k}{1+\tau_k f^k} \sigma_k k^k \rho_{ik} \right\} \tag{4.111}$$

Using exactly the same method we used for the volatility drift under a terminal measure, we have

$$\gamma = -\frac{\mu_i}{\sigma_i \kappa^i}$$

$$= -\sum_{j=\alpha}^{\beta-1} \left\{ (2\mathbb{I}_{i>j} - 1) \omega_j \sum_{k=\min(i,j)+1}^{\max(i,j)} \frac{\tau_k \sigma_k k^k}{1+\tau_k f^k} \rho_{ik} \right\} \tag{4.112}$$

But we also know that

$$\eta_i = -R_{ii} \gamma \nu_i \tag{4.113}$$

Therefore

$$\eta_i = R_{ii} \nu_i \sum_{j=\alpha}^{\beta-1} \left\{ (2\mathbb{I}_{i>j} - 1) \omega_j \sum_{k=\min(i,j)+1}^{\max(i,j)} \frac{\tau_k \sigma_k k^k}{1+\tau_k f^k} \rho_{ik} \right\} \tag{4.114}$$

This gives us both the forward rate and volatility drifts in the swap measure. We note in passing that these expressions coincide with the equations provided without derivation in Henry-Labordere (2007). R_{ii} is just the market-given, β-dependent SABR correlation between a swap rate and its own volatility. Any choice of the exponent β that makes the term R_{ii} smaller will also make the volatility drift terms smaller, making life computationally easier (and possibly justifying some approximations of these terms).

Part II

Implementation and Calibration

Chapter 5

Calibrating the LMM-SABR Model to Market Caplet Prices

5.1 The Caplet-Calibration Problem

We assume in this section that the SABR parameters for a set of caplets are already available from market prices from a previous SABR fitting for all the maturities and strikes or interest. They implicitly determine the market caplet smile surface. Our goal is to determine the parameters of our LMM-SABR model in such a way that the caplet prices it produces for all the same strikes and maturities are as close as possible to the SABR caplet prices. As usual, we want to do so in a financially desirable way. Therefore, given a collection of SABR caplets parameters $(\sigma_0^{T_i}, \rho_{SABR}^{T_i}, \nu^{T_i}, \beta_{SABR}^{T_i})$ spanning the maturity range of interest (i.e., for $i = 1, 2, \ldots, N$), we call the 'caplet calibration problem' the choice of

- the parameters of the two volatility functions $g(\cdot)$ and $h(\cdot)$;

- the exponent, β, in the LMM-SABR model;

- the correlations, R_{ii}, between each forward rate and its own volatility in the LMM-SABR model; and

- the initial values, k_0^T, of the processes k_t^T

in such a way that the SABR market prices are recovered as closely as possible.

For ease of reference we present again the SABR dynamics of a generic forward rate $f_t^{T_i}$ resetting at time T_i and paying at time $T_{i+1} = T_i + \tau$ which is driftless under the terminal measure, $\mathbb{T}_i$:

$$df_t^{T_i} = \sigma_t^{T_i} \left(f_t^{T_i} \right)^{\beta_{SABR}^{T_i}} dz_t^{T_i} \tag{5.1}$$

$$\frac{d\sigma_t^{T_i}}{\sigma_t^{T_i}} = v^{T_i} dw_t^{T_i} \tag{5.2}$$

$$\mathbb{E}\left[dz_t^{T_i} dw_t^{T_i}\right] = \rho_{\text{SABR}}^{T_i} dt \tag{5.3}$$

The SABR dynamics are therefore fully described by the initial conditions, $f_0^{T_i}, \sigma_0^{T_i}$, and by the expiry-dependent parameters $\beta_{\text{SABR}}^{T_i}, \rho_{\text{SABR}}^{T_i}, v^{T_i}$. As for the LMM-SABR specification, we obtain our results for the caplets under the same terminal measure under which the forward rate is driftless.

We can re-express the forward rate dynamics under the LMM-SABR specification on the same forward rate f_t^i, resetting at time T_i and paying at time $T_{i+1} = T_i + \tau$, under its terminal measure $\mathbb{T}_i$ as

$$df_t^i = \left(f_t^i\right)^{\beta_i} s_t^{T_i} dz_t^i \tag{5.4}$$

$$ds_t^{T_i} = g_t^{T_i} dk_t^{T_i} \tag{5.5}$$

$$\frac{dk_t^{T_i}}{k_t^{T_i}} = \mu_k^i dt + h_t^{T_i} dw_t^i \tag{5.6}$$

$$\mathbb{E}[dz_t^i dz_t^j] = \rho_{ij} dt \tag{5.7}$$

$$\mathbb{E}[dw_t^i dw_t^j] = r_{ij} dt \tag{5.8}$$

$$\mathbb{E}[dw_t^i dz_t^j] = R_{ij} dt \tag{5.9}$$

with $g_t^T = g(T - t)$. Note that if $k_t^{T_i} \equiv s_t^{T_i}/g_t^{T_i}$ were a deterministic function of t and T_i (or a constant) we would be in the traditional deterministic-volatility LMM setting.

As for the drift term, μ_k^i, for an arbitrary numeraire in general this term is non-zero for all the forward-rate volatilities. We have derived it in Chapter 4.

For the reasons explained in Chapter 4, we impose that the volatility of volatility should have the time-homogeneous form

$$h(t, T) = h(T - t) \tag{5.10}$$

with the function $h(\cdot)$ parametrized by a set of parameters $[l, m, n, \ldots]$. Therefore

$$k_t^T = k_0^T \exp\left[\int_0^t \left\{-\frac{1}{2}h^2(T - s)ds + h(T - s)dw_s\right\}\right] \tag{5.11}$$

and

$$s_t^T = g_t^T k_t^T = g_t^T k_0^T \exp\left[\int_0^t \left\{-\frac{1}{2}h^2(T - s)ds + h(T - s)dw_s\right\}\right] \tag{5.12}$$

With these constitutive equations in place we can move to the choice of the parameters. We follow Rebonato (2007b).

5.2   Choosing the Parameters of the Function, $g(\cdot)$, and the Initial Values, k_0^T

Let us start from the determination of the parameters of the function $g(\cdot)$ and of the initial values, k_0^T. Recall from Chapter 2 that in a deterministic-volatility setting the quantities $\{k^T\}$ would be fully determined by the requirement that each caplet should be perfectly priced:

$$\widehat{\sigma}^2 T = \left(k^T\right)^2 \int_0^T g(u, T)^2 du \tag{5.13}$$

where $\widehat{\sigma}$ is the implied Black volatility of the caplet. For future reference we can profitably express the deterministic-volatility factor k^T in terms of the root-mean-squared volatility, $\widehat{g}(T_i)$:

$$\widehat{g}(T) \equiv \sqrt{\frac{1}{T} \int_0^T g(u, T)^2 du} \Rightarrow k^T = \frac{\widehat{\sigma}}{\widehat{g}(T)} \tag{5.14}$$

Clearly, this relationship no longer holds in the stochastic-volatility setting. We therefore need another way to determine the initial value, k_0^T, of the processes k_t^T. Note in passing that in this book we denote by $\widehat{f}$ the root-mean-square of a generic time-dependent function, f, and by $\widehat{\sigma}$ the Black implied volatility. This choice is not as bad as it looks, because, in a Black world, if the volatility is a deterministic function of time, $\sigma(t)$, then the correct input in the Black formula to obtain the option price is just the root-mean-squared volatility, $\widehat{\sigma}$.

In order to determine the initial values, $k_0^{T_i}$, we begin by noting that, given the SABR process for the volatility, the expectation at time 0 of the volatility at time t is simply given by σ_0:

$$\mathbb{E}_0\left[\sigma(t)\right] = \sigma_0 \tag{5.15}$$

This follows immediately because the SABR volatility, $\sigma(t)$, at a generic time $t > t_0$ is given by

$$\sigma(t) = \sigma_0 \exp\left[-\frac{1}{2} \int_0^t \sigma_s^2 ds + \int_0^t \sigma(s) dz(s)\right] \tag{5.16}$$

and

$$\mathbb{E}_0\left[\exp\left(-\frac{1}{2} \int_0^t \sigma_s^2 ds + \int_0^t \sigma(s) dz(s)\right)\right] = 1 \tag{5.17}$$

We can then heuristically impose that the parameters of the deterministic-volatility LMM-SABR function, $g(t, T)$ (in our case a, b, c and d) should be chosen in such a way as to match as closely as possible the expectation, σ_0^T, at time 0 of the SABR volatility, σ_s^T. (Later we will provide a different argument to derive the same result.) In the light of Equation (5.13), it is therefore plausible to set this expectation to be as close as possible to the root-mean-squared value of $g(t, T)$, $\widehat{g}(T_i)$. At this stage, we therefore simply minimize over the parameters of the deterministic-volatility function, $g(t, T)$, the sum, χ^2, of the squared discrepancies:

$$\chi^2 = \sum_i^N \left[\sigma_0^{T_i} - \widehat{g}(T_i) \right]^2 \tag{5.18}$$

where the sum over i runs over the N caplet expiries and (for our parametrization of the function $g(\cdot)$):

$$\widehat{g}(T_i) = \sqrt{\frac{1}{T_i} \int_0^{T_i} \left[(a + b\tau_i) \exp(-c\tau_i) + d \right]^2 d\tau_i} \tag{5.19}$$

In general, the quantities $\widehat{g}(T_i)$ will not exactly match the market-given SABR initial volatilities, $\sigma_0^{T_i}$. The initial values $k_0^{T_i}$ in Equation (5.13) are therefore chosen so as to provide exact recovery of the quantities $\sigma_0^{T_i}$:

$$k_0^{T_i} = \frac{\sigma_0^{T_i}}{\widehat{g}(T_i)} \tag{5.20}$$

Note the similarity between Equation (5.20) and Equation (5.14). If the chosen function $g(\tau)$ allows for a good fit to the dependence of the initial SABR value $\sigma_0^{T_i}$ on the maturities T_i, the initial values of the processes $k_t^{T_i}$ will all be close to 1. This is a nice result: in our setting, in fact, we would like the stochasticity in the volatility function to appear as a stochastic perturbation to a deterministic function that displays, on average, the correct 'physical' behaviour (in our case, the humped behaviour).[1]

5.3   Choosing the Parameters of the Function $h(\cdot)$

We now move to the second function, $h_t^T = h(T - t)$, which describes the volatility of volatility. Again, we assume that the SABR maturity-dependent volatility-of-volatility coefficients, v^{T_i}, are already available from a previous market fit. We want to make use of these exogenous inputs to determine the parameters of the volatility-of-volatility function, h_t^T.

   In the original paper (Rebonato (2007b)), one of us (RR) recommended using a function of the form

$$h_\tau = (\alpha + \beta\tau) \exp(-\gamma\tau) + \delta \tag{5.21}$$

with $\tau = T - t$. The parameters α, β, γ and δ were then chosen to minimize the sum, χ^2, of the squared discrepancies:

$$\chi^2 = \sum_i^N \left[v^{T_i} - \widehat{h}(T_i) \right]^2 \tag{5.22}$$

---

[1]Needless to say, it would not matter if all the quantities $k_0^{T_i}$ were equal to a constant other than 1, as long as this constant, which could be absorbed in the function $g(\tau)$, is the same for all the forward rates.

where now $\widehat{h}(T_i)$ denotes the root-mean-squared value of the function h to time T_i. Small correction factors, ξ_i, were then applied to ensure the exact recovery of the root-mean-squared volatility of volatility,$\widehat{h}(T_i)$:

$$v^{T_i} = \xi_i \widehat{h}(T_i) \tag{5.23}$$

Here we propose a modification of this procedure that significantly improves its accuracy. The degree of improvement is shown in Section 5.5. The rationale for the new approximation is as follows.

In the limit as the volatility of volatility goes to zero, we can clearly guarantee that the distributions of a given forward rate under the SABR and LMM-SABR processes, f_{SABR} and f_{LMM}, respectively, match at option expiry by imposing

$$(\sigma_0)^2 T = k_0 \int_0^T g(T, t)^2 dt \tag{5.24}$$

If we do so, in a deterministic-volatility setting all the European option prices would match as well, because, in general, all that matters for the pricing of a European option (such as a caplet) is the final (terminal) distribution of the associated forward rate. In a deterministic-volatility setting, the fulfilment of Equation (5.24) is therefore all that matters for pricing caplets correctly.

When the volatility is stochastic, however, the terminal distribution of a forward rate (and hence the price of the associated caplet) is not uniquely determined either by the terminal value of its volatility (or its variance) or by the average value of the volatility of volatility over the life of the European option. *When* the volatility of volatility occurs matters.

To see why this is the case, consider the two time-dependent volatility-of-volatility functions, $h_A(t)$ and $h_B(t)$, depicted in Figure 5.1 against the same function $g(t)$. The two

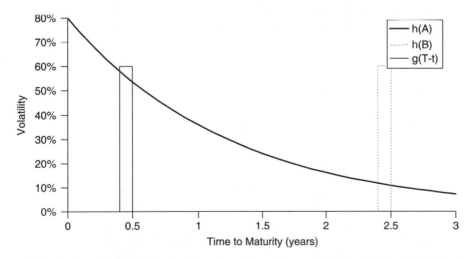

Figure 5.1   A time-decaying volatility function, $g(t)$, and two stylized volatility-of-volatility functions, $h_A(t)$ and $h_B(t)$, with the same root-mean-squared value, but a very different effect on option prices. See the text for a discussion.

volatility-of-volatility functions have been constructed to have the same root-mean-squared volatility, $\widehat{h}(T_i)$. Despite this, it is easy to see that it *does* matter for caplet pricing when the high volatility of volatility period occurs. To begin with, if, for instance, the volatility of volatility were high when the volatility itself were low (curve labelled $h(B)$ in Figure 5.1), this stochasticity of the volatility would effectively be 'wasted'. More importantly, even if the function $g(\cdot)$ were flat, *when* the volatility of volatility is concentrated has a large effect on curvature of the smile: if it were concentrated towards the expiry, for instance, it is easy to see that it would have a small impact on option prices.

The upshot of this is that just imposing the matching of the average volatilities or variances of a forward rate under the SABR and LMM-SABR processes is not enough to ensure the same pricing for caplets. We therefore approach the problem from a different angle. Our strategy will be to make rather heroic, *but identical*, approximations both for the SABR and the LMM-SABR models, hoping that the errors introduced by the approximations will cancel out in the two similar SABR and LMM-SABR models.

Let's start from the SABR model. First, we define the integral of the stochastic volatility squared as

$$\Gamma_T = \int_0^T (\sigma_t)^2 \, dt \tag{5.25}$$

Clearly, Γ_T is itself a stochastic quantity, and we define a particular realization[2] of this integral as γ_T.

We then note that the price of a European option conditional on a particular realization of the path of the stochastic volatility is

$$Call|\text{vol-path} = p(0, T)\mathbb{E}\left[(f_T - k)^+|\text{vol-path}\right] \tag{5.26}$$

where the symbolic expression $\mathbb{E}\left[x|\text{vol-path}\right]$ means 'expectation of x conditional on a particular volatility path having been realized'. Then the tower rule[3] gives

$$Call_{\text{SABR}} = p(0, T)\mathbb{E}\left[\mathbb{E}\left[(f_T - k)^+|\text{vol-path}\right]\right] \tag{5.27}$$

where the outer expectation is taken over the volatility paths. If the correlation between the forward rate and its own volatility in the SABR model, ρ_{SABR}, were zero, we could replace the vol-path by Γ_T. We therefore would have

$$Call_{\text{SABR}} = p(0, T)\mathbb{E}\left[\mathbb{E}\left[(f_T - k)^+\Big|\Gamma_T = \gamma_T\right]\right]$$

$$= p(0, T)\int_{-\infty}^{\infty} \mathbb{E}\left[(f_T - k)^+\Big|\Gamma_T = \gamma_T\right]\phi(\gamma_T)d\gamma_T \tag{5.28}$$

where $\phi(\gamma_T)$ is the unknown density of Γ_T. This is our first approximation.

---

[2]Here we follow the usual notation of using a capital letter to denote a random variable/distribution, and the lower case letter to denote a particular draw from that distribution.

[3]Also known as the law of total expectation, or the law of iterated expectations.

Since, of course, we do not know $\phi(\gamma_T)$, we now approximate this unknown density, $\phi(\gamma_T)$, by a Dirac delta at its expectation,

$$\phi(\gamma_T) \simeq \delta(\gamma_T - \mathbb{E}[\Gamma_T]) \qquad (5.29)$$

and obtain

$$Call_{SABR} \approx p(0, T) \int_{-\infty}^{\infty} \mathbb{E}\left[(f_T - k)^+ \Big| \Gamma_T = \gamma_T \right] \delta(\gamma_T - \mathbb{E}[\Gamma_T]) d\gamma_T$$

$$= p(0, T) \mathbb{E}\left[(f_T - k)^+ \Big| \Gamma_T = \mathbb{E}[\Gamma_T] \right]$$

$$= p(0, T) \mathbb{E}\left[(f_T - k)^+ \Big| \Gamma_T = \mathbb{E}\left[\int_0^T \sigma_t^2 dt \right] \right] \qquad (5.30)$$

So much for our rough handling of the SABR caplet pricing.

Recall that our strategy is to make similar approximations for the SABR and the LMM-SABR models. Following the same reasoning that leads to Equation (5.30) we can directly write the expression for the LMM-SABR model equivalent to Equation (5.30):

$$Call_{LMM} \approx p(0, T) \mathbb{E}\left[(f_T - k)^+ \Big| \Gamma_T = \mathbb{E}\left[\int_0^T g(t)^2 k(t)^2 dt \right] \right] \qquad (5.31)$$

We do not claim that either of these approximations is accurate (they are not!), but we try to make the same errors when dealing with the SABR and the LMM dynamics, and we rely on cancellation of errors. Looking at Equations (5.30) and (5.31), it is clear that in order to match the call prices we must impose the condition

$$\mathbb{E}\left[\int_0^T \sigma_t^2 dt \right] = \mathbb{E}\left[\int_0^T g(t)^2 k(t)^2 dt \right] \Rightarrow$$

$$\int_0^T \mathbb{E}[\sigma_t^2] dt = \int_0^T g(t)^2 \mathbb{E}[k(t)^2] dt \Rightarrow$$

$$\left(\frac{\sigma_0}{v}\right)^2 \left(e^{v^2 T} - 1 \right) = (k_0)^2 \int_0^T g(t)^2 e^{t \widehat{h}_t^2} dt \qquad (5.32)$$

where, as above, the quantity $\widehat{h}_t$,

$$\widehat{h}_t = \sqrt{\frac{1}{t} \int_0^t (h_s)^2 \, ds} \qquad (5.33)$$

denotes the root-mean-squared value of $h(\cdot)$ to time t. Taylor expanding both sides of Equation (5.32) gives

$$(\sigma_0)^2 T + \frac{(\sigma_0)^2 v^2 T^2}{2} + \frac{(\sigma_0)^2 v^4 T^3}{3!} + \dots$$

$$= (k_0)^2 \int_0^T g(t)^2 dt + (k_0)^2 \int_0^T g(t)^2 \widehat{h}_t^2 t \, dt + \frac{(k_0)^2}{2} \int_0^T g(t)^2 \widehat{h}_t^4 t^2 dt + \dots \qquad (5.34)$$

Let's look carefully at the first two terms in this expansion. Equating the first term gives

$$(\sigma_0)^2 \, T = (k_0)^2 \int_0^T g(t)^2 dt$$

Reassuringly, this is exactly the same condition we had obtained before (see Equation (5.24)).

Let's now look at the second term. This is where the more interesting results appear. Equating second-order terms in fact gives

$$\frac{\left(\sigma_0 v_{\mathrm{SABR}}^T\right)^2 T^2}{2} = (k_0)^2 \int_0^T g(t)^2 \widehat{h_t}^2 t \, dt \Rightarrow \qquad (5.35)$$

$$v_{\mathrm{SABR}}^T = \frac{k_0}{\sigma_0 T} \left(2 \int_0^T g(t)^2 \widehat{h_t}^2 t \, dt\right)^{1/2} \qquad (5.36)$$

This is the equation we were looking for – i.e., a relationship between the market-given quantity, v_{SABR}^T, and the parameters of our LMM-SABR model. Note that in Equation (5.36) the integral depends on the interaction between the deterministic-volatility function, $g(t)$, and the root-mean-squared volatility-of-volatility out to time t, $\widehat{h_t}$. In other words, the approximation that we have obtained depends on *when* the volatility and the volatility of volatility are large or small. This squares with the qualitative discussion given above and correctly mirrors our intuition.

So, the final result is the following: if the first two terms in the expansion are matched (and the functions $g(\cdot)$ and $h(\cdot)$ are not too pathological) then we can hope that further terms in the expansion will not be too dissimilar. This means that we can hope that, by choosing the functions $g(t)$ and $h(t)$ in such a way that Equations (5.35) and (5.36) are satisfied, the prices of caplets under the SABR and LMM-SABR models will be very similar – this is the reason for expanding *both* sides of Equation (5.32).

5.4   Choosing the Exponent, β, and the Correlation, ϕ_{SABR}

For the above to hold, it is necessary that $\rho_{\mathrm{SABR}} \approx \rho_{\mathrm{LMM}}$ and $\beta_{\mathrm{SABR}} \approx \beta_{\mathrm{LMM}}$. So finally, the plausible choices are made:

$$\rho_{\mathrm{SABR}} = \rho_{\mathrm{LMM}} \qquad (5.37)$$

$$\beta_{\mathrm{SABR}} = \beta_{\mathrm{LMM}} \qquad (5.38)$$

We note in passing that condition (5.37) is natural enough when we deal with caplets, but is no longer so when we move to swaptions.

5.5   Results

Many of the arguments presented so far have been heuristic in nature. Their ultimate justification therefore lies in the numerical quality of the approximation over parameter ranges likely to be found in practice. We present two sets of figures: the first set of figures (Figures 5.2

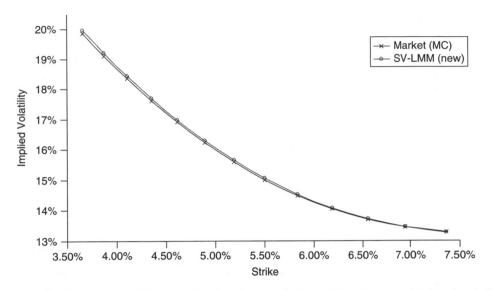

Figure 5.2   The accuracy of the approximation discussed in the text for a 5-year caplet. The (market) SABR parameters were: $f_0 = 5.19\%$, $\sigma_0 = 3.5\%$, $\beta = 0.5$, $\rho = -0.45$, and $\nu = 33.5\%$.

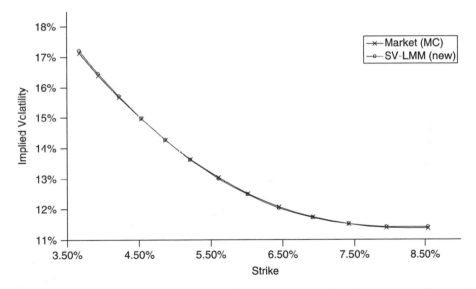

Figure 5.3   The accuracy of the approximation discussed in the text for a 10-year caplet. The (market) SABR parameters were: $f_0 = 5.60\%$, $\sigma_0 = 3.05\%$, $\beta = 0.5$, $\rho = -0.395$, and $\nu = 28.25\%$.

and 5.3) go straight to the point and show the quality of our approximation against a Monte Carlo simulation; the second set of figures (Figures 5.4 and 5.5) provide further information about the accuracy with comparisons to the Hagan formula and the approximation presented in Rebonato (2007b). More precisely, the lines in this second set of figures are:

- the implied volatilities obtained by inputting the SABR parameters into the Hagan *et al.* (2002) approximate formula – curve labelled 'Market (Hagan)';

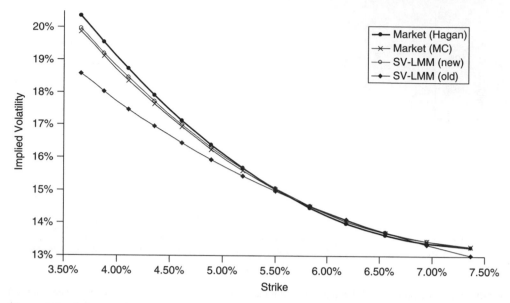

Figure 5.4   Same as Figure 5.2 with additional information as explained in the text.

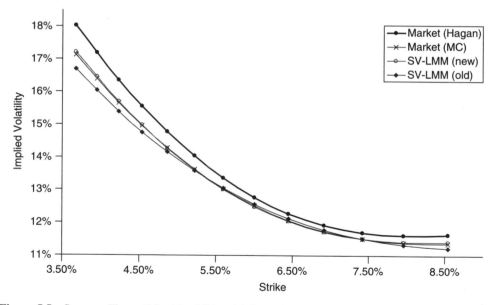

Figure 5.5   Same as Figure 5.3 with additional information as explained in the text.

- the implied volatilities obtained by inputting the SABR parameters into a Monte Carlo simulation of the true SABR process – curve labelled 'Market (MC)'; this is our benchmark;

- the implied volatilities obtained using the approximation presented in Rebonato (2007b) – curve labelled 'SV-LMM (old)';

- the implied volatilities obtained using the approximation suggested above (Equation (5.36)) – curve labelled 'SV-LMM (new)'; this is the curve to be most directly compared with the benchmark.

The agreement between the SABR (market) prices and the LMM-SABR prices can be seen to be extremely good. In particular the new approximation for the volatility of volatility performs considerably better than the original approximation in Rebonato (2007b): the largest error for the 5-year (10-year) caplet is of 11 (9) basis points in volatility for a strike of 3.66% (3.67%) when the forward is at 5.19% (5.60%), *five to ten times smaller than what was obtained with the previous approximation*.

These results substantiate the correctness of the idea behind our identical, if rough, approximations for determining the volatility of volatility. They confirm that the accuracy of the approximation does not depend on the correlation between the forward rate and its volatility being close to zero (this is what we needed to manipulate the tower law as in Equation (5.28)), or on a vanishing volatility of volatility (that would make the use of the Dirac-δ approximation exact), but on a cancellation of errors.

So far we have tested the approximations against hypothetical SABR prices. The next section discusses the nature of actual fits to market data.

5.6 Calibration in Practice: Implications for the SABR Model

5.6.1 Looking at Caplets in Isolation

We present in this section the results of actual calibration to market caplet prices. We focus on two particular trading dates: 13th June 2006 and 4th March 2008. The former is taken as a representative date for a normal market period, the second for an excited date. We want to comment on the quality of the fit, and on what the fit tells us about the SABR and LMM-SABR models.

Let's begin with the fitted parameters. These are shown in Table 5.1.

We obtained a, b, c and d from matching the root-mean-squared of the function $g(\cdot)$ to the SABR market values $\sigma_0^{T_i}$ for date 13-06-06 as described in the text – see Equations (5.18) to (5.20). The quantities α, β, γ and δ were obtained using Equation (5.36).

The very high quality of the fit is shown in Figure 5.6. Figure 5.7 shows similar results for the 'excited' day 04-03-08. The fitted excited parameters are shown in Table 5.2. The initial values $k_0^{T_i}$ determined using Equation (5.20) are shown in Figure 5.8. From the closeness to 1 of the fitted values $k_0^{T_i}$ one can see that the fit has worked very well, and that the

Table 5.1 The parameters a, b, c and d for function $g(\cdot)$ and α, β, γ and δ for function $h(\cdot)$ for a 'normal-day' fit.

Fitted values	$a(\alpha)$	$b(\beta)$	$c(\gamma)$	$d(\delta)$
$g(\cdot)$	-1.13%	0.0287	0.5272	2.68%
$h(\cdot)$	57.27%	0.0002	2.3035	27.57%

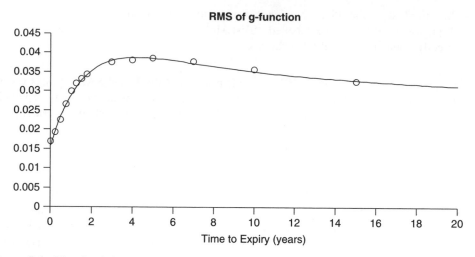

Figure 5.6   The fit of the parameters of the root-mean-squared of the $g(\cdot)$ function to the market quantities $\sigma_0^{T_i}$ for day 13-06-06. The open circles denote the market inputs.

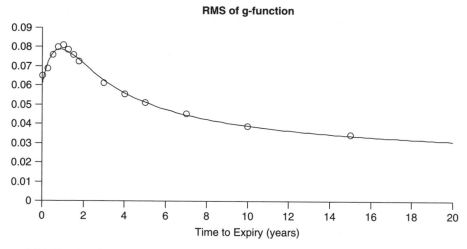

Figure 5.7   The fit of the parameters of the root-mean-squared of the $g(\cdot)$ function to the market quantities $\sigma_0^{T_i}$ for day 04-03-08. The open circles denote the market inputs.

evolution of the smile surface will be almost exactly time homogeneous. Similar, and even better, results (not shown for the sake of brevity) are found for the 'normal' trading day 13-06-08.

The volatility function $g(\cdot)$ and volatility-of-volatility function $h(\cdot)$ obtained from the fit for the chosen 'normal' and 'excited' days are shown in Figures 5.9 and 5.10. The fits deserve some observations.

The fitted function $g(\cdot)$ for the excited date suggests that the maximum volatility (uncertainty in rates) will be attained approximately half a year from the spot date, and that it will then quickly decline. The fit for the normal state indicates that the maximum volatility

Table 5.2 Same as Table 5.1 for date 04-03-08.

Fitted values	$a(\alpha)$	$b(\beta)$	$c(\gamma)$	$d(\delta)$
$g(\cdot)$	4.06%	0.1538	1.2447	2.02%
$h(\cdot)$	111.38%	0.0002	1.9833	30.69%

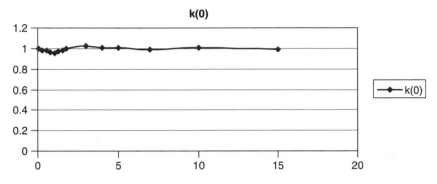

Figure 5.8 The initial values $k_0^{T_i}$ determined using Equation (5.20). Note how close to 1 they all are, showing the high quality of the fit.

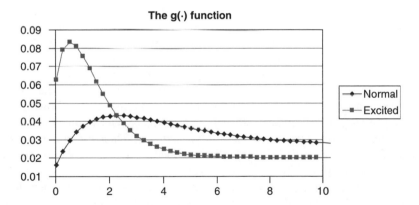

Figure 5.9 The volatility function $g(\cdot)$ obtained from the fit for the chosen 'normal' and 'excited' days.

will be reached after about two years and will then decrease slowly. This makes intuitive sense. The volatility function $g(\cdot)$ tends as $\tau \to 0$ towards 0.0155 on the normal day, and towards 0.0606 on the excited day. Also this is more or less as we expect. But what about the values attained by the function $h(\cdot)$ for very short residual time expiry?

Let's look at the volatility-of-volatility function $h(\cdot)$ more carefully. For the normal day the volatility of volatility approaches 84.82% ($\alpha + \delta = 57.27\% + 27.57\%$) as the time to maturity decreases, i.e., in the limit $\lim_{\tau=T-t \to 0} h(\tau)$. For the excited day the same function approaches 142.07% (111.38% + 30.69%). This is consistent with the interpretation of 'normal' and 'excited' days, but why are both these values so much higher than typical market values for v^T that tend to range between 20% and 50%?

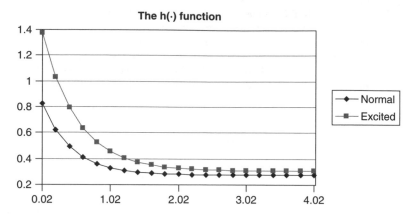

Figure 5.10   The volatility-of-volatility function $h(\cdot)$ obtained from the fit for the chosen 'normal' and 'excited' days.

The reason for this is that a typical SABR ν parameter (of the order of 20%–50%) is usually quoted for expiries no shorter than a few weeks. The values quoted above (84.82% and 142.07%), however, refer to a vanishingly short expiry. As the option expiry is reduced, the stochastic-volatility SABR model (and the LMM-SABR model) are not really able to reproduce the smile curvature observed in the market. For such short expiries discontinuous jumps, reflecting the possibility of large 'surprises', are priced in by the market, and give rise even for vanishing expiries to a non-zero smile curvature. A stochastic-volatility model, however, does not allow for such discontinuities. As the Black formula is almost exactly linear in the volatility at-the-money, in order to produce the required smile curvature the (LMM)-SABR model has to increase, in the limit to infinity, the volatility of volatility.

Let's look into this a bit more carefully. As a first approximation, and neglecting any correlation between the forward rate and the volatility, one can think of the following toy model as a proxy for pricing an option under stochastic volatility: we can assume that the volatility can be in either of two equiprobable states, high and low. Then the option price will be the average of one deterministic-volatility price obtained with a high-volatility path and one deterministic-volatility price obtained with a symmetrically positioned low-volatility path. Recall now that, at-the-money, the Black formula is linear in volatility. Then the average of the two prices will be little different from the price obtained with the average volatility. In order to get deviations from linearity – i.e., to have an effect from the stochasticity of volatility – one must extend the range of values explored by the underlying: the high and low volatility states must be widely separated, the more so, the shorter the option expiry. In order to do so for shorter and shorter expiries, a stochastic-volatility model therefore requires higher and higher volatilities of volatilities. This would not be the case for a model with jumps (e.g., if the underlying were driven by a Levy process). Ultimately, this is because with a diffusive process as the time step goes to zero the probability of an up or a down move remains constant, but the size of the move scales as the square root of the time step. With a jump process, on the other hand, as the time step goes to zero the size of the move does not change, but its probability scales linearly with time. See Merton (1992). Jump processes are therefore better suited at capturing a non-zero curvature of smiles for very short expiries. This is an intrinsic shortcoming not only of the (LMM)-SABR model, but also of all models that rely purely on stochastic volatility to introduce curvature to the smile.

5.6.2   Looking at Caplets and Swaptions Together

The discussion above suggests another interesting observation. Let's consider the predicted price of the 5y × 5y swaption obtained for these two trading days *after fitting as described above to the caplet prices only*. Figure 5.11 shows the excellent quality of the prediction obtained using the caplet calibration to the 'normal' caplet market. It also shows what the prediction would have been if the volatility functions had been chosen to be flat, i.e.,

$$g_i(\tau) = d_i \tag{5.39}$$

with the values d_i chosen to price exactly the caplet market. This is the curve labelled 'Model (Flat Curve)'. Why is the prediction of the swaption price obtained in normal market conditions with time-dependent volatilities so much better? We will discuss how to fit the LMM-SABR model to swaptions in the next chapter, but we can already easily understand the link between swaption and caplet volatilities, and why the flat-volatility prediction is not only worse, but higher.

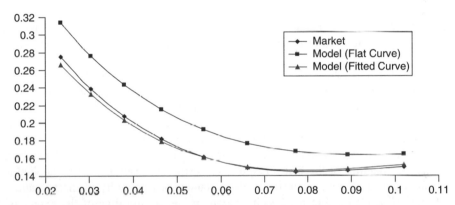

Figure 5.11   The market smile during a 'normal' day for a 5y × 5y swaption (US$) (curve labelled 'Market'); the model price of the same swaption obtained using the parametrization described in Chapter 6 and flat volatilities (curve labelled 'Model (Flat Curve)'); the model price of the same swaption obtained using the parametrization described in Chapter 6 and time-dependent (humped) volatilities (curve labelled 'Model (Fitted Curve)').

To follow the discussion it is useful to develop some intuition about the effect of the time dependence of the volatility of forward rates on the swaption implied volatility. This can be achieved by analysing the example depicted in Figure 5.12 of a semi-annual 3y × 3y swaption.[4] The instantaneous volatilities of the six forward rates have been assumed to be given by Equation (2.11) with a choice of parameters that gives rise to a hump. The first forward rate in the swaption (labelled 'Fwd_1') will come to its own expiry by expiry of the swaption. At time 0 (today) it will therefore have the volatility of a 3-year residual-maturity forward rate. Given the time homogeneity of the volatility function, and given that this function displays a hump in approximately a year's time, as time increases from today

---

[4]The swaption notation '$m \times n$' indicates an option expiring in m-years' time on an n-year swap.

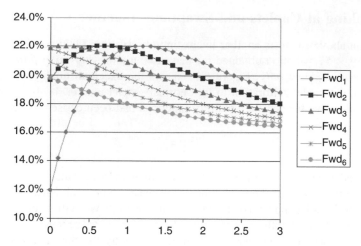

Figure 5.12   The time dependence of the instantaneous volatility of the six forward rates in a 3y × 3y semi-annual swaption. The time on the x-axis indicates the time to expiry of the swaption.

the instantaneous volatility of the first forward rate will rise slowly to reach a maximum approximately 12 months from today, and then will begin to decline sharply as its expiry approaches.

The second forward rate (i.e., the forward rate labelled 'Fwd_2', that will expire half a year after the expiry of the swaption) has at time 0 the volatility 'appropriate' to a forward rate with three and a half years to expiry. As seen from 'today' (time 0) its instantaneous volatility then keeps increasing for approximately 18 months (i.e., 6 months more than the first forward rate). By the swaption expiry (i.e., three years from today), it will still have half a year to its own expiry, and its instantaneous volatility will therefore not have declined as much as the volatility of the first forward rate. A similar reasoning can be applied to all the other forward rates, and, for instance, the instantaneous volatility of the last and sixth forward rate ('Fwd_6') has not reached its maximum yet by the time of the expiry of the European swaption.

Now, in a deterministic-volatility setting the Black swaption implied volatility is a weighted sum of covariance elements of the form

$$[\widehat{\sigma}^{SR_i}]^2 T_{\exp} \propto \sum_{j,k} \int_0^{T_{\exp}} \rho_{jk}(t)\sigma_j(t)\sigma_k(t)dt$$

$$\propto \sum_{j,k} \int_0^{T_{\exp}} \rho_{jk}(t)g_j(t)g_k(t)dt$$

where $\widehat{\sigma}^{SR_i}$ is the swaption implied volatility, $\sigma_j(t)$ is the instantaneous volatility of the jth forward rate in the swap, $g_j(t)$ is its time-homogeneous component and is the correlation between the ith and the jth forward rate. See Rebonato (2006) for a detailed derivation.

By the discussion above, the value of this covariance integral will therefore strongly depend on whether, over the integration interval, any two volatilities have high and low values 'in phase' or 'out of step' with each other. For a given instantaneous correlation, the values of these integrals, which directly determine the European swaption price, will therefore depend strongly on the relative shape of the various instantaneous volatility functions over the integration time, and not just on their root-mean-squares. In particular, looking at Figure 5.12, one can see that the covariance element between, say, the first and the sixth forward rates will be much lower than the product of their root-mean-squared volatilities, even if the instantaneous correlation were exactly equal to one, since one volatility is large when the other is small, and *vice versa*. In general, the more the instantaneous volatility function displays a significant hump, the more this effect will be pronounced.

This discussion explains why the prediction of the implied volatility for the 5y × 5y swaption obtained with flat volatilities for the forward rates was not only worse (because the market 'knows' about time dependence of volatilities, but flat-volatility calibrations ignore this piece of information), but *higher* (because flat volatilities do not provide enough decorrelation among forward rates).

Let's now look, however, at the prediction of the price of the same 5y × 5y swaption obtained using the same calibration to caplets during the excited day (04-03-08). See Figure 5.13. It is the prediction with time-dependent volatilities that is now bad, and much poorer than the flat-volatility prediction. What is going on?

To understand what is happening, recall that the fit to caplets to which Figure 5.13 refers was obtained during a period of extreme market volatility. When these conditions prevail, however, the market 'knows' that this high volatility will only persist for a relatively short period of time, and it assumes that, after a small number of weeks or months, the trading environment will go back to more normal conditions. Long-expiry options will therefore be priced with only a relatively limited period of high volatility. Their 'implied volatility' will therefore be only marginally higher than if the market currently were in a normal state – the more so, the longer the expiry of the option.

We can see this clearly by looking at Figure 5.14, which presents the fit to the swaption matrix carried out during a (different) excited period. To obtain these curves we used both a deterministic, time-homogeneous volatility model (curves labelled 'Deterministic Model')

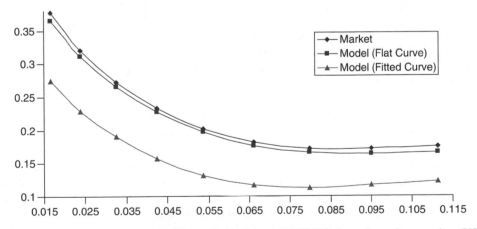

Figure 5.13 The market smile during an 'excited day' (04-03-08) for a 5y × 5y swaption (US$) (curve labelled 'Market'); the model price of the same swaption obtained using the parametrization described in Chapter 6 and flat volatilities (curve labelled 'Model (Flat Curve)'); the model price of the same swaption obtained using the parametrization described in Chapter 6 and time-dependent (humped) volatilities (curve labelled 'Model (Fitted Curve)').

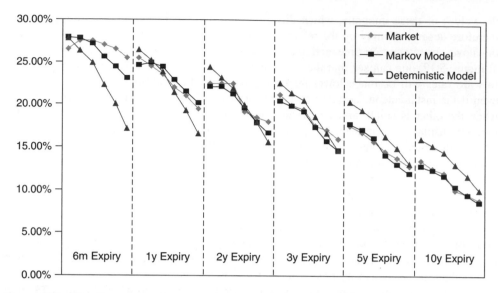

Figure 5.14 The fit to the at-the-money volatilities of the whole swaption matrix (US$) obtained using a deterministic-volatility LMM as described in Rebonato (2006) (curves labelled 'Deterministic Model'), and a two-state Markov-chain model for volatility (curves labelled 'Markov Model'), as described in White and Rebonato (2008).

and a two-state Markov-chain model for volatility (curves labelled 'Markov Model'). See White and Rebonato (2008) for a fuller description. Each panel of the figure shows the at-the-money implied volatilities for options into swaps of different maturities. The results of the two models are compared with the market implied volatilities by showing the curves labelled 'Market'. The important thing to note is that the overall fit to the whole swaption matrix using time-homogeneous, deterministic-volatility functions finds an acceptable solution only for expiries of approximately two years. The same time-homogeneous fit, however, produces volatilities that are far too low for the short ('excited') expiries, and far too high for the long expiries (which refer to options for which the overall volatility to expiry is only marginally affected by the present-day turbulence). There is nothing better that a deterministic, time-homogeneous model can do in situations of market excitation, and virtually identical results are found during periods of excitation across markets and models that share these fundamental (and usually desirable) features of time homogeneity. We note in passing that a two-state Markov-chain model for the volatility (which 'knows' that excited states do not last forever) does a much better job at accounting for swaption prices across the expiry spectrum. This is not the point of the present discussion, however. The relevant observation here is that no model with a time-homogeneous volatility structure can handle the transition from excited to normal market conditions. It is the very time-homogeneity condition (desirable in normal markets) that causes the problem, in that it propagates forward in time the same (exceptionally excited) smile that applies to short-dated options.

The explanation appears plausible, but, looking again at Figure 5.13, a new question arises: if the market was in an excited state at the time of the fit, we expect the prediction of the swaption price made with time-dependent volatilities fitted to caplets to be lower than the flat-volatility solution (and indeed it is). But why was it also lower *than the market price*? And why is the flat-volatility solution almost correct?

To answer these further questions, we must look again at Figure 5.9. Given the current market excitation, the short-expiry caplets require very high values of the function $g(\cdot)$ to match the high root-mean-squared volatility observed in the market. The volatility, however, is assumed to be time homogeneous. Longer-maturity caplets are therefore made to experience, when close to expiry, the same very high volatility – even if, by the time the long-expiry forward rates approach their own expiry market, conditions will probably be close to normal. But since the market implies values of long-term root-mean-squared volatilities for these caplets which are close to normal (for the reasons explained above), *the $g(\cdot)$ function has to become very low as the residual time to expiry increases in order to match the market*. Indeed, note how the 'excited' $g(\cdot)$ function dips and remains below the 'normal' $g(\cdot)$ function for residual time to expiry greater than approximately two years.

This explains what happens to the prediction for the 5y × 5y swaption volatility in the excited state. The forward rates that make up this swaption will traverse during the life of the swaption very different portions of the volatility 'life cycle': according to the model calibrated to the excited market state, the front forward rate will indeed experience very high volatility, *but only in the last two years of its life*; for three years of its life it will actually experience a *lower* volatility than if the $g(\cdot)$ function had been calibrated in normal market conditions. And as for the last forward rate in the swaption (the one that, at the start of the trade, is 9.5 years from its own expiry, and will be approximatcly 5 years to its own reset by swaption expiry), *it will experience a very low volatility throughout the whole life of the swaption*. Not surprisingly, the net effect of a rapidly decaying time-homogeneous volatility function (dictated by the fit to the market) is therefore to creatc a *low* overall volatility for all longer-dated options. Paradoxically, this low volatility is just a result of the high volatility of the short-dated options (combined, of course, with time homogeneity).

5.7 Implications for Model Choice

For the reasons discussed above, we have shown that using flat, rathcr than time-dependent, volatilities in conditions of market excitation can raise the value of longer-datcd swaption volatility (because of less decorrelation among rates) and happens in this casc to bring about a better match to the market observed prices. In general, however, two wrongs cannot be counted on to make a right. The good prediction for the 5y × 5y swaption obtained with flat volatilities was not a result with a deep reason, but little more than a coincidence, and nothing much should be read into the fact that the compensating shortcomings of flat volatilities magically appear to bring us back right onto market.

We said 'little more' rather than 'nothing'. Flat volatilities, as we know, produce a strongly time-inhomogeneous evolution of the smile surface. Normally, this is a very unpleasant feature. But in conditions of exceptional market excitation, the future does *not* look like the present, and it may fortuitously happen that the change in the 'smile world' brought about by flat volatilities will contain a grain of truth, and cause less of a problem than an uncritical use of time-homogeneous models.

A more convincing solution would require a different line of attack: a modelling approach that is built to know about normal and excited states and about the relative degree of persistence. A Markov-chain model for volatilities can provide one such modelling framework. See, e.g., Rebonato and Kainth (2004), White and Rebonato (2008). As we said, these approaches are unfortunately computationally much more expensive and currently do not lend themselves to the pricing of complex derivative products, which often combine path dependence with callability. For this reason, we present in Chapter 15 an approximate way to incorporate the insight from these regime-switching models into a robust hedging strategy that can be used with the LMM-SABR approach. And, in any case, if a trader were in an excited state, the 'thoughtful' time-inhomogeneous volatility functions presented in Section 4.8 can offer a simple and potentially very effective solution of the problem.

Chapter 6

Calibrating the LMM-SABR Model to Market Swaption Prices

6.1 The Swaption Calibration Problem

In the previous chapter we looked at how to determine the parameters of the LMM-SABR so that they are compatible with a set of SABR market prices for caplets. In this chapter we look at a different problem. We assume that the market prices of a set of swaptions are given. These swaptions could be the whole swaption matrix (not just the at-the-money volatilities – we should really speak of the swaption cube, which gives the implied volatilities as a function of expiry, swap tail and strike!) or a significant subset of it (where the meaning of 'significant' depends on the problem at hand). Given these market prices of swaptions, we want to determine the parameters of a *forward-rate-based* LMM-SABR model that best recover these prices. We can do this by a non-linear optimization over the space of the model parameters. It could be a good idea to undertake a Bayesian estimation, with the prior given by econometric information about the plausible range of the parameters. We do not pursue this study in what follows.

The outstanding question, of course, is: how do we calculate the swaption prices given the LMM-SABR parameters of the forward-rate processes? The 'brute-force' approach would be, of course, to obtain the swaption prices corresponding to the chosen set of parameters from a Monte Carlo simulation of the process of the forward rates and to vary the parameters until an optimal solution has been reached. In practice this is not a practical option, because each Monte Carlo evaluation is computationally expensive. The main contribution of this chapter is therefore the derivation of fast but accurate analytic approximations to the swaption prices that a set of forward-rate LMM-SABR parameters *would* produce if they were used as inputs to a Monte Carlo simulation.

Once the fast approximation to the prices we present below is available, one can carry out a minimization of (squared) errors by varying the model parameters. (The squared errors, of course, are the squares of the differences between the model and the market prices or implied volatilities.) By so doing one will find the best overall recovery of the swaption prices obtainable with a forward-based LMM-SABR approach. Of course, there is no guarantee that the recovery will be perfect – or indeed even good. This could be due either to a model mis-specification or to a lack of congruence between the caplet and swaption markets (and to the difficulty in arbitraging away these supply-and-demand-induced discrepancies). In the authors' experience, for a model like the LMM-SABR the latter explanation is likely to be much more likely than the first. See also Jamshidian (1997) on this point in the context of the deterministic-volatility LMM.

Typically, a complex book or a complex product will depend more strongly on some swaptions than on others. (Or, to look at the problem from a different angle, the hedging of a complex book or a complex product will require taking larger hedging positions in a subset of the available swaptions.) It therefore makes sense to recover the prices of these swaptions more accurately. This can be achieved giving non-constant importance weights to the (squared) errors in recovering these important prices. As one of us (RR) discusses in Rebonato (2002), using non-constant importance weights can be a good idea. However, it is important not to get carried away, lest pathological solutions are found (see the discussion in Rebonato (1999b)).

Finally, it should be kept in mind that the LMM-SABR model can be specified with a large number of degrees of freedom (mainly coming from the correlation matrix). The temptation to use these degrees of freedom to fit with abandon everything in sight is all the greater because some of the correlation inputs (say, between a 5-year forward rate and the volatility of a 30-year forward rate) are believed to be knowable with confidence only by fools and mad econometricians. For this reason we caution against throwing the full force of the $2N \times 2N$ matrix into the 'implied' recovery of the swaption prices. We strongly advise using instead parsimonious and transparent parametrizations of the correlation matrix. We cover this topic in Chapters 7 and 10.

6.2   Swap Rate and Forward Rate Dynamics

Recall the LMM-SABR forward rate dynamics as presented in Chapter 4 (and specifically in Equations (4.16) through (4.18)), which for ease of reference we report below:

$$df_t^i = \mu_t^i dt + \left(f_t^i\right)^{\beta_i} s_t^i \sum_{j=1}^{M} e_{ij} dy_{j,t} \qquad (6.1)$$

$$= \mu_t^i dt + \left(f_t^i\right)^{\beta_i} s_t^i dz_t^i \qquad (6.2)$$

$$ds_t^i = g(t, T_i) dk_t^i \qquad (6.3)$$

$$\frac{dk_t^i}{k_t^i} = \mu_t^{k_i} dt + h_t^i \sum_{j=1}^{M} e_{N+i,j} dy_{j,t} \qquad (6.4)$$

$$= \mu_t^{k_i} dt + h_t^i dw_t^i \qquad (6.5)$$

where $\{dy_{k,t}\}$ are the increments of independent Brownian motions

$$\mathbb{E}\left[dy_{i,t} dy_{j,t}\right] = \delta_{ij} dt \tag{6.6}$$

and

$$P = ee^{\dagger} \tag{6.7}$$

$$= \begin{bmatrix} \rho & R \\ R^{\dagger} & r \end{bmatrix} \tag{6.8}$$

so that

$$\mathbb{E}\left[dz_t^i dz_t^j\right] = \rho_{ij} dt \tag{6.9}$$

$$\mathbb{E}\left[dw_t^i dw_t^j\right] = r_{ij} dt \tag{6.10}$$

$$\mathbb{E}\left[dz_t^i dw_t^j\right] = R_{ij} dt \tag{6.11}$$

The price of a caplet only depends on one forward rate, its volatility, and the correlation between the forward rate and its own volatility. For products with more complex payoffs (e.g., swaptions), however, we must fully specify the parameters in Equations (6.1) to (6.11), i.e., we must also define the correlations among the forward rates, among the volatilities and between a forward rate and a volatility other than its own, i.e., the non-diagonal elements $R_{ij}, i \neq j$. This is because from the SABR market prices of caplets we only have information about the diagonal of the sub-matrix R.

The sub-matrices of P could be parameterized, for example, by

$$\rho_{ij} = \eta_1 + (1 - \eta_1) \exp\left[-\lambda_1 \left(|T_i - T_j|\right)\right] \tag{6.12}$$

$$r_{ij} = \eta_2 + (1 - \eta_2) \exp\left[-\lambda_2 \left(|T_i - T_j|\right)\right] \tag{6.13}$$

$$R_{ij} = \text{sign}(R_{ii}) \sqrt{|R_{ii} R_{jj}|} \exp\left[-\lambda_3 \left(T_i - T_j\right)^+ - \lambda_4 \left(T_j - T_i\right)^+\right] \tag{6.14}$$

The pros and cons of these, and other, parametrizations are discussed at length in Chapter 2 in Part I and Chapters 7 and 10 in Part III. For the goals of this chapter, the results that we derive do not depend on the particular parametrization of P chosen, as they are all expressed simply in terms of the elements ρ_{ij}, r_{ij} and R_{ij}, however obtained.

In order to proceed with the calibration of the swaption market to the LMM-SABR forward-rate model, we begin by recalling that a forward swap rate $SR_t^{\alpha\beta}$ spanned by $\beta - \alpha$ forward rates f_t^{α} to $f_t^{\beta-1}$ can be expressed as a weighted sum of forward rates

$$SR_t^{\alpha\beta} = \sum_{i=\alpha}^{\beta-1} \omega_i f_t^i \tag{6.15}$$

(refer to Equation (4.95) for the definition of the weights ω_i). We will often drop in the following α, β superscripts and the summation limits unless they are required for clarity. We assume for swap rate, SR_t, SABR dynamics of the type:[1]

$$dSR_t = (SR_t)^B \Sigma_t dZ_t \tag{6.16}$$

$$\frac{d\Sigma_t}{\Sigma_t} = V dW_t \tag{6.17}$$

$$\mathbb{E}[dZ_t dW_t] = R_{\text{SABR}} dt \tag{6.18}$$

In the following we will use as an intermediate step the instantaneous volatility of the swap rate in the LMM-SABR model. Recall our convention of using as much as possible Greek letters for the SABR-model symbols and Latin letters for the LMM-SABR symbols, and lower-case symbols for forward rates and upper-case symbols for swap rates. We therefore denote this LMM-SABR swap-rate instantaneous volatility by S_t where

$$dSR_t = (SR_t)^B S_t dZ'_t \tag{6.19}$$

and $S_t = S_t (\{f_t\}, \{s_t\}, \{\rho\})$ is a stochastic-volatility process dependent on the underlying LMM-SABR forward rates. We stress that we only need the instantaneous volatility of the swap rate, S_t, as a piece of scaffolding that will be removed once the task of determining an approximation for Σ_0 is finished.

As anticipated in the introductory section, for a given set of forward-rate parameters our goal is to approximate analytically (i.e., without making use of a Monte Carlo approximation) the SABR parameters of the swaption-based prices implied by the LMM-SABR dynamics of the forward rates. Therefore we need to 'guess' (i.e., to imply from the parameters of the forward-rate-based LMM-SABR model) the initial values of four SABR quantities:

1. the swap-rate volatility, Σ_0;

2. the correlation between the volatility of the swap rate and the swap rate itself, R_{SABR};

3. the exponent B; and

4. the volatility of the swap-rate volatility, V;

as a function of the forward-rate parameters or functions, $g(\tau_i)$, β_i, P, $h(\tau_i)$, f_0^i, $i = \alpha, \ldots, \beta - 1$.

6.3   Approximating the Instantaneous Swap Rate Volatility, S_t

Our goal in this section is to obtain an approximate expression for the instantaneous volatility of the swap rate, S_t, in the LMM-SABR swap-rate model. The strategy employed is

---

[1]To help the reader through the maze of symbols, we have used the convention of employing upper-case symbols for swaptions and lower-case for forward rates. Whenever possible (sometimes jumping between the Greek and Latin alphabets), the same letters have been used in lower- or upper-case for the same quantities relating to forward rates or swap rates, respectively.

based on the usual 'freezing' of suitable quantities to their initial values. As explained in Jaeckel and Rebonato (2002) and Rebonato (2002), the success of the freezing strategy rests both on the frozen quantities having a small volatility, and on their expectation being centred around the frozen values. In order to create variables with small volatilities, we use ratios of forward rates to swap rates: presumably, if a swap rate attains a 'high' value, its corresponding forward rates are likely to be rather high as well. The ratio should therefore have a lower volatility than either the swap rate or the forward rates in isolation. The details of the derivation can be found in the appendix (Section 6.10). The results for the swap rate instantaneous volatility, S_t, are

$$S_t = \sqrt{\sum_{k,m=1,n_j} W_k^0 W_m^0 s_t^k s_t^m \rho_{k,m}} \tag{6.20}$$

with

$$W_k^t = \omega_k \frac{\left(f_t^k\right)^{\beta_k}}{(SR_t)^B} \tag{6.21}$$

We use in the following this approximation as our starting point to derive further approximations for the swaption SABR quantities Σ_0 (initial volatility), R (swap-rate/swap-rate-volatility correlation), V (volatility of volatility of the swap rate) and B (exponent) implied by forward-rate LMM-SABR parameters.

We find that several, *a priori* equally plausible, approximations could be made. Interestingly enough, however, surprisingly few approximations provide a recovery of the SABR parameters for a one-period swaption (i.e., for a caplet). We therefore use this condition as a useful guide when devising our approximations.

6.4 Approximating the Initial Value of the Swap Rate Volatility, Σ_0 (First Route)

The first route is very straightforward, but, as we shall see, does not lend itself to obvious generalizations. We equate the SABR initial value of the volatility, Σ_0, to the root-mean-squared value of S_t. See Equation (6.24). In order to calculate the root-mean-squared value of S_t we use the expression (6.20) obtained above for the time-dependent volatility of the swap rate in the LMM-SABR model, S_t.

So, using the trick of 'freezing the initial values', one can assume

$$(\Sigma_0)^2 T \simeq \int_0^T (S_t)^2 dt \tag{6.22}$$

$$= \sum_{k,m} W_k^0 W_m^0 \int_0^T s_t^k s_t^m \rho_{k,m} dt \tag{6.23}$$

$$\Sigma_0 = \sqrt{\frac{1}{T} \sum_{k,m} W_k^0 W_m^0 \int_0^T s_t^k s_t^m \rho_{k,m} dt} \tag{6.24}$$

where T is the expiry of the swaption, and T_i is the expiry of a particular forward rate f_t^i (and, of course, $T_i \geq T$). Further freezing the terms k_t^i to their initial values gives the following approximation for the initial value of Σ_t, Σ_0:

$$\Sigma_0 = \sqrt{\frac{1}{T}\sum_{k,m} W_k^0 W_m^0 k_0^k k_0^m \int_0^T g_t^k g_t^m \rho_{k,m} dt} \qquad (6.25)$$

One can verify that in the limit of a one-period swaption (i.e., a caplet) Equation (6.25) gives

$$\Sigma_0 \equiv \sigma_0 = k_0^T \sqrt{\frac{1}{T}\int_0^T \left(g_t^T\right)^2 dt} \qquad (6.26)$$

This expression coincides with Equation (5.20) and is therefore perfectly consistent with the caplet set-up.

6.5   Approximating Σ_0 (Second Route) and the Volatility of Volatility of the Swap Rate, V

We want to derive the same approximation using a second approach, one that will allow us to obtain, at the same time, an expression for the volatility of volatility, V. Recall that the SABR dynamics of the swap rate are

$$dSR_t = \Sigma_t (SR_t)^B dZ_t \qquad (6.27)$$

$$d\Sigma_t = V\Sigma_t dW_t \qquad (6.28)$$

with $\mathbb{E}[dZ_t dW_t] = R_{SABR} dt$. We first use the approximation for the swap-rate instantaneous volatility, S_t, derived in (6.20),

$$S_t^2 = \sum_{k,m} W_k^0 W_m^0 s_t^k s_t^m \rho_{k,m} \qquad (6.29)$$

to equate the expectation of the total variance of the swap rate to expiry under the SABR model (LHS of Equation (6.30)) and under the LMM-SABR model (RHS of Equation (6.30)). We then proceed as we did for caplets to obtain

$$\mathbb{E}\left[\int_0^T S_t^2 dt\right] = \mathbb{E}\left[\int_0^T \left(\sum_{i,j} W_j^0 W_j^0 s_t^i s_t^j \rho_{i,j}\right) dt\right] \qquad (6.30)$$

The SABR expectation can be easily calculated:

$$\mathbb{E}\left[\int_0^T \Sigma_t^2 dt\right] = \left(\frac{\Sigma_0}{V}\right)^2 \left(e^{V^2 T} - 1\right) \tag{6.31}$$

Therefore we have

$$\left(\frac{\Sigma_0}{V}\right)^2 \left(e^{V^2 T} - 1\right) = \sum_{i,j} \left(\rho_{ij} \int_0^T g_t^i g_t^j \mathbb{E}\left[W_i^t W_j^t k_t^i k_t^j\right] dt\right)$$

$$\approx \sum_{i,j} \left(\rho_{ij} W_i^0 W_j^0 \int_0^T g_t^i g_t^j \mathbb{E}\left[k_t^i k_t^j\right] dt\right) \tag{6.32}$$

What remains to be evaluated is the expectation $\mathbb{E}\left[k_t^i k_t^j\right]$. To simplify notation we first define the cross root-mean-square volatility of volatility by

$$\widehat{h}_{ij}(t) = \sqrt{\frac{1}{t}\int_0^t h^i(s) h^j(s) ds} \tag{6.33}$$

With this definition it is easy to show that

$$\mathbb{E}\left[k^i(t) k^j(t)\right] = k_0^i k_0^j \exp\left[r_{ij}\widehat{h}_{ij}(t)^2 t\right] \tag{6.34}$$

From this we have the expression

$$\left(\frac{\Sigma_0}{V}\right)^2 \left(e^{V^2 T} - 1\right) = \sum_{i,j} \left(\rho_{ij} W_i^0 W_j^0 k_0^i k_0^j \int_0^T g_t^i g_t^j \exp\left[r_{ij}\widehat{h}_{ij}(t)^2 t\right] dt\right) \tag{6.35}$$

Taylor-expanding both sides and equating terms of the same order finally gives

$$\Sigma_0 = \sqrt{\frac{1}{T}\sum_{i,j}\left(\rho_{ij} W_i^0 W_j^0 k_0^i k_0^j \int_0^T g_t^i g_t^j dt\right)} \tag{6.36}$$

$$V = \frac{1}{\Sigma_0 T}\sqrt{2\sum_{i,j}\left(\rho_{ij} r_{ij} W_i^0 W_j^0 k_0^i k_0^j \int_0^T g_t^i g_t^j \widehat{h}_{ij}(t)^2 t\, dt\right)} \tag{6.37}$$

Using this procedure, we obtain two results: first, an expression for V; second, we also note that the equation we have obtained for the SABR initial value of the swap rate, Σ_0, using a Taylor expansion coincides with the expression for the same quantity we had obtained in the previous section invoking freezing.

Finally, we can quickly verify that Equation (6.37) coincides with Equation (5.36) in the one-period-swaption case.

6.6   Approximating the Swap-Rate/Swap-Rate-Volatility Correlation, R_{SABR}

In order to approximate the correlation between a swap rate and its volatility, R_{SABR}, it would be tempting to suggest a simplistic expression such as

$$R_{SABR} = \sum_{k=1,n_j} \omega_k R_{kk} \tag{6.38}$$

This would, however, be inaccurate, the more so, the more the forward rates are imperfectly correlated with each other. To see this, consider the limiting case when the volatilities of forward rates are strongly correlated with their own forward rates, but the forward rates themselves have zero correlation among themselves. In this situation, the correlation between the change in a given underlying forward rate and the swap rate could be low (the more so, the longer the swap), and so would therefore be the correlation between the swap rate and its own volatility. However, if we estimated the correlation between the swap rate and its own volatility using Equation (6.38), we would find a high value for R_{SABR}. Given the discussion just presented, this would be wrong. We must ensure that our approximation reflects this intuition.

The derivation is presented in the appendix (Section 6.11). The result is

$$R_{SABR} = \sum_{i,j} \Omega_{ij} R_{ij} \tag{6.39}$$

with the matrix Ω defined as

$$\Omega_{ij} = \frac{2\rho_{ij} R_{ij} W_i^0 W_j^0 k_0^i k_0^j \int_0^T g^i g^j \widehat{h}_{ij}(t)^2 t \, dt}{(V\Sigma_0 T)^2} \tag{6.40}$$

An important and pleasant feature of this approximation is that the quadruple summations[2] that would come from a brute-force application of the expressions obtained above are avoided.

6.7   Approximating the Swap Rate Exponent, B

Finally, for the exponent B we simply set

$$B = \sum_{k=1,n_j} \omega_k \beta_k \tag{6.41}$$

---

[2]Using symmetry, the quadruple summations can be reduced to triple summations. For very long-dated swaptions the computational burden is still unpleasant.

This *Ansatz* is clearly heuristic, as the (approximate) sum of CEV variables with exponent β is in general not a CEV variable with the same exponent. We know, however, that in the log-normal case the approximation is good (see Rebonato (1999a)), and that in the normal case it is exact. As the CEV exponent β is between 1 and 0, the approximation should be at least as good as in the log-normal case, and increasingly better as β approaches 0.

It is trivial to verify that in the limit of a one-period swaption the approximation is exact.

6.8 Results

6.8.1 Comparison between Approximated and Simulation Prices

The most direct way (but not the only way – see below) to check the accuracy of the approximations above is, of course, to compare the swaption prices as obtained by a full Monte Carlo simulation with the prices produced by the approximations suggested above. We performed these checks by using the following inputs. For the forward-rate parameters we used values similar to those typically observed in the calibration to market caplet prices of the forward-rate-based LMM-SABR model. As for the various components of the correlation super-matrix P, we made the following choices:

- in the absence of direct market information we used as inputs a variety of correlation structures for the volatility/volatility correlations, r;

- the diagonal elements of the sub-matrix of correlations between the forward rates and their volatilities, R, were obtained from the market forward-rate LMM-SABR model;

- the off-diagonal elements of the sub-matrix R were obtained using formula (6.14);

- finally, the forward-rate/forward-rate correlations were set around typical values reported in the literature (see Rebonato (2002) and references therein and Chapter 10).

For each set of forward-rate parameters and correlations we calculated the 'true' swaption prices by running a Monte Carlo simulation of the forward-rate processes and we turned these prices into 'true' implied volatilities. We call this simulation the LMM-SABR simulation. We then used the expressions presented above to calculate the swaption SABR parameters, Σ_0, R_{SABR}, B, V. We input these parameters both in the Hagan *et al.* (2002) SABR formula and in a separate Monte Carlo simulation of the SABR process, which we call the SABR simulation. We do so in order to ascertain to what extent small differences between the prices coming from our approximate formulae differ from the prices of the true SABR process because of the well-known limitations of the Hagan *et al.* (2002) SABR formula. The swaption 'true' implied volatilities from the LMM-SABR simulations are then compared with the implied volatilities obtained using our 'guessed' SABR swaption parameters, Σ_0, R_{SABR}, B, V, used either in the Hagan *et al.* (2002) formula or in the SABR simulation.

The accuracy of the approximations above is shown in Figures 6.1 to 6.7 where we display the swaption implied volatilities under Monte Carlo simulation of the *LMM-SABR forward-rate* process against the swaption implied volatilities under a Monte Carlo simulation of the *SABR swap-rate* process using the approximated parameters.

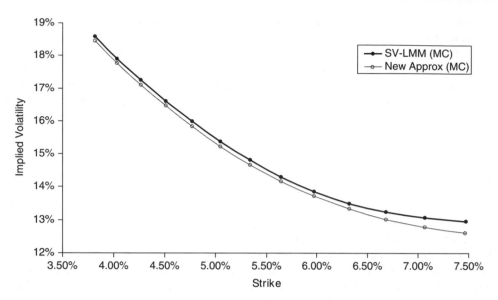

Figure 6.1   Accuracy of the approximations discussed in the text for the 5y × 2y swaption.

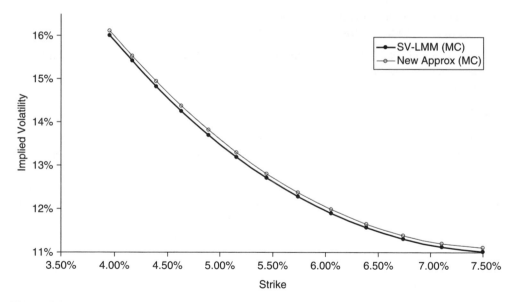

Figure 6.2   Accuracy of the approximations discussed in the text for the 5y × 5y swaption.

Certainly the errors appear very 'small'. But how small is small? To put the accuracy of the approximations in context we also display a different set of figures with a much richer set of information. So, in Figures 6.8 to 6.14:

- the curves labelled 'SV-LMM (MC)' report the implied volatilities corresponding to the swaption prices obtained running a Monte Carlo simulation of the LMM-SABR forward-rate processes;

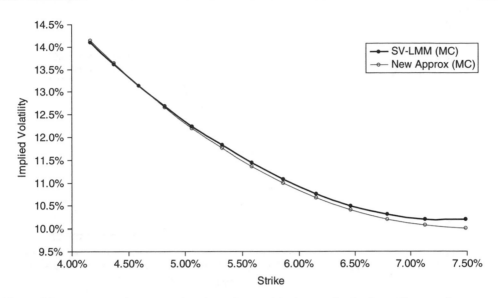

Figure 6.3 Accuracy of the approximations discussed in the text for the 5y × 10y swaption.

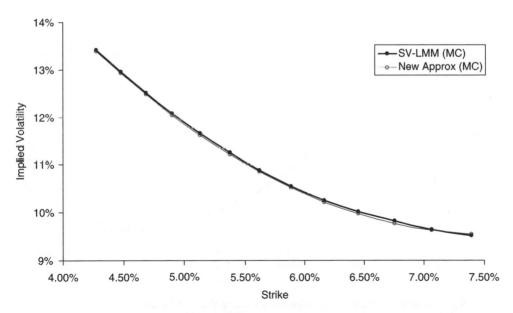

Figure 6.4 Accuracy of the approximations discussed in the text for the 5y × 15y swaption.

- the curves labelled 'New Approx (MC)' report the implied volatilities corresponding to the swaption prices obtained running a Monte Carlo simulation of the SABR swaption-rate process with the parameters 'guessed' using our approximation;

- the curves labelled 'New Approx (Hagan)' report the implied volatilities corresponding to the swaption prices obtained inputting the parameters 'guessed' using our approximation in the Hagan *et al.* (2002) SABR formula;

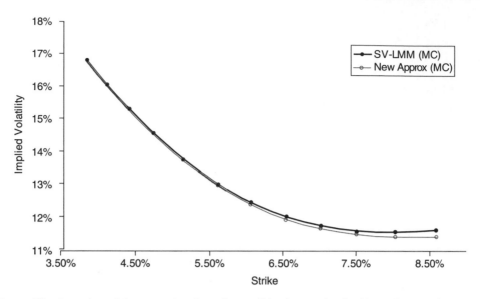

Figure 6.5 Accuracy of the approximations discussed in the text for the 10y × 2y swaption.

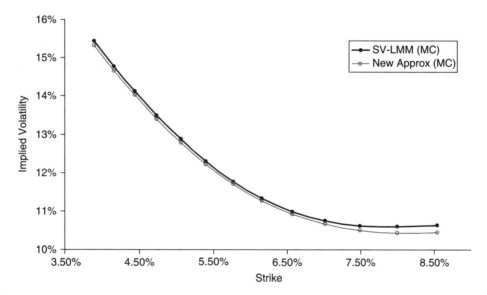

Figure 6.6 Accuracy of the approximations discussed in the text for the 10y × 5y swaption.

- the curves labelled 'Market (Hagan)' report the implied volatilities corresponding to the swaption prices obtained inputting in the Hagan formula the parameters used by the market for swaptions on the same day the forward-rate parameters were obtained;

- the curves labelled 'Market (MC)' report the implied volatilities corresponding to the swaption prices obtained running a Monte Carlo simulation of the SABR swaption-rate process with the parameters used by the market for swaptions on the same day the forward-rate parameters were obtained.

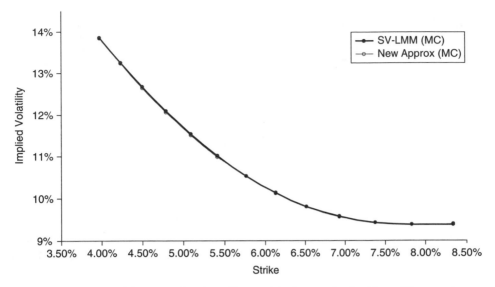

Figure 6.7   Accuracy of the approximations discussed in the text for the 10y × 10y swaption.

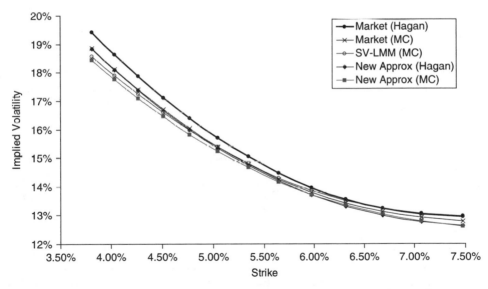

Figure 6.8   Accuracy of the approximations discussed in the text for the 5y × 2y swaption compared with several market and model inputs as described in the text.

We stress that no direct comparison should be made between the curves labelled 'New Approx' and the curves labelled 'Market (Hagan)' and Market (MC). The two distinct sets of curves are presented together only to give a yardstick to gauge the accuracy of our approximations. If the reader finds these figures too busy, it is Figures 6.1 to 6.7 that tell the punch line.

From these graphs we see that even in the worst cases our approximation is of the same order of accuracy as the asymptotic expansion of the SABR model, and often much

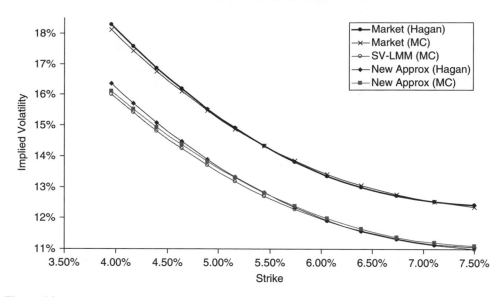

Figure 6.9   Accuracy of the approximations discussed in the text for the 5y × 5y swaption compared with several market and model inputs as described in the text.

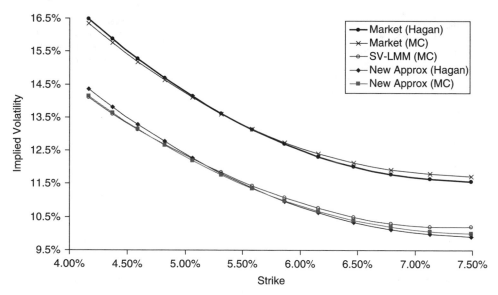

Figure 6.10   Accuracy of the approximations discussed in the text for the 5y × 10y swaption compared with several market and model inputs as described in the text.

better. We note that the approximations display greater accuracy for 'long-tail' swaptions than for 'short-tail' ones and for short-expiry than for long-expiry swaptions. For instance, the 10y × 10y curves for the swaption implied volatilities obtained using our approximate parameters in a Monte Carlo simulation and via direct simulation of the forward-rate LMM-SABR process are virtually on top of each other: that is why in Figure 6.14 there

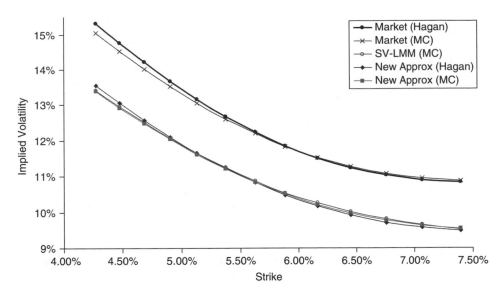

Figure 6.11 Accuracy of the approximations discussed in the text for the 5y × 15y swaption compared with several market and model inputs as described in the text.

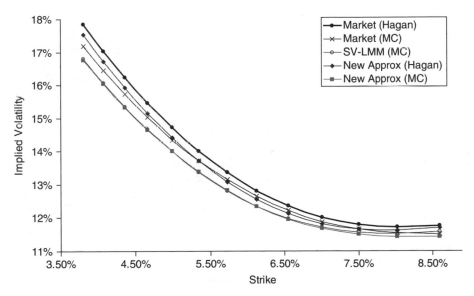

Figure 6.12 Accuracy of the approximations discussed in the text for the 10y × 2y swaption compared with several market and model inputs as described in the text.

appear to be only four curves instead of five. On the other hand, the accuracy of the approximation is worst for the 5y × 2y swaption. Since the caplet approximation is excellent (see Figures 5.2 and 5.3), this suggests that one source of weakness of the approximations we have proposed stems from the difficulty in capturing correctly the integral cross-terms between the functions $h(\cdot)$ and $g(\cdot)$ when these change rapidly. This would also explain

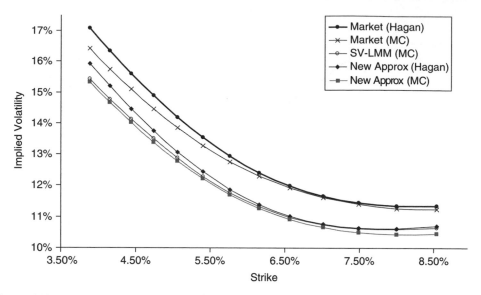

Figure 6.13   Accuracy of the approximations discussed in the text for the 10y × 5y swaption compared with several market and model inputs as described in the text.

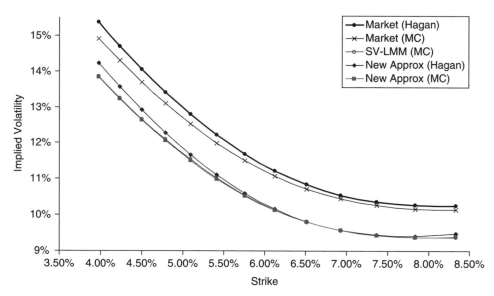

Figure 6.14   Accuracy of the approximations discussed in the text for the 10y × 10y swaption compared with several market and model inputs as described in the text.

why long-expiry, 'long-tail' swaptions are very well captured: the longer the underlying swap rate, the larger the number of forward rates that, by swaption expiry, are still in a very-flat-volatility environment and the smaller the importance of the correct handling of the time variation of the functions $g(\cdot)$ and $h(\cdot)$. Similarly, if the expiry is long, for most of the time the cross-integrals of the functions $h(\cdot)$ and $g(\cdot)$ will be rather flat.

6.8.2 Comparison between Parameters from the Approximations and the Simulations

An alternative way to understand the accuracy of our approximations is the following. We first calculated using a Monte Carlo simulation the prices of the swaptions for several strikes implied by a given set of forward-rate LMM-SABR parameters. As a second step, we fitted a swap-based SABR 'model' (i.e., the Hagan *et al.* (2002) formula) to these prices. To avoid multiple minima – in the SABR model the exponent and the correlation coefficient tend to 'play against each other' (see Chapter 3 and, e.g., Castagna, Mercurio and Tarenghi (2007)) – we anchored the numerical search around the exponent given by Equation (6.41). We then compared the SABR coefficients obtained by this search with the coefficients estimated using the approximations above. This analysis allows us to appreciate which of the various approximations are more effective.

The results are shown in Table 6.1. For each section, the row labelled 'SV-LMM' displays the SABR coefficients fitted to the prices obtained using the Monte Carlo simulation of the forward-rate processes, and the row labelled 'Approx' displays the SABR coefficients as guessed by our approximate formulae[3] using as input the parameters of the forward-rate processes and the matrix P.

Table 6.1 Fitted SABR parameters for full LMM Monte Carlo and our approximation.

		Σ_0	B	R_{SABR}	V
5y Caplet	SV-LMM	3.51%	0.5	−43.7%	30.46%
(Fig. 5.2)	Approx	3.49%	0.5	−42.7%	30.45%
10y Caplet	SV-LMM	2.98%	0.5	−36.41%	25.85%
(Fig. 5.3)	Approx	3.00%	0.5	−36.73%	24.87%
5y × 2y Swaption	SV-LMM	3.35%	0.5	−37.38%	29.91%
(Fig. 6.1	Approx	3.34%	0.5	−40.88%	28.51%
5y × 5y Swaption	SV-LMM	2.92%	0.5	−40.44%	26.92%
(Fig. 6.2)	Approx	2.95%	0.5	−40.58%	27.08%
5y × 10y Swaption	SV-LMM	2.65%	0.5	−35.68%	25.80%
(Fig. 6.3)	Approx	2.64%	0.5	−38.25%	26.08%
5y × 15y Swaption	SV-LMM	2.55%	0.5	−40.18%	24.98%
(Fig. 6.4)	Approx	2.54%	0.5	−39.22%	25.52%
10y × 2y Swaption	SV-LMM	2.84%	0.5	−33.22%	26.52%
(Fig. 6.5)	Approx	2.86%	0.5	−35.13%	25.56%
10y × 5y Swaption	SV-LMM	2.62%	0.5	−34.12%	25.55%
(Fig. 6.6)	Approx	2.61%	0.5	−35.58%	24.65%
10y × 10y Swaption	SV-LMM	2.46%	0.5	−36.17%	24.26%
(Fig. 6.7)	Approx	2.45%	0.5	−35.59%	24.38%

---

[3]Actually, it shows the SABR fit to the smile produced by running a Monte Carlo simulation on the SABR dynamics 'guessed' by our approximation. This is more appropriate when comparing to the LMM.

We see that the approximation (6.25) estimates in all conditions very accurately the initial value of the volatility, Σ_0 (minimum relative error 0.2%, maximum relative error 0.8%, average relative error 0.5%). As this parameter is mainly linked to the level of the smile, we understand why our approximate curves are always well centred at the at-the-money level. The approximation for the parameter V, which mainly controls the degree of curvature of the smile, is the second most accurate (minimum relative error 0.5%, maximum relative error 4.9%, average relative error 2.4%). The approximation for the parameter R_{SABR}, which mainly controls the slope of the smile, is the least accurate (minimum relative error 0.3%, maximum relative error 8.6%, average relative error 4.2%). This explains why the small errors in implied volatilities tend to have opposite signs moving from deeply in- to deeply out-of-the-money swaptions.

6.9 Conclusions and Suggestions for Future Work

We have presented analytical approximations of the swaption prices implied by a set of parameters for the forward-rate-based SABR-LMM model. In the range of parameter values associated with market fits, the approximations have been shown to be very accurate and to do at least as well as, and very often better than, the generally market-accepted SABR formula – the errors in this latter case stem from the approximate nature of the underlying asymptotic expansion.

En route to obtaining these results we have presented an improvement on the approach presented in Rebonato (2007b) to calibrating the same forward-rate-based SABR-LMM model to caplet prices.

This work can be of great use in calibrating a forward-rate-based SABR-LMM to (subsets of) the swaption matrix, or in obtaining a joint calibration to caplets and swaptions for mixed products (e.g., products with LIBOR-based payoffs and callability features).

The approximations can also be useful in order to obtain a consistent drift correction for CMS products in a forward-rate-based LMM approach. Hagan (2003) has in fact shown that the correction can be expressed as an integral over swaption prices. From a set of forward-rate parameters and correlations, in fact, one can use our approximations to obtain directly the SABR parameters for swaptions, obtain from these the swaption Black 'implied volatilities' using the Hagan *et al.* (2002) formula and input these into the Black formula for swaptions under the sign of the integral as in Hagan (2003).

Finally, the approximations we have presented would be very useful to investigate the congruence of the swaption and caplet markets and to explore whether the correlation super-matrix P can be profitably 'implied' from market prices of caplets and swaptions.

6.10 Appendix: Derivation of Approximate Swap Rate Volatility

Let's apply Ito's lemma to Equation (6.15) using Equation (6.2) and the approximation[4] $\frac{\partial \omega_k}{\partial f_t^j} = 0$ and let's focus on the volatility part of the resulting expression for the swap-rate

---

[4]This approximation is not required, and could be replaced by the more cumbersome expression in Jaeckel and Rebonato (2002). The effect is generally small, and exactly zero for a flat term structure of rates.

volatility, S_t (we concur with Henry-Labordere (2007) that the contribution in dt to the following expressions is negligible):[5]

$$S_t (SR_t)^B dZ'_t = \sum_k \frac{\partial SR_t}{\partial f_t^k} \left(f_t^k\right)^{\beta_k} s_t^k dz_t^k$$

$$\simeq \sum_k \omega_k \left(f_t^k\right)^{\beta_k} s_t^k dz_t^k \qquad (6.42)$$

Consider now equating and squaring the above expressions

$$(S_t)^2 (SR_t)^{2B} = \sum_{k,m} \omega_k \omega_m \left(f_t^k\right)^{\beta_k} \left(f_t^m\right)^{\beta_m} s_t^k s_t^m \rho_{k,m} \qquad (6.43)$$

where

$$\rho_{k,m} dt = \mathbb{E}\left[dz_t^k dz_t^m\right] \qquad (6.44)$$

From Equation (6.43) we have

$$(S_t)^2 = \frac{\sum_{k,m} \omega_k \omega_m \left(f_t^k\right)^{\beta_k} \left(f_t^m\right)^{\beta_m} s_t^k s_t^m \rho_{k,m}}{(SR_t)^{2B}}$$

$$= \sum_{k,m} \left\{ \omega_k \frac{\left(f_t^k\right)^{\beta_k}}{(SR_t)^B} \right\} \left\{ \omega_m \frac{\left(f_t^m\right)^{\beta_m}}{(SR_t)^B} \right\} s_t^k s_t^m \rho_{k,m} \qquad (6.45)$$

Define

$$W_k^t = \omega_k \frac{\left(f_t^k\right)^{\beta_k}}{(SR_t)^B} \qquad (6.46)$$

Equation (6.45) becomes

$$S_t = \sqrt{\sum_{k,m} W_k^t W_m^t s_t^k s_t^m \rho_{k,m}} \qquad (6.47)$$

Comparing with Equation (6.16) gives

$$dSR_t = (SR_t)^B \sqrt{\sum_{k,m} W_k^t W_m^t s_t^k s_t^m \rho_{k,m}} dZ'_t \qquad (6.48)$$

Up to this point no approximations have been made (apart from the avoidable $\frac{\partial \omega_k}{\partial f_t^j} = 0$).

Let us now assume that the variation over time of the ratio $\left(f_t^k\right)_k^\beta/(SR_t)^B$ can be considered small compared with the variation in the functions s_t^m. This is plausible because swap rates are strongly correlated with the underlying forward rates. Then, following usual

---

[5]Note, the limits of the summation Σ_k are not shown below for clarity but for a $SR_t^{\alpha\beta}$ the summation is $\Sigma_{k=\alpha}^{\beta-1}$.

practice (see, e.g., Hull and White (2000), Jaeckel and Rebonato (2002)), it is reasonable to assume that the 'weights' W_k^t could be frozen with little loss of precision. (See, however, Henry-Labordere (2007) for a discussion of the limitations of this approach.) This would give

$$S_t = \sqrt{\sum_{k,m} W_k^0 W_m^0 s_t^k s_t^m \rho_{k,m}} \qquad (6.49)$$

6.11   Appendix: Derivation of Swap-Rate/ Swap-Rate-Volatility Correlation, R_{SABR}

We want to choose the parameters of the forward-rate process in such a way that

$$\mathbb{E}[dZ_t dW_t] = R_{\text{SABR}} dt \qquad (6.50)$$

Differentiating expression (6.49) gives

$$dS_t = d\left(\sqrt{\sum_{k,m} W_k^0 W_m^0 s_t^k s_t^m \rho_{k,m}}\right) \qquad (6.51)$$

Using Ito's lemma gives (see the appendix (Section 6.12))

$$\frac{dS_t}{S_t} = A dt + \sum_{k,m_j} W_k^0 W_m^0 \rho_{k,m} \Psi_t^k \Psi_t^m h_t^k dw_t^k$$

with

$$\Psi_t^k \equiv \frac{s_t^k}{S_t} \qquad (6.52)$$

The terms in dt (also given in the appendix (Section 6.12)) are irrelevant for the future discussion. So

$$VAR\left[\frac{dS_t}{S_t}\right] = \sum_{k,m,n,l} \left\{W_k^0 W_m^0 W_n^0 W_l^0 \Psi_t^k \Psi_t^m \Psi_t^n \Psi_t^l \rho_{k,m} \rho_{n,l} h_t^k h_t^n r_{kn}\right\} \qquad (6.53)$$

Freezing the Ψ_t^k terms gives

$$V \approx \sqrt{\frac{1}{T_j} \sum_{k,m,n,l} \left\{W_k^0 W_m^0 W_n^0 W_l^0 \Psi_0^k \Psi_0^m \Psi_0^n \Psi_0^l \rho_{k,m} \rho_{n,l} r_{kn} \int_0^T h_t^k h_t^n dt\right\}} \qquad (6.54)$$

From Equation (6.54) it would be tempting to try to achieve $E[dZ_t dW_t] = R dt$ simply by approximating

$$\mathbb{E}\left[\frac{d(SR_t)}{(SR_t)^B}\frac{dS_t}{S_t}\right] = \mathbb{E}\left[\left(\sum_r W_r^0 k_0^r g_t^r dz_t^r\right)\left(\sum_{k,m} W_k^0 W_m^0 \rho_{k,m} \Psi_t^k \Psi_t^m h_t^k dw_t^k\right)\right]$$

$$= \sum_{k,m,r} k_0^r W_r^0 W_k^0 W_m^0 \rho_{k,m} \Psi_t^k \Psi_t^m R_{rk} g_t^r h_t^k dt \tag{6.55}$$

i.e., one could set

$$R_{SABR} = \frac{\sum_{k,m,r} k_0^r W_r^0 W_k^0 W_m^0 \Psi_t^k \Psi_t^m \rho_{k,m} R_{rk} \frac{1}{T}\int_0^T g_t^r h_t^k dt}{\Sigma_0 V} \tag{6.56}$$

or, after pulling the functions $g(\cdot)$ inside the integral,

$$R_{SABR} = \frac{\sum_{k,m,r} k_0^k k_0^m k_0^r W_r^0 W_k^0 W_m^0 \rho_{k,m} R_{rk} \int_0^T g_t^k g_t^m g_t^r h_t^k dt}{(\Sigma_0)^3 VT} \tag{6.57}$$

However, from Equations (6.57) or (6.56) together with Equation (6.37) one can see that the correct one-period-swaption (caplet) limit would in general not be recovered unless

$$\frac{\int g_t^T h_t^T dt}{\left(2\int_0^T g(t)^2 \hat{h}_t^2 t dt\right)^{1/2}} = 1 \tag{6.58}$$

or

$$\frac{\int_0^T (g_t^T)^3 h_t^T dt}{\left(\frac{1}{T}\int_0^T g(t)^2 dt\right)\left(2\int_0^T g(t)^2 \hat{h}_t^2 t dt\right)^{1/2}} = 1 \tag{6.59}$$

according to whether approximation (6.56) or (6.57) is used. This will not happen for non-trivial cases. In order to fix this problem, we use Equations (6.56) and (6.57) as an indication of the overall structure of the expression we are looking for, and Equations (6.58) and (6.59) as a hint of the problems we must avoid. We therefore proceed by defining the matrix Ω as

$$\Omega_{ij} = \frac{2\rho_{ij} R_{ij} W_i^0 W_j^0 k_0^i k_0^j \int_0^T g^i g^j \hat{h}_{ij}(t)^2 t dt}{(V\Sigma_0 T)^2} \tag{6.60}$$

From Equation (6.37) we then have

$$\Omega_{ij} \geq 0 \text{ and } \sum_{i,j} \Omega_{ij} = 1 \tag{6.61}$$

i.e., the quantities Ω_{ij} have the properties of weights. If we now propose the following expression for R_{SABR}:

$$R_{\text{SABR}} = \sum_{i,j} \Omega_{ij} R_{ij} \tag{6.62}$$

the structure of the approximation reflects the intuition mentioned at the start of the section and what was suggested by Equations (6.56) and (6.57), but, at the same time, the correct one-period swaption limit is recovered.

6.12   Appendix: Approximation of dS_t/S_t

Start from

$$\frac{dS_t}{S_t} = \frac{\sum\limits_{k,m} W_k^0 W_m^0 \rho_{k,m} d(s_t^k s_t^m)}{2\,(S_t)^2} \tag{6.63}$$

Consider the terms $d(s_t^k s_t^m)$. Each term is equal to

$$d(s_t^k s_t^m) = \left(s_t^m ds_t^k + s_t^k ds_t^m + ds_t^m ds_t^k \right) \tag{6.64}$$

Taking one term at a time gives

$$
\begin{aligned}
s_t^m ds_t^k &= k_t^m g_t^m d\left(k_t^k g_t^k \right) \\
&= k_t^m g_t^m \left(g_t^k k_t^k h_t^k dw_t^k + k_t^k g_t'^k dt \right)
\end{aligned}
\tag{6.65}
$$

and

$$
\begin{aligned}
ds_t^m ds_t^k &= d\left(k_t^m g_t^m \right) d\left(k_t^k g_t^k \right) \\
&= g_t^m g_t^k k_t^m k_t^k h_t^m h_t^k r_{mk} dt
\end{aligned}
\tag{6.66}
$$

Putting the various terms together gives

$$
\begin{aligned}
d(s_t^k s_t^m) &= \left(s_t^m ds_t^k + s_t^k ds_t^m + ds_t^m ds_t^k \right) \\
&= k_t^m g_t^m \left(k_t^k g_t^k h_t^k dw_t^k + k_t^k g_t'^k dt \right) \\
&\quad + k_t^k g_t^k \left(k_t^m g_t^m h_t^m dw_t^m + k_t^m g_t'^m dt \right) \\
&\quad + k_t^k k_t^m g_t^k g_t^m h_t^k h_t^m r_{km} dt
\end{aligned}
\tag{6.67}
$$

After collecting terms in dt and dw we have

$$
\begin{aligned}
d(s_t^k s_t^m) &= \left[k_t^m k_t^k \left(g_t^m g_t'^k + g_t^k g_t'^m \right) + k_t^k k_t^m g_t^k g_t^m h_t^k h_t^m r_{km} \right] dt \\
&\quad + k_t^m k_t^k g_t^m g_t^k h_t^k dw_t^k + k_t^k k_t^m g_t^k g_t^m h_t^m dw_t^m
\end{aligned}
$$

Equation (6.63) therefore becomes

$$
\frac{dS_t}{S_t} = \frac{\sum_{k,m} W_k^0 W_m^0 \rho_{k,m} d(s_t^k s_t^m)}{2 (S_t)^2}
$$

$$
= \frac{1}{2 (S_t)^2} \sum_{k,m} \left\{ W_k^0 W_m^0 \rho_{k,m} \left[k_t^m k_t^k \left(g_t^m g_t'^k + g_t^k g_t'^m \right) + k_t^k k_t^m g_t^k g_t^m h_t^k h_t^m r_{km} \right] \right\} dt
$$

$$
+ \sum_{k,m} \left\{ \frac{W_k^0 W_m^0 \rho_{k,m} k_t^k k_t^m g_t^m g_t^k h_t^k}{\left(S_t^j \right)^2} dw_t^k \right\} \tag{6.68}
$$

Call A all the terms in dt. Also, define

$$
\Psi_t^k \equiv \frac{s_t^k}{S_t} \tag{6.69}
$$

Then

$$
\frac{dS_t}{S_t} = A dt + \sum_{k,m=1,n_j} W_k^0 W_m^0 \rho_{k,m} \Psi_t^k \Psi_t^m h_t^k dw_t^k \tag{6.70}
$$

Chapter 7

Calibrating the Correlation Structure

7.1 Statement of the Problem

Before discussing the calibration of the LMM-SABR model to the target correlation function it is important to distinguish clearly between the input and the model correlation matrices. If N is the number of forward rates in the problem, the input correlation matrix is the full-rank $2N \times 2N$ real symmetric matrix that we can in principle estimate using statistical techniques, or from correlation-dependent market prices. If we could afford a $2N$-factor model, this is the matrix ideally we would like to work with. Then there is the model correlation matrix. This is the matrix, typically of lower rank, that our LMM-SABR model sees. Only rarely will the two be the same.

With the deterministic-volatility LIBOR market model, we do not normally worry too much about the input matrix (this may be a pity, especially for products like CMS spread options, but this is another story). When it comes to the LMM-SABR model, however, matters are different. As we mentioned in Chapter 3, creating a valid (i.e., positive definite) input correlation matrix of full dimensionality is not a trivial task. This is because N of the $N(N-1)/2$ elements are exogenously fixed by the SABR market-given correlations between each forward rate and its own volatility. As we show below, this may require some compromises to be made if we want our input matrix to be positive definite (i.e., a *bona fide* correlation matrix).

When we implement the LMM-SABR model, we will probably want to reduce the number of factors from $2N$ to a more manageable number. This will introduce a further distortion to the correlation matrix, i.e., a transformation from the input matrix to the model matrix. This is simply due to the fact that the fewer factors we retain, the fewer Fourier components we will be able to recover in our model correlation matrix. These problems are well known, and have been discussed at length in Rebonato and Cooper (1995), Rebonato (2002) and

Rebonato (2004a), among others. In the deterministic-volatility LIBOR market model this is the only 'compromise' one should worry about. We stress that this is no longer the case with the LMM-SABR model. It is important to keep the different sources of 'corruption' conceptually distinct.

A last remark: ultimately, the only matrix that matters is the one the model 'sees'. So, if the input matrix is not positive definite, but the model correlation matrix is, no great harm would have been done. However, the model correlation matrix will typically be made to 'resemble' as closely as possible the input matrix. If the latter is too far removed from a possible correlation matrix (because some eigenvalues, for instance, are large and negative), we would be approximating with a possible correlation matrix something that does not look like a correlation matrix at all. This is not a good place to start. Therefore it is a good idea to find ways to make sure our input matrix is as close as possible to a *bona fide* correlation matrix and reflects all the available market information. This task is undertaken in Chapter 10. In this chapter we will assume that this good work has already been done, and we tackle the problem of finding a good model correlation matrix.

7.2   Creating a Valid Model Matrix

For N forward rates, the full correlation matrix, P, is a $2N \times 2N$ real symmetric matrix defined as

$$P = \begin{pmatrix} \rho & R \\ R^\dagger & r \end{pmatrix} \tag{7.1}$$

where ρ is the forward-rate/forward-rate correlation matrix, r is the volatility/volatility correlation matrix and R is the forward-rate/volatility matrix.[1] The only elements that affect the caplet prices are the diagonal elements of the sub-matrix R–these are the ρ_{SABR} parameters of the SABR model. Any scheme to reduce the number of factors must preserve the diagonal elements, $R_{ii} = \rho^i_{SABR}$, of R.

Recall from Chapter 4 that, neglecting the drifts, the equations of motion can be written for N forward rates and volatilities as

$$\frac{df^i_t}{\left(f^i_t\right)^{q_i}} = s^i_t \sum_{j=1}^{M} e_{ij} dz_j, \ i = 1 \text{ to } N \tag{7.2}$$

$$ds^i_t = g(t, T_i) dk^i_t \tag{7.3}$$

$$\frac{dk^i_t}{k^i_t} = h^i_t \sum_{j=1}^{M} e_{N+i,j} dz_j, \ i = 1 \text{ to } N \tag{7.4}$$

with

$$M = N_F + N_V \tag{7.5}$$

---

[1] This is not a standard correlation matrix since the correlation between the ith forward rate and the jth volatility is not necessarily the same as the correlation between the jth forward rate and the ith volatility.

for N_F forward-rate factors and N_V volatility factors, and

$$\mathbb{E}\left[dz_i dz_j\right] = \rho_{ij} dt \qquad (7.6)$$

$$\sum_{j=1}^{M} e_{ij}^2 = 1 \qquad (7.7)$$

In matrix form this can be rewritten as

$$dx = q \cdot E \cdot dz \qquad (7.8)$$

where

- dx is a $[2N, 1]$ vector whose first N elements are given by $\frac{df_t^i}{(f_t^i)^{q_i}}$, and its last N elements are given by $\frac{dk_t^i}{k_t^i}$, $i = 1, 2, \ldots, N$;

- q is the $[2N, 2N]$ diagonal matrix whose first N diagonal elements are given by s_t^i and its last N diagonal elements are given by h_t^i, $i = 1, 2, \ldots, N$;

- E is a $[2N, M]$ matrix of elements e_{ij} and of the stacked form

$$E = \begin{bmatrix} B \\ C \end{bmatrix} \qquad (7.9)$$

- B is the $[N, M]$ matrix with elements b_{ij}, $i = 1, 2, \ldots, N$ and $j = 1, 2, \ldots, M$ (and similarly for matrix C of elements c_{ij});

- dz is the $[M, 1]$ vector of elements dz_j.

Of course, if $M = 2N$ then we have a full factor model and recover P exactly. This is no longer the case when $M < 2N$. In this case we want to determine the 'mixing' matrices B and C in such a way that they 'resemble' the P matrix (in some sense to be defined) as closely as possible:

$$BB^{\dagger} \approx \rho$$
$$CC^{\dagger} \approx r$$
$$BC^{\dagger} \approx R \qquad (7.10)$$

To do this, we treat the ith row of B as the $[1 \times M]$ vector b^i, and the ith row of C as the $[1 \times M]$ vector c^i. We have two constraints on these vectors:

- the normalization constraint

$$b^i \cdot b^i = \sum_{j=1}^{M} b_{ij}^2 = c^i \cdot c^i = \sum_{j=1}^{M} b_{ij}^2 = 1 \quad \forall i \qquad (7.11)$$

- the SABR correlation constraint

$$b^i \cdot c^i = R_{ii} \qquad (7.12)$$

So b^i and c^i are unit vectors in an M-dimensional space.

There are many ways to solve this problem with the above constraints (and many 'optimal' solutions since we have not specified what we mean by 'approximate'). We present two solutions, based on different definitions of distance between two vectors. The first will recover the elements R_{ii} exactly; the second gets arbitrarily close to them, but in general recovers other portions of the P matrix better.

7.2.1   First Strategy, Stage 1: Diagonalize P

Since P is a real symmetric matrix it is easy and quick to diagonalize. We write

$$P = \Lambda D \Lambda^{\dagger} \qquad (7.13)$$

where D is a diagonal matrix of the (real) eigenvalues of P and Λ is a matrix with the eigenvectors of P as its columns.

If all the eigenvalues are positive then P is positive definite (or positive semi-definite if some are zero). If, however, the matrix is not positive semi-definite we can still proceed provided the number of positive eigenvalues is greater than or equal to $M-$ this is a standard way of dealing with a non-positive semi-definite correlation matrix.

The vectors b^i and c^i are then defined as

$$b^i_j = B_{ij} = \frac{\Lambda_{ij} D_j^{1/2}}{\sum_{k=1}^{M} \Lambda_{ik} D_k^{1/2}} \qquad (7.14)$$

$$c^i_j = C_{ij} = \frac{\Lambda_{i+N,j} D_j^{1/2}}{\sum_{k=1}^{M} \Lambda_{i+N,k} D_k^{1/2}} \qquad (7.15)$$

These relationships preserve b^i and c^i as unit vectors, and satisfy Equation (7.10). In general, however, the constraint of Equation (7.12) will not be satisfied. We take care of this as follows.

7.2.2   First Strategy, Stage 2: Analytic Optimization of c^i

Recall that the SABR constraint can be written as

$$b^i \cdot c^i = R_{ii} \qquad (7.16)$$

We want to keep the vectors b^i fixed and adjust the vectors c^i – which we call $\tilde{c}^i$ – in turn in such a way that

1. the SABR constraint is satisfied;

2. the vectors $\tilde{c}^i$ remain of unit norm; and

3. the distance from the original c^i is minimized.

First of all, note that the vectors b^i and $\tilde{c}^i$ define a plane (as long as they are not parallel). Think of placing the origin of the vectors $\tilde{c}^i$ to coincide with the origin of b^i. The SABR constraint (7.16) prescribes an angle, say R_{ii}, between b^i and c^i. Let $\phi_i = b^i \cdot \tilde{c}^i$ then be the (known) angle between b^i and $\tilde{c}^i$.

The vectors $\tilde{c}^i$ sweep a cone with vertex at the common origin of b^i and $\tilde{c}^i$. Therefore, in order to minimize the distance between c^i and $\tilde{c}^i$, c^i must lie in the plane defined by b^i and $\tilde{c}^i$ and is found by the intersection of this plane with the cone described above. The vector c^i can therefore be written as a linear combination of the two (non-orthogonal) 'basis' vectors b^i and $\tilde{c}^i$:

$$c^i = \lambda_1 b^i + \lambda_2 \tilde{c}^i \tag{7.17}$$

What we do not know are the coefficients λ_1 and λ_2 in the expansion of the solution vector c^i. To find these quantities we proceed as follows.

Keeping in mind that the required vectors must have unit length, we have

$$c^i \cdot c^i = \lambda_1^2 + \lambda_2^2 + 2\lambda_1\lambda_2\phi_i = 1 \tag{7.18}$$

$$b^i \cdot c^i = b^i \cdot \left(\lambda_1 b^i + \lambda_2 \tilde{c}^i\right) = \lambda_1 + \lambda_2\phi_i = R_{ii} \tag{7.19}$$

This gives

$$\lambda_2 = \sqrt{\frac{1 - R_{ii}^2}{1 - \phi_i^2}} \tag{7.20}$$

The value λ_2 can then be substituted in Equation (7.17) to solve for λ_1. The simple procedure can be repeated sequentially for each vector c^i to find its 'optimal' value.

There is some financial justification for the procedure, which treats the matrix B (which is related to the forward-rate/forward-rate portion of the correlation matrix P) as more 'privileged' than the matrix C. One can in fact reasonably assume that the forward-rate/forward-rate matrix is better and more reliably known than the volatility/volatility or the volatility/forward-rate blocks. The exact recovery of their elements is therefore a less stringent requirement (apart from the SABR-related diagonal elements R_{ii}).

7.2.3   Second Strategy: Optimizing over Angles

The second route to optimizing places different weights on the elements of the matrix P and structures the problem so as to carry out an unconstrained non-linear optimization. It is very similar to the strategy proposed by Rebonato (1999b) to calibrate a deterministic-volatility LMM to an exogenously assigned correlation matrix. The intuition is very simple: consider the trigonometric relationship

$$\sin^2\theta + \cos^2\theta = 1 \tag{7.21}$$

which holds for any angle θ. If two quantities, say e_1 and e_2, are set equal to the sine and cosine terms above, the constraint on the sum of their squares, $e_1^2\theta + e_2^2\theta = 1$ (see Equation (7.11)) is automatically satisfied. The generalization to M variables is immediate: we simply have to use as optimization variables the $(M - 1)$ angles that define the surface of an $(M - 1)$-dimensional hypersphere[2] of unit radius (with one such set of angles for each variable – forward rate or volatility):

$$e_{ik} = \cos\theta_{ik}\,\Pi_{j=1}^{k-1}\sin\theta_{ij} \quad k = 1, 2, \ldots, M - 1 \tag{7.22}$$

$$e_{ik} = \Pi_{j=1}^{k-1}\sin\theta_{ij} \quad k = M \tag{7.23}$$

with $i = 1, 2, \ldots, 2N$.

The optimization is then achieved

- by starting from an initial inspired guess for the angles (or, failing that, from random variates drawn from the uniform $\mathcal{U}\,[0, 2\pi]$) distribution;

- by obtaining the trial correlation matrix by

$$P = ee^\dagger \tag{7.24}$$

- by calculating the distance χ^2 between the trial (P) and target ($\widetilde{P}$) correlation matrices as, for example,

$$\chi^2 = \sum_{ij} w_{ij}\left(P_{ij} - \widetilde{P}_{ij}\right)^2 \tag{7.25}$$

- by minimizing this distance in an unconstrained manner over the angles.

The requirement that the elements R_{ii} are 'very important' can be translated by giving very high weights to the associated elements of $\widetilde{P}_{ij}$. Similarly, if we believe, as we normally do, that we can trust the forward-rate/forward-rate portion of the correlation matrix more than other parts, we can assign higher weights to these entries.

There is one numerical problem – what we call the Greenland-on-a-world-map effect. Its origin lies in the fact that the mapping from the quantities we want to optimize over to the angles is very non-linear, and the original surface is locally very strongly deformed (much as Greenland is deformed on a two-dimensional map of the world). In other words, a uniform probability distribution over the angles is very non-uniform in the space of the variables we are interested in. So, minima in the original space can become extremely steep (and easy-to-miss) wells in angle space. The more so, the higher the dimensions of the sphere.

Doust (2007) has suggested an inspired guess to fix this problem. This is presented in Appendix 7.5. However, we show in the next section the result of a simple optimization using Equations (7.22) and (7.23) to a plausible and realistically complex correlation surface. The outcome, as we shall see, is very satisfactory.

---

[2]Mathematicians (and relativists) define such a surface as an S^{k-1} sphere, where k are the dimensions of the space in which the surface is embedded, and $k - 1$ the number of *intrinsic* coordinates necessary to specify a point on the surface. So, the perimeter of a circle is an S^1 sphere, and the surface of a 3d sphere is an S^2 sphere. We do not use this terminology.

7.3   A Case Study: Calibration Using the Hypersphere Method

We study the case of 10 forward rates and 10 volatilities. We assume that the forward-rate/forward-rate block of the correlation matrix is given by a Doust-like correlation, displayed in Table 7.1 and Figures 7.1 and 7.2. The volatility/forward-rate portion of the correlation is assumed to have a market-realistic value of −0.2 along the main diagonal, and a constant value of −0.1 for all the other entries. As for the volatility/volatility block of the overall correlation matrix a Doust-like shape has been assumed, but with a much higher value for the overall level of correlation (between 85% and 100%). This is also market-plausible. See Table 7.2. Figure 7.3 shows the overall correlation matrix. It is useful to pause and familiarize oneself with its shape, because it certainly does not resemble any forward-rate/forward-rate correlation matrix the reader may be familiar with.

We stress that this matrix was set up on plausibility grounds, but it was not even checked whether its eigenvalues were all positive definite. (It turned out that 14 of the 20 eigenvalues were positive.) Warts and all, this is our target matrix.

We then chose six factors for our LMM-SABR model (we could have chosen up to 14, given the number of positive eigenvalues of the target correlation matrix). We generated

Table 7.1   The forward-rate/forward-rate portion of the target correlation matrix.

	1	2	3	4	5	6	7	8	9	10
1	1.000	0.819	0.684	0.583	0.507	0.445	0.395	0.357	0.330	0.323
2	0.819	1.000	0.835	0.712	0.619	0.543	0.482	0.436	0.403	0.395
3	0.684	0.835	1.000	0.852	0.741	0.651	0.577	0.522	0.482	0.472
4	0.583	0.712	0.852	1.000	0.869	0.763	0.677	0.613	0.566	0.554
5	0.507	0.619	0.741	0.869	1.000	0.878	0.779	0.705	0.651	0.638
6	0.445	0.543	0.651	0.763	0.878	1.000	0.887	0.803	0.741	0.726
7	0.395	0.482	0.577	0.677	0.779	0.887	1.000	0.905	0.835	0.819
8	0.357	0.436	0.522	0.613	0.705	0.803	0.905	1.000	0.923	0.905
9	0.330	0.403	0.482	0.566	0.651	0.741	0.835	0.923	1.000	0.980
10	0.323	0.395	0.472	0.554	0.638	0.726	0.819	0.905	0.980	1.000

Forward-Rate/Forward-Rate Correlation

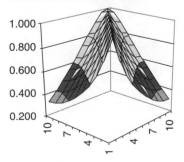

Figure 7.1   The forward-rate/forward-rate portion of the target correlation matrix.

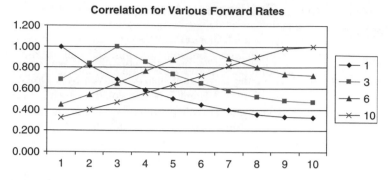

Figure 7.2   Selected cross-sections of the forward-rate/forward-rate portion of the target correlation matrix.

Table 7.2   The volatility/volatility portion of the target correlation matrix.

	1	2	3	4	5	6	7	8	9	10
1	1	0.97531	0.95361	0.93473	0.91851	0.90371	0.89025	0.87919	0.87045	0.86827
2	0.97531	1	0.97775	0.95839	0.94176	0.92658	0.91279	0.90145	0.89248	0.89025
3	0.95361	0.97775	1	0.98020	0.96319	0.94767	0.93356	0.92196	0.91279	0.91051
4	0.93473	0.95839	0.98020	1	0.98265	0.96681	0.95242	0.94059	0.93123	0.92890
5	0.91851	0.94176	0.96319	0.98265	1	0.98388	0.96923	0.95719	0.94767	0.94530
6	0.90371	0.92658	0.94767	0.96681	0.98388	1	0.98511	0.97287	0.96319	0.96079
7	0.89025	0.91279	0.93356	0.95242	0.96923	0.98511	1	0.98758	0.97775	0.97531
8	0.87919	0.90145	0.92196	0.94059	0.95719	0.97287	0.98758	1	0.99005	0.98758
9	0.87045	0.89248	0.91279	0.93123	0.94767	0.96319	0.97775	0.99005	1	0.99750
10	0.86827	0.89025	0.91051	0.92890	0.94530	0.96079	0.97531	0.98758	0.99750	1

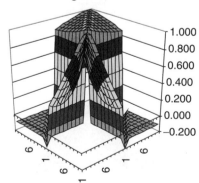

Figure 7.3   The whole target correlation matrix.

a $[20 \times 5]$ matrix of random numbers drawn from the $\mathcal{U}[0\ 1]$ uniform distribution. From this matrix we derived the zeroth iteration weights, e_{ik}, $i = 1, 2, \ldots, 20$, $k = 1, 2, \ldots, 6$ (i.e., a $[20 \times 6]$ matrix) using Equations (7.22) and (7.23). We calculated the zeroth iteration $[20 \times 20]$ model correlation matrix by using

$$\widetilde{P} = ee^{\dagger} \tag{7.26}$$

We calculated the distance between the target and the model correlation matrix using

$$\chi^2 = \sum_{ij} w_{ij} \left(P_{ij} - \widetilde{P}_{ij}\right)^2 \tag{7.27}$$

All the importance weights were set by default to 1, with the following exceptions:

- All the entries of the forward-rate/forward-rate block were given an importance weight of 8 – this reflects the fact that we 'trust' the entries of the forward-rate/forward-rate block more.

- The diagonal entries of the forward-rate/volatility block (which correspond to the SABR entries) were given an importance weight of 40 – this reflects our attempt to recover the elements R_{ii} very closely. We do not know at this stage whether a weight of 40 is too 'light' or an overkill.

The unconstrained search procedure took approximately 1 minute of real time on a standard IBM laptop computer. Figures 7.4 and 7.5 show the excellent results for the overall correlation matrix.

Since 3d graphs are dazzling, but difficult to read, Figure 7.5 shows selected sections of the forward-rate/forward-rate portion of the correlation matrix for the target and the optimized model. Figures 7.6 and 7.7 do the same for the forward-rate/volatility and volatility/volatility sub-matrices. Note from Figure 7.7 that for the forward-rate/volatility sub-matrix the model recovers very accurately the all-important diagonal elements. See Table 7.3. It does not do a great job at recovering the correlation elements adjacent to the main diagonal – but, for the stylized example that we have presented, this may not be a

The Overall Model Correlation Matrix

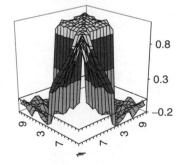

Figure 7.4   The outcome of the best-fit (second method) to the target correlation matrix depicted in Figure 7.3 obtained using six factors.

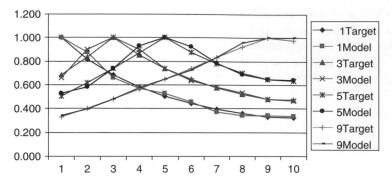

Figure 7.5   Selected cross-sections of the target and fitted portions referring to forward rates of the correlation matrices shown in Figures 7.3 and 7.4, respectively. A line labelled, say, as 3Target or 3Model shows the target and fitted correlation between the third forward rate and the others. The results were obtained using six factors.

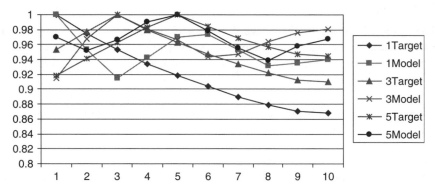

Figure 7.6   Selected cross-sections of the target and fitted portions referring to volatilities of the correlation matrices shown in Figures 7.3 and 7.4, respectively. A line labelled, say, as 3Target or 3Model shows the target and fitted correlation between the third volatility and the others. The results were obtained using six factors.

bad thing, as the discontinuity we assumed for the target matrix (all diagonal elements at −0.2 and all other elements at −0.1) may, after all, not be very 'physical'. Had we used the functional form suggested in Equation (6.14) we would have probably obtained better overall results.

In sum, the important components of the overall target correlation matrix (i.e., the forward-rate/forward-rate and the diagonal of the forward-rate/volatility sub-matrices) have been recovered really well. The remaining portions are not perfectly recovered, but, given the much lower number of factors (6) than variables (20), we are hitting against the intrinsic limitations of low-dimensionality models explored at length in Rebonato and Cooper (1995) and Rebonato (2002). We have no reason to believe that the model's shortcomings are due to numerical deficiencies of the chosen approach.

Indeed, as we increase the number of factors from 6 to 10 we observe a steady improvement of the solution, as shown in Figures 7.8 to 7.11. The improvement is particularly marked for the off-diagonal elements of the **R** matrix.

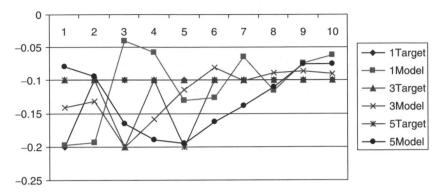

Figure 7.7 Selected cross-sections of the target and fitted portions referring to forward rates and volatilities of the correlation matrices shown in Figures 7.3 and 7.4, respectively. A line labelled, say, as 3Target or 3Model shows the target and fitted correlation between the third volatility and the other forward rates. Note that for all the forward rates shown in these cross-sections the elements R_{ii} are recovered almost exactly – recall that their common target value was −0.2. The results were obtained using six factors.

Table 7.3 Forward-rate/volatility diagonal.

	Model	Target
1	−0.2	−0.19776
3	−0.2	−0.19961
5	−0.2	−0.19544
7	−0.2	−0.19416
9	−0.2	−0.19401

The Overall Model Correlation Matrix (10 factors)

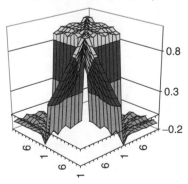

Figure 7.8 As Figure 7.4, with 10 factors.

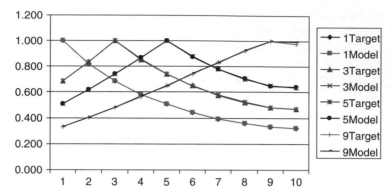

Figure 7.9   As Figure 7.5, with 10 factors.

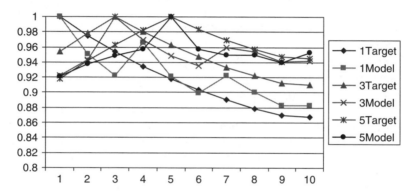

Figure 7.10   As Figure 7.6, with 10 factors.

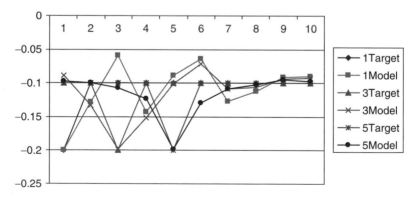

Figure 7.11   As Figure 7.7, with 10 factors.

7.4   Which Method Should One Choose?

We have presented two methods, one analytic and one numeric, to calibrate the LMM-SABR model to a target correlation matrix. In general, analytic methods are thought to be superior (and faster). Why should one consider the numerical method at all? There are two possible reasons.

Let's start from the target correlation matrix. Since this matrix contains a number of exogenously assigned (and negative[3]) entries, it is likely not to be a feasible correlation matrix (i.e., not to have all positive eigenvalues). The analytic procedure suggests performing an orthogonalization first, and retaining at most as many factors as the number of positive eigenvectors. This is perfectly correct, but the number of factors one is left to work with is outside the control of the modeller. If, say, only two eigenvalues are positive, no model implementation with four, six or 10 factors will be possible.

The second, and closely related, potential problem (or advantage, depending on the point of view) is that the analytic solution provides an *exact* recovery of the SABR correlation R_{ii}. Why is getting an *exact* recovery a bad thing? Because there is no way of introducing a trade-off between a very small error in recovering some of the R_{ii} elements and increasing the number of positive eigenvalues. Perhaps if we accepted, say, $R_{22} = -0.1975$ instead of $R_{22} = -0.200$ we could have six instead of four positive eigenvalues, but the analytic procedure has no concept of the fact that an overall more desirable solution may be lurking just 'nearby' (in solution space).

This is where the numerical (and imperfect) method can provide an advantage. If the target correlation matrix has all positive eigenvalues, then the analytic method should certainly be used. The same applies if it has at least as many positive eigenvalues as factors the trader wants to retain. But if the target correlation matrix happens to have fewer positive eigenvalues than the desired number of factors, then the numerical approach *can* provide a better solution. It can do so by finding the positive-definite correlation matrix (of whatever rank up to $2N$) that is closest to a perhaps poorly specified target matrix. The more factors in the model, the closer one can get to the 'wrong' target matrix, while remaining within the set of positive-definite real symmetric matrices.

We should mention a last possible advantage of the numerical procedure. We pointed out in Section 4.4 that, when we use the more symmetric matrix of loadings e, which treats all the variables (forward rates and volatilities) on the same footing, there is no exact way to impose that, say, four of our six factors should be devoted to recovering the forward-rate/forward-rate portion of the correlation matrix and only two to the poorly known volatility part. (We may want to do so perhaps because we trust the forward-rate portion more, or because we consider it more important for the pricing of the product at hand.) This remains true if we use the analytic calibration described above. However, if we use the numerical procedure with non-constant importance weights we are implicitly specifying how we want to use our silver bullets (i.e., the degrees of freedom afforded by the number of factors that we have decided to retain). Assigning importance weights, say, 10 times as large for the forward-rate/forward-rate portion of the correlation matrix as for the volatility/volatility portion does something very similar to assigning far more factors

---

[3]Negative entries in a correlation matrix reduce considerably the set of possible solutions with positive eigenvalues.

to the description of the forward rates than of the volatilities. The relationship between weights and number of factors assigned to a given portion is clearly complex, and certainly non-linear. Nonetheless, the choice of the importance weights performs a very similar role to the choice of the number of factors for the various drivers.

7.5   Appendix[4]

Various problems involve a constrained maximization or minimization over quantities whose squares must sum to 1. Denoting by p_i these n squared quantities, this means that the constraints to be satisfied are

$$\sum_{i=1}^{n} p_i = 1, \qquad p_i \geq 0 \ \text{ for all } i \tag{7.28}$$

Without loss of generality we can think of the squared quantities as probabilities. One way of satisfing these conditions automatically (see Section 7.2.3) is to use internal variables θ_j ($j = 1$ to $n - 1$) where

$$p_i = p_i(\theta_j) = \begin{cases} \cos^2 \theta_1 & i = 1 \\ \sin^2 \theta_1 \cos^2 \theta_2 & i = 2 \\ \sin^2 \theta_1 \sin^2 \theta_2 \cos^2 \theta_3 & i = 3 \\ \cdots & \\ \sin^2 \theta_1 \ \cdots \ \sin^2 \theta_{n-2} \cos^2 \theta_{n-1} & i = n - 1 \\ \sin^2 \theta_1 \ \cdots \ \sin^2 \theta_{n-2} \sin^2 \theta_{n-1} & i = n \end{cases} \tag{7.29}$$

and where $0 \leq \theta_j < \pi/2$.

However, assuming that numerical methods are being used to solve the problem at hand, Doust (2007, 2008) points out that Equation (7.29) is sub-optimal because a uniform probability distribution for each θ_i implies $E(p_i) \sim 2^{-i}$, which is highly non-uniform.

A better framework is to use the following algorithm:

$$\begin{aligned} n = 2 \quad & \begin{cases} p_1 = \cos^2 \theta_1 \\ p_2 = \sin^2 \theta_1 \end{cases} \\[2mm] n = 3 \quad & \begin{cases} p_1 = \cos^2 \theta_1 \cos^2 \theta_2 \\ p_2 = \sin^2 \theta_1 \\ p_3 = \cos^2 \theta_1 \sin^2 \theta_2 \end{cases} \\[2mm] n = 4 \quad & \begin{cases} p_1 = \cos^2 \theta_1 \cos^2 \theta_2 \\ p_2 = \sin^2 \theta_1 \cos^2 \theta_3 \\ p_3 = \cos^2 \theta_1 \sin^2 \theta_2 \\ p_4 = \sin^2 \theta_1 \sin^2 \theta_3 \end{cases} \end{aligned} \tag{7.30}$$

---

[4]The following is taken from Doust (2008) with thanks.

$$n = 5 \begin{cases} p_1 = \cos^2 \theta_1 \cos^2 \theta_2 \cos^2 \theta_4 \\ p_2 = \sin^2 \theta_1 \cos^2 \theta_3 \\ p_3 = \cos^2 \theta_1 \sin^2 \theta_2 \\ p_4 = \sin^2 \theta_1 \sin^2 \theta_3 \\ p_5 = \cos^2 \theta_1 \cos^2 \theta_2 \sin^2 \theta_4 \end{cases}$$

$$n = 6 \begin{cases} p_1 = \cos^2 \theta_1 \cos^2 \theta_2 \cos^2 \theta_4 \\ p_2 = \sin^2 \theta_1 \cos^2 \theta_3 \cos^2 \theta_5 \\ p_3 = \cos^2 \theta_1 \sin^2 \theta_2 \\ p_4 = \sin^2 \theta_1 \sin^2 \theta_3 \\ p_5 = \cos^2 \theta_1 \cos^2 \theta_2 \sin^2 \theta_4 \\ p_6 = \sin^2 \theta_1 \cos^2 \theta_3 \sin^2 \theta_5 \end{cases}$$

and so on.

Although it is hard to write down a closed-form formula for this framework, the rule to generate the formulae is easy to specify. To generate the formulae for $n = m$ given the formulae for $n = m - 1$, work down the formulae for $n = m - 1$ starting at p_1 and locate the first p_i with fewer sin/cos terms than p_1. Then multiply this p_i by $\cos^2 \theta_{m-1}$ and define p_m by using the original p_i but multiplied by $\sin^2 \theta_{m-1}$. If $m - 1$ is a power of 2 then all the p_i have the same number of terms, so modify p_1 to create p_m.

For (7.30), if the θ_i are uniformly distributed then $E(p_i)$ just depends on how many sin/cos terms the formula for p_i contains. If n is such that $2^{m-1} < n < 2^m$, all p_i will have either $m - 1$ or m sin/cos terms and $E(p_i) = 2^{-m-1}$ or 2^{-m} accordingly. Furthermore if $n = 2^m$ then $E(p_i) = 2^{-m}$ for all i and in these special cases the distribution will be uniform across the p_i.

For both (7.29) and (7.30) the derivatives $\frac{\partial p_i}{\partial \theta_j}$ are easy to calculate if needed. Again this is more easily specified by a rule rather than a formula, as follows:

$$\frac{\partial p_i}{\partial \theta_j} = \begin{cases} \frac{2 p_i}{\tan(\theta_j)} & \text{if } p_i \text{ contains a term in } \sin^2 \theta_j \\ -2 p_i \tan(\theta_j) & \text{if } p_i \text{ contains a term in } \cos^2 \theta_j \\ 0 & \text{otherwise} \end{cases} \tag{7.31}$$

Note that (7.28) guarantees

$$\sum_i \frac{\partial p_i}{\partial \theta_j} = 0 \tag{7.32}$$

Part III

Empirical Evidence

Chapter 8

The Empirical Problem

> ... The government are very keen on amassing statistics. They collect them, add them, raise them to the nth power, take the cube root and prepare wonderful diagrams. But you must never forget that every one of these figures comes in the first instance from the village watchman, who just puts down what he damn pleases ...
>
> Anonymous English Judge, quoted by Sir Josiah Stamp in *Some Economic Matters in Modern Life* (1929).[1]

8.1 Statement of the Empirical Problem

For a full specification of the LMM-SABR model one has to specify

1. the functional form and the parameters of the forward-rate instantaneous volatility function;

2. the functional form and the parameters of the function that describes the volatility of volatility of the forward rates;

3. the correlation among the forward rates;

4. the correlation among the volatilities;

5. the correlation among forward rates and volatilities;

6. the exponent β of the CEV process.

In this part of the book we would like to make use of actual historical information extracted from the time series of forward rates to assess how well specified the SABR and LMM-SABR models are. In a perfect world, we would like to estimate directly from real market data all the quantities above. As we shall show below, this task is a tall order, and sometimes we will have to make compromises. The basic reason for this is that the volatility is an unobservable (latent) quantity, whose features can only be indirectly gleaned from the time series of the forward rates it affects. In principle, the volatility leaves its signature mark

---

[1] Many thanks to Dr Charkes Jenkins of the Australian National University for providing this quote.

on several quantities related to the forward rate. For instance, it can appear in the kurtosis and variance of the distribution of the forward rate returns. Indeed, we present in Section 8.3 some analytic results about the moments of the forward-rate distribution produced by the SABR model as a function of the model parameters. This is all well and good in theory, but we show in Section 8.4 that, for time series of reasonable financial length, the noise of naive estimators is often so large that we are left almost none the wiser about the properties of the volatility process than before the analysis. If this is the case, why don't we just make use of more data? Because we strongly believe in using 'relevant' data, i.e., data that have been collected in market conditions relatively similar to the current ones. One of us (RR) has written (almost) a whole book about this (see Rebonato (2007a)).

So, only using forward-rate data we can reasonably estimate the expiry and time dependence of the volatility. With some considerable efforts we can also get an idea of the magnitude of its own volatility. But when we move to subtler effects, such as the correlation between the volatility and the forward rates or the time dependence of the volatility of volatility, direct time series analysis of the forward rates can tell us relatively little.

As for the exponent β, the only way to extract some information from the data is to use *very* long time series. We must hope, in doing so, that the dependence of the change in rates on the rate level is a quasi-universal property, independent of the vagaries of transient market conditions. We do not know whether this is true – and, *prima facie*, the idea seems rather implausible. However, the quality of the fit to the data to a simple and intuitive model that we introduce is such (see Section 8.5) that we at least hold out the hope that we have actually stumbled on a rather fundamental regularity.

When direct time series analysis of forward rates cannot take us very far not all hope is lost. We can take the time series of the SABR-fitted quantities, $\sigma_0(T_i)$, as the market estimate of the instantaneous volatility of the forward rate. If the market were truly so clever (not to say supernaturally omniscient) as to obtain unbiased estimates of this unobservable quantity,[2] then all of a sudden the time series of the volatility becomes available to us with very little effort, and all kind of wonderful quantities can be estimated. It doesn't take much, for instance, to calculate the correlation between the now-revealed volatility and the forward rate, or its own volatility.

Do we have any confidence that the market estimates, $\sigma_0(T_i)$, truly contain some information about the time series of the underlying latent stochastic volatility? Or are they just fitting parameters? We show below that there are some very encouraging signs of an unexpected degree of coherence between the time series of fitted quantities, $\sigma_0(T_i)$, and the latent volatility. In reality, we have been surprised ourselves by the degree of congruence between what we can only painfully and imprecisely estimate, and the 'market guess'. Therefore, much as we would prefer to make use of forward rate information only, we will also make judicious use of indirect market-implied information.

Ultimately, we should not lose sight of the fact that the reason why we are interested in this econometric information is two-fold: in the correlation case, it is because we *have to* provide a reasonable estimate of the super-correlation matrix in order to get started; as for the other quantities (volatility, volatility of volatility, etc.), our interest arises from the belief that successful hedging only works when the underlying model is reasonably well specified, i.e., when it reflects what really happens in reality. We therefore want to convince ourselves

---

[2]More precisely, even if the market were efficient, from fitted data the drift of the volatility process could still not be directly estimated because of the Girsanov transformation from the objective to the pricing measure. However, the higher moments would be measure-invariant.

that the LMM-SABR model captures well, albeit in a possibly simplified manner, important features of market dynamics.

Finally, we conclude this introductory section with a word of reassurance for the reader. Whatever estimation procedure we propose (or discard), we always test its effectiveness by simulating synthetic (i.e., fake) SABR data series of the same approximate length as the ones we do have and by applying our estimators to the perfect but limited data thus generated. Only if we can recover the ingredients of the soup at least in the ideal case of synthetic data, do we go on and apply the same estimators to real data. We love fancy estimators no less than the next econometrician, but we also share Surly's sceptical disposition in the quote that opens the next chapter. (*Faith, I have a humour/I would not willingly be gull'd.*)

8.2   What Do We Know from the Literature?

The description of the volatility as a geometric diffusion is a common modelling choice in the literature. See, e.g., Taylor (2005), who refers to the log-normal volatility model as 'the standard choice when a continuous distribution is used for volatility', in that it prevents negative volatilities, it allows the calculation of moments and is compatible with any degree of excess kurtosis in the return distribution. It must be noted, however, that the typical specification of the log-normal volatility process found in the literature is as an AR(1) (auto-regressive order 1) process. This is because the autocorrelations of volatility are proportional to those of the absolute value of returns (of the percentage changes of forward rates in our case), and these have often been observed to decrease slowly. In this respect the (LMM)-SABR differs sharply from the more common specifications in the econometric literature, in that in this model the innovations in both forward rates and volatilities are assumed to be conditionally serially independent.

We also note that, to incorporate asymmetry in the return distribution, the most common models in the econometric literature postulate that returns and volatilities have innovations dz_t and dw_t distributed according to

$$\begin{bmatrix} dz_t \\ dw_{t+1} \end{bmatrix} \sim \text{i.i.d. } \mathcal{N}\left(\begin{bmatrix} 0 \\ 0 \end{bmatrix}, \begin{bmatrix} \sigma^2 & \rho v \sigma \\ \rho v \sigma & v^2 \end{bmatrix} \right) \tag{8.1}$$

so that ρ is the correlation between dz_t and dw_{t+1}. Despite the superficial similarity, this specification differs from the LMM-SABR model, in that the latter imposes a *contemporaneous* correlation between dz_t and dw_t. This feature is thought to be undesirable because the returns process (in our case of the forward rates) is no longer serially uncorrelated. This is only true, however, if an AR(1) process has been chosen for the volatility. (See, e.g., the discussion in Taylor (2005), Chapter 11.) As in our case this choice is not made, lack of serial correlation in the changes in forward rates is compatible with a structure of the type

$$\begin{bmatrix} dz_t \\ dw_t \end{bmatrix} \sim \text{i.i.d. } \mathcal{N}\left(\begin{bmatrix} 0 \\ 0 \end{bmatrix}, \begin{bmatrix} \sigma^2 & \rho v \sigma \\ \rho v \sigma & v^2 \end{bmatrix} \right) \tag{8.2}$$

A further comment is in order: in the literature (that is mainly concerned with returns in prices rather than rates), returns are almost invariably assumed to be *percentage* returns. The burden to produce a skew in the distribution of log-returns (when this is deemed desirable) is therefore placed entirely on the shoulders of the correlation coefficient, ρ. In the CEV specification that constitutes the backbone of the (LMM)-SABR models, however, both the correlation ρ and the exponent β affect the skewness of the distribution. See Section 3.5. In the more general CEV context, speaking of a correlation coefficient therefore only makes sense conditional on a particular choice for the exponent β. More precisely, if we define returns, R_β, as

$$R_\beta = \frac{f_{\text{new}} - f_{\text{old}}}{(f_{\text{old}})^\beta} \tag{8.3}$$

it is clear that the existence of a residual functional dependence of the power-law type between the returns and the volatility will be revealed as a non-zero correlation in a time series analysis.

Now, it may well be the case that the AR(1) description common in the literature better describes financial 'reality'. Our goal, however, is to estimate from market data quantities *conditional on the assumption that some generalization of the (LMM)-SABR model is correct*. This is no different from what one implicitly does when one assumes, say, that returns are normally distributed (as is done in one version of CAPM), or that they follow a geometric diffusion (as in the Merton–Black–Scholes model). In our case the process for the underlying simply has a less illustrious pedigree (but, perhaps, more realism). So, we part company almost from the start with much of the econometric tradition in stochastic-volatility modelling, and prescribe the following specification for the evolution of a forward rate in the form:

$$df_t^T = m_f dt + s(f_t^T, t, T)dz_t^T \tag{8.4}$$

$$ds(f, t, T) = \mu_\sigma dt + v(s_t^T, f_t^T, t, T)dw_t^T \tag{8.5}$$

$$E\left[df_t^T ds_t^T\right] = c_t^T \tag{8.6}$$

If one believes that it is plausible to assume that the dependence of the function $s(f_t, t, T)$ on the forward rate f should be of the separable type, and, furthermore, that it should be of the power-law type (with $0 \leq \beta \leq 1$), then for one particular $\widetilde{\beta}$ one can write

$$\frac{df_t^T}{\left(f_t^T\right)^{\widetilde{\beta}}} = \mu_f^{\widetilde{\beta}} dt + \sigma_{\widetilde{\beta}}(t, T)dz_t^T \tag{8.7}$$

$$d\sigma_{\widetilde{\beta}}(t, T) = \mu_\sigma dt + v'(\sigma_t^T, f_t^T, t, T)dw_t^T \tag{8.8}$$

$$E\left[df_t^T d\sigma_t^T\right] = C_t^T \tag{8.9}$$

with $C \neq c$ and $\sigma(t, T)$ now purely a function of t and T. Clearly, for any other $\beta \neq \widetilde{\beta}$, even if the true process were indeed of the separable CEV type, there will be some residual dependence on f in the volatility function:

$$\sigma = \sigma_{\widetilde{\beta}}(t, T) \quad \text{for } \beta = \widetilde{\beta} \tag{8.10}$$

$$\sigma = \sigma_\beta(f, t, T) \quad \text{for } \beta \neq \widetilde{\beta} \tag{8.11}$$

The LMM-SABR specification has a volatility which is purely a function of calendar time, t, and of the expiry of the forward rate, T. Since, as stated above, it is our intention to find the best statistical description of the yield curve dynamics compatible with the assumptions of the LMM-SABR model, one could try to choose the exponent β in such a way as to make the volatility function as much as possible a pure function of t and T. Since the volatility is not directly observable, in order to do so we will have to make use of indirect evidence, such as, for instance, the skewness of the β-dependent distribution of returns, R_β. Our returns will therefore be defined by Equation (8.3), and all descriptive statistics (e.g., variance, skewness, kurtosis, etc.) and their behaviour as a function of, say, maturity will implicitly depend on the choice of β.

We mentioned above that one of the routes taken in the literature in order to impute the parameters of a posited process for the forward rates and their volatilities has been to look at selected features of the distribution of the forward rates – these features should, in theory, contain a 'signature' of the process: for instance, the exponent β and the correlation ρ should affect the skewness of the distribution; the volatility of volatility ν should have an impact not only on its kurtosis, but also on the variance, etc. The links between the process parameters and the distribution are typically available in the literature for the type of processes commonly used in econometric studies. As our process is somewhat different, we provide below the equivalent links between model parameters and the moments of the distribution generated by the SABR process.

In order to obtain results simple to interpret, we consider a somewhat simplified model for the forward rate and volatility processes:

$$df_t = \mu(t)dt + \sigma_t dw_t \tag{8.12}$$

$$d\sigma_t = \eta(t)dt + v d\widetilde{w}_t \tag{8.13}$$

So, formally we can write

$$f_T = f_0 + \int_0^T \mu(t)dt + \int_0^T \sigma_t dw_t$$

$$= f_0 + \int_0^T \mu(t)dt + \int_0^T \left(\sigma_0 + \int_0^t \eta(s)ds + \int_0^t v d\widetilde{w}_s \right) dw_t$$

$$= f_0 + \int_0^T \mu(t)dt + \int_0^T (\alpha_t + v\widetilde{w}_t)\, dw_t \tag{8.14}$$

where $\alpha_t = \sigma_0 + \int_0^t \eta(s)ds$. Using the results derived in the appendix (Section 8.6), we can write immediately the moments of f_T:

$$\mathbb{E}\left[f_T\right] = f_0 + \int_0^T \mu(t)dt \tag{8.15}$$

$$\mathrm{var}\left[f_T\right] = \int_0^T \left(\alpha_t^2 + v^2 t \right) dt = \int_0^T \left(\sigma_0 + \int_0^t \eta(s)ds \right)^2 dt + \frac{v^2 T^2}{2} \tag{8.16}$$

$$\mathrm{skew}\left[f_T\right] = \rho \left(6v \int_0^T \alpha_t \left\{ \int_0^t \alpha_s ds \right\} dt + v^3 T^3 \right) \tag{8.17}$$

If both drifts happen to be constant (or are 'frozen'), one has

$$\mathbb{E}\left[f_T\right] = f_0 + \mu T \tag{8.18}$$

$$\text{var}\left[f_T\right] = \sigma_0^2 T + \left(\sigma_0 \eta + v^2/2\right) T^2 + \frac{\eta^2 T^3}{3} \tag{8.19}$$

$$\text{skew}\left[f_T\right] = \rho v T^2 \left(3\sigma_0^2 + \left(3\sigma_0 \eta + v^2\right) T + \frac{3\eta^2 T^2}{4}\right) \tag{8.20}$$

So the variance is a function of σ_0, η and v, and the skew a function of σ_0, η, v and ρ. These results have been verified by Monte Carlo simulation using a very large amount of simulated data. But is the amount of relevant market data available in practice sufficient for the estimation of the parameters? We will address this question in the following.

8.3   Data Description

In this study we have used 30 evenly spaced 12 month forward rates in USD and EUR. The final maturity date of the ith forward rate coincided with the reset of the $(i + 1)$th forward rate. We had at our disposal 1826 data points, corresponding to trading days from 6-November-2000 to 5-November-2007. These forward rates were obtained from the traded 1, 2, 3, 4, 5, 7, 10, 12, 15, 20 and 30-year LIBOR equilibrium swap rates. To obtain the forward rates an interpolation had to be used. It is important to discuss this aspect in some detail.

The 11 equilibrium swap rates mentioned above are the actively traded reference market rates. Their values ('broker quotes') are visible daily on screens updated by data providers. The position of a trader will typically consist of forward rates resetting on a variety of dates, in general not coinciding with the reset dates of the reference market rates. These off-date positions may arise from 'old' plain-vanilla rates that were originally transacted with standard maturities, but have since then 'aged'; but they may also come from non-standard swaps or from structured transactions whose value depends on the future fixings of forward rates resetting on dates other than the reference ones.

A trader with an exposure to these forward rates or to these off-date swap rates will not in general hedge himself in the market by offsetting the exact positions. Rather, he will first map ('grid') his delta risk positions onto the actively traded reference swap rates, and then enter hedging transactions into these instruments. The gridding is the combination of the mapping from a series of forward rates to the reference rates that would give the forward rates and an interpolation procedure. The mapping is, of course, only unique once an interpolation procedure is specified.

The trader's exposure to forward rates that do not reset on reference dates therefore depends on the interpolation chosen. The resulting off-date forward rates may not be reference rates and may not be actively traded among traders, but they nonetheless affect the value of the trader's positions. So, despite the fact that they are not quoted on data information screens and reported by data providers, they nonetheless have an economic effect on the positions of the trading community.

The fine details of the interpolation are, of course, house-specific, but the general market consensus is that the interpolation should be carried out using (natural) cubic splines. Linear interpolation is not favoured by traders. The reason for this is illustrated in Figure 8.1, which shows a hypothetical (and not necessarily realistic) yield curve. Despite the fact that, in this example, the 5- and 7-year rates are both at 5%, given the values of the 10- and 4-year rates it is plausible to surmise that the non-directly observed 6-year rate should trade *below* both the 5- and the 7-year rates. A linear interpolation would not give this result, while a cubic-spline approach would.

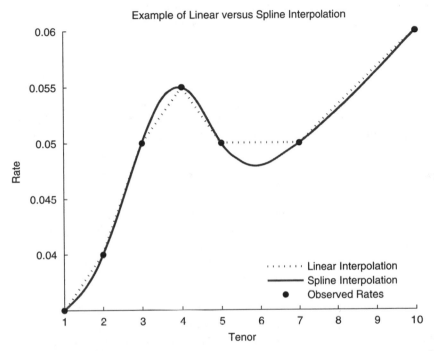

Figure 8.1   The effect of cubic spline interpolation: despite the fact that the 5- and 7-year rates trade at the same level, the 6-year rate is interpolated by the cubic spline procedure to lie below the 5- and 7-year rates because of the influence of the 4- and 10-year rates.

In order to reduce oscillations away from the nodes induced by the cubic spline procedure it is also common to use natural splines, i.e., splines for which the second derivatives at both ends of the interpolation spectrum, x_{min} and x_{max}, are set to zero. (It is well known that this choice gives rise to the spline-interpolated curve, $g(x)$, with the minimum overall curvature, i.e., to a curve $g(x)$ that minimizes $\int_{x_{min}}^{x_{max}} g''(x)dx$ – see, e.g., Press *et al.* (1992).) When traders construct their interpolated yield curve using this procedure, they find themselves 'on market' to within one-eighth of a basis point when they transact off-market rates, i.e., on those occasions when they do have to enter an off-date interbank transaction.

In this study we look both at forward rates that are directly 'visible' from the market, and forward rates that have been obtained by interpolation. When one studies the volatility of, and correlation among, quantities that have been spline-interpolated one is clearly introducing two sources of variation: one coming from the directly observable market moves in the reference rates (the 'nodes' of the splines); and one stemming from the chosen interpolation scheme. To the extent that the interpolation scheme is market-agreed-upon, these derived rates are, however, just as 'real' and (almost) unique as the reference ones. Despite not being directly quoted, they have a direct economic effect, as their value will change the valuation of the non-plain-vanilla, non-reference trades. Therefore, *they will dictate different amounts of hedging in the reference trades*. If a trader were to construct his interpolation using a different procedure, he would soon discover that this is the case because his trades would be off-market.

In the study presented below it will be apparent that the interpolated rates display a behaviour different from the reference rates. This difference in behaviour is indeed likely to be caused by the interpolation procedure. It would be wrong, however, to dismiss and exclude this information from the analysis: the interpolated rates are different, but as real and important as the reference ones. An analysis purely conducted on the reference rates would give no information about the correlations and volatilities of forward rates, for instance, that directly enter the pricing of structured products, such as the CMS trades that we will consider in some detail below. Interpolated rates may not be 'pleasing' but they are not metaphysical constructs and, given the market consensus as to how to build them, their analysis brings information about market quantities, not about numerical artefacts.

8.4   Distributional Analysis and Its Limitations

The results presented in this section show that trying to 'read off' the parameters β, ρ and ν of the SABR process directly from the distribution of the forward rates may be a good idea in theory (and that is why we worked out the moments of their distribution), but it does not work well enough in practice. For this direct idea to work the time series at our disposal would have to be far longer than what we can consider 'relevant' to current market conditions.[3]

The difficulty can easily be seen in Figures 8.2 to 8.4. Here we simulated 1000 SABR processes with $f_0 = 5\%$, $\sigma_0 = 25\%$ (β was chosen equal to 1 for this test) with daily observations over 5 years under two volatility-of-volatility and correlation assumptions: $\nu = 20\%$, $\rho = -20\%$ and $\nu = 40\%$, $\rho = -40\%$. We see from the figures that although the distributions of volatility, skewness and excess kurtosis do exhibit some differences, their variances are so large that it will be difficult to glean much useful information about ν and ρ from our market data from these statistics alone – within one standard deviation of the distribution of skewness, for instance, one cannot even tell with confidence the sign of the skewness.

While an estimation of the parameters of the SABR process from direct analysis of the moments of the changes in forward rates is problematic, we may still be able to draw some general observations or see some broad patterns. We take 1- through 10-day changes in forward rates (again under the assumption of $\beta = 1$) for our USD and EUR data. We plot the skewness and kurtosis in Figures 8.5 and 8.6 for the 10-day difference assumptions across the 20 forward rates.

Despite the noise, note the different qualitative behaviour of skewness and kurtosis in the two currencies. In the skewness figure, USD forward rates exhibit a high skew at the short end which becomes smaller at the long end while the EUR rates seem to exhibit little skew at the short end and a larger skew at the longer end. The pattern is very similar when one looks at excess kurtosis: USD rates exhibit fatter tails at the short end which diminish at the longer end while EUR rates appear to exhibit fatter tails as a function of maturity.

---

[3]Let's not forget, for instance, that forward rate smiles before 1998 were monotonically decaying – and that they did not exist as recently as the mid-1990s for currencies other than JPY.

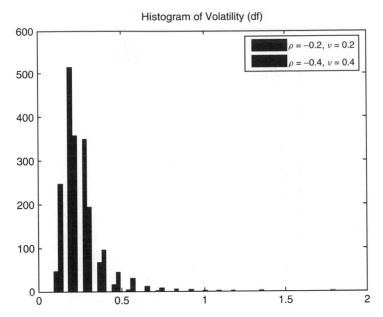

Figure 8.2   Distribution of volatility for simulated SABR processes. $f_0 = 5\%$, $\sigma_0 = 25\%$ under two cases: $\nu = 20\%$, $\rho = -20\%$ and $\nu = 40\%$, $\rho = -40\%$.

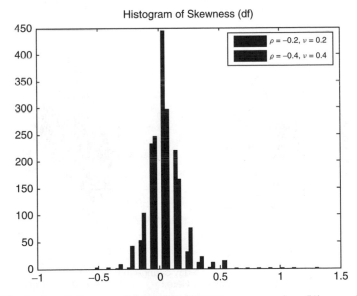

Figure 8.3   Distribution of skewness for simulated SABR processes. $f_0 = 5\%$, $\sigma_0 = 25\%$ under two cases: $\nu = 20\%$, $\rho = -20\%$ and $\nu = 40\%$, $\rho = -40\%$.

One conclusion that can be drawn from this is that we should expect, based on the historical data, to see more volatility of volatility and stronger (negative) correlation between the forward rate and volatility in shorter-expiry USD forward rates and in the longer-expiry EUR forward rates. Comparison with market data shows that this is certainly the case, at least for USD.

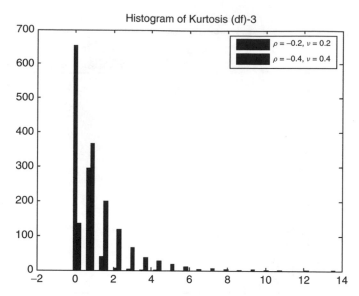

Figure 8.4   Distribution of excess kurtosis for simulated SABR processes. $f_0 = 5\%$, $\sigma_0 = 25\%$ under two cases: $\nu = 20\%$, $\rho = -20\%$ and $\nu = 40\%$, $\rho = -40\%$.

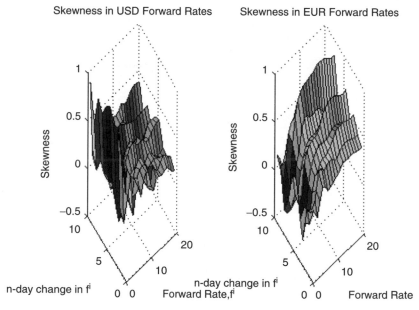

Figure 8.5   Skewness in USD and EUR 1-year forward rates (1–20y tenors) for 1- through 10-day changes in the rate.

We will show in the next chapter other ways in which we can tease out useful information from selected distributional statistics, but that we will have to do some degree of pre-processing in order to make the results more stable and reliable. Before moving to that task we tackle the important question of the 'correct' β exponent in the SABR model. This

Excess Kurtosis in USD Forward Rates   Excess Kurtosis in EUR Forward Rates

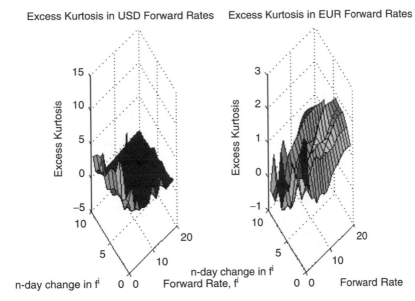

Figure 8.6   Excess kurtosis in USD and EUR 1-year forward rates (1–20y tenors) for 1- through 10-day changes in the rate.

is *the* one area where, in order to derive our results, we make use of as much data as possible, without worrying too much whether these data may still be relevant. The results are extremely interesting, and we leave it to the reader to judge whether they can be trusted in current market conditions.

8.5   What is the True Exponent β?

We have explained in Part I that the market seems to have settled on a choice of 0.5 for the SABR exponent β. This choice is rarely questioned, but, as we saw, it has deep consequences: volatility of volatility can be made to appear or disappear with different choices of β; rates can be allowed to become, or prevented from becoming, negative; most importantly, for some values of β zero can become an absorbing barrier. So, what exponent β should one choose? Can empirical analysis address this question?

The most directly relevant answers to these questions we are aware of are reported in de Guillaume (2008), who refined original ideas by Burridge (2007). They looked at appropriately rescaled changes in rates in USD, GBP, CHF and JPY using daily data going back to the 1960s. The reason for using JPY and CHF as well as USD and GBP data was to explore the behaviour of rates when they are very low. More precisely, Burridge (2007) undertook an empirical analysis along the following lines.

They first combined all the data points from the four currencies into one master data set. Then they defined the rate observed on day i ($i = 1, 2, \ldots, n$) by y_i. (Since they used 40 years' worth of data, for each currency and tenor the integer n is of the order of 10 000.) Let $\Delta y_i = y_{i+1} - y_i$ be the observed *absolute* change in rates when the rate level was y_i. One can then

- make a list of rates, $y_1, y_2, \ldots, y_{n-1}$;

- make a shifted list of rates, $y_2, y_3, \ldots, y_n$;
- create the absolute difference of list 1 and list 2: $y_2 - y_1 = \Delta y_1$, $y_3 - y_2 = \Delta y_2, \ldots,$ $y_n - y_{n-1} = \Delta y_{n-1}$;
- sort lists 1 and 3 by the elements of the first list, i.e., sort $\{y_i, \Delta y_i\}$ by $\{y_i\}$;
- after sorting, create buckets of rates sorted by level containing 100 points – given the size of the data set we will have hundreds of such buckets;
- calculate the standard deviation, σ^k, $k = 1, 2, \ldots, n/100$, of the entries Δy_i in each bucket, k;
- plot these standard deviations against the average level of the bucket.

The results are shown in Figure 8.7. Looking at this plot Burridge (2007) and de Guillaume (2008) found that *for all currencies* the relationship between observed changes in rates and rate level can be well modelled by the function $p(y)$:

$$p(y) = \Delta y_i \frac{y}{y_{\text{low}}} \quad \text{for } y \le y_{\text{low}} \tag{8.21}$$

$$p(y) = \Delta y_i \quad \text{for } y_{\text{low}} \le y \le y_{\text{high}} \tag{8.22}$$

$$p(y) = 1 + K\left(y - y_{\text{high}}\right) \tag{8.23}$$

with $y_{\text{low}} = 1.2\%$, $y_{\text{high}} = 5.6\%$ and $K = 29$.

What is this telling us? That *for rates of all currencies and all tenors* below y_{low} – the extremely low-rate regime – the dependence of changes on the level of rates is approximately proportional to the level itself – *we are in a log-normal regime*. For rates between

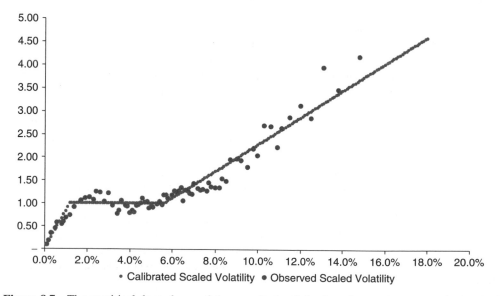

Figure 8.7   The empirical dependence of the magnitude of absolute changes in rates on the level of rates compared with the Burridge–de Guillaume function $p(y)$. See the text for details.

y_{low} and y_{high}, the dependence of the standard deviation on the changes disappears – *we move into a normal regime*. Finally, for rates above y_{high}, the proportionality between changes and level reappears – *we are back in a log-normal regime*.

This tallies well with traders' lore and with our intuition: when rates are 'rather low', the accepted wisdom in the trading room is that moves are independent of the level of rates: 'a 25 bp rate cut is a 25 bp rate cut is a 25 bp rate cut', the folk theorem goes. On the other hand, when rates are *extremely* low (as they were in Japan in the second part of the 1990s), they do not go negative. If this is the case, the moves must stop being normal below some low levels of rates (below 1.25%, Burridge and de Guillaume would say) and become proportional to the level itself. As for the high-rates regime, most traders are too young to remember how rate changes behaved in the early 1990s, but extrapolating from what happens to credit spreads, a log-normal behaviour sounds more right than a normal one.

What does this tell us about the market choice of $\beta = 0.5$? On the one hand, one may look at it as a one-size-fits-all, not-too-good/not-too-bad reasonable compromise between the 'true', level-dependent exponents of 1, 0 and 1 for the very low, medium and high regimes, respectively. However, this compromise solution creates at least one important problem: real data show no evidence of an absorbing barrier at zero. This is, however, a prominent feature of the $\beta = 0.5$ exponent – see the discussion in Section 3.10.2 – and it is a feature that, when rates are low, *does* have a strong impact on pricing.

So, a more desirable, second-generation (LMM)-SABR model could be developed along the following lines:

$$df = f^\beta \sigma dz \tag{8.24}$$

$$\frac{d\sigma}{\sigma} = v dw \tag{8.25}$$

$$\mathbb{E}\,[dzdw] = \rho dt \tag{8.26}$$

$$\beta = \beta\,(f) \tag{8.27}$$

with the function $\beta\,(f)$ chosen so as to reflect the Burridge–de Guillaume findings – see Equation (8.21) and *passim*. It looks simple enough. Unfortunately, there are no nice Hagan approximations for this richer formulation, and even the Monte Carlo simulations we have carried out as an experiment proved to be numerically trickier than one would *a priori* imagine. If someone found some nice analytic approximations (Richard, when are you coming back from your world tour?), this could in our opinion be the most profitable development of the SABR model. As things stand, this is its most glaring current shortcoming.

8.6 Appendix: Some Analytic Results

This appendix provides some results used in Section 8.2 to obtain (approximations to) the moments of SABR-generated forward rates.

Some preliminaries to start with. Consider $Y_t = W_t^2$. From Ito's lemma we have

$$dY_t = 2W_t dW_t + dW_t^2$$

$$= 2W_t dW_t + dt \tag{8.28}$$

It then follows that

$$\int_0^T W_t dW_t = \frac{1}{2}\left(W_T^2 - T\right)$$

The moments are

$$\mathbb{E}\left[\int_0^T W_t dW_t\right] = \frac{1}{2}(T - T) = 0$$

$$\text{var}\left[\int_0^T W_t dW_t\right] = \frac{T^2}{4}\text{var}\left[Z^2\right] = \frac{T^2}{2}$$

$$\text{skew}\left[\int_0^T W_t dW_t\right] = \sqrt{8}$$

$$\text{kurt}\left[\int_0^T W_t dW_t\right] = 12$$

Let $\Theta_T = \int_0^T W_t dW_t$. By the càdlàg property of a Wiener process, we have

$$\mathbb{E}[W_t dW_t] = \mathbb{E}[W_t]\mathbb{E}[dW_t] = 0 \times 0 = 0$$
$$\Rightarrow \mathbb{E}[\Theta_T] = 0 \tag{8.29}$$

The variance is simply calculated by

$$\text{var}[\Theta_T] = \mathbb{E}\left[\Theta_T^2\right]$$
$$= \int_0^T \int_0^T \mathbb{E}[W_t W_s]\mathbb{E}[dW_t dW_s]$$
$$= \int_0^T t\, dt = \frac{T^2}{2} \tag{8.30}$$

Now let $\Theta_T = \int_0^T W_t d\widetilde{W}_t$. Again the expectation is zero. We calculate the variance as above:

$$\text{var}[\Theta_T] = \mathbb{E}\left[\Theta_T^2\right]$$
$$= \int_0^T \int_0^T \mathbb{E}[W_t W_s]\mathbb{E}\left[d\widetilde{W}_t d\widetilde{W}_s\right]$$
$$= \int_0^T t\, dt = \frac{T^2}{2} \tag{8.31}$$

Now define $\int_0^t \gamma_s dw_s = \Gamma_t$ and let $\Theta_T = \int_0^T \Gamma_t d\widetilde{W}_t$. As above the expectation is zero. The variance is

$$
\begin{aligned}
\mathrm{var}\,[\Theta_T] &= \mathbb{E}\left[\Theta_T^2\right] \\
&= \int_0^T \int_0^T \mathbb{E}\,[\Gamma_t \Gamma_s]\,\mathbb{E}\left[d\widetilde{W}_t d\widetilde{W}_s\right] \\
&= \int_0^T \mathbb{E}\left[\Gamma_t^2\right] dt = \int_0^T \left\{\int_0^t \gamma_s^2 ds\right\} dt
\end{aligned}
\tag{8.32}
$$

The distribution of Θ_T is a (shifted) squared-Gaussian distribution – i.e., a chi-square distribution of degree 1.

Consider now the increments, dw_t and $d\widetilde{w}_t$, of two standard Brownian motions (Wiener processes). One should always specify the measure they inhabit, but we will only do so when there is room for ambiguity (e.g., when we switch between measures using Girsanov's theorem). We require that the two processes should be correlated:

$$
\langle dw_t d\widetilde{w}_t \rangle = \rho_t dt
\tag{8.33}
$$

For future reference we recall the following well-known stochastic integrals for the increments dw_t and $d\widetilde{w}_t$:

$$
\int_0^t dw_s = W_t \quad \text{where } W_t \sim \mathcal{N}(0, t)
\tag{8.34}
$$

$$
\int_0^t \gamma_s dw_s = \Gamma_t \quad \text{where } \Gamma_t \sim \mathcal{N}\left(0, \int_0^t \gamma_s^2 ds\right)
\tag{8.35}
$$

where $\mathcal{N}(0, t)$ is the normal distribution of mean 0 and variance t and γ_t is a deterministic function of time. Keeping the same notation, a less well-known integral is

$$
\int_0^t \Gamma_s \beta_s d\widetilde{w}_s = \int_0^t \left\{\int_0^s \gamma_u dw_u\right\} \beta_s d\widetilde{w}_s = \Theta_t
\tag{8.36}
$$

where β_t is also a deterministic function of time. The terminal distribution of Θ_T is not Gaussian. However, we can calculate its moments:

$$
\mathbb{E}\,[\Theta_T] = 0
\tag{8.37}
$$

$$
\mathrm{var}\,[\Theta_T] = \int_0^T \beta_t^2 \left\{\int_0^t \gamma_s^2 ds\right\} dt
\tag{8.38}
$$

$$
\mathrm{skew}\,[\Theta_T] = 6\int_0^T \beta_t^2 \left\{\int_0^t \rho_s \gamma_s \beta_s \left\{\int_0^s \gamma_u^2 du\right\} ds\right\} dt
\tag{8.39}
$$

If the functions β and γ are just constants, the expressions for the variance and the skew become

$$\text{var}\,[\Theta_T] = \beta^2 \gamma^2 \frac{T^2}{2} \tag{8.40}$$

and

$$\text{skew}\,[\Theta_T] = \rho \beta^3 \gamma^3 T^3 \tag{8.41}$$

so the normalized skew[4] is just $\sqrt{8}\rho$.

For future reference we generalize slightly Equation (8.36) to

$$\int_0^t (\alpha_s + \Gamma_s \beta_s)\, d\tilde{w}_s = \int_0^t \left\{ \alpha_s + \beta_s \int_0^s \gamma_u \, dw_u \right\} d\tilde{w}_s \tag{8.43}$$

where, again, α_t is deterministic. The expectation is of course still zero. The higher moments now are

$$\text{var}\,[\Theta_T] = \int_0^T \left(\alpha_t^2 + \beta_t^2 \left\{ \int_0^t \gamma_s^2 ds \right\} \right) dt \tag{8.44}$$

$$\text{skew}\,[\Theta_T] = 6 \int_0^T \alpha_t \beta_t \left\{ \int_0^t \alpha_s \gamma_s \rho_s ds \right\} dt$$

$$+ 6 \int_0^T \beta_t^2 \left\{ \int_0^t \rho_s \gamma_s \beta_s \left\{ \int_0^s \gamma_u^2 du \right\} ds \right\} dt \tag{8.45}$$

and for constant functions β and γ

$$\text{var}\,[\Theta_T] = \alpha^2 T + \beta^2 \gamma^2 \frac{T^2}{2} \tag{8.46}$$

and

$$\text{skew}\,[\Theta_T] = \rho \gamma \beta T^2 \left(3\alpha^2 + \beta^2 \gamma^2 T \right) \tag{8.47}$$

For $T \to \infty$ this gives the usual normalized skew of $\sqrt{8}\rho$.

---

[4]For $n > 2$ the nth central moment is defined as

$$M_n = \frac{E\left[(x - \mu)^n\right]}{\left(E\left[(x - \mu)^2\right]\right)^{n/2}} \tag{8.42}$$

so is dimensionless.

Chapter 9

Estimating the Volatility of the Forward Rates

> *Mammon*   You are incredulous.
> *Surly*   Faith, I have a humour
>   I would not willingly be gull'd.
>
> Ben Johnson, *The Alchemist*, Act 2, Scene 1, in which Surly tells Mammon that he
> wants to make sure that the volatility process in the SABR model is well specified.

In this chapter we go down several avenues in order to estimate various properties of the volatility of the forward rates:

- estimation based on the normality of the residuals;

- direct calculation of rolling standard deviations;

- modification of a maximum-likelihood criterion;

- direct estimation from the time series of the SABR parameters, $\sigma(T_i)$.

By comparing the results from these very different methods, we can try to understand to what extent they paint a congruent picture. As it turns out, the results are surprisingly encouraging, in the sense that the (LMM)-SABR model appears better specified than it would be reasonable to expect – at least under normal market conditions.

These lines of attack do not exhaust all the possible avenues. There are other promising, and possibly more powerful, statistical approaches – for instance, using Kalman filters (see, e.g., Taylor (2005) and Rachev *et al.* (2008) and references therein). We do not pursue them here, however, for two reasons: first, because they would require too much of a detour from the main thrust of the book; and, second, because ultimately as users of the LMM-SABR model we are only interested in whether the estimated volatility roughly behaves as the SABR model predicts – i.e., if the model is reasonably well specified. For instance, we would like to be able to answer questions like: Is the empirical evidence at all compatible with stochastic volatility? Does the estimated volatility track the best-fitted SABR parameter $\sigma(T_i)$? If we can arrive at a reasonable estimate of the volatility of volatility, does it turn out to have at least the same order of magnitude as the best-fitted SABR parameter ν?

As we shall see, the answers to these questions will indeed give us comfort in our use of the LMM-SABR model. However, there is precious little calibration of the volatility structure that we can do once the exogenous market quantities $\sigma(T_i)$ are given, and once we enforce the time-homogeneity condition – and we are not going to give up on this one very easily. As a consequence, our interest in the estimation of the volatility is more of a fundamental and 'academic' nature, but not as crucial as the estimation of the correlation super-matrix P (dealt with in Chapter 10) without which we cannot really even get started with a real implementation of the LMM-SABR model. This is why we stick to relatively simple estimation techniques in this chapter, and refer the interested reader to work by Rebonato and McKay (2009) for fancier extensions.

9.1 Expiry Dependence of Volatility of Forward Rates

In this section we start by looking at a simple and fundamental property of the volatility of forward rates. The justification for taking a time-homogeneous function (the $g(\cdot)$ function) as the backbone both of our deterministic-volatility and of our stochastic-volatility treatment is that, to first order, the only relevant variable that distinguishes one forward rate from the other should be its residual time to maturity. We also posit a financial 'story' (see Section 2.2), according to which this time-homogeneous function should have a humped shape, with a maximum somewhere between 12 and 24 months – at least in normal market conditions. Is our story borne out by the data?

To answer this question we calculated from eight years' worth of market data 20 12-month forward rates as described in the previous chapter. For each maturity and for each business day we looked at the differences:

$$x_t^i = \frac{f_{t+1}^i - f_t^i}{\left(f_t^i\right)^\beta} \tag{9.1}$$

(where the superscript refers to the expiry and the subscript to the business day). Each time series represents the SABR-compatible changes in a forward rate *of constant residual time to expiry*. We therefore calculated the annualized standard deviations of these 20 time series (using $\beta = 0.5$). These are reasonable proxies for the SABR instantaneous volatilities of the forward rates of the same expiry. The results are shown in Figures 9.1 and 9.2 for USD and EUR.

The results are encouraging. The shape is consistent with our financial story, as is the location of the maximum. When the two currencies are normalized, the shape, magnitude and location of the peaks are remarkably similar, and the overall agreement between the two normalized curves is high. This gives us confidence that the backbone of our approach is solid and well founded. We therefore move to subtler features of the volatility functions.

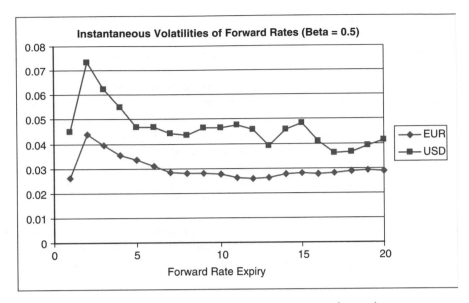

Figure 9.1   The annualized standard deviations of the changes $x_t^i = \dfrac{\left(f_{t+1}^i - f_t^i\right)}{\left(f_t^i\right)^\beta}$ for USD and EUR.

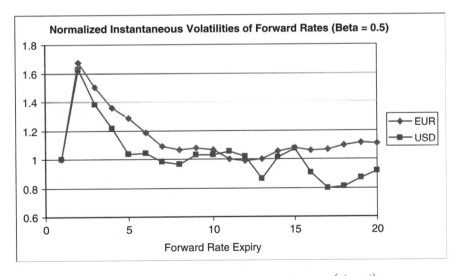

Figure 9.2   The annualized standard deviations of the changes $x_t^i = \dfrac{\left(f_{t+1}^i - f_t^i\right)}{\left(f_t^i\right)^\beta}$ for USD and EUR,

divided by the volatility of $x_t^1 = \dfrac{\left(f_{t+1}^1 - f_t^1\right)}{\left(f_t^1\right)^\beta}$.

9.2   Direct Estimation

We now tackle the estimation of the volatility and of the volatility of volatility. This is our first line of attack.

This approach is the most brute-force one, based as it is on taking a fixed-length rolling-window standard deviation of the changes in forward rates, and taking the resulting time series of estimated standard deviations as a proxy for the latent volatility. Figure 9.3 shows with simulated data that the approach, despite its simplicity, produces reasonable results. For instance, we simulated a SABR process with exponent $\beta = 0$, volatility of volatility $\nu = 40\%$, a SABR correlation $\rho = -25\%$, an initial value for the forward rate and the volatility of 5% and 0.011, respectively, and obtained the estimates in Table 9.1 for the volatility of volatility (the left-most column shows the number of business days in the window).

Table 9.1 shows that the estimates are of the right order of magnitude, but that they rather strongly depend on the length of the window: take the window too short, and the estimates of the volatility will jump around too much, giving rise to too high an estimate of

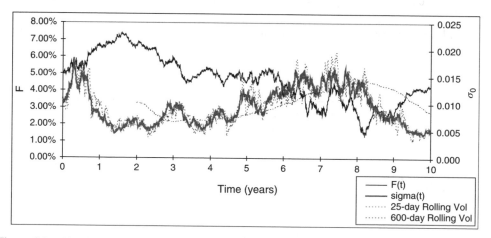

Figure 9.3   Simulation of a SABR forward rate and volatility process with realized volatility calculated with a rolling window of 25 and 600 days.

Table 9.1   Estimation of the volatility of volatility with simulated SABR data using rolling windows of different length (shown in the left-hand column). The volatility of volatility used to produce the synthetic SABR data was 40%.

n-Day window	ν (est)	ν (true)
25	72.4%	40%
150	34.51%	40%
300	34.60%	40%
600	27.96%	40%

the volatility of volatility; take the window too long, and the estimated volatility will be too slowly moving, giving rise to too low an estimate of the volatility of volatility. But what is 'too short' and 'too long'? How do we know where to stop?

This is where the idea introduced in the next section can help: we examine the distribution of residuals, and we accept results for window lengths such that we cannot reject the hypothesis of normality.

What does this approach give us for real data? For such a crude first approximation the results are surprisingly good. Figure 9.4 shows the realized volatility of realized volatility on 10-day changes in the forward rates of USD and EUR (from April 2004 through November 2007) using rolling volatility windows of length 30 and 50. When we use the 50-day window the USD rates show a volatility of volatility decaying from around 55% to 20% for the 50-day window length. Using a 30-day window gives a volatility of volatility decaying from 75% to 45%. EUR rates show a similar decay when we use the 30-day windows and a flat-to-moderately-increasing behaviour with the 50-day windows.

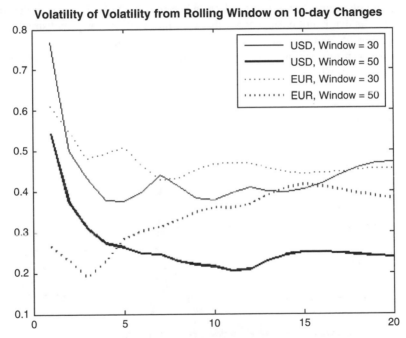

Figure 9.4 The realized volatility of realized volatility on 10-day changes in the forward rates of USD and EUR (from April 2004 through November 2007).

The results are very encouraging on two fronts: first, the magnitude of the estimated volatility of volatility is very similar with the implied SABR values of the parameter ν – which is typically implied from fits to market data; second, the qualitative shape, at least in USD, of the dependence of the volatility of volatility on the time to expiry of the forward rate is roughly consistent with our functional specification of the dependence of the volatility-of-volatility function $h(\cdot)$ on the residual time to expiry.

We expand on this approach in the next section by considering the distribution of the residuals in order to refine this method.

9.3 Looking at the Normality of the Residuals

One of the problems mentioned in the previous section was how to decide the right size of the rolling window. As we shall see, this is a recurring problem for several of the approaches to estimating the volatility of volatility. One way to tackle it is to look at the normality of the residuals (or lack thereof). The idea is that if the volatility is indeed stochastic it should show in the fatness of the tails of the forward rate returns.

To see why this is the case, let's consider a simpler case. Suppose that the volatility can be in two Gaussian states, with high and low variance, but we erroneously believe that there is only one Gaussian volatility state. Starting from this wrong assumption, we first estimate the only one volatility that we believe applies by calculating the annualized standard deviation of the returns. We then associate to each move in the forward rates a standardized move, Z_i, by subtracting the mean and dividing by the standard deviation. Under our (false) assumption of a single Gaussian regime, the Z_is should of course be distributed as $\mathcal{N}(0, 1)$. But since our wrong model interprets the observed standardized returns as either too high (when the true volatility was low) or too low (when the true volatility was high), we find a distribution of Z_is that is not normal at all: there are far too many large and small draws, and not enough draws of 'medium' size – this is just the definition of a leptokurtic distribution.

How do we turn this simple insight into a way to estimate the latent volatility? Let's start with a test case, where we can see everything very clearly. See Figure 9.5.

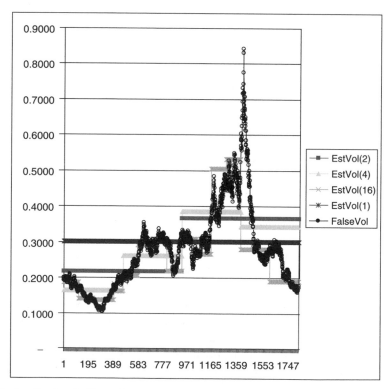

Figure 9.5 Realized volatility of a simulated SABR process calculated over 1, 2, 4 and 16 sub-intervals versus the true, latent, volatility process.

First, we simulated forward rates and volatilities for a SABR process using approximately as many days, N, as in our data record (as usual, there is little point in showing that a method would work well if we had 300 years' worth of data). To generate the time series of volatilities we used a volatility of volatility, v, of 40%. The initial volatility level of the volatility was 20% (in equivalent percentage terms).

Our first assumption (H_0) was that the series of forward rates had been generated by a non-stochastic and constant volatility, equal to the standard deviation of the measured log-differences in forward rates (20.08%).

Under this assumption we then estimated how many standard deviations each standardized move would have been. Call this set of numbers $Z_i(1)$, $i = 1, 2, \ldots, N$. We then looked at the mean, variance and excess kurtosis of $Z_i(1)$, which turned out to be 0, 1 and 2.996, respectively. The mean and the variance were just right, but the excess kurtosis was far too high (for a correctly specified model it should be 0, because we are dealing with the *excess* kurtosis). We can certainly reject H_0.

As a next step we now suppose that *two* distinct volatilities prevailed, one in the first and one in the second half. We estimate these volatilities as the standard deviation of the measured log-differences in forward rates for the two halves. Under this assumption we then estimate how many standard deviations each move would have been. Call this set of numbers $Z_i(2)$. The mean, variance and excess kurtosis of $Z_i(2)$ now turn out to be 0, 1 and 1.263, respectively. Better, but not quite there yet.

We continue in the same way, creating $Z_i(4)$, $Z_i(8)$, $Z_i(16)$, and calculate their mean, variance and excess kurtosis as above. See the results in Table 9.2.

Table 9.2   Estimates of the volatility of volatility (columns labelled 'vol of vol') and of the excess kurtosis (columns labelled 'ex kurt') for different values of the theoretical input v (top row) and various numbers of sub-divisions of the whole data set (left-most column).

	$v = 20\%$		$v = 30\%$		$v = 40\%$	
	vol of vol	ex kurt	vol of vol	ex kurt	vol of vol	ex kurt
2	21.2%	2.87	15.4%	2.28	6.87%	1.81
4	22.9%	1.19	23.4%	1.25	26.8%	1.21
8	31.6%	0.46	33.0%	0.61	35.5%	0.76
16	44.6%	1.43	49.5%	1.44	54.5%	1.28
928	2539%	−2.00	2539%	−2.00	2540%	−2.00

Finally, we created $Z(928)$, i.e., we calculated the standard deviation using each and every pair of log-changes in forward rates. The mean, variance and excess kurtosis of $Z(928)$ are now 0, 1 and −2.001. We have 'chopped up' the data too much. Somewhere between 8 and 16 sub-divisions the excess kurtosis gets as close to 0 as our data sample allows. That is the number of optimal sub-divisions of the time series that will give the best stepwise approximation to the latent volatility. Figure 9.5 shows the results, together with the latent true path of the volatility (about which, of course, we didn't know anything during the estimation procedure). The agreement is acceptably good given the crudeness of the estimation.

Now comes the interesting bit. With the piecewise linear estimate of the latent volatility process we calculate the volatility of the volatilities obtained using 1, 2, 4, 8, 16 and 928 sub-divisions of the time series. Doing this may seem strange, because the time series of volatilities thus created are series of steps. A moment's thought, however, shows that the standard deviation of the stepwise volatility time series does not depend on the order of the realizations.

When we do so we obtain for the volatility of volatility values of 0, 15.8%, 33.0%, 32.9%, 47.0% for 1, 2, 4, 8, 16 partitions and 2515.3% for 928 partitions. Recall that the true value was 40%. Table 9.2 gives some estimates of the volatility of volatility (columns, labelled 'vol of vol') and of the excess kurtosis (columns labelled 'ex kurt') for different values of the theoretical input v (top row) and various numbers of sub-divisions of the whole data set (left-most column).

It is interesting to observe that, with one exception, the best guess of the unknown volatility of volatility is obtained for the level of sub-divisions (8) that also brings about the closest agreement to the theoretical excess kurtosis.

This method therefore suggests that our estimate of the best stepwise approximation to the unknown volatility and to its volatility of volatility will be in the range of the values of sub-divisions, N, when we can no longer reject the hypothesis that the realizations of the deviates have been obtained from $N(0, 1)$, i.e., when the excess kurtosis becomes close to 0. By the way, looking at the excess kurtosis has a good pedigree in Independent Component Analysis, where it is used exactly to identify (and, in that context, to amplify) deviations from normality. See, e.g., Hyvarinen, Karhunen and Oja (2001) and references therein. Of course, one doesn't have to focus just on the kurtosis: one can run richer tests, such as using a Kolmogorov–Smirnov, Anderson–Darling or Kuiper test to reject the hypothesis of normality for the residuals. See Rebonato and McKay (2009) for further details.

How well does this approach work with our real forward-rate data? We split three and a half years of daily USD and EUR forward-rate observations into 15 and 30 sections. We calculated the realized volatility for each of these sections and then the volatility of this realized volatility. We show in Figures 9.6 and 9.7 the realized volatility across the 20 forward rates for each of the 30 sections. These figures broadly confirm the results of the previous section, indicating a hump-shaped $g(\cdot)$ as a function of residual time to expiry.

In order to examine the normality of the residuals, recall that we assume that the volatility, σ_k, is constant over each of the time sections $k = 1, \ldots, K$. For each day and for each forward-rate expiry T we therefore calculate the quantity

$$ x_{t,k}^T = \frac{f_{t+1}^T - f_t^T}{\left(f_t^T\right)^\beta} \frac{1}{\sigma_k} \qquad (9.2) $$

(where the subscript k identifies the time section). From the time series of $x_{t,k}^T$ we then calculate the excess kurtosis across the 20 forward rates in USD and EUR. These are shown in Figure 9.8. The excess kurtosis appears to be lower when we divide the sample into $K = 30$ sections than into $K = 15$ sections. With this number of sub-divisions, except for the first forward rate the excess kurtosis is quite close to zero. In general, the distribution of residuals for EUR forward rates is closer to normal than for the forward USD rates.

Given that the distribution of the normalized forward-rate changes $x_{t,k}^T$ has acceptably normal tails when the data set is divided into 30 sections, we can now look at what this implies for the volatility of volatility.

The results, shown in Figure 9.9, are remarkably consistent with those of the approach presented in the previous section. Recall that with the rolling-window method we found

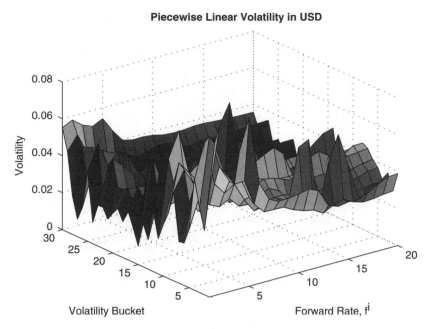

Figure 9.6 The realized volatility across the 20 forward rates for each of the 30 sections for USD.

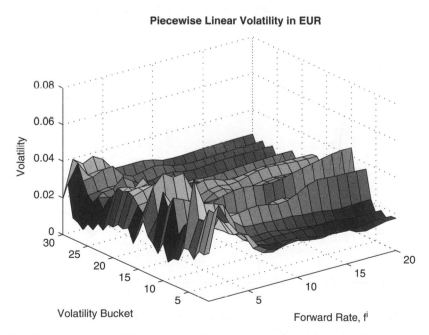

Figure 9.7 The realized volatility across the 20 forward rates for each of the 30 sections for EUR.

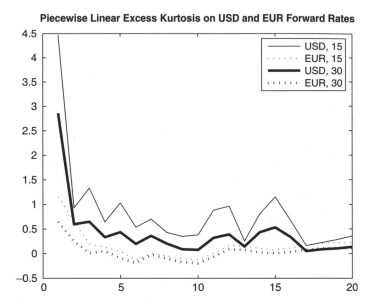

Figure 9.8   Excess kurtosis for $x_{t,k}^T$ for $T = 1, \ldots, 20$ with constant estimated volatility over each of $K = 15$ and $K = 30$ sections for USD and EUR.

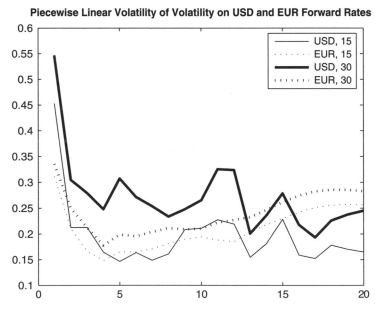

Figure 9.9   Volatility of σ_k^T, $T = 1, \ldots, 20$ with constant estimated volatility over each of $K = 15$ and $K = 30$ sections for USD and EUR.

for USD rates a volatility of volatility decaying from around 55% to 20% or from 75% to 45% for the 50-day or 30-day windows, respectively. The piecewise linear method gives a volatility decaying from 53% to 23% when 50 sections were used, and from 77% to 48% with 30 windows.

We can also compare these results, *derived entirely from analysis of the forward rates*, with observations from the swaption market. The results are very encouraging, on three accounts.

- First, if one looks at the time series of the SABR market quantities, $\sigma_{T_i}(0)$ (the market's estimate of the instantaneous volatility), one sees in Figures 9.10–9.12 that for the 6m × 1y, 2y × 2y and 5y × 5y swaptions it is tracked rather closely by the stepwise constant approximation to the latent volatility created by the technique above.

- More interestingly, and to some extent more surprisingly, the estimated volatility of volatility of the stepwise constant approximation matches the average of the market quantities ν_{T_i} over the period better than it would be reasonable to expect. For instance, the average market volatility of volatility and the corresponding estimates are 61% and 49% for the 6m × 1y swaption, 45% and 46% for the 2y × 2y swaption and 49% and 37% for the 5y × 5y swaption.

- The fitted function $h(\cdot)$, which describes the expiry dependence of the volatility of volatility and which is determined purely on the basis of market data and of the assumption of time homogeneity, is broadly consistent with the empirical dependence of the estimated volatility of volatility on the expiry of the forward rate.

In sum, the two crude methods described so far to estimate the volatility and the volatility of volatility have produced some surprisingly interesting and encouraging results. Not only

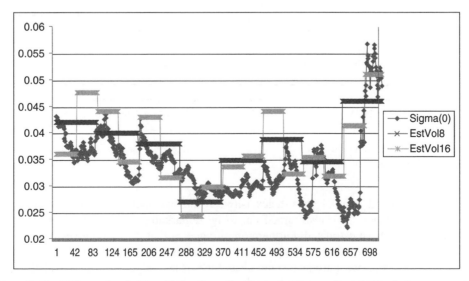

Figure 9.10 Estimated volatility of the 6m × 1y forward rate over 8 and 16 windows versus the swaption SABR parameter σ_0.

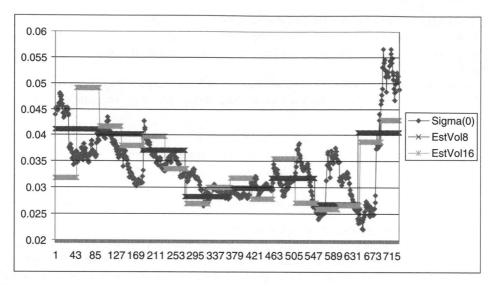

Figure 9.11   Estimated volatility of the 2y × 2y forward rate over 8 and 16 windows versus the swaption SABR parameter σ_0.

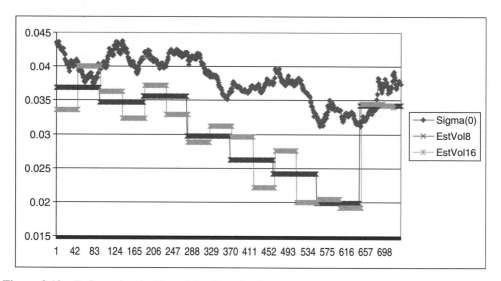

Figure 9.12   Estimated volatility of the 5y × 5y forward rate over 8 and 16 windows versus the swaption SABR parameter σ_0.

have we found good internal consistency between the two methods. The market-implied values for $\sigma(0)$ and ν have also turned out to be remarkably close to the corresponding quantities that we have estimated. Furthermore, it appears that the qualitative shape posited for the $g(\cdot)$ and $h(\cdot)$ functions are appropriate (at least as a first approximation).

In the next section we introduce some ideas for further refinement of the volatility and volatility of volatility estimation problem. These are dealt with in detail in Rebonato and McKay (2009).

9.4 Maximum-Likelihood and Variations on the Theme

In theory, a maximum-likelihood approach to the estimation of the latent volatility may seem promising. The idea is the following.

For simplicity, let's consider the simple case where the forward rate and volatility processes are uncorrelated, and the exponent β is equal to 1. The more general case brings about a more cumbersome notation, but the intuition remains the same.

Let's suppose that we have a time series of forward rate changes, and that, somehow, we have correctly guessed the initial value of the volatility, σ_0. To get started, let's also assume for the moment that we know the volatility of volatility, ν. We observe the magnitude of the change in forward rate from time 1 to time 2, $\Delta f_1 = f_2 - f_1$. The probability of observing a change of this magnitude will be given by

$$p(\Delta f_1) = p(\Delta f_1|\sigma_1)\, p(\sigma_1|\sigma_0) \qquad (9.3)$$

The term $p(\Delta f_1|\sigma_1)$ is a function of the volatility at time 1, σ_1. In turn, for a given ν, the probability of a given σ_1 depends on its 'distance' from σ_0. One can therefore find the value σ_1 that maximizes $p(\Delta f_1)$.

The intuition behind the procedure is clear. Suppose that the observed move Δf_1 is very large. In itself such a 'large' move should be unlikely. However, it can become more likely if σ_1 is also large. Whether a large σ_1 is likely depends, however, on the value of σ_0: if σ_0 is also large, then a large σ_1 is likely; if σ_0 is small, then the probability of a large σ_1 is small. The overall probability of observing a given Δf_1 is therefore a trade-off between making $p(\Delta f_1|\sigma_1)$ large enough, and not making the term $p(\sigma_1|\sigma_0)$ too small. We want the value of σ_1 that maximizes the overall probability $p(\Delta f_1|\sigma_1)\, p(\sigma_1|\sigma_0)$.

If we gloss over the fact that we assumed knowledge of σ_0, this procedure has given us an estimate of σ_1. We could proceed in this same way by looking now at Δf_2 and looking at the value of σ_2, conditioned on the value σ_1 we have just estimated, that maximizes

$$p(\Delta f_2) = p(\Delta f_2|\sigma_2)\, p(\sigma_2|\sigma_1) \qquad (9.4)$$

The procedure seems appealing, and indeed by repeating this procedure for the whole length of the time series, we obtain an acceptable reconstruction of the latent volatility. If the forward rate series is driven by

$$\sigma_t = \sigma_{t-1} + \nu\sigma_{t-1}z_t^\sigma \qquad (9.5)$$

$$f_t = f_{t-1} + \sigma_{t-1}f_{t-1}^\beta z_t^f \qquad (9.6)$$

for some f_0, σ_0, ν, β, with normally distributed z_t^σ and z_t^f with variance Δt, then

$$p(\sigma_t|\sigma_{t-1}) = \frac{1}{\sqrt{2\pi}\,\nu\sigma_{t-1}\sqrt{\Delta t}} \exp\left[-\frac{1}{2}\frac{(\sigma_t - \sigma_{t-1})^2}{\left(\nu\sigma_{t-1}\sqrt{\Delta t}\right)^2}\right] \qquad (9.7)$$

$$p(\Delta f_t|\sigma_{t-1}) = \frac{1}{\sqrt{2\pi}\,\sigma_{t-1}f_{t-1}^\beta\sqrt{\Delta t}} \exp\left[-\frac{1}{2}\frac{(f_t - f_{t-1})^2}{\left(\sigma_{t-1}f_{t-1}^\beta\sqrt{\Delta t}\right)^2}\right] \qquad (9.8)$$

This expression can be rearranged to find the σ_{t-1} which maximizes the likelihood, L, given by

$$L = \frac{1}{2\pi v\sigma_{t-1}\sigma_{t-1}f_{t-1}^{\beta}\Delta t} \exp\left[-\frac{1}{2}\frac{(\sigma_{t-1} - \sigma_{t-2})^2}{\left(v\sigma_{t-2}\sqrt{dt}\right)^2} - \frac{1}{2}\frac{(f_t - f_{t-1})^2}{\left(\sigma_{t-1}f_{t-1}^{\beta}\sqrt{\Delta t}\right)^2} \right] \qquad (9.9)$$

Taking logs and ignoring the terms which are not dependent on σ_t we have

$$\log L' = -\log\sigma_{t-1} - \frac{1}{2}\frac{(\sigma_{t-1} - \sigma_{t-2})^2}{\left(v\sigma_{t-2}\sqrt{\Delta t}\right)^2} - \frac{1}{2}\frac{(f_t - f_{t-1})^2}{\left(\sigma_{t-1}f_{t-1}^{\beta}\sqrt{\Delta t}\right)^2} \qquad (9.10)$$

to maximize.

We provide a test example where we simulate a volatility and forward-rate process and, assuming the correct initial state σ_0 and parameters v and β, we estimate the volatility series from the 'observable' forward rate series. We then plot the estimated volatility series against the 'unobservable' simulated volatility series. See Figure 9.13. Optically, the result is very poor: the estimated volatility fails to track the latent volatility with any accuracy. Furthermore, the volatility of the volatility that can be calculated from the volatility we have estimated turns out to be much smaller (about 1.3%) than the volatility of volatility that was used in the simulation and as a parameter in the estimation procedure (40%).[1] What went wrong?

The problem is that, after the first step, in reality we have *a full distribution* of possible values for σ_1. Our procedure assumes instead that we have a single value. In other terms, we collapse this distribution into a Dirac-δ function centred at the most likely value. This makes the problem very easily tractable, as an impossibly many-dimensional integral is iteratively reduced to a single function. Unfortunately, we pay a heavy price. If one just wants to estimate the centre of the volatility distribution the Dirac-δ approximation can just about work, but it is clearly no good to estimate its true dispersion – which is of course linked to the volatility of the volatility. A more precise discussion of this point can be found in Rachev *et al.* (2008). A proper way around this problem involves the use of Kalman filtering techniques, but, as we said, introducing this technique would entail too much of a detour. The interested reader is referred to Rebonato and McKay (2009).

Instead, we describe below a simpler binomial-tree approach that, despite its crudeness, overcomes some of the shortcomings of the naive maximum-likelihood estimation presented above. Lest one misses the wood for the trees, the important point to note about this binomial method is that it (crudely) samples all the possible volatility paths, and therefore keeps track in a simplified manner of the whole distribution of the latent volatility, not just of its expectations. This was exactly the missing feature in the maximum-likelihood method presented above. The ability to capture this feature, albeit in an approximate fashion, is enough to allow a satisfactory estimation both of the volatility and of the volatility of volatility.

---

[1] Had the procedure worked, the idea would of course have been then to vary the estimation parameter v until it matched the estimated volatility of volatility. In fact, however, more went wrong than just this. This approach drives a very smooth volatility process as it does not allow σ to vary much. In fact, if we don't condition on the correct starting value of σ_0, the estimated volatility series will tend towards the true volatility but very, very slowly. So slow, in fact, that if we guess σ_0 wrong by a factor of 3, the estimated series does not even approach the latent volatility in our five-year simulated example.

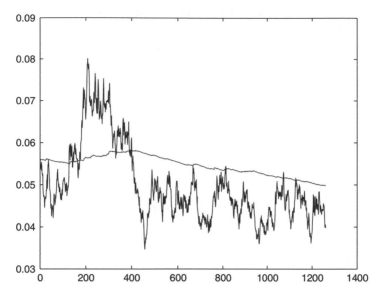

Figure 9.13   The volatility from a simulated SABR process with the maximum likelihood estimated volatility.

Let us map the process for the volatility onto a recombining (CRR-like) binomial tree. Since we need to keep track of the whole volatility path (and not just of the terminal nodes) this process is rapidly going to be limited by the number of time steps in our tree. With 12 time steps we have $2^{12} = 4096$ possible paths through the tree; about the most we will be able to evaluate in a reasonable amount of time. In the volatility tree we construct an 'up' move defined as $u = \exp\left[\nu\sqrt{\Delta t}\right]$ and a 'down' move defined as $d = 1/u = \exp\left[-\nu\sqrt{\Delta t}\right]$. The tree starts at σ_0. So the problem is to find the best starting point σ_0, the best volatility of volatility parameter ν, and the best path along the tree such that the innovations in the forward rate are approximately normally distributed. We therefore choose as our test criterion maximizing the P-value of the Kuiper test of normality. When we run this procedure on simulated data we get very good results. Figure 9.14 shows the outcome of the procedure for a typical simulation.

What happens when we apply this method to real data, e.g., to the 1-year forward-rate time series? We obtain the result shown in Figure 9.15, i.e., a volatility with a mean of about 0.05 and a volatility of volatility of 35%, 65% and 40% in our best three cases. We also plot in this figure the SABR-fitted σ_t series for the 6m × 1y swaption to get a feel for market volatility over this time horizon.

The estimated volatility path is not very satisfactory, but perhaps not as poor as it first appears. Admittedly, it tracks poorly to the swaption-implied SABR state variable σ_0 around nodes 4, 5 and 6. However, Figure 9.15 shows that jumps in the forward rate occurred during the turbulent time period surrounding these nodes. Since our model does not 'know' about jumps, they are interpreted as draws from a distribution with an extremely large volatility (about 90% in our case). This is the first estimation error (which did not occur with our synthetic data, because, of course, these did not contain 'impossible' jumps). Once the volatility has been pushed to such high values by the 'misinterpretation' of the jump, it can only decay as fast as our binomial tree can allow it to.

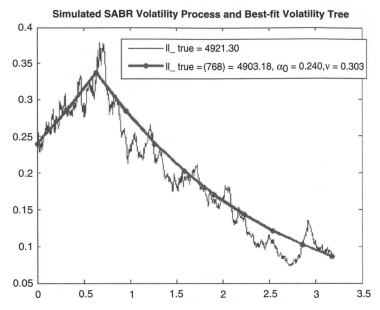

Figure 9.14   The volatility from a simulated SABR process with the 10-step estimated volatility binomial tree.

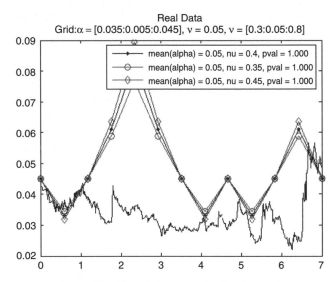

Figure 9.15   The estimated volatility binomial tree on the 6m forward. For comparison the SABR quantity σ_0 for the 6m × 1y swaption is plotted as a proxy for the true, latent, volatility process.

In short, the jumps in the forward rate around time 1 (accompanied by a large increase in σ_0 required to explain them) caused the volatility estimate to spike; then the coarseness of the tree meant that it was slow to fall back to more normal levels.

The main point of this discussion is that we must be very careful when we apply methods that are prone to misinterpreting large ('jumpy') moves in the forward rates as being due to an extremely large volatility. The more sophisticated and black-box-like these methods are (we are thinking of Kalman filtering methods often recommended in the literature as state-of-the-art), the more difficult it may be to understand what can go wrong. These sophisticated methods can work very well if the true process is indeed a perfect stochastic-volatility process – and, in these situations, can beat hands down the cruder methods, like the rolling-window approach, that we presented above. However, the crude methods, which, by and large, are more local and have less 'memory', can be more robust when pitted against real and imperfect data.

This is the most important message from the lengthy analysis presented in this chapter, and this is the reason why we spent so much time analysing not only what works, but also what doesn't. Once again, like Surly we 'have a humour we would not willingly be gull'd'.

9.5 Information About the Volatility from the Options Market

So far we have attempted to estimate the volatility process by making use only of forward-rate information. Can we complement this with 'implied' information from the options market, and from fitted SABR parameters in particular? Can we say something about the congruence of these 'implied' estimates with the purely statistical analysis presented so far? In short, can we try to establish if the SABR description of the volatility process is reasonably well specified?

The SABR model makes the assumption that the volatility at time t of the quantity

$$x_i = \frac{\Delta f(t_i)}{f(t_i)^\beta} \tag{9.11}$$

should be a stochastic quantity with a value at time t_i equal to $\sigma_{t_i}^T$. Incidentally, given the choice of the process for the volatility, this 'initial' (time-t_i) value coincides with the time-t_i expectation of the future volatility, given by $\mathbb{E}_{t_i}\left[\sigma_\tau^T\right] = \sigma_0^T, 0 \leq \tau \leq T$. Given the time series x_i, we can therefore compare its annualized volatility with the SABR volatility $\sigma(t_i)$ averaged over all the data points in our sample.[2] The results are shown in Tables 9.3 and 9.4.

Table 9.3 The SABR quantity $\sigma(t_i)$ averaged over all the data points in our sample ($\beta = 0.5$).

	1y	2y	5y	10y
6m	0.034	0.037	0.038	0.035
1y	0.038	0.039	0.039	0.037
2y	0.041	0.041	0.040	0.037
5y	0.040	0.040	0.038	0.036
10y	0.035	0.034	0.033	0.031

[2]For all the results in this section a value of 0.5 was always used for the exponent β, as this appears to be a standard market practice.

Table 9.4   The annualized volatility of the quantity $x_i = \frac{\Delta f(t_i)}{f(t_i)^\beta}$ (daily changes).

	1y	2y	5y	10y
6m	0.038	0.037	0.034	0.031
1y	0.037	0.036	0.033	0.031
2y	0.035	0.035	0.032	0.031
5y	0.031	0.031	0.031	0.030
10y	0.032	0.031	0.030	0.030

We note that the two sets of quantities are in surprisingly close agreement, with a small negative bias for the realized volatility. We observe that the implied results display a mild hump as a function of expiry, while the realized volatility appears to be monotonically decreasing with swaption expiry. The effect is, however, small. As for the difference in level, one can interpret the small negative bias as a 'risk premium': for all expiries and tails (except one) it would have been profitable on average to sell volatility. The seller would, however, be exposed to rare, large, non-normal moves in volatility, as discussed below.

We must stress how encouraging and, to some extent, surprising these results are. We are in fact comparing the model-dependent (time averages of the) market estimate of an unobservable quantity (the instantaneous volatility) with the sample standard deviation of an observable and model-independent time series, $x_i = \frac{\Delta f(t_i)}{f(t_i)^\beta}$. *A priori*, we would not have expected an agreement better than at the order-of-magnitude level. Instead we were positively surprised to find an average error of the order 15–20%.

We want to look more carefully into this striking correspondence. To do so, we perform a regression of the time series market SABR-fitted quantities $\Delta\sigma(t_i|\theta_i)$ with the SABR-fitted quantities $\Delta\sigma(t_i|\theta_{i-1})$, where now the parameters ρ, ν and β are kept at the values obtained from the previous-day SABR fitting. See Rebonato, Pogudin and White (2008). We do so because, if the SABR model were poorly specified, after each time step a large change

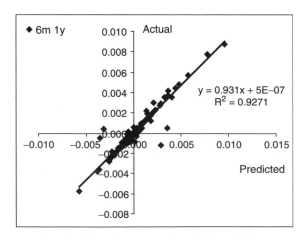

Figure 9.16   Regression of $\Delta\sigma(t_i|\theta_i)$ against $\Delta\sigma(t_i|\theta_{i-1})$ (6m × 1y).

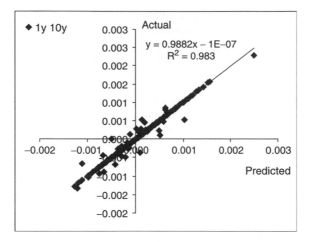

Figure 9.17   Regression of $\Delta\sigma(t_i|\theta_i)$ against $\Delta\sigma(t_i|\theta_{i-1})$ (1y × 10y).

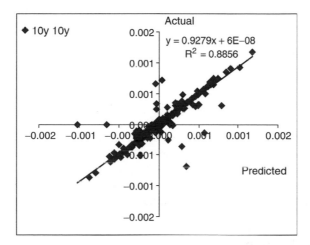

Figure 9.18   Regression of $\Delta\sigma(t_i|\theta_i)$ against $\Delta\sigma(t_i|\theta_{i-1})$ (10y × 10y).

in the parameters $\{\theta_i\}$ would be required to fit the new market prices and the time series $\sigma(t_i|\theta_i)$ and $\sigma(t_i|\theta_{i-1})$ would display a low correlation (low R^2) in the regression, and a slope different from 1. In reality (see Figures 9.16 to 9.18) we find that this is not the case: for all the swaptions the slope of the regression is very close to 1 and the quality of the linear fit is very high (max $R^2 = 0.99$, min $R^2 = 0.77$, average $R^2 = 0.93$).

We then look at the distributional features of the time series $\{\Delta\sigma(t_i|\theta_{i-1})\}$. Since the volatility of volatility is invariant under a change of measure, if the SABR model were correctly specified the distribution would be log-normal, and its annualized standard deviation would be equal to the SABR-fitted volatility of volatility parameter, v. Not surprisingly, we can reject the assumption of log-normality (there is far too much positive skew and the kurtosis is far too high, especially for short expiries and short tails). This observation should be linked to the remarks made about the apparent profitability on average of the strategy of selling volatility during the period under analysis: the seller would be exposed to rare but

Table 9.5 Market-fitted volatility of volatility (SABR ν) averaged over all the days in our sample ($\beta = 0.5$).

	1y	2y	5y	10y
6m	0.61	0.60	0.58	0.57
1y	0.47	0.46	0.44	0.43
2y	0.39	0.39	0.37	0.37
5y	0.32	0.33	0.32	0.32
10y	0.27	0.28	0.27	0.27

Table 9.6 Annualized standard deviation of the distribution of the daily changes in volatility, $\{\Delta\sigma(t_i | \theta_{i-1})\}$.

	1y	2y	5y	10y
6m	0.46	0.35	0.27	0.25
1y	0.28	0.25	0.20	0.18
2y	0.20	0.19	0.16	0.15
5y	0.15	0.14	0.13	0.13
10y	0.14	0.14	0.13	0.13

large losses arising from the large moves that populate the right fat tails of the volatility distribution.

Having said this, the standard deviation of the distribution is reasonably close to the SABR-fitted volatility of volatility, ν. Furthermore, it is encouraging that both the fitted ν and the measured standard deviation display the same qualitative features of declining both with increasing expiries and with increasing swap tails. A small but noticeable systematic bias is, however, present. See Tables 9.5 and 9.6.

9.6   Overall Conclusions

What conclusions can we draw from these analyses? We have found a very encouraging degree of coherence between two sets of quantities: on the one hand, among the various statistical estimates obtained by looking only at forward-rate data; and, on the other hand, between these estimates and the SABR model. Recall that the statistical estimate only made use of time series of (functions of) forward rates to estimate first- and second-order statistics of an unobservable quantity (the instantaneous volatility). This is a tall order. Even more interesting is the observation that these internally congruent statistical estimates compare well with the market-implied values for the same quantities derived from the SABR model. This points, at the same time, to a good model specification and to a high degree of market informational efficiency.

We cautioned the reader in Chapter 3 that one should not be carried away too much by certain apparently very encouraging features of the SABR model – such as the fact that many parameters that the model assume to be constant indeed remain almost constant for long stretches of time – and we hinted at a 'sociological' interpretation of this observation based on traders' behaviour.[3] The results of this chapter may suggest that perhaps we have been too cynical and 'post-modern' in those pronouncements, and that the (LMM)-SABR model, at least in normal market conditions, may actually contain a larger grain of truth than even we originally suspected.

We conclude by pointing out that more sophisticated studies (which we do not report here for brevity, but which the reader can find in Rebonato and McKay (2009)) paint a more complex, but fundamentally unaltered, picture.

---

[3]See Section 3.9.

Chapter 10

Estimating the Correlation Structure

10.1   What We are Trying to Do

With the LMM-SABR model the correlation super-matrix, P, plays a subtler and more complex role than for the LMM and other interest-rate models. As we mentioned above, this is partly because the diagonal elements of the forward-rate/volatility block, R, must be set (almost exactly) equal to the market-chosen SABR parameters, ρ_{SABR}, if one wants to recover the caplet prices correctly.

In Chapter 7 we tackled the problem of how best to calibrate the model to a target correlation matrix given a chosen number of driving factors. This implicitly assumed that we had already established what the correlation matrix should look like. In this chapter we fill in the gaps, i.e., we show how to determine the correlation elements to which the model must be calibrated.

Even this task is not totally straightforward. We could show how much discernible information there actually is in the super-matrix, P, suggest how best to estimate its $2N \times 2N$ elements, and leave it at that. However, when we use the LMM-SABR model in practice we would like to hedge at the very least against the modes of deformation of the covariance surface it knows about. (See the discussion in Chapters 11 and 14 on this point.) Effective hedging can only be accomplished if one has a relatively small number of parameters at one's disposal that synthetically describe how a much larger number of variables co-vary. Any such reduced-form parametrization almost inevitably involves some loss of information. The real art of parameter hedging lies in finding the right trade-off between computational tractability and intuition on the one hand, and information loss on the other. So, for instance, one-factor interest-rate models *are* very synthetic, but the information about the co-movements of forward rates is too condensed to be of pricing quality. Models of the LMM family, on the other hand, tend to be profligate in their use of degrees of freedom unless tightly controlled. We want to strike an inspired balance between these two extremes.

In practice we show that two parameters for the forward-rate/forward-rate correlation block, ρ, two parameters for the volatility/volatility correlation block, r, and two parameters for the forward-rate/volatility correlation block, R, do an excellent job at describing the whole super-matrix, P. As the latter can easily have hundreds of entries, the reduction in complexity is vast, especially considering how little information is thrown away.

So, here is the plan of this chapter. First of all (Section 10.2) we present some results from random matrix theory and from information theory that will be used in the rest of the chapter. This will keep the theoretical material clearly in mind in the background, but out of the way of the empirical discussion. In the next section we explain how we have estimated the various blocks of the super-correlation matrix. Then (Sections 10.3 and 10.4) we move to a more descriptive part. As a next step (Section 10.5) we try to understand how much information there actually is in the empirical correlation blocks we have determined in Section 10.4. We use some simple results from random matrix theory for the task.

We then put to the test (Section 10.6) the correlation models already introduced in Chapter 2. We want to establish how well these perform in practice, in the sense of recovering the signal that the analysis in Section 10.5 has shown the empirical matrices to contain – the empirical matrices, for instance, can well give rise after orthogonalization to dozens of eigenvalues, but if only three or four of these make it above the noise-significance threshold, there may be little reason for the model to chase the random eigenvalues. Also for this test we use some results from random matrix theory. Finally, in the final part of the chapter we introduce some new tools (Rebonato and McKay, 2008) that make use of information-theoretical criteria (cross-entropy or relative entropy) in order to assess the quality of a correlation model.

10.2   Some Results from Random Matrix Theory

Random Matrix Theory has been extensively used in physics for a number of years (e.g., Wigner (1951), Mantegna and Stanley (1999)). More recently, it has been applied to the study of the correlation matrices one finds in finance (mainly, in portfolio theory and in derivatives pricing). Some of the more relevant financial applications can be found in Bouchaud and Potters (2003).

Random Matrix Theory can be applied in its most common form to all real symmetric matrices (i.e., to all matrices that can be orthogonalized). A subset of applications is concerned with real symmetric matrices with positive eigenvalues.

Let's start from an empirical correlation matrix, $\rho(N, T)$, of size $N \times N$, estimated using T synchronous N-dimensional vectors of empirical observations. (So, to be clear, T is the length of the time series and N the number of variables.) The argument T has been included in the notation $\rho(N, T)$ to emphasize that we are dealing with a noisy estimate of the true underlying correlation, $\rho(N)$, and that the degree of noise in our estimate will in general depend on the length of the time series, T.

Let's assume that we have orthogonalized the matrix $\rho(N, T)$ and that we have obtained N eigenvalues, $\{\lambda_i(T)\}$, $i = 1, 2, \ldots, N$. Again, the argument T reminds us that we are dealing with noisy estimates of the true ('Platonic') eigenvalues.

One of the important questions in Random Matrix Theory is then the following. Let's suppose for a second that there is no correlation at all among the N underlying variables, and that the off-diagonal elements of the correlation matrix we have estimated are non-zero just because of statistical noise. If this were the case, what would be the distribution of the eigenvalues from a population of identically obtained noisy $\rho(N, T)$ matrices?

One fundamental result in Random Matrix Theory is of help in answering this question: *in the limit of very large matrices*,[1] *the distribution of the eigenvalues, $\phi(\lambda(T))$, is a function of the ratio $Q = T/N \geq 1$ only:*

$$\phi(\lambda) = \frac{Q}{2\pi\sigma^2} \frac{\sqrt{(\lambda_{max} - \lambda)(\lambda_{min} - \lambda)}}{\lambda} \tag{10.1}$$

with

$$\lambda_{max} = \sigma^2 \left(1 + \frac{1}{Q} + 2\sqrt{\frac{1}{Q}}\right) \tag{10.2}$$

$$\lambda_{min} = \sigma^2 \left(1 + \frac{1}{Q} - 2\sqrt{\frac{1}{Q}}\right) \tag{10.3}$$

This limit distribution is shown in Figure 10.1 for a few values of Q. The most important feature is that, in the infinite limit, there are sharp boundaries for the upper and lower limits of the distribution: if the correlation matrix were truly random no eigenvalues should appear either below or above the cut-off points λ_{max} and λ_{min}. For finite T the edges of the distribution are smoothed out (as shown in Section 10.5).

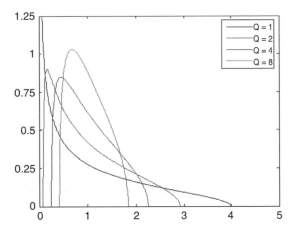

Figure 10.1 The distribution of eigenvalue for selected values of the ratio $Q = T/N$ (see text) in the infinite size limit.

A moment's reflection shows that these results are less surprising than they *prima facie* appear. First of all, there obviously *must* be an upper cut-off: if we are orthogonalizing a correlation (as opposed to a covariance) matrix, the sum of all the eigenvalues must equal the sum of the (unit) variances of the underlying variables, and must therefore be equal to N. As all the eigenvalues must be non-negative (we are dealing with *bona fide* correlation matrices), no eigenvalue can therefore possibly be larger than N. So much for an upper

---

[1]This means, in the limit as $N \to \infty$, while Q remains constant.

cut-off. Suppose now that one did find that the sum of a small number of eigenvalues were smaller than, but very close in magnitude to, N. Then all the other eigenvalues *could* be very close to zero. But having a single large eigenvalue (or a small number of large eigenvalues) runs just opposite to our intuition of how a random matrix should behave: the more we can explain the overall variability with one eigenvalue (or a small number of eigenvalues), the less we expect the underlying joint process to be made up of independent components – think, for instance, of one-factor models. Therefore, both very large *and very small* eigenvalues are intuitively incompatible with a random correlation matrix. This is where the cut-offs come from. And as for the finite-size effects, when T is finite, we leave the door open to the possibility of spurious structure (hence large eigenvalues, hence small ones) being created by noise fluctuations: the eigenvalues spill over on either side of the sharp band that obtains when $T \to \infty$; the more so the smaller N (for a fixed Q).

How does one know whether one is close enough to the very-large-matrix limit for the results above to apply? Not coincidentally, the question – and the answer – are similar in spirit to knowing whether enough variables have been added for the Central Limit Theorem (CLT) to apply. (See Bouchaud and Potters (2003) for a CLT-inspired derivation of the results above.) In practice, one should always carry out some simulation work to make sure that the formula (10.1) can be safely applied.

How do we make use of these results? The reasoning goes as follows. One looks at the eigenvalues of the real (empirical) matrix and checks whether they all fall within the bounds of the random matrix distribution – in which case one is likely to be dealing with uncorrelated variables. In practice, however, the first eigenvalue (the 'level' or 'market' eigenvalue) will typically lie well outside the allowed band prescribed by Random Matrix Theory. One therefore 'subtracts' the contribution from the largest eigenvalue and repeats the analysis. One continues until the residual eigenvalues all fall comfortably within the band allowed for by Random Matrix Theory. See, e.g., Bouchaud and Potters (2003).

This is not the only way to use Random Matrix Theory, or, rather, this is not the only way to analyse the eigenvalues of a real, positive, symmetric matrix. If one is dealing with a chosen model for the correlation (such as one of the models presented below), one can ask the question whether the differences between the observed correlation matrix and the best-fit model can be ascribed to noise. One way to answer this question is to generate (by simulation) a distribution of the eigenvalues from the model using for each simulation exactly as many 'observations' (the length, T, of the time series) as in the real data. Then one can see whether the eigenvalues of the market correlation matrix fall within the respective simulated distribution. This is the approach followed below – and in greater detail in Rebonato and McKay (2008).

Yet another line of approach is the following. One can look at the differences between the best-fit model and the empirical correlation matrix. The difference matrix is no longer positive definite (and hence is no longer a correlation matrix), but it is still real and symmetric and can therefore be orthogonalized. By doing so one can obtain the eigenvalues of the difference matrix. As a next step one can simulate as above 'noisy' correlation matrices (using pseudo-time series of length T created assuming the chosen model to be true) and take the difference between the noisy and the 'Platonic' model correlation matrix. One can orthogonalize each of these difference matrices, calculate their eigenvalues (now positive and negative) and construct a distribution for each eigenvalue. Finally, one can compare the difference eigenvalues for (market–model) with the distribution of the eigenvalues (noisy model–model). Also this line of attack is explained in greater detail in Rebonato and

McKay (2009). Intuitively, if the eigenvalues with 'high-frequency' eigenvectors have a lot of weight in the orthogonalization of the (market–model) matrix, it means that there is a lot of 'structure' to the errors, and that these are unlikely to have been obtained just by noise.

Let us see how these techniques can be applied to the problem at hand.

10.3 Empirical Estimation

In the rest of this chapter we look one by one at the three blocks of the super-matrix P. For the forward-rate/forward-rate correlation block we directly estimate its entries using time series data of forward rates. Given the difficulties with estimating the unobservable volatility, in order to estimate the volatility/volatility sub-matrix and the volatility/forward-rate correlation blocks we make use of the SABR-fitted quantities, $\sigma(T_i)$ – and light a few votive candles to the Gods of Boundless Market Efficiency.[2]

In all cases the models we pit our empirical matrices against are the 'tent' model (simple decaying exponential) and the Doust model (either with full or restricted parametrization) – which nests the tent model as a special case. These are described in detail in Chapter 2. For ease of reference, recall that the Doust correlation matrix is of the form

$$
\begin{bmatrix}
1 & a_1 & a_1 a_2 & \cdots & a_1 a_2 \ldots a_n \\
a_1 & 1 & a_2 & \cdots & a_2 \ldots a_n \\
a_1 a_2 & \cdots & 1 & \cdots & a_{n-1} a_n \\
\cdots & \cdots & \cdots & 1 & \cdots \\
a_1 a_2 \ldots a_n & a_2 \ldots a_n & \cdots & a_n & 1
\end{bmatrix}
\tag{10.4}
$$

The conventional 'tent' model is a simple one-parameter function of $a_k = \exp[-\beta]$ for each k. In order to get the dome shape typically observed empirically, we require some dependence of the speed of decorrelation on the tenor of the forward rate. We achieve this by introducing the 'one-parameter Doust' model, given by $a_k = \exp[-\beta/k]$ and the 'two-parameter Doust' model, given by $a_k = \exp[-\beta/k^\gamma]$, which allows greater control over the rate of decorrelation. As for the 'full-parameter Doust' model, it simply allows each a_k to be fit separately. If the reader prefers a different model, the blue-print presented here can be used with little conceptual modification.

10.4 Descriptive Statistics

10.4.1 The Forward-Rate/Forward-Rate Correlation Matrix

We show in Figure 10.2 the $[20 \times 20]$ empirical correlation matrix $[\rho]$ pertaining to the first 20 equally spaced 1-year forward LIBOR rates. The first five eigenvalues are 17.52, 1.86, 0.28, 0.14, 0.08. So, the first, second, third and fourth eigenvalues account for 87.6%, 96.9%, 98.3% and 99%, respectively, of the total variability. This suggests that a substantial amount of the variance of the underlying variables can be recovered with a small number of judiciously chosen factors.

---

[2]Perhaps we shouldn't be such doubting Thomases: see the discussion in Section 9.5.

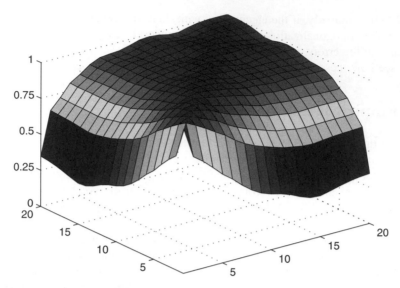

Figure 10.2   The correlation among 20 equally spaced 12-month LIBOR rates. Note how, looking down the main diagonal, the shape of the correlation surface changes from convex to concave.

We highlight an important qualitative feature of the matrix $[\rho]$: if one looks down the main diagonal the surface is convex in the region of the front forward rates, and concave at the back. This indicates that the decorrelation between two forward rates is not just a function of the 'distance' between the two rates, but also of the expiry of the first. Casual inspection of the data therefore supports the intuition that the decorrelation between, say, the first and second forward rate should be greater than between, say, the 19th and the 20th. It is precisely this change from convexity at the front end to concavity at the back end that has led us to adopt the Doust parametrization of the correlation matrix.

We note that this feature has important economic consequences for the pricing of some of the currently most-popular structured products, such as the CMS spread range accruals. In their simplest form, these products pay a *pro rata* fraction of a coupon for any day that a difference between two constant-maturity swap rates (typically, the 2-year rate and the 10-year, 20-year or 30-year rate) remains within a given band. The contractual maturity of these products can be very long, sometimes 10, 20 years or even longer. In its simplest form, this structured product can therefore be seen as a series of short- and long-dated digital options on the spreads. So, the value today of a CMS range accrual will depend, for instance, on the volatility of the spread between the 2-year and 10-year rates in many years' time. (See further discussion in Section 10.7.1.)

The volatility of the spread is a function of the volatilities of the two constant-maturity rates and of the correlation between the two. Whether the very long-expiry forward rates that underlie the relevant swap rates decorrelate as fast as the front forward rates or not therefore makes a very big difference to the volatility of the spread,[3] to the probability of the spread remaining within the accrual band and, ultimately, to the price of the product. The

---

[3]This is particularly important because for very long-dated forward rates the instantaneous volatility function becomes virtually flat (see, e.g., Rebonato (2002)). So, the *terminal* decorrelation that matters for pricing is dominated by the instantaneous correlation rather than by the time dependence of the instantaneous volatility.

ability to capture the change in shape of the forward-rate correlation matrix from concave to convex is therefore of great practical importance for the pricing of these products.

10.4.2 The Forward-Rate/Volatility Correlation Block

We highlight the following qualitative features of the forward-rate/volatility correlation block, R (see Figure 10.3). If one looks down the main diagonal of the sub-matrix R (i.e., if one looks down the market-given element $R_{ii} = \rho^i_{SABR}$) one notices the following features:

- The off-diagonal elements tend to be less negative than the diagonal elements, supporting the intuition that there should be a weaker (less negative) correlation between a forward rate and the volatility of another forward rate than between a forward rate and its own volatility.

- The correlation between a forward rate and its own volatility becomes weaker (less negative) as a function of increasing forward rate maturity for the front than for the back forward rates. For instance, along the main diagonal the correlation between the forward rate and its own volatility decreases (in absolute terms) from around $R_{1,1} = -64\%$ to $R_{10,10} = -51\%$.

- There is a marked asymmetry in this block of the matrix. It is seen by noting that the correlation between, say, the first forward rate and the 10th volatility is $R_{1,10} = -48\%$ but between the 10th forward rate and the first volatility is only $R_{10,1} = -34\%$. This is despite the fact that the two pairs of forward rates and volatilities are separated by the same 'distance'. We currently do not have a simple convincing explanation for this feature.

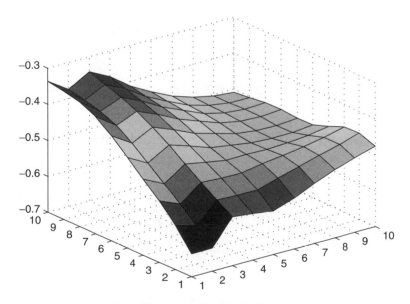

Figure 10.3 The forward-rate/volatility correlation block, R.

10.4.3   The Volatility/Volatility Correlation Matrix

There are few surprises in the volatility/volatility r sub-matrix, shown in Figure 10.4. The 10×10 volatility/volatility correlation matrix of the 73 non-overlapping 10-day changes in the forward rate and σ_0 values of our swaption data gives for the first three eigenvalues 8.65, 1.01, 0.23, which together account for 86.5%, 96.6% and 98.9% of the total variability.

The most noteworthy feature is that the correlation among volatilities is an increasing function of the index of the associated forward rate. So, for instance, $r_{1,2}$ is 81%,[4] but $r_{9,10}$ is 99%, despite the fact that the distance between the underlying forward rates is the same. We also note a change in convexity when one looks down the main diagonal (from mildly convex at the front to concave at the back).

Both these features are shared with the forward-rate/forward-rate correlation block. So, if we find a good model for ρ, it is likely to work well for the r sub-matrix as well.

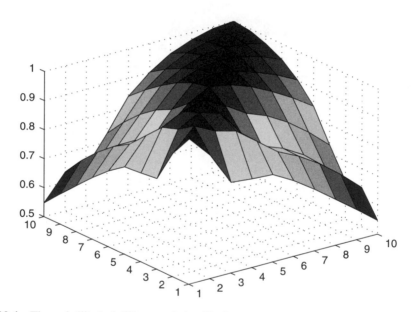

Figure 10.4   The volatility/volatility correlation block, r.

10.5   Signal and Noise in the Empirical Correlation Blocks

In this section we want to ascertain how many of the eigenvectors of the different correlation blocks pass the noise test (i.e., are likely to be produced by true signal rather than by noise).

10.5.1   The Forward-Rate/Forward-Rate Correlation Matrix

Recall that the results of Random Matrix Theory quoted above apply to matrices in the limit as $T \to \infty$. We therefore show in Figure 10.5 that the formulae presented above are still

---

[4]Note that $r_{1,2} = 92\%$ is a slightly unusual observation in this matrix. This is due to the interpolation scheme used in estimating the 1-year volatilities from the 6 m, 1y, 2y, 5y, 7y and 10y option expiry data.

applicable with the dimensions of our finite matrix. In the simple experiment we simulate 1000 random matrices with $N = 20$ and $T = 73$ and plot the theoretical and simulated distribution of the eigenvalues.[5] Note that the empirical distribution has smoother edges for the hard upper- and lower-limits than in the infinite-size distribution, but that the overall theoretical shape is preserved.

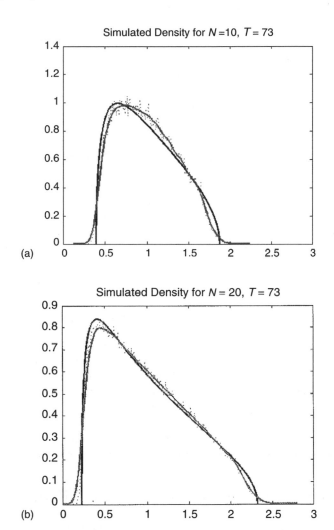

Figure 10.5   The theoretical and simulated distribution of the eigenvalues of r. (a) $N = 10$, $T = 73$; (b) $N = 20$, $T = 73$.

The largest eigenvalue of the forward-rate/forward-rate correlation block (based on 73 non-overlapping 10-day changes in the first 20 forward rates extracted from our swap data set between December 2004 through October 2007) has a value of 17.52. As we would expect, this is clearly outside the theoretical limits of [0.23, 2.32] of eigenvalues

---

[5]The length of the time series was 73 because we looked at 10-day changes in forward rates.

for $Q = 73/20 = 3.65$. This is obviously going to be the case as the principal mode of deformation controls the level of the rates and will have a commanding impact on all of them (i.e., the level effect will certainly make the correlation matrix a non-random matrix).

The next question is whether the second eigenvalue is also significantly outside the distribution of eigenvalues from a random matrix. One way to answer this question (see, e.g., Bouchaud and Potters (2003)) is to remove the contribution of the first eigenvalue and recalculate the distribution of the remaining eigenvalues. To do this we adjust the variance in Equation (10.1) to $\sigma^2 = 1 - \lambda_1/N = 1 - 17.52/20 = 0.1240$ and recalculate the limits to find the theoretical range [0.0282, 0.2878]. The second eigenvalue of 1.86 is again clearly outside this interval but the third eigenvalue lies just inside this region. However, if we correct again the distribution of the eigenvalue limits to take into account the contribution of the first and second eigenvalues, we find the third to lie outside. Therefore it appears to be significant.

10.5.2   The Volatility/Volatility Correlation Matrix

Recall that the 10×10 volatility/volatility correlation matrix of the 73 non-overlapping 10-day changes in the forward rate and σ_0 values of our swaption data has the first three eigenvalues 8.65, 1.01, 0.23. Again, the first is safely outside the theoretical bounds [0.3968, 1.9772] of a purely random matrix. When we correct the limits for the contribution of the first eigenvalue the new limits are [0.05, 0.25]. Now the second eigenvalue is well outside and the third is just inside the upper bound. When we correct for the contribution of the first and second eigenvalues, the third eigenvalue appears to be significant.

10.5.3   The Forward-Rate/Volatility Correlation Block

This block is not a true correlation matrix (it is not symmetric or positive definite). We cannot apply Random Matrix Theory to the forward-rate/volatility matrix of correlations directly, but we can apply it to the 20×20 correlation super-matrix, P, made up of the three 10×10 sub-matrices calculated from our swaption data. This has eigenvalues [13.77, 4.28, 1.23, 0.35, 0.22, . . .]. Together they explain 68.9%, 90.2%, 96.4% and 98.2% of the overall variability.

Repeating the procedure described above, we find that the first, second and third eigenvalues lie above the variance-adjusted limits of the eigenvalue distribution.

10.6   What Does Random Matrix Theory Really Tell Us?

Random Matrix Theory tells us how many of the eigenvalues of a noisy correlation matrix can be considered due to signal. This is clearly informative and important, but should not be regarded as the be-all-and-end-all of correlation analysis. In general, we find that probably too much emphasis is placed in the literature on the analysis of the eigenvalues. The main result typically quoted – and that we find as well – is that a handful of eigenvalues account for a very high fraction, say, 99%, of the total variance. From here, the leap is made to the conclusion that, if we keep this handful of eigenvectors, 'we recover 99% of the original correlation matrix'. When we make this leap, we jump from a well-defined (and true) statement about the variance of the original variables to a rather vague and woolly statement about the correlation matrix in its entirety. In reality, what eigenvalue analysis tells us is that we have been able to find a small number of linear combinations of the original variables (the eigenvectors) that have the property that the variance of the latter is almost completely recovered. But there is more to a set of variables than their variance. As Rebonato and Cooper (1995) have shown, for a tent-like correlation matrix, for instance, even a relatively large number of eigenvectors can fail to recover the shape of the true correlation matrix, even if they do account for a very high fraction of the overall variability. A synthetic, quantitative description of the shape of matrix is more difficult to capture with a small number of quantities – and this probably is why less attention has been paid to it. However, as we have argued above (see also Section 10.7.1), the concavity or convexity of the correlation matrix does have important economic consequences for products such as CMS range accruals, and for spread options in general. Yet, eigenvalue analysis is ill-suited to dealing with these issues.

There is more: Rebonato and McKay (2008) report the following. They start from a target Doust-like correlation matrix. They try to find by least-squared fitting the optimal parameters of a two-factor Doust model correlation matrix. This would have, by construction, the ability to produce a change in convexity along the main diagonal. However, Rebonato and McKay do not optimize the parameters of their model matrix by minimizing the sum of the squared differences between the entries of the target and model matrices. Instead, they minimize the squared differences between the first three target and model eigenvalues – the eigenvalues above the noise threshold. By construction, the leading eigenvalues could not be better recovered, and, indeed, the optimization brings about an extremely close match between model and target eigenvalues. However, this fitting procedure stubbornly fails to recover the shape of the target model, and recovers instead the tent shape for the best-fit model matrix, *even if the model could very easily reproduce – indeed, is built to reproduce – the mixed convex–concave shape*!

Again, matrix orthogonalization (Principal Component Analysis) finds the linear combinations of the original variables that most efficiently recover the total variance. This is important, and in some applications this may well be the most important feature to capture. However, the linear combinations produced by matrix orthogonalization are emphatically not the best linear combinations to recover the shape of a correlation matrix. Whether this matters or not depends on the application at hand. As we have shown, and discuss again in Section 10.7.1, there are situations when accurate recovery of the shape of the matrix does have an important economic relevance. And as Rebonato and McKay show, small differences in the recovery of the first eigenvalues can bring about large differences in the shape of the correlation surface. Eigenvalues *are* important, but do not tell the full story.

10.7 Calibrating the Correlation Matrices

We have highlighted the empirical features of the correlation blocks we want to model. We now move to the next problems: given this information, how can we best fit the model of our choice, and how good will the fit be? More details can be found in Rebonato and McKay (2008), who also deal with alternative parametrizations and fitting schemes. For this section, however, we simply fit the Doust correlation matrix (see Section 2.5.2 and passim) to our forward-rate/forward-rate and volatility/volatility correlation matrices and the White matrix

$$R_{ij} = \text{sign}(R_{ii})\sqrt{|R_{ii}R_{jj}|}\exp\left[-\lambda_A\left(T_i - T_j\right)^+ - \lambda_B\left(T_j - T_i\right)^+\right] \qquad (10.5)$$

to the forward-rate/volatility correlation block (see Section 6.2) by minimizing the sum of squared differences between the empirical and model entries of the matrices.

We have three empirical (target) matrices which we need to parametrize in order to construct the super-correlation matrix P. First, there is the 20×20 forward-rate/forward-rate correlation matrix from our 20 one-year spanning LIBOR forward rates. For the lower-right block we have a 10×10 volatility/volatility correlation matrix (calculated from the swaption data). Finally, we have the 10×10 matrix relating to the forward-rate/volatility block.

We choose to model the correlation matrices ρ and r using the Doust (2008) approach so that we can (1) work with a flexible, valid, positive definite, correlation matrix, (2) easily calibrate the matrix with a small number of parameters, and (3) embed as a base-case the conventional tent-shaped correlation matrix for comparison where necessary. The White parametrization is used for the R block because it is a simple intuitive form which retains the diagonal elements as required for correct recovery of caplet prices and can be made to square, at least at a qualitative level, with the empirical evidence reported above.

10.7.1   The Fitting Procedure

In the results that follow we obtain the best fit by minimizing the sum of the squared differences between the empirical and model matrices. Alternative fitting approaches are discussed in Rebonato and McKay (2008). For the sake of brevity we do not dwell on the different approaches in detail, but mention one variation of the standard methodology that has relevance for the discussion of CMS products mentioned above.

Rebonato and McKay find that minimization of the differences based on Fisher z-transformed correlations has particular merit in cases where the *relative* differences in correlations are as important as absolute differences, as can be the case for spread-options products. It is easy to see why absolute changes can be inappropriate: think of applying a perturbation of 0.1 to a correlation of 0.4 or 0.95. If we want to move the two correlations 'by the same amount' (whatever that means), we clearly have to move them by different *absolute* amounts. In order to treat on a similar footing changes in correlation at very high and very low levels, one can carry out the Fisher transformation, which maps the correlation, ρ – which takes values in the interval $[-1, +1]$ – into a new variable, z – which takes values in the interval $(-\infty, +\infty)$:

$$z = \log \left[\frac{1 + \rho}{1 - \rho} \right] \tag{10.6}$$

This transformation stretches the correlation interval to the whole of the real line so that small changes in ρ near 1 have more comparable distances to much bigger changes nearer to 0. It also has the nice feature that the z variable is almost normally distributed.

In what follows we simply minimize the sum of squared differences between the target and model matrix in ρ space, but keep this observation in the back of our minds.

10.7.2   Results

We show the best fits for the various forward-rate/forward-rate fitted models in Figures 10.6 through 10.8. Figure 10.6 shows the traditional exponentially decaying correlation: $a_k = \exp[-\beta]$; Figure 10.7 displays the results for the one-parameter Doust correlation, given by

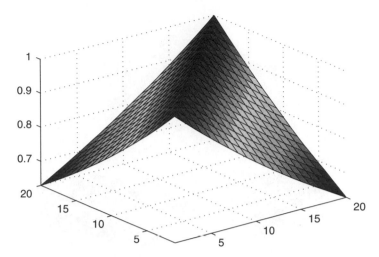

Figure 10.6 Best fit to the forward-rate/forward-rate part of the correlation obtainable using the tent model.

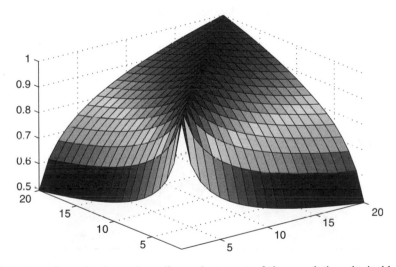

Figure 10.7 Best fit to the forward-rate/forward-rate part of the correlation obtainable using the one-parameter Doust model.

$a_k = \exp\left[-\beta/k\right]$; and Figure 10.8 shows the best fit for the two-parameter Doust model, given by $a_k = \exp\left[-\beta/k^\gamma\right]$.

Figure 10.9 shows the calibrated volatility/volatility matrix with the two-parameter Doust model. Figure 10.10 shows the target and calibrated White model for the forward-rate/volatility matrix.

The forward-rate/forward-rate 'tent' model has parameter $\beta_{\text{tent}} = 0.0121$ for $a_k = \exp\left[-\beta_{\text{tent}}\right]$. The one-parameter Doust specification has parameter $\beta_{\text{Doust}(1)} = 0.0968$ for $a_k = \exp\left[-\beta_{\text{Doust}(1)}/k\right]$ and the two-parameter Doust specification has $\{\beta_{\text{Doust}(2)}, \gamma\} = \{0.2020, 1.5456\}$ for $a_k = \exp\left[-\beta_{\text{Doust}(2)}/k^\gamma\right]$.

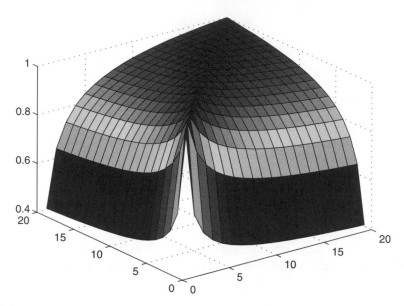

Figure 10.8 Best fit to the forward-rate/forward-rate part of the correlation obtainable using the two-parameter Doust model.

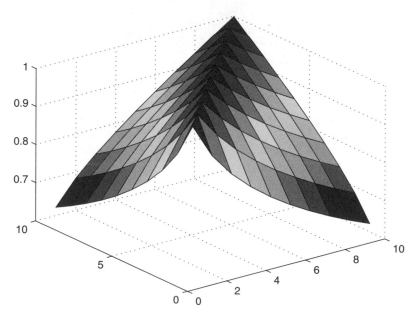

Figure 10.9 Best fit to the volatility/volatility part of the correlation obtainable using the two-parameter Doust model.

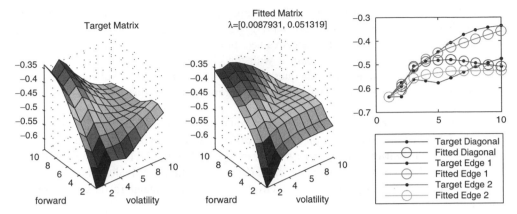

Figure 10.10 Best fit to the volatility/forward-rate part of the correlation obtainable using the two-parameter White model.

The equivalent parameters for the volatility/volatility matrix are $\beta_{\text{tent}} = 0.0248$, $\beta_{\text{Doust}(1)} = 0.0855$ and $\{\beta_{\text{Doust}(2)} = 0.0465, \gamma = 0.4417\}$, respectively.

10.8 How Much Information Do the Proposed Models Retain?

Now we ask a different question: how much worse off are we if instead of using the empirical matrix we used a best-fit model of our choice? Surely the best-fit model will not recover the empirical correlation matrix in all its nooks and crannies. But are we throwing away information or noise? How much 'structure' is there in the errors?

To answer these question we use the calibrated models from the previous section, and begin by comparing the eigenvalues of the true and model correlation matrices.

10.8.1 Eigenvalues of the Correlation Blocks

The largest three eigenvalues of the two-parameter Doust fitted forward-rate/forward-rate correlation matrix (Figure 10.8) have values of 17.3587, 1.2513, 0.5813 against the eigenvalues of the empirical target correlation matrix of 17.5246, 1.8648, 0.2800. We note that both the first eigenvalue and the sum of the first three eigenvalues are very similar (19.18 versus 19.66). There is a limited trade-off in the magnitudes of the second and third eigenvalues (recall that the third empirical eigenvalue was found to be at the boundary of the noise region), but it is difficult to say *a priori* whether it is significant, or, indeed, what should be read into it if it were.

Similarly, the best-fit two-parameter Doust volatility/volatility correlation matrix shown in Figure 10.9 has eigenvalues 8.5412, 0.8232, 0.2591 (compared with 8.6536, 1.0057, 0.2343 from the empirical target correlation matrix). Again, here the third eigenvalue is bigger in the model matrix than in the empirical matrix.

In order to understand the significance of these results, we investigate the distribution of eigenvalues created by simulating the calibrated model. We proceed as follows. We start by assuming that our fitted model perfectly reflects reality. Using all of its eigenvalues we simulate thousands of time series of the same length as the empirical one, and from each of these we derive a correlation matrix. We orthogonalize each of these synthetic correlation matrices and obtain their eigenvalues. Finally, we look at the distribution of the eigenvalues thus obtained and compare it with the eigenvalues of our target (empirically observed) matrix. We can now ask the question: with what confidence level can we say that the eigenvalues of our empirical matrix have been drawn from the distribution of the model eigenvalues?

Under the tent model for forward/forward correlation, the fitted model has a first eigenvalue of 17.1363 against the empirical eigenvalue of 17.5246. From our simulated correlation matrices using the tent model we observe a mean eigenvalue of 17.11 with standard deviation of 0.4785. The tent model therefore safely captures the first eigenvalue. It also captures the second but not the third or fourth eigenvalues within two standard deviations of the simulated distribution.

For the two-parameter Doust model we capture the first eigenvalue better, but not the next three. Under this performance test the two-parameter Doust model appears to perform worse than the 'tent' model if one is more concerned about capturing the first few eigenvalues, but better if it is more important to recover the principal eigenvalue. We should point out that the two-parameter Doust model not only recovers the qualitative shape of the target correlation surface much better, but also gives a much lower sum of the squared differences. This cautions us again against giving too much weight to criteria based on analysis of eigenvalues alone.

10.8.2   Eigenvalues of Differences in the Correlation Blocks

If tests based on the recovery of the first eigenvalues have such low discriminatory power between good and bad models, are there alternative ways to look at the quality of a model? In order to find better indicators of good and bad models, we simulated 1000 random correlation matrices from the model (as above), and created the distribution of eigenvalues of the matrix $\rho^{model} - \rho^{simulation}$. Note that this is not a correlation matrix, but it is still real and symmetric and can therefore be orthogonalized. We compared the eigenvalues of this difference matrix to the eigenvalues of the matrix $\rho^{model} - \rho^{market}$, and asked a similar question to the one posed before: could the eigenvalues of the difference matrix, $\rho^{model} - \rho^{market}$, be drawn from the population of the eigenvalues of the difference matrix $\rho^{model} - \rho^{simulation}$?

Figure 10.11 shows the distribution of the eigenvalues of the simulated $\rho^{model} - \rho^{simulation}$ where the model is the 'tent' model and Figure 10.12 shows the distribution using the two-parameter Doust model. The figures also plot the largest (absolute) eigenvalues of $\rho^{model} - \rho^{market}$. The largest three eigenvalues ($-2.27, 1.35, 0.69$) of the tent model lie well outside two standard deviations of the distribution for the 'tent' model. The two-parameter Doust model gives difference eigenvalues of ($-0.59, 0.40, -0.22$). Now the first eigenvalue is within the two-standard-deviation band; the other two eigenvalues ($-0.59, 0.40, -0.22$) are outside the distribution, but much closer to its body than the tent model. This criterion confirms that the two-parameter Doust model does a better job than the tent model.[6]

For comparison, when all parameters of the Doust matrix are permitted to be freely fit (i.e., the full-parameter Doust model), the largest three eigenvalues of the matrix difference

---

[6]What we are looking for, of course, is not a quantitative criterion to confirm our prejudices, but a tool that can give us guidance when the superiority of one model over another is not such a no-brainer.

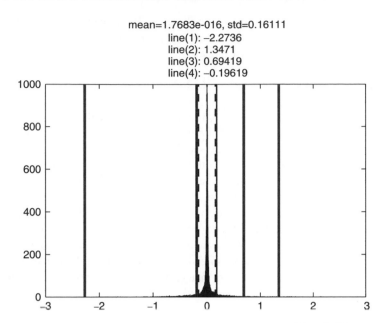

Figure 10.11 The distribution of the eigenvalues of the simulated $\rho^{\text{model}} - \rho^{\text{simulation}}$ where the model is the 'tent' model.

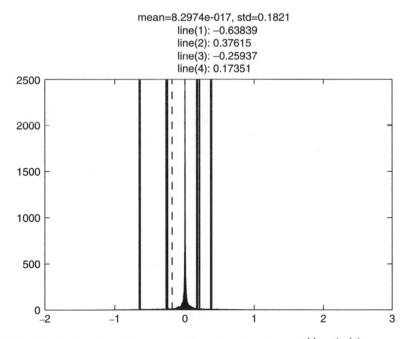

Figure 10.12 The distribution of the eigenvalues of the simulated $\rho^{\text{model}} - \rho^{\text{simulation}}$ where the model is the two-parameter Doust model.

are $(-0.59, 0.40, -0.22)$. That is, there is a large improvement in moving from the tent model to the one- or two-parameter Doust models, but little additional benefit in moving from these to the full-parameter Doust model.

10.8.3   Entropy Measures

Can we get a better idea of how much 'structure' there is in the errors after the best fit allowed by a given model has been carried out? The intuition here is that two models with the same total sum of squared differences should not be regarded as equally good if one showed all the errors concentrated, say, in the top right corner of the matrix. Such a high degree of structure in the errors would suggest that one of the models fails to capture some systematic features of the target correlation matrix.

How can we make this intuition more precise? The method is described in detail in Rebonato and McKay (2008) and outlined here briefly. This approach borrows from the entropy literature. The intuition is the following: if the errors were all concentrated in one area of the correlation, they would be spread in a very non-random manner. Entropy is the standard information-theory criterion that tells us how 'informative' (non-random) a distribution is. See, e.g., Ash (1965), Cover and Thomas (2006) or MacKay (2003). This is how we can adapt it to our purposes.

Given a probability distribution

$$P\,[X = x_k] = p_k \tag{10.7}$$

for $k = 1, 2, \ldots, K$, let *entropy* be defined by

$$H\,(P) = -\sum_k p_k \log\left[\frac{1}{p_k}\right] \tag{10.8}$$

Entropy therefore describes the degree of information in a given distribution. The more a distribution is sharply peaked, the more informative it is, the smaller its entropy. If we know nothing about a random variable, the uniform distribution applies, and the entropy is maximum.

Given some other probability distribution, Q, we can define the *cross-entropy* between P and Q as

$$H\,(P, Q) = -\sum_k p_k \cdot \log\left[\frac{1}{q_k}\right] \tag{10.9}$$

When a problem naturally defines two distributions, a related measure, the Kullback–Leibler divergence (or *relative entropy*), can be defined as

$$D_{KL}\,(P\|Q) = \sum_k p_k \cdot \log\left[\frac{p_k}{q_k}\right] = H\,(P, Q) - H\,(P) \geq 0 \tag{10.10}$$

where $D_{KL}\,(P\|Q) = 0 \Leftrightarrow P = Q$. If two probability distributions are identical they will have zero relative entropy. The relative entropy is positive and unbounded as the two distributions diverge from one another.

We apply this concept to our problem as follows. Recall that we want to identify structure ('information') in our errors: our *desideratum* is that a model with low structure in the errors (large entropy) will be more desirable than a model with high structure (small entropy).

As a first step we have to convert our correlation matrix into something that 'looks like' a probability (i.e., weighs p_k in the interval $[0, 1]$ such that $\sum_k p_k = 1$). We take the $N(N-1)/2 = 190$ elements in the upper triangle of the forward-rate/forward-rate correlation matrix and normalize them by dividing by their sum.[7] Then, we assume the chosen model to be true, and carry out 1000 simulations identical to the ones described in the previous sections. We calculate the correlation matrix from the simulated vectors, and apply the relative entropy calculation to the model and simulated matrices. As a last step, we calculate the relative entropy between the model and the empirical matrix, and we construct a distribution of the relative entropies thus obtained.

The distributions for the tent, one-parameter Doust, two-parameter Doust and full-parameter Doust models are shown in Figures 10.13 to 10.16. We see that under the tent model the relative-entropy distance between the market and the model lies well outside the distribution of the relative-entropy distances between the model and the noisy simulations. Already for the one-parameter Doust model we find a marked improvement, in that the empirical relative entropy lies just inside the simulated distribution. For the two-parameter Doust model the relative entropy is clearly inside the distribution. By this measure of divergence the empirical correlation matrix could easily have been drawn from our calibrated two-parameter Doust matrix. For the full-parameter Doust model the results are nearly identical, suggesting that very little additional benefit is reaped by increasing the number of parameters.

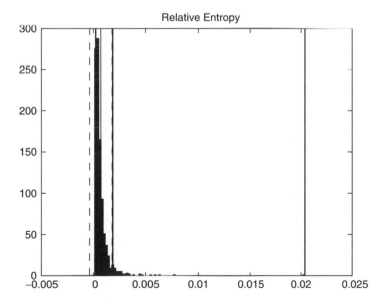

Figure 10.13 Distribution of relative entropies for the tent model.

---

[7]The procedure as described can only be used if all the correlation elements are positive. For correlations among forward rates this poses no problems.

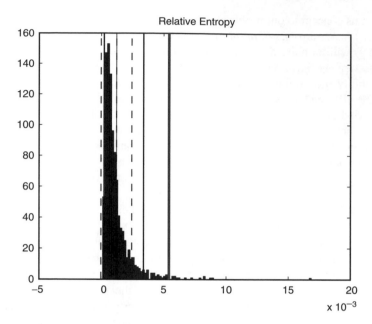

Figure 10.14   Distribution of relative entropies for the one-parameter Doust model.

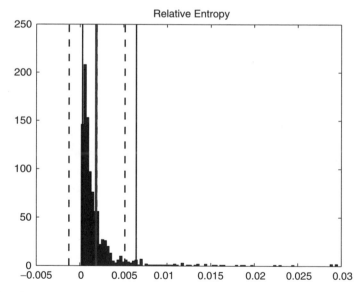

Figure 10.15   Distribution of relative entropies for the two-parameter Doust model.

What is this measure telling us? The 'entropy distance' between two correlation matrices (transformed to look like probabilities) is sensitive to the localization of the errors, and therefore gives us information about the degree of structural mis-specification of a given model. If used in conjunction with the more traditional eigenvalue methods, it can give a better picture of the appropriateness of a given model.

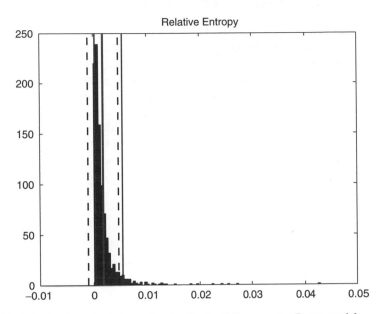

Figure 10.16 Distribution of relative entropies for the full-parameter Doust model.

Table 10.1 Market-fitted correlation (SABR ρ) averaged over all the days in our sample ($\beta = 0.5$).

	1y	2y	5y	10y
6m	−0.25	−0.24	−0.12	−0.08
1y	−0.30	−0.29	−0.21	−0.18
2y	−0.33	−0.33	−0.30	−0.28
5y	−0.30	−0.32	−0.34	−0.33
10y	−0.30	−0.33	−0.36	−0.35

Table 10.2 Statistically measured realized correlation obtained using the procedure described in the text (daily changes).

	1y	2y	5y	10y
6m	−0.27	−0.28	−0.23	−0.18
1y	−0.37	−0.36	−0.33	−0.29
2y	−0.41	−0.42	−0.38	−0.36
5y	−0.38	−0.38	−0.39	−0.39
10y	−0.42	−0.39	−0.41	−0.41

10.8.4   The Forward-Rate/Volatility Correlation Block

For the forward-rate/volatility correlation block we make use of the information provided by SABR fits to the swaption market. We analyse the correlation between the changes in volatilities, $\{\Delta\sigma(t_i|\boldsymbol{\theta}_{i-1})\}$, and the changes in swap rate, $\{\Delta f(t_i)\}$: for each swaption we calculate this quantity and compare it with the corresponding SABR correlation. The notation $\Delta\sigma(t_i|\boldsymbol{\theta}_{i-1})$ emphasizes that on the ith fitting day the best-fit value is obtained for the volatility keeping the parameters of the model fixed at their $i-1$ values.

We find that the agreement is very good, as shown by Tables 10.1 and 10.2. This again supports the view that, with some *caveats* that we discuss in the following chapters, the SABR model is essentially well specified.

Part IV

Hedging

Chapter 11

Various Types of Hedging

There are more things in heaven and earth, Horatio, than are dreamt of in your philosophy

Hamlet (Act I, Scene V, 166–167), warning Horatio not to trust in-model hedging too much.

11.1 Statement of the Problem

Any model is only as good as the hedges it recommends. In this chapter we therefore look at how successful the delta and vega hedging suggested by the SABR and by the LMM-SABR models are in practice. Ultimately, these are the acid tests of the quality of a model, but neither aspect has so far been quantitatively investigated for the (LMM)-SABR model.

Successful hedging is linked to how well the model predicts the changes in the option prices (the implied volatilities) given the changes in the state variables (in the case of the SABR model, the forward rates and their volatilities). It has nothing to do with how the prices of options change as a function of strike. Since we know that the risk-neutral density for a given horizon T is fully determined if we give the T-expiry option prices for all strikes,[1] this means that many different processes can give rise to the same terminal density, but they would provide different hedges.[2] Indeed, the wrong qualitative behaviour of hedges produced by local-volatility models was Hagan *et al.*'s (2002) motivation when they introduced the SABR model. To evaluate the quality of hedging we need *dynamic* information (call prices versus changes in the stochastic state variables) not *static* information (call prices versus strikes).

Hedging is made up of two distinct parts. First, one tries to discover how the price of a traded instrument changes when the quantities on which this price depend change (by a small amount). Then, one tries to assess how and to what extent this dependence can be

---

[1]It is just proportional to the second derivatives of the call price with respect to the strike.

[2]This can be shown by construction. Think of any process (jump-diffusion, stochastic volatility, Levy process, whatever). Generate the prices of European calls for all strikes at a given horizon. From these prices, impute the local volatility $\sigma(S, t)$ that produces exactly the same prices. By construction, the risk-neutral density will be the same, and the change in call prices as a function of strike will also be the same. Given our assumption about the 'true' generating process, however, the 'true' hedges will in general be different from those suggested by the perfectly calibrated local-volatility model.

neutralized by taking offsetting positions in another traded instrument. It sounds very simple and straightforward, but there are at least three important aspects that are glossed over by this simple definition. We must look at them in some detail in order to appreciate how to make hedging work in practice.

11.2   Three Types of Hedging

11.2.1   In- and Out-of-Model Hedging

Every model has a set of state variables (variable quantities that, roughly speaking, determine that state of the system) and parameters (quantities that the model assumes to be fixed). What is a state variable and what is a parameter often depends on the model. So, volatility is a parameter for the Black model, but a state variable for the SABR model.

Hedging is on firm theoretical ground when it comes to determining the sensitivity of a price with respect to a state variable, because the model 'knows' that this quantity is supposed to change, and prescribes how it can do so. This is what we call in-model hedging. For the Black model, delta hedging with respect to the underlying is in-model hedging. For every model, 'delta' hedging with respect to the stochastic driver(s) of that model is always an instance of in-model hedging.

In practice, however, traders typically want to discover how the price of an instrument changes also when quantities that the model assumes constant are allowed to vary. How can constant quantities move? There are two reasons. The first is that, typically, these model parameters are determined either by an 'implied' procedure (i.e., backing them out from a single-time cross-section of traded prices) or by a historical procedure (i.e., estimating them from a time series of financial quantities). In either case, both these procedures give rise to an estimation variation (uncertainty) in supposedly fixed quantities. The second – and practically more important – reason is the following: traders tend to give a very high importance to fitting the plain-vanilla market as closely as possible. If the model were correctly specified, and the market informationally efficient, the trader should in principle try to impute the values of the state variables and of the parameters by fitting them to the observed market prices. When this is done, however, the fits to market prices tend to be poor. Traders, who are not proud, at this point throw one theoretical nicety out of the window after the other. So, they keep on the pretence that markets are informationally efficient, but day after day they refit to market prices not only the values of the state variables (which should have changed), but also of the model parameters (which should have stayed put). This gives rise to a daily variation in the model parameters, which the trader, having got himself into this unavoidable mess, will now have to hedge against. Not pretty, but pragmatically unavoidable. The hallmark of a useful, if not perfect model, can be found in the almost-constancy of the fitted parameters. We look at this important aspect in Chapter 14.

Be that as it may, the trader will want to protect himself against changes in quantities that the model assumes constant. This is what we call out-of-model hedging. An example is hedging against correlation or the volatility of volatility in the SABR model.

It all sounds very plausible, but we must remember that, when we deal with out-of-model hedging, we are on conceptually shaky ground, as we are examining the sensitivity of a price that would be different if the quantity we are perturbing could change at all. We must hope in cancellation of errors. So, for instance, if a model 'knew' that the correlation could be stochastic it would give a different price than the SABR model. When we calculate the *change* in price for a small change in correlation we must hope that this price *difference* would not be too different in the SABR and in the 'true' (stochastic-correlation) model.

11.2.2   Functional-Dependence Hedging

So much for in- and out-of-model hedging. In practice hedging is, however, often carried out in a way that by-passes this neat distinction. This is what we call functional-dependence hedging, and this practice often mixes in- and out-of-model hedging in a rather opaque way. From the discussion in the previous subsection, it is clear that only a courageous – or foolhardy – trader would rely only on in-model hedging. In this subsection we explain why even out-of-model hedging may not be enough.

To understand what functional-dependence hedging means, suppose that I want to hedge a complex instrument. Consider then any hedging instrument, or portfolio of hedging instruments, whose value displays a functional dependence (not just a degree of correlation!) on the state variables and/or parameters of the chosen model. A hedging instrument, for instance, could be a swaption of a given maturity, tail and strike.[3] If we work with the SABR model, we can see that there is functional dependence, via the Black and the Hagan formulae, of the price of this swaption on the two state variables and three model parameters.

A hedge can then be put in place by determining by how much the value of the complex instrument we want to hedge changes when the hedging instruments[4] undergo a given small move. Let's look at this more closely. Suppose that the hedging instruments are plain-vanilla European swaptions. Then we can do the following:

1. determine the parameters of the model via a best fit to the market swaption matrix (or a relevant portion thereof) – i.e., we calibrate our model to the hedging instruments we have chosen;

2. price the complex instrument using the model thus calibrated;

3. 'bump' in turn each element of the swaption matrix;

4. recalibrate the model as best we can after each 'bump', using as target the pseudo-market swaption matrix with one element perturbed at a time;

5. reprice the complex instrument with the 'bumped' parameters;

6. calculate the change in value of the complex instrument before and after each 'bump';

7. finally, determine using this information as many 'hedge ratios' as instruments we have bumped.

One can see from this description that functional-dependence hedging scrambles in- and out-of-model hedging in a rather complex way. To begin with, in general the functional relationship between the change in price of the hedging instrument on the one hand and of the state variables and parameters of the model on the other is unfortunately not one-to-one – the more so, the more one has to deal with numerical noise. In practice, one will in fact recalibrate the model after each shock to the hedging instruments (step 4 above). In general,

---

[3]Similarly, a portfolio of hedging instruments could be, for instance, the group of at-the-money swaptions in the neighbourhood of an important reference swaption, such as, for instance, the 10y × 10y swaption.

[4]Usually, their Black implied volatilities rather than their prices.

however, several combinations of model state variables and parameters can recover to an almost identical degree of numerical precision the 'bumped' prices. These different combinations may well lie on 'iso-price lines' for the hedging instruments, but these different combinations of model state variables and parameters can give rise to different changes in price for the complex instrument. Think, for instance, of the case where the price of the complex product we want to hedge depends more strongly on, say, the correlation than the price of the hedging instrument does (a concrete example could be a CMS range accrual – see the discussion in Section 10.4.1). Suppose also that two sets of model state variables and parameters recover the bumped swaption prices just as well (within numerical noise), but that one solution implies a greater change in the correlation parameter than the other. (With the SABR model this is not a fanciful example at all, as β and ρ play against each other.) The two sensitivities (hedge ratios) will then be very different. But which one do we believe?

Despite this important *caveat*, functional-dependence hedging is very widespread. Why is that? *Because both in- and out-of-model hedging can only explore deformations of the smile surface that the model 'knows' (or can be 'made to know') about.* If reality is more complex than what the model allows (even after shocking its supposedly constant parameters) the trader will fail to hedge against real sources of risk. To understand why this is the case, suppose that we use a deterministic-volatility LMM, for instance, perhaps with a displaced-diffusion implementation (see Rebonato (2002) and Rebonato (2004a)). By shocking the displacement coefficient (a case of out-of-model hedging) we can, to some extent, get an idea of the sensitivity to a change in the *slope* of the smile. But there is no way to explore the sensitivity of a product to an increase in the *curvature* of the smile, irrespective of whether we engage in in- or out-of-model hedging. It is to overcome these shortcomings that functional-dependence hedging is introduced. In its most brute-force incarnation, we shock every single relevant price (implied volatility, really) of the smile surface, and we therefore attempt to 'leave nothing behind'.

Let's look at what functional-dependence hedging does in a more precise way. We have written above that a 'hedge can be put in place by determining by how much the value of the complex instrument we want to hedge changes when the hedging instrument undergoes a given small move'. But this is a strange way to think about the drivers of the price of the complex instrument! If we denote by $\{\theta\}$ the set of state variables and parameters of a model, we are naturally led to think of the price, P, of a complex instrument as $P = P(\{\theta\})$. With functional-dependence hedging we instead think of the dependence of the complex instrument as $P = P(\{S\})$, where $\{S\}$ is the (much larger!) set of prices of the hedging instruments that we decide to bump.

So, with functional-dependence hedging we first completely forget about our chosen model, and say that the value of our complex instrument depends on the hedging instruments – for instance, if the complex instrument is a 10-year, quarterly Bermudan swaption, we could consider the price of the swaption as dependent, in a way that we have not specified yet, on the prices of the 40 underlying co-terminal European swaptions. Then, we step back into the model framework, in order to be able to specify the precise nature of this dependence. More precisely, when we do functional-dependence hedging, we implicitly write

$$\Delta P = \sum_{j=1}^{N} \frac{\partial P(\{S\})}{\partial S_j} \Delta S_j \qquad (11.1)$$

(where N is the possibly very large number of hedging instruments we have chosen to bump), instead of the more natural expression

$$\Delta P = \sum_{j=1}^{n} \frac{\partial P(\{\boldsymbol{\theta}\})}{\partial \theta_j} \Delta \theta_j$$

(where n is the much smaller number of parameters and state variables of the model). The hedge ratio, h_j, with functional-dependence hedging is given by

$$h_j = \frac{\Delta P}{\Delta S_j} \tag{11.2}$$

and

$$\Delta P = \sum_{j=1}^{N} h_j \Delta S_j \tag{11.3}$$

The bridge between the terms $\frac{\partial P(\{S\})}{\partial S_j}$ and the hedge ratios is given by the model-dependent recalibration procedure described above. The root of the potential problem becomes clear if we expand each of the terms $\frac{\partial P(\{S\})}{\partial S_k}$ a bit further by writing

$$\frac{\partial P(\{\mathbf{S}\})}{\partial S_k} = \sum_{j=1}^{n} \frac{\partial P(\{\boldsymbol{\theta}\})}{\partial \theta_j} \frac{\partial \theta_j}{\partial S_k} \tag{11.4}$$

The term to focus on is, of course, $\frac{\partial \theta_j}{\partial S_k}$, i.e., how much the jth parameter changes when the kth hedging instrument changes a bit. If there is a well-defined inverse function

$$\theta_j = f_j^{-1}(\mathbf{S}) \tag{11.5}$$

then Equation (11.4) makes perfect sense and we are on safe ground. But if, as explained above, the relationship between prices and parameters is not one-to-one, then there are potential problems. To see when functional-dependence hedging works well and when it doesn't, suppose that one and only one parameter or state variable of our chosen model can produce a parallel move upward in implied volatilities. In the case of a deterministic-volatility LMM model, the 'correction' factor $k_0^{T_i}$ for a given forward rate (see Equation (2.26) in Chapter 2) could be one such parameter. Let's now bump upward by a small amount the implied volatility of a given forward rate. Then, in our deterministic-volatility LMM model, the 'correction' factor $k_0^{T_i}$ for that forward rate, *and only that forward rate*, will be recalibrated upward by the refitting procedure described above. In a situation like this, functional-dependence hedging *can* make sense and *can* help in controlling against risk factors. But what if we had changed the tilt of a smile (when our underlying model is the LMM-SABR model)? What do we do if moving either the exponent or the correlation (or some combination of both) gives the same quality of refitting? We can only hope that, if the choice of which parameter is moved does not matter too much for the hedging instruments, it will not matter too much for the complex instrument either. It is in situations like this when one has to make ample recourse to the cardinal virtues of faith and hope.[5]

In sum: by looking at the dependence of the price of the complex product on a set of 'price state variables' (which are, of course, very strongly dependent on each other, the more so, the larger N is) we, like Horatio, are reminded by functional-dependence hedging that there are more things between heaven and earth than our hedging philosophy knows about, *and we are given a tool to hedge risks our model does not know about.*

The price to pay for this over-complete description is two-fold: conceptual, for the possible lack of uniqueness explained above and for the over-reliance on 'fudge factors' to achieve the deformations we desire; and practical, because of the computational burden, that for real swaption matrices (with smiles!) can soon become prohibitive.

The best of all worlds would, of course, be a model that knew, via its state variables and parameters, about all the possible relevant modes of deformation. This would indeed be the best of all possible worlds because in this case we could simply perform always-well-defined derivatives of the type $\frac{\partial P(\{\boldsymbol{\theta}\})}{\partial \theta_j}$, while resting assured that no important sources of risk are being ignored. So, in the present and in the next two chapters we want to understand to what extent the (LMM)-SABR models approach this kind of hedging nirvana.

11.3   Definitions

As the discussion above suggests, we have to be careful when we take derivatives. This is because hedging is often expressed in terms of price sensitivities to quantities that are unambiguously defined only in the Black model. For instance, calculating the vega exposure makes perfect sense (as an instance of out-of-model hedging) in the Black model. For this model it is unambiguously given by the sensitivity of the price to a change in *the* volatility. We do not have to explain carefully whether we are dealing with the true model volatility or the Black 'implied' volatility, because they are one and the same thing. But as soon as we move away from the Black model matters become subtler: what do we mean by vega in the context of the SABR model, for instance? The price sensitivity to a 1% change in the 'true' SABR volatility, or to a 1% change in the Black volatility? And, what is the meaning of the Black volatility when we are dealing with the SABR model?

To see clearly into these matters, we must first remember the definition of implied volatility (Rebonato, 1999a, 2004a) as

> the wrong number to put in the wrong (Black) formula to get the right price of a plain-vanilla option

---

[5]Note also that a fitted model typically contains a relatively small number of state variables and parameters (for the LMM-SABR model the latter are the fitted values of the volatility and correlation functions), plus a large number of 'fudge factors' (again, for the LMM model the forward-rate-specific values $k_0^{T_i}$, for the LMM-SABR model the forward-rate-specific values ξ^{T_i}). As in the example above, the hard work in recalibrating the model after the bump is often done by the 'fudge factors', i.e., precisely by those *dei ex machina* the model is not too proud about, but that it nonetheless needs to achieve a good fit. To the extent that these fudge factors should ideally be absent from a well-specified model, the whole procedure leaves a lot to be desired.

With this sound bite in mind, we can now define

- by $C(x; K, T)$ the true price (as given by our model calibrated to market inputs) of a call of strike K and expiry T when the underlying price has value x;

- by $\widehat{\sigma}(K, T)$ the implied volatility for a call of strike K and expiry T;

- by $\widehat{C}(x|K, T)$ the Black formula with implied volatility x, strike K and expiry T;

- by $\widehat{C}(\widehat{\sigma}(K, T)|K, T)$ an alternative way of expressing the true price of the call via the intermediate Black step;[6]

- by $\Delta C^{\text{mkt}}(x; K, T)$, $\Delta C^{\text{mod}}(x; K, T)$ and $\Delta C^{\text{Black}}(x; K, T)$ the change in the market, model and Black price, respectively, of a call of strike K and expiry T when the underlying price has value x.

Note that, when we call $C(x; K, T)$ the 'true' price, we do not mean that our model is perfect and therefore perfectly describes the market dynamics. We simply imply that our model has been (perfectly) calibrated to market prices and that, therefore, at least in a static sense market and model prices perfectly coincide today. It is when it comes to *changes* in prices that the differences between our model, the reference Black model and the market matter (hence the definitions in the last bullet points).

Why make use at all of Black prices and implied volatilities, given that, in general, they are 'wrong'? Because doing so allows us to deal with hedging in a way that cuts across the idiosyncracies of different models. Let's see how this happens.

11.4   First-Order Derivatives with Respect to the Underlyings

11.4.1   Delta Hedging

In this subsection we develop a discussion based on the original delta with respect to the forward rate, as presented in the paper by Hagan *et al.* (2002). We show in the next chapter that, in general, this expression does *not* provide the best hedge, if by best hedge we mean the optimal position in the forward rate to minimize the variance of the hedged portfolio returns. However, for simplicity and clarity of exposition, we start with the 'traditional' formula first, and present the refinement after.

In the SABR model the model delta, $\Delta_K^T|_{\text{mod}}$, is given by

$$\Delta_K^T|_{\text{mod}} = \frac{\partial C(f; K, T)}{\partial f} \tag{11.6}$$

---

[6]To lighten notation we will often write $\widehat{\sigma}_K^T$ and $\widehat{C}_K^T$.

We can also write the model delta as

$$\Delta_K^T|_{\text{mod}} = \frac{\partial \widehat{C}(K,T)}{\partial f} + \frac{\partial \widehat{C}(K,T)}{\partial \widehat{\sigma}_K^T} \frac{\partial \widehat{\sigma}_K^T}{\partial f}|_{\text{mod}} \qquad (11.7)$$

Note that, in moving from Equation (11.6) to Equation (11.7) we have changed from the 'true' price functional to the Black formula. Despite the fact that in Equation (11.7) we are making use of the 'wrong' Black formula and of the 'wrong' Black volatility, this expression is *not* an approximation, but it is perfectly correct[7] whatever the true underlying model might be. Let's look in turn at the various terms that make up this correct expression.

The meaning of the 'wrong' terms $\frac{\partial \widehat{C}(K,T)}{\partial f}$ and $\frac{\partial \widehat{C}(K,T)}{\partial \widehat{\sigma}_K^T}$ is transparent: they are the Black delta and the Black vega. It is the term $\frac{\partial \widehat{\sigma}_K^T}{\partial f}|_{\text{mod}}$ that requires a few words. It is given by the model change in implied volatility (i.e., by the change of the wrong number to put in the wrong formula) when the underlying changes by an infinitesimal amount. If we are using the SABR model this term is very easy to calculate, because it just entails taking a derivative of the Hagan formula. We cannot know how this term behaves just by looking at the Black formula. It is this term that gives us a way of telling whether the model behaves as it should. It is by looking at this term, for instance, that we can tell that the Black model (see Rebonato (2006)) and the local-volatility model (see Hagan *et al.* (2002)) do not produce the right hedges. This is the only place in Equation (11.7) where the true-model-specific information comes in – and this is where all the real action is.

This ability to use a common, model-independent framework when dealing with different models makes the apparently cumbersome detour via the ultimately irrelevant Black model useful. But there is another advantage. Both Equation (11.6) and Equation (11.7) lend themselves well to the *calculation* of what the model delta *should be* like given the functional form of a particular model, which is tentatively assumed to be 'true'. However, a small modification of Equation (11.7) allows us to *estimate* what the true delta *is* like in reality, by focussing on how the observable market implied volatility surface changes when the forward rate changes. This slightly different formulation is the following:

$$\Delta_K^T|_{\text{mkt}} = \frac{\partial \widehat{C}(K,T)}{\partial f} + \frac{\partial \widehat{C}(K,T)}{\partial \widehat{\sigma}_K^T} \frac{\partial \widehat{\sigma}_K^T}{\partial f}|_{\text{mkt}} \qquad (11.8)$$

The difference is in the term $\frac{\partial \widehat{\sigma}_K^T}{\partial f}|_{\text{mkt}}$. It describes how the market implied volatility for strike K and expiry T changes when the underlying changes by an infinitesimal amount. By comparing the model term $\frac{\partial \widehat{\sigma}_K^T}{\partial f}|_{\text{mod}}$ with the 'experimental' $\frac{\partial \widehat{\sigma}_K^T}{\partial f}|_{\text{mkt}}$ we can tell how good a model is at suggesting the right delta. (Indeed, this is just what we do in Chapter 14.) As we shall see below, the same reasoning can be repeated for the vega and for higher-order sensitivities. Before doing that, however, we trivially rewrite Equation (11.8) in a way that will lend itself to generalizations, as follows:

$$\Delta_K^T|_{\text{mkt}} = \frac{\partial \widehat{C}(K,T)}{\partial f} + \frac{\partial \widehat{C}(K,T)}{\partial \widehat{\sigma}_K^T} \left(\frac{\partial \widehat{\sigma}_K^T}{\partial f}|_{\text{mod}} - A_K^T \right) \qquad (11.9)$$

---

[7]Actually, as we show in the next chapter, a term is missing – but this is a different story.

with

$$A_K^T = \frac{\partial \widehat{\sigma}_K^T}{\partial f}\Big|_{\text{mod}} - \frac{\partial \widehat{\sigma}_K^T}{\partial f}\Big|_{\text{mkt}} \tag{11.10}$$

To see why the tautology in Equation (11.9) helps, suppose for a moment that our model is the Black one. Then the term $\frac{\partial \widehat{\sigma}_K^T}{\partial f}\Big|_{\text{mod}}$ is identically equal to zero (because, according to the Black model, the volatility is a constant and therefore does not depend on the forward rate), and Equation (11.9) reduces to the well-known formula

$$\Delta_K^T\Big|_{\text{mkt}} = \frac{\partial \widehat{C}(K,T)}{\partial f} + \frac{\partial \widehat{C}(K,T)}{\partial \widehat{\sigma}_K^T}\frac{\partial \widehat{\sigma}_K^T}{\partial f}\Big|_{\text{mkt}} \tag{11.11}$$

In other words, the Black model does none of the work in the interesting term $\frac{\partial \widehat{C}(K,T)}{\partial \widehat{\sigma}_K^T}\left(\frac{\partial \widehat{\sigma}_K^T}{\partial f}\Big|_{\text{mod}} - A_K^T\right)$, the term A_K^T is just equal to

$$A_K^T = -\frac{\partial \widehat{\sigma}_K^T}{\partial f}\Big|_{\text{mkt}}$$

and the burden of obtaining the right change in price is all taken by the market correction, $\frac{\partial \widehat{\sigma}_K^T}{\partial f}\Big|_{\text{mkt}}$. Consider instead a 'perfect' model, i.e., a model that perfectly describes the dynamics of the underlying – in particular, a model that perfectly describes how the implied volatility moves when the forward rate moves. Then Equation (11.9) becomes

$$\Delta_K^T\Big|_{\text{mkt}} = \frac{\partial \widehat{C}(K,T)}{\partial f} + \frac{\partial \widehat{C}(K,T)}{\partial \widehat{\sigma}_K^T}\frac{\partial \widehat{\sigma}_K^T}{\partial f}\Big|_{\text{mod}} \tag{11.12}$$

In this case we do not need any correction term at all because $A_K^T = \frac{\partial \widehat{\sigma}_K^T}{\partial f}\Big|_{\text{mod}} - \frac{\partial \widehat{\sigma}_K^T}{\partial f}\Big|_{\text{mkt}}$ is by definition identically equal to zero.

In reality, for any decent-but-not-perfect model we will be somewhere between these two extremes ('useless' model and 'perfect' model), and the term

$$A_K^T = \frac{\partial \widehat{\sigma}_K^T}{\partial f}\Big|_{\text{mod}} - \frac{\partial \widehat{\sigma}_K^T}{\partial f}\Big|_{\text{mkt}} \tag{11.13}$$

will quantify exactly where on this spectrum our model lies – i.e., it will tell us by how much we have to correct the model-predicted changes in prices in order to obtain the market changes.

11.4.2 Vega Hedging

So much for the delta. We have not dealt with the sensitivity of a price to the volatility yet, but we can proceed exactly along the same lines. The model vega, $Vg_K^T\big|_{\text{mod}}$, will be given by

$$Vg_K^T|_{\text{mod}} = \frac{\partial C(f, \sigma; K)}{\partial \sigma} = \frac{\partial \widehat{C}(K, T)}{\partial \widehat{\sigma}_K^T} \frac{\partial \widehat{\sigma}_K^T}{\partial \sigma}|_{\text{mod}} \qquad (11.14)$$

Once again, given the availability of the Hagan formula, the expression $\frac{\partial \widehat{C}(K,T)}{\partial \widehat{\sigma}_K^T} \frac{\partial \widehat{\sigma}_K^T}{\partial \sigma}|_{\text{mod}}$ gives the easiest way to calculate the model vega. We can then define the market vega as

$$Vg_K^T|_{\text{mkt}} = \frac{\partial C(f, \sigma; K)}{\partial \sigma} = \frac{\partial \widehat{C}(K, T)}{\partial \widehat{\sigma}_K^T} \frac{\partial \widehat{\sigma}_K^T}{\partial \sigma}|_{\text{mkt}} \qquad (11.15)$$

where the term $\frac{\partial \widehat{\sigma}_K^T}{\partial \sigma}|_{\text{mkt}}$ tells us how the implied volatility moves when the second state variable of the SABR model, the true volatility, moves by an infinitesimal amount. *Mutatis mutandis*, the reasoning proceeds exactly along the same lines.

For the SABR model the definitions above cover all the possible instances of first-order hedging against the state variables.

We now move to the second-order derivatives.

11.5   Second-Order Derivatives with Respect to the Underlyings

11.5.1   Vanna and Volga[8]

Let us look along the same lines at higher-order sensitivities with respect to the true volatility, i.e., the vanna, Vn_K^T, and the volga, Vl_K^T (that is, the sensitivity of the delta or of the vega, respectively, to changes in the true volatility). We can write

$$Vn_K^T|_{\text{mod}} = \frac{\partial}{\partial \sigma}\left(\frac{\partial C(f; K, T)}{\partial f}\right) = \frac{\partial \Delta_K^T|_{\text{mod}}}{\partial \sigma} = \frac{\partial}{\partial f}\left(Vg_K^T|_{\text{mod}}\right)$$

$$= \frac{\partial}{\partial f}\left(\frac{\partial \widehat{C}(K, T)}{\partial \widehat{\sigma}_K^T} \frac{\partial \widehat{\sigma}_K^T}{\partial \sigma}|_{\text{mod}}\right)$$

$$= \left(\frac{\partial}{\partial f}\widehat{Vg}_K^T\right)\frac{\partial \widehat{\sigma}_K^T}{\partial \sigma}|_{\text{mod}} + \frac{\partial \widehat{C}(K, T)}{\partial \widehat{\sigma}_K^T}\left(\frac{\partial^2 \widehat{\sigma}_K^T}{\partial f \partial \sigma}|_{\text{mod}}\right) \qquad (11.16)$$

and

$$Vl_K^T|_{\text{mod}} = \frac{\partial Vg_K^T}{\partial \sigma}|_{\text{mod}} = \frac{\partial}{\partial \sigma}\left(\frac{\partial C(f, \sigma; K)}{\partial \sigma}\right)$$

$$= \frac{\partial}{\partial \sigma}\left(\frac{\partial \widehat{C}(K, T)}{\partial \widehat{\sigma}_K^T} \frac{\partial \widehat{\sigma}_K^T}{\partial \sigma}|_{\text{mod}}\right)$$

$$= \left(\frac{\partial}{\partial \sigma}\widehat{Vg}_K^T\right)\frac{\partial \widehat{\sigma}_K^T}{\partial \sigma}|_{\text{mod}} + \frac{\partial \widehat{C}(K, T)}{\partial \widehat{\sigma}_K^T}\left(\frac{\partial^2 \widehat{\sigma}_K^T}{\partial \sigma^2}|_{\text{mod}}\right) \qquad (11.17)$$

---

[8]Caution: sometimes the definitions for vanna and volga are interchanged.

where $\widehat{Vg}_K^T$ is the true-model-independent Black vega

$$\widehat{Vg}_K^T \equiv \frac{\partial \widehat{C}(K, T)}{\partial \widehat{\sigma}_K^T} \tag{11.18}$$

Changing the subscript 'mod' to 'mkt' turns the expressions above to the equivalent market vega, vanna and volga.

Two terms, namely $\frac{\partial}{\partial \sigma}\left(\widehat{Vg}_K^T\right)$ and $\frac{\partial}{\partial f}\left(\widehat{Vg}_K^T\right)$, now appear in these expressions whose meaning is not immediately obvious. What are we to make of them? What does it mean to take the derivative with respect to a true variable (such as f or σ) of a 'wrong' Black quantity like the Black vega? We can give a meaning to, say, the first derivative term as follows.

- First, we calibrate the state variables (f and σ) and parameters of our model to all the available current market prices and translate these prices into implied volatilities.

- Given these implied volatilities, we calculate for each strike and maturity the Black vega.

- Given our true stochastic-volatility model, we perturb the value of the calibrated model volatility by a small amount.

- With these perturbed values for the model input we compute 'perturbed' prices, and translate them into 'perturbed' implied volatilities.

- With these perturbed implied volatilities we compute the perturbed Black vega.

- We then estimate the derivative $\frac{\partial}{\partial \sigma}\left(\widehat{Vg}_K^T\right)$ as the limit of the ratio of the difference in Black vega over the difference in true volatility.

Clearly, we can proceed in the same manner for the term $\frac{\partial}{\partial f}\left(\widehat{Vg}_K^T\right)$.

Note the subtle differences between this procedure and taking derivatives with respect to the implied volatility – which is basically a case of functional-dependence hedging. We explain why this is the case in the next section.

11.6 Generalizing Functional-Dependence Hedging

Let's go back for a moment to the distinction between derivatives with respect to the true and the implied volatility. When we take a derivative with respect to the implied volatility we are doing the simplest case of functional-dependence hedging. To see why this is the case, let's look again at the simplest possible case, i.e., let's offer an alternative definition of vega as the derivative of the true model price with respect to the Black implied volatility, $\widehat{Vg}_K^T$:

$$\widehat{Vg}_K^T = \frac{\partial C(f, \sigma; K)}{\partial \widehat{\sigma}_K^T} \tag{11.19}$$

What does expression (11.19) mean? What information does it convey? To give precise meaning to this quantity – which is just what is estimated when one 'bumps' a single swaption volatility – we must think in the following terms.[9]

- First, we calibrate our model to all the available current market prices (implied volatilities), and obtain the model parameters (and, in the case of the SABR model, the implied value of the unobservable true volatility).

- We denote the set of parameters thus determined by $\{\boldsymbol{\theta}\}$.

- We now shift by a small amount a particular implied volatility (or, for that matter, a number of pre-chosen implied volatilities).

- Then we recalibrate our model using shifted current market prices (implied volatilities), and obtain the new model parameters and the new value for the unobservable true volatility; the shifted market prices are obtained (for all the strikes and maturities used in the fit) by using the Black formula, $\widehat{C}_K^T(x)$, with the shifted implied volatilities: $\widehat{C}_K^T(\widehat{\sigma}_K^T + \Delta\widehat{\sigma}_K^T)$.

- We denote the set of recalibrated 'shifted' parameters thus determined by $\{\boldsymbol{\theta} + \Delta\boldsymbol{\theta}\}$.

- The derivative $\frac{\partial C(f,\sigma;K)}{\partial \widehat{\sigma}_K^T}$ is then approximated as

$$\widehat{V}_{gK}^T = \frac{\partial C(f,\sigma;K)}{\partial \widehat{\sigma}_K^T} \simeq \frac{C(f;\boldsymbol{\theta} + \Delta\boldsymbol{\theta}) - C(f;\boldsymbol{\theta})}{\Delta\widehat{\sigma}_K^T} \qquad (11.20)$$

This shows clearly that what we have just defined is one particular instance of functional-dependence hedging. Despite the fact that this approach seems less natural (and certainly more cumbersome), taking derivatives with respect to the implied volatility has one important advantage, which becomes apparent by generalizing a bit the step-by-step procedure above. We can proceed as follows.

Note that the procedure outlined in the bullet points above is well defined for *any* shift we may give to the implied volatility surface. We could have moved several implied volatilities at the same time – as we make clear in the third bullet point. Of course, doing so is only interesting to the extent that the chosen shift is a common mode of deformation of the real implied volatility surface. But how do we choose a 'common mode of deformation'? There are obvious candidates: for instance, we can move all the implied volatilities upwards in parallel. But we can also produce more interesting changes. One could define, for instance, the sensitivity of the price of a product to a 'risk-reversal' move in the implied volatility – perhaps by moving the 25-delta implied volatility up by 1% and the 75-delta implied volatility down by the same amount, and linearly interpolating or extrapolating the other moves in implied volatilities accordingly. The same procedure of initial calibration to market inputs, pricing with these inputs, appropriately 'deforming' the volatility surface, recalibration and repricing could be applied.

---

[9]Note that what we are doing is the mirror image of what we discussed before. We were there discussing how to give meaning to a term like $\frac{\partial}{\partial \sigma}\left(\widehat{V}_{gK}^T\right)$, i.e., to a derivative of a 'wrong' Black quantity with respect to a 'true' state variable (in this case the volatility). Now we want to give meaning to a derivative, like $\frac{\partial C(f,\sigma;K)}{\partial \widehat{\sigma}_K^T}$, of a 'true' price with respect to a 'wrong' Black implied volatility.

This sensitivity is informative and important, but our choice of risk reversal shock was somewhat arbitrary. Can we generalize this *modus operandi* and make it more systematic? Indeed, we can do so in at least two different ways: the former relies more strongly on pure statistical analysis, the latter places more reliance on the fact that a good model should 'know' about the fundamentals of this statistical analysis. This is how it all works.

The implied volatility surface can of course change in an infinity of ways. Traders, however, are interested in market-significant modes of deformation of the implied volatility surface. These could be identified, for instance, using principal-component or independent-component analysis. We can think – and traders certainly do – of these dominant modes of deformation as a parallel shift, a tilt and a change in curvature in the smile surface. Let's denote these three components by $\widehat{\sigma}_1$, $\widehat{\sigma}_2$ and $\widehat{\sigma}_3$. Note that we no longer show a dependence on K and T, because these are now collective modes of the whole surface. How can we recast the equations above in this new framework? A natural extension of Equations (11.9) and following is:

$$\Delta_K^T|_{\text{mkt}} = \frac{\partial \widehat{C}(K,T)}{\partial f} + \sum_i^{1,3} \frac{\partial \widehat{C}(K,T)}{\partial \widehat{\sigma}_i} \left(\frac{\partial \widehat{\sigma}_i}{\partial f}\Big|_{\text{mod}} - A_i \right) \tag{11.21}$$

with

$$A_i = \frac{\partial \widehat{\sigma}_i}{\partial f}\Big|_{\text{mod}} - \frac{\partial \widehat{\sigma}_i}{\partial f}\Big|_{\text{mkt}} \tag{11.22}$$

and $\widehat{\sigma}_i$, $i = 1, 2, 3$ now denoting the ith model of deformation of the volatility surface.

Of course, we can do exactly the same for the vega, i.e., we can define the quantities

$$Vg_K^T|_{\text{mkt}} = \frac{\partial \widehat{C}(K,T)}{\partial \sigma} + \frac{\partial \widehat{C}(K,T)}{\partial \widehat{\sigma}_K^T} \left(\frac{\partial \widehat{\sigma}_K^T}{\partial \sigma}\Big|_{\text{mod}} - B_K^T \right) \tag{11.23}$$

with

$$B_K^T = \frac{\partial \widehat{\sigma}_K^T}{\partial \sigma}\Big|_{\text{mod}} - \frac{\partial \widehat{\sigma}_K^T}{\partial \sigma}\Big|_{\text{mkt}} \tag{11.24}$$

$$Vg_K^T|_{\text{mkt}} = \frac{\partial \widehat{C}(K,T)}{\partial \sigma} + \sum_i^{1,3} \frac{\partial \widehat{C}(K,T)}{\partial \widehat{\sigma}_i} \left(\frac{\partial \widehat{\sigma}_i}{\partial \sigma}\Big|_{\text{mod}} - B_i \right) \tag{11.25}$$

with

$$B_i = \frac{\partial \widehat{\sigma}_i}{\partial \sigma}\Big|_{\text{mod}} - \frac{\partial \widehat{\sigma}_i}{\partial \sigma}\Big|_{\text{mkt}} \tag{11.26}$$

We must stress again that if we use terms $\frac{\partial \widehat{\sigma}_K^T}{\partial f}\Big|_{\text{mkt}}$ or $\frac{\partial \widehat{\sigma}_K^T}{\partial \sigma}\Big|_{\text{mkt}}$ (where we look at each individual implied volatility, $\widehat{\sigma}_K^T$), we avail ourselves of a more comprehensive description of the smile deformation – a description that 'knows' about all its possible modes of deformation. In a way, every single swaption, of every expiry and strike, is treated as a state variable.

On the other hand, when one uses terms like $\frac{\partial \widehat{\sigma}_i}{\partial f}$ or $\frac{\partial \widehat{\sigma}_i}{\partial \sigma}$ one is relying on the chosen modes of deformation to reflect all the relevant modes of deformation of the smile that matter for the complex product.

If this is the case, why not simply estimate the terms $\frac{\partial \widehat{\sigma}_K^T}{\partial f}|_{\text{mkt}}$ and $\frac{\partial \widehat{\sigma}_K^T}{\partial \sigma}|_{\text{mkt}}$ and use them to construct our hedge ratios? Because to do so we would have to run regressions of the changes in implied volatility against changes in the underlying for every strike and every maturity of our hedging instruments. And, of course, the task would become even heavier when we look at the vega, vanna and volga statistics. And if you thought that estimating from empirical data a term like $\frac{\partial \widehat{\sigma}_2}{\partial f}|_{\text{mkt}}$ might be difficult (i.e., estimating how the 'risk-reversal' mode of deformation changes when the forward rate changes), imagine the practical difficulties in estimating for all strikes, expiries and tail lengths the terms $\frac{\partial \widehat{\sigma}_K^T}{\partial f}|_{\text{mkt}}$.[10]

What we need is therefore a 'decent' model that takes up most of the burden of producing an acceptable $\frac{\partial \widehat{\sigma}_K^T}{\partial f}|_{\text{mod}}$ for any strike K and expiry T, so that our need to use correction terms $\frac{\partial \widehat{\sigma}_K^T}{\partial f}|_{\text{mkt}}$ can be reduced. If the model did an overall acceptable job, then one could hope to impart relatively broad-brush corrections. What we need, in other words, is a model that knows about the important modes of deformation of the smile surface. This is where the (LMM)-SABR model can help. Let's see how.

The modes of deformation of the smile surface could be assigned in a systematic manner by looking at the first few principal components of the changes in the implied volatility surface. Careful, though: if you are dealing with the deformation of the smile of a swaption matrix (which is actually a cube, once the strike dimension is taken into account!), your principal components can become rather complex and difficult to interpret: Rebonato and Joshi (2002), for instance, already show pretty complex and difficult-to-interpret eigenvectors in their analysis of the US$ swaption matrix, and they only look at at-the-money implied volatilities!

To get around this problem, and try to regain an intuitive grip on the problem, one could simply try to assign user-defined parallel shifts, tilts and changes in curvature to the smile surface. But since we are dealing with a surface and not with a single curve, practical questions immediately arise: for the parallel move, by how much should I move (in parallel) the 10-year expiry relative to the 1-month expiry? How fast should my user-assigned tilt decay along the maturity spectrum? What about the curvature? And, when we look at swaption matrices, should I tilt across strikes the 5y × 5y volatility as much as the 5y × 1m volatility? One is therefore faced with the task of assigning not three numbers, not three lines, but three surfaces!

Luckily, there is a good compromise. We saw in Chapter 2 that these changes in principal components are nicely mimicked by the changes in the smile surface brought about by changes in the SABR quantities $\sigma_0^{T_i}$ (level), ρ (tilt) and ν (curvature). This is (yet another) reason why we think the SABR model is a good modelling approach: by 'trusting' the SABR model we can find a systematic way to assign almost orthogonal modes of deformation to the smile surface along the strike, expiry and swap tail axes, and when we do so we empirically

---

[10]Note that, if we follow this more informative and synthetic route, and if we want to have small correction terms A_i, it is essential for a model to 'know' about the possibility of these modes of deformation. For instance, if the model does not allow for a tilt in the smile, the term $\frac{\partial \widehat{\sigma}_2}{\partial f}|_{\text{mod}}$ will be identically zero, and all the burden will be taken up by the term $\frac{\partial \widehat{\sigma}_2}{\partial f}|_{\text{mkt}}$.

find that the model-produced deformations are not too dissimilar from the way the swaption implied volatilities actually move in reality. This therefore brings us to our punch line.

> If we perform in-model and out-of-model hedging with respect to the SABR state variables and parameters, our hedge ratios will be very similar to what we would obtain if we did functional-dependence hedging with respect to the first three principal components.

11.7 How Does the Model Know about Vanna and Volga?

Let's go back to the vanna and volga taken with respect to the true volatility, i.e., with the quantities Vn_K^T and Vl_K^T, rather than $\widehat{Vn}_K^T$ and $\widehat{Vl}_K^T$. To see what information these risk statistics offer, consider the case when a trader wants to hedge a given complex instrument with a set of hedging instruments. The trader has made himself vega-neutral, but his resulting portfolio is negative volga. As the volatility increases, the vega of the portfolio decreases. (This is just the definition as being short volga.) Since the trader had built a vega-neutral portfolio, he will now be short vega. Therefore, in order to remain vega-neutral the trader will have to buy more volatility, just when the price for volatility has gone up.

Conversely, suppose that the volatility had decreased. Since the trader is short volga, this means that the vega of the portfolio has increased. To remain vega-neutral the trader will have to sell the now-cheaper volatility.

In either case, the trader is not in a nice place. In volatility space the situation is the exact equivalent of being short gamma. The compensation for being short gamma is an option premium (and being long theta). If the model the trader uses does not know about the fact that volatility can be stochastic, it cannot know about being short volga, and therefore cannot ask for the correct compensation for the risk taken on board, i.e., cannot ask for the correct premium.

What does it mean for the model 'to know about volga'? With a stochastic-volatility model (like SABR), as a first approximation one can think of the price as a suitable weighted average over different volatility paths.[11] Being long or short 'volatility gamma' (i.e., volga) stems from the non-linearity of the price in volatility. If the conditional prices are such that the prices with the volatility *above or below* are locally lower than the price with the reference volatility, then the product is short volga. As all these conditional prices are below the reference-volatility case, the overall price produced by the model will also be lower than if the model had had no volatility of volatility. If a given product displays negative volga, the stochastic-volatility model therefore will suggest for it a lower price than a deterministic-volatility model. As a consequence, the trader will be less aggressive in his bidding.

In this case, the difference in prices between the deterministic-volatility and the stochastic-volatility case is the 'premium' to compensate the trader for the short volga. *Vice versa*, if the local average of the conditional prices for volatility paths above and below the reference volatility case is greater than the price for the zero-volatility-of-volatility case, the stochastic-volatility model will produce a higher price. The trader can be more

---

[11]Of course, the correlation between the volatility and the underlying complicates matters, but, for simplicity, let's leave this valid objection aside.

aggressive in his bidding because he will have volga on his side: he will buy volatility when it becomes cheaper, and sell it when it becomes dearer. Volatility theta is now against him. This is how the model 'knows about volga'.

The reader can extend this line of reasoning to the analysis of vanna.

11.8   Choice of Hedging Instrument

The last important observation is that, no matter how good a model is, no sensible trader should blindly follow its hedging prescriptions without choosing very carefully which hedging instrument to use. On this all-important point the model is totally silent: should the trader offset the vega, vanna and volga exposure from, say, a Bermudan swaption using caplets or swaptions? If swaptions are chosen, which ones? With which strike? The co-terminal ones? All of them?

Ultimately, all hedging ratios fundamentally rely for their effectiveness on a substantial cancellation of errors. It is the art of the trader to choose the liquid plain-vanilla instruments that most resemble the exotic product she wants to hedge, so as to maximize this cancellation of errors, and minimize the reliance on the output of a necessarily crude model. In Chapter 15 we will try to give some more systematic suggestions as to how to maximize the benefits of this cancellation of errors. For the moment we just stress that it is in practice extremely important. The reader should keep this in mind in all of the discussion that follows.

Chapter 12

Hedging against Moves in the Forward Rate and in the Volatility

As we indicated in the previous chapter, the formulae we derived for delta and vega hedging are not quite correct. When the diffusive processes for the volatility and the forward rate are correlated, there is a term missing in the naive expressions we obtained above. Conceptually, this term does not change the overall picture by much – and this is the reason why we did not include it in our previous discussion – but in practice it does make a noticeable difference.

12.1 Delta Hedging in the SABR-(LMM) Model

In order to understand where this extra term comes from, let's start from the SABR equations again:

$$df_t^T = \left(f_t^T\right)^{\beta^T} \sigma_t^T dz_t^T \tag{12.1}$$

$$\frac{d\sigma_t^T}{\sigma_t^T} = \nu^T dw_t^T \tag{12.2}$$

$$\mathbb{E}^{\mathbb{Q}^T}\left[dz_t^T dw_t^T\right] = \rho^T dt \tag{12.3}$$

For simplicity we will work in the (terminal) measure under which both the forward rate and its own volatility are martingales. To keep notation light, we do not explicitly show in the rest of this section the measure dependence on the Brownian increments.[1]

Let's call $C(f, \sigma)$ the value of a call option under the SABR model. As the SABR model produces (approximate) expressions for the Black implied volatility, $\widehat{\sigma}$ (see Equations (3.4) to (3.8) in Chapter 3), we can also consider the call price as a function of the forward rate

---

[1] We thank Dr Andrei Pogudin for the material in this section, which is part of his M.Sc. thesis.

and of the implied volatility: $C = \widehat{C}(f, \widehat{\sigma})$. The Black implied volatility is therefore also a function of the true volatility and of the forward rate: $\widehat{\sigma} = \widehat{\sigma}(\sigma, f)$. We can therefore apply Ito's lemma to this function, to obtain:

$$d\widehat{\sigma} = \frac{\partial \widehat{\sigma}}{\partial \sigma} d\sigma + \frac{\partial \widehat{\sigma}}{\partial f} df$$

$$+ \frac{1}{2} \left[\frac{\partial^2 \widehat{\sigma}}{\partial \sigma^2} <d\sigma^2> + \frac{\partial^2 \widehat{\sigma}}{\partial f^2} <df^2> + 2\frac{\partial^2 \widehat{\sigma}}{\partial f \partial \sigma} <d\sigma df> \right]$$

$$= \frac{\partial \widehat{\sigma}}{\partial \sigma} d\sigma + \frac{\partial \widehat{\sigma}}{\partial f} df + [A]dt \tag{12.4}$$

where the term $[A]dt$ denotes terms in dt that will disappear in the variance calculation that follows and the symbols $<\ldots>$ signify the quadratic variation or co-variation, as appropriate.

Next we also apply Ito's lemma to the function $C = \widehat{C}(f, \widehat{\sigma})$, and obtain:

$$dC = \frac{\partial \widehat{C}}{\partial \widehat{\sigma}} d\widehat{\sigma} + \frac{\partial \widehat{C}}{\partial f} df$$

$$+ \frac{1}{2} \left[\frac{\partial^2 \widehat{C}}{\partial \widehat{\sigma}^2} <d\widehat{\sigma}^2> + \frac{\partial^2 \widehat{C}}{\partial f^2} <df^2> + 2\frac{\partial^2 \widehat{C}}{\partial f \partial \widehat{\sigma}} <d\widehat{\sigma} df> \right] \tag{12.5}$$

We can now substitute the expression for $d\widehat{\sigma}$ derived above. This gives us

$$dC = \frac{\partial \widehat{C}}{\partial \widehat{\sigma}} \left[\frac{\partial \widehat{\sigma}}{\partial \sigma} d\sigma + \frac{\partial \widehat{\sigma}}{\partial f} df + Adt \right] + \frac{\partial \widehat{C}}{\partial f} df$$

$$+ \frac{1}{2} \left[\frac{\partial^2 \widehat{C}}{\partial \widehat{\sigma}^2} <d\widehat{\sigma}^2> + \frac{\partial^2 \widehat{C}}{\partial f^2} <df^2> + \frac{\partial^2 \widehat{C}}{\partial f \partial \widehat{\sigma}} <d\widehat{\sigma} df> \right] \tag{12.6}$$

Rearranging terms gives

$$dC = \frac{\partial \widehat{C}}{\partial \widehat{\sigma}} \frac{\partial \widehat{\sigma}}{\partial \sigma} \sigma v dw + \left[\frac{\partial \widehat{C}}{\partial \widehat{\sigma}} \frac{\partial \widehat{\sigma}}{\partial f} + \frac{\partial \widehat{C}}{\partial f} \right] f^\beta \sigma dz_t$$

$$+ \frac{1}{2} \left[\frac{\partial^2 \widehat{C}}{\partial \widehat{\sigma}^2} <d\widehat{\sigma}^2> + \frac{\partial^2 \widehat{C}}{\partial f^2} <df^2> + 2\frac{\partial^2 \widehat{C}}{\partial f \partial \widehat{\sigma}} <d\widehat{\sigma} df> \right] + \frac{\partial \widehat{C}}{\partial \widehat{\sigma}} A dt \tag{12.7}$$

We collect all the terms in dt to give

$$dC = \frac{\partial \widehat{C}}{\partial \widehat{\sigma}} \frac{\partial \widehat{\sigma}}{\partial \sigma} \sigma v dw + \left[\frac{\partial \widehat{C}}{\partial \widehat{\sigma}} \frac{\partial \widehat{\sigma}}{\partial f} + \frac{\partial \widehat{C}}{\partial f} \right] f^\beta \sigma dz + B dt \tag{12.8}$$

with

$$Bdt = \frac{1}{2} \left[\frac{\partial^2 \widehat{C}}{\partial \widehat{\sigma}^2} <d\widehat{\sigma}^2> + \frac{\partial^2 \widehat{C}}{\partial f^2} <df^2> + 2\frac{\partial^2 \widehat{C}}{\partial f \partial \widehat{\sigma}} <d\widehat{\sigma}df> \right] + \frac{\partial \widehat{C}}{\partial \widehat{\sigma}} Adt \qquad (12.9)$$

Clearly, we have two sources of uncertainty (dw and dz) and we cannot therefore hope to neutralize them both with a Δ position, no matter how cleverly chosen, in the forward rate. (See the painfully detailed discussion in Rebonato (2006).) However, even if setting up a *zero*-variance portfolio is impossible, we can still try to put together a *minimum*-variance portfolio, Π:

$$d\Pi = dC - \Delta df$$

$$= \frac{\partial \widehat{C}}{\partial \widehat{\sigma}} \frac{\partial \widehat{\sigma}}{\partial \sigma} \sigma v dw + \left[\frac{\partial \widehat{C}}{\partial \widehat{\sigma}} \frac{\partial \widehat{\sigma}}{\partial f} + \frac{\partial \widehat{C}}{\partial f} - \Delta \right] f^{\beta}\sigma dz + Bdt \qquad (12.10)$$

The variance of this quantity is given by

$$\mathrm{var}\,(d\Pi) = \mathbb{E}\left[d\Pi^2\right] - (\mathbb{E}\,[d\Pi])^2$$

$$= \left[\frac{\partial \widehat{C}}{\partial \widehat{\sigma}} \frac{\partial \widehat{\sigma}}{\partial f} + \frac{\partial \widehat{C}}{\partial f} - \Delta \right]^2 f^{2\beta}\sigma^2 dt + \left[\frac{\partial \widehat{C}}{\partial \widehat{\sigma}} \frac{\partial \widehat{\sigma}}{\partial \sigma} \right]^2 \sigma^2 v^2 dt$$

$$+ 2 \left[\frac{\partial \widehat{C}}{\partial \widehat{\sigma}} \frac{\partial \widehat{\sigma}}{\partial \sigma} \right] \left[\frac{\partial \widehat{C}}{\partial \widehat{\sigma}} \frac{\partial \widehat{\sigma}}{\partial f} + \frac{\partial \widehat{C}}{\partial f} - \Delta \right] \rho\sigma^2 v f^{\beta} dt \qquad (12.11)$$

To find the 'amount of forward rate', Δ, that minimizes the variance of the portfolio we just take the derivative of $\mathrm{var}\,(d\Pi)$ with respect to Λ, and set it to zero:

$$\frac{d\,[\mathrm{var}\,(d\Pi)]}{d\Delta} = 0$$

$$\Rightarrow \left[\frac{\partial \widehat{C}}{\partial \widehat{\sigma}} \frac{\partial \widehat{\sigma}}{\partial f} + \frac{\partial \widehat{C}}{\partial f} - \Delta \right] f^{\beta}\sigma + \frac{\partial \widehat{C}}{\partial \widehat{\sigma}} \frac{\partial \widehat{\sigma}}{\partial \sigma} \rho\sigma v = 0 \qquad (12.12)$$

The position in the forward rate, Δ, that minimizes the variance is therefore

$$\Delta_{\mathrm{opt}} = \frac{\partial \widehat{C}}{\partial f} + \frac{\partial \widehat{C}}{\partial \widehat{\sigma}} \left(\frac{\partial \widehat{\sigma}}{\partial f} + \frac{\partial \widehat{\sigma}}{\partial \sigma} \frac{\rho v}{f^{\beta}} \right)$$

$$= \frac{\partial \widehat{C}}{\partial f} + \frac{\partial \widehat{C}}{\partial \widehat{\sigma}} \frac{\partial \widehat{\sigma}}{\partial f} + \frac{\partial \widehat{C}}{\partial \widehat{\sigma}} \frac{\partial \widehat{\sigma}}{\partial \sigma} \frac{\rho v}{f^{\beta}} \qquad (12.13)$$

We therefore see that the minimum-variance delta is made up of three components:

1. the 'naive' Black delta term, $\frac{\partial C}{\partial f}$;

2. the familiar correction term, $\frac{\partial \widehat{C}}{\partial \widehat{\sigma}} \frac{\partial \widehat{\sigma}}{\partial f}$, that comes from any deterministic dependence, $\frac{\partial \widehat{\sigma}}{\partial f}$, of the implied volatility, $\widehat{\sigma}$, on the forward rate, f, scaled by the 'Black vega', $\frac{\partial \widehat{C}}{\partial \widehat{\sigma}}$, i.e., by the sensitivity of the call price to a change in implied volatility;

3. a new correction term, $\frac{\partial \widehat{C}}{\partial \widehat{\sigma}} \frac{\partial \widehat{\sigma}}{\partial \sigma} \frac{\rho v}{f^\beta}$, that now depends on how much the call price changes as the SABR volatility changes, $\frac{\partial \widehat{C}}{\partial \widehat{\sigma}} \frac{\partial \widehat{\sigma}}{\partial \sigma}$, times a term, $\frac{\rho v}{f^\beta}$, that depends on the correlation between the forward rate and its own volatility.

The first two terms appear in Hagan *et al.*'s (2002) original formula. Can we understand better the intuition behind the third term? To gain some understanding about the origin of the last term, we follow a different derivation for Equation (12.13), due to Bartlett (2006). The idea is that, if f and σ are correlated, when the forward rate changes, the volatility will change as well, *and will not do so in an independent manner*. Let's call $\delta_f \sigma$ the average change in σ caused by a change in f. Somewhat heuristically, let's therefore shock the call price, C, by simultaneously perturbing its two state variables, f and σ:

$$f \rightarrow f + \Delta f \tag{12.14}$$

$$\sigma \rightarrow \sigma + \delta_f \sigma \tag{12.15}$$

Let's now rewrite the SABR equation in a slightly different form, by expressing the increment dw in terms of dz and of an independent Wiener increment, dB (as we can always do):

$$dw = \left[\rho dz + \sqrt{1 - \rho^2} dB \right] \tag{12.16}$$

$$\Rightarrow df = f^\beta \sigma dz \tag{12.17}$$

$$d\sigma = \sigma v \left[\rho dz + \sqrt{1 - \rho^2} dB \right] \tag{12.18}$$

But, since

$$dz = \frac{df}{f^\beta \sigma} \tag{12.19}$$

we can also write

$$d\sigma = \frac{\sigma v \rho}{f^\beta \sigma} df + \sigma v \sqrt{1 - \rho^2} dB \tag{12.20}$$

As Bartlett points out, the evolution of the volatility has been decomposed into two components, one perfectly linked to the change in forward rate, $\frac{\sigma v \rho}{f^\beta \sigma} df$, and one totally independent, $\sigma v \sqrt{1 - \rho^2}$. This interpretation shows that the average change in σ, $\delta_f \sigma$, given a change, df, in the forward rate, is given by

$$\delta_f \sigma = \frac{\rho v}{f^\beta} df \tag{12.21}$$

Following this reasoning, the change in call price becomes

$$dC = \left[\frac{\partial \widehat{C}}{\partial f} + \frac{\partial \widehat{C}}{\partial \widehat{\sigma}} \left(\frac{\partial \widehat{\sigma}}{\partial f} + \frac{\partial \widehat{\sigma}}{\partial \sigma} \frac{\rho v}{f^{\beta}} \right) \right] df \qquad (12.22)$$

which gives a new Δ:

$$\Delta = \frac{\partial \widehat{C}}{\partial f} + \frac{\partial \widehat{C}}{\partial \widehat{\sigma}} \left(\frac{\partial \widehat{\sigma}}{\partial f} + \frac{\partial \widehat{\sigma}}{\partial \sigma} \frac{\rho v}{f^{\beta}} \right) \qquad (12.23)$$

A glance at Equation (12.13) shows that the new delta we have just obtained coincides with the optimal Δ_{opt} that we had derived by imposing the minimum-variance condition for the delta-hedged portfolio. This joint treatment allows us to understand better both derivations: the Bartlett Δ corresponds to the delta that gives rise to a minimum-variance portfolio; the new term in the minimum-variance portfolio is linked to the average value, $\frac{\rho v}{f^{\beta}} df$, of the volatility move, given a move df in the forward rate.

Does this term make a difference? Yes, it does, as demonstrated by work we did with Pogudin (2008). First, we simulated a perfect SABR world, with known parameters and known initial value for the volatility (incidentally, the initial value of the volatility was correctly reverse-engineered by the fitting to the model prices because we knew the correct β and ρ).[2] Our goal was to hedge a receiver swaption with expiry at inception of 0.5 years. The forward rate was assumed to be at 5% and the strikes were at-the-money and 150, 100, 50 bps on each side of at-the-money. The simulation of the replicating strategies was carried out until the residual option expiry was 0.25 years (i.e., for three months), at which point the difference between the option value and the value of the replicating portfolio was recorded. This difference is the quantity reported in Figures 12.1 to 12.3. The initial value of the volatility, σ_0, was 0.05, the correlation, ρ, was -0.5, the volatility of volatility, v, was 50% and the exponent, β, was the market standard 0.5. These are all market-typical values for a short-dated swaption. See also Tables 12.1 to 12.3.

With this set-up we engaged in three distinct hedging strategies of the European swaption:

1. The first strategy was based on the naive Black formula, without including the correction term ($\frac{\partial \widehat{\sigma}}{\partial f}$) that takes into account the dependence of the smile on the forward rate – we availed ourselves, however, of the knowledge of the correct average quadratic variation.

2. The second strategy was based on the Hagan delta formula, $\frac{\partial \widehat{C}}{\partial f} + \frac{\partial \widehat{C}}{\partial \widehat{\sigma}} \frac{\partial \widehat{\sigma}}{\partial f}$, plus perfect knowledge of the parameters of the SABR process.

3. The third strategy was based on the Bartlett–Pogudin formula, $\frac{\partial \widehat{C}}{\partial f} + \frac{\partial \widehat{C}}{\partial \widehat{\sigma}} \frac{\partial \widehat{\sigma}}{\partial f} + \frac{\partial \widehat{C}}{\partial \widehat{\sigma}} \frac{\partial \widehat{\sigma}}{\partial \sigma} \frac{\rho v}{f^{\beta}}$, plus, again, knowledge of the SABR parameters.

The hedging performance was assessed on the basis of the variance of the difference between the terminal option payoff and value at option expiry of the three self-financing trading strategies 1, 2 or 3.

---

[2]Useful discussions with Dr Andrei Pogudin and his calculations are gratefully acknowledged. Further details on his work can be found in Pogudin (2008).

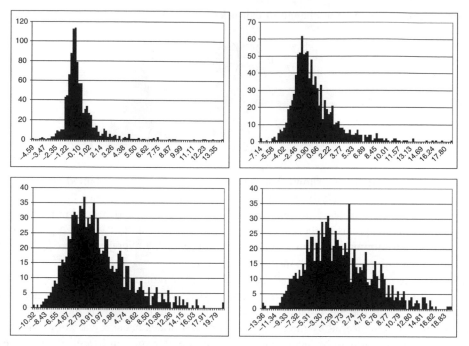

Figure 12.1   The distribution of the differences between the hedging portfolio and the call price at 3 months from expiry when the naive Black formula was used for hedging (term $\frac{\partial C}{\partial f}$ only).

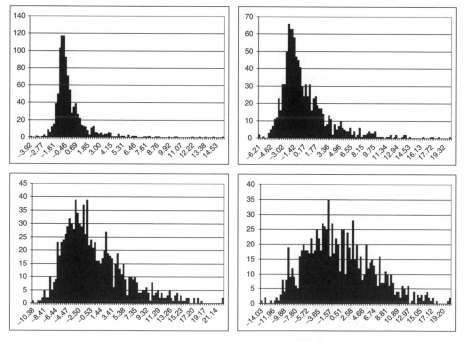

Figure 12.2   The distribution of the differences between the hedging portfolio and the call price at 3 months from expiry when the naive Hagan formula was used for hedging (terms $\frac{\partial C}{\partial f}$ and $\frac{\partial C}{\partial \hat{\sigma}} \frac{\partial \hat{\sigma}}{\partial f}$).

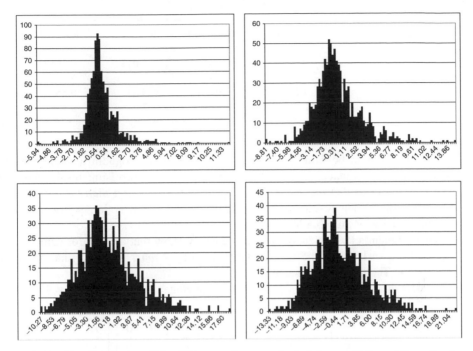

Figure 12.3 The distribution of the differences between the hedging portfolio and the call price at 3 months from expiry when the Bartlett–Pogudin formula was used for hedging (terms $\frac{\partial C}{\partial f}$, $\frac{\partial \widehat{C}}{\partial \widehat{\sigma}} \frac{\partial \widehat{\sigma}}{\partial f}$ and $\frac{\partial \widehat{C}}{\partial \widehat{\sigma}} \frac{\partial \widehat{\sigma}}{\partial \sigma} \frac{\rho v}{f^\beta}$).

Table 12.1 Pogudin BS.

Pogudin BS	K+/−150	K+/−100	K+/−50	K+/−0
m	0.02	0.053	0.099	0.11
std	1.78	3.25	4.9	5.74
m_3	3.1	1.8	0.99	0.54
m_4	18	7.8	4.1	3.1

Table 12.2 Pogudin SABR.

Pogudin SABR	K+/−150	K+/−100	K+/−50	K+/−0
m	0.03	0.074	0.14	0.16
std	1.92	3.5	5.25	6.1
m_3	3.4	1.9	1	0.5
m_4	19	8.1	4	3

Table 12.3   Pogudin SMART.

Pogudin SMART	K+/−150	K+/−100	K+/−50	K+/−0
m	−0.0037	0.0077	0.018	0.0017
std	1.6	2.93	4.45	5.23
m_3	1.6	0.94	0.63	0.55
m_4	11	5.3	3.6	3.4

There are no prizes to be won by guessing that the Bartlett–Pogudin formula provided the best hedging performance, i.e., the lowest variance. The surprising result shown by Figures 12.1 to 12.3 was that *the naive Black formula often did better than the more sophisticated Hagan formula*. The result was robust across a variety of swaption expiries and tails. Can we understand why this should be the case?

Following Pogudin's (2008) analysis, one can easily show that at least for some parameters the portfolio variance of the simple Hagan strategy 2 *must* be worse than the naive Black strategy 1. The reasoning goes as follows.

Consider the difference between the Black and the Hagan portfolio variance:

$$\text{var}_{\text{Black}}\,(d\Pi) - \text{var}_{\text{Hagan}}\,(d\Pi) = \left[\frac{\partial \widehat{C}}{\partial \widehat{\sigma}}\frac{\partial \widehat{\sigma}}{\partial f}\right]^2 f^{2\beta}\sigma^2 dt + 2\left[\frac{\partial \widehat{C}}{\partial \widehat{\sigma}}\frac{\partial \widehat{\sigma}}{\partial \sigma}\right]\left[\frac{\partial \widehat{C}}{\partial \widehat{\sigma}}\frac{\partial \widehat{\sigma}}{\partial f}\right]\rho\sigma^2 v f^{\beta} dt$$

(12.24)

This difference between the variances *can* be smaller than zero:

$$\text{var}_{\text{Black}}\,(d\Pi) - \text{var}_{\text{Hagan}}\,(d\Pi) < 0 \quad \text{if}$$

$$\left[\frac{\partial \widehat{C}}{\partial \widehat{\sigma}}\frac{\partial \widehat{\sigma}}{\partial f}\right]^2 f^{\beta} + 2\left[\frac{\partial \widehat{C}}{\partial \widehat{\sigma}}\frac{\partial \widehat{\sigma}}{\partial \sigma}\right]\left[\frac{\partial \widehat{C}}{\partial \widehat{\sigma}}\frac{\partial \widehat{\sigma}}{\partial f}\right]\rho v < 0$$

(12.25)

Can this inequality ever be satisfied? Yes it can! Consider, for instance, the case $\beta = 1$. Then

$$\left[\frac{\partial \widehat{C}}{\partial \widehat{\sigma}}\frac{\partial \widehat{\sigma}}{\partial f}\right]^2 f + 2\left[\frac{\partial \widehat{C}}{\partial \widehat{\sigma}}\frac{\partial \widehat{\sigma}}{\partial \sigma}\right]\left[\frac{\partial \widehat{C}}{\partial \widehat{\sigma}}\frac{\partial \widehat{\sigma}}{\partial f}\right]\rho v < 0 \quad \text{[for } \beta = 1] $$

(12.26)

But for close-to-at-the-money options

$$\frac{\partial \widehat{\sigma}}{\partial f} = -\frac{\rho v}{2f} > 0 \quad \text{if } \rho < 0$$

(12.27)

$$\frac{\partial \widehat{\sigma}}{\partial \sigma} \simeq 1$$

(12.28)

Therefore Equation (12.26) is *always* smaller than zero for close-to-at-the-money options, at least when $\beta = 1$. We stress that Pogudin (2008) has *proven* that this is the case when

$\beta = 1$, but *empirically finds* outperformance of the naive Black strategy over the Hagan strategy (in minimum-variance terms) also for other values of the exponent β. See Pogudin (2008) for further details.

The intuition behind this result is very interesting: whether the naive Black or the Hagan strategy wins depends on the relative magnitude of the terms $\frac{\partial \widehat{\sigma}}{\partial f}$ and $\frac{\partial \widehat{\sigma}}{\partial \sigma} \frac{\rho \nu}{f^\beta}$. Let's look at their interplay. When the correlation ρ is negative the second term, $\frac{\partial \widehat{\sigma}}{\partial \sigma} \frac{\rho \nu}{f^\beta}$, is obviously always negative. The first term, $\frac{\partial \widehat{\sigma}}{\partial f}$, would also seem to be always negative – after all, doesn't the implied volatility move *up* when the underlying forward rate moves *down*? And, if it is negative, it has the same sign as the correction term $\frac{\partial \widehat{\sigma}}{\partial \sigma} \frac{\rho \nu}{f^\beta}$. How can it do any harm? Shouldn't then it always provide a contribution to the total delta in the right direction, if not of the right magnitude?

Yes and no. When we engage in actual hedging, we do not deal with miraculously always-at-the-money options, but with real options of a given strike. If a given *fixed-strike* option was, say, at-the-money before the move in the forward rate, it will no longer be so after the move. Therefore, in order to decide the sign of the first term, $\frac{\partial \widehat{\sigma}}{\partial f}$, we must go back to the discussion at the end of Section 3.3: it is indeed true that the *at-the-money* implied volatility will move upwards for a downward move in the forward rate; but, *for a fixed strike option*, there is also a sliding of the implied volatility down the smile (for $\beta < 1$). If the second effect prevails, the naive Hagan term *will therefore even have the wrong sign* – this is why, in these situations, it does more harm than good compared to the naive Black formula.

When would one use these formulae in practice? The obvious application is for the trader who has either 'bought cheap volatility' or 'sold expensive volatility', i.e., for the trader who perceives the Black implied volatility to be over-sold or over-bid. If the trader wants to monetize the correctness of her view, she cannot, of course, vega hedge – by so doing, she would be exactly giving up the market opportunity she perceives. She will, instead, have to 'trade the gamma' (see the discussion in Rebonato (2004a)), i.e., engage in delta hedging and try to capture the value arising from the discrepancy between the implied and realized volatility. The formulae presented above are just what she needs.

But what about the situation when the trader engages in vega hedging – either because she is hedging a complex trade or because she is engaging in relative value trading in vega space? We turn to this question in the next section.

12.2   Vega Hedging in the SABR-(LMM) Model

Following the same reasoning as above, Bartlett (2006) shows that, by imparting to the forward rate and the volatility the shocks

$$f \to f + \delta_\sigma f \tag{12.29}$$

$$\sigma \to \sigma + \Delta \sigma \tag{12.30}$$

one finds that

$$\delta_\sigma f = \frac{\rho f^\beta}{\nu} \Delta \sigma \tag{12.31}$$

The change in the option value is now

$$dC = \frac{\partial \widehat{C}}{\partial \widehat{\sigma}} \left(\frac{\partial \widehat{\sigma}}{\partial \sigma} + \frac{\partial \widehat{\sigma}}{\partial f} \frac{\rho f^{\beta}}{\nu} \right) \Delta \sigma \tag{12.32}$$

A portfolio of options $\{ \widehat{C}(K_i, T_j) = \widehat{C}_{ij} \}$ is then vega-neutral if

$$\sum_{i,j} \frac{\partial \widehat{C}_{ij}}{\partial \widehat{\sigma}} \left(\frac{\partial \widehat{\sigma}_{ij}}{\partial \sigma} + \frac{\partial \widehat{\sigma}_{ij}}{\partial f} \frac{\rho f^{\beta}}{\nu} \right) = 0 \tag{12.33}$$

Chapter 13

(LMM)-SABR Hedging in Practice: Evidence from Market Data

13.1 Purpose of this Chapter

In the two previous chapters we have looked at different types of hedging (Chapter 11) and at the best formulae for delta and vega hedging that would apply if we lived in a perfect SABR world (Chapter 12). In this chapter we make use of empirical information about the evolution of the swaption matrix (including full smile information) in order to assess how well the SABR model can be expected to perform in practice. We approach this problem by gauging how well specified the SABR model is. We want to see, in other words, how close the sub-lunar empirical market universe is to the Platonic SABR world. We have explained in Section 11.2 why looking at the degree of variation of the time series of the supposedly constant model parameters can give a useful indication of the success of the hedging programme.

If the (LMM)-SABR were indeed found to be close-to-well-specified, then the analysis of the previous chapter would become more directly applicable. If it weren't, then the analysis presented in Chapter 11 – out-of-model hedging, functional-dependence hedging, etc. – would have to be more heavily relied upon. As it turns out, the SABR model appears to be surprisingly well specified, at least in normal market conditions. In situations of market stress the analysis presented in Chapter 15 will come in handy.

13.2 Notation

For a set of trading days $\{t_i\}$, $i = 0, 1, 2, \ldots, N$, we denote:

- the set of SABR parameters $\{\beta, \rho \text{ and } \nu\}$ at time t_i by $\{\theta_i\}$, $i = 0, 1, 2, \ldots, N$;

- the same set of SABR parameters at time t_i augmented by the time t_i-value of the unobservable state variable $\sigma(t_i)$ by $\{\boldsymbol{\theta}'_i\}$: $\{\boldsymbol{\theta}'_i\} = \{\beta, \rho, \nu \cup \sigma_{t_i}\}$, $i = 0, 1, 2, \ldots, N$;

- the difference in the swap rate between day $i - 1$ and day i by $\Delta f(t_i) \equiv f(t_i) - f(t_{i-1})$, $i = 1, 2, \ldots, N$;

- the difference in the volatility between day $i - 1$ and day i by $\Delta\sigma(t_i|\boldsymbol{\theta}_{i-1}) \equiv \sigma(t_i|\boldsymbol{\theta}_{i-1}) - \sigma(t_{i-1}|\boldsymbol{\theta}_{i-1})$, or by $\Delta\sigma(t_i|\boldsymbol{\theta}) \equiv \sigma(t_i|\boldsymbol{\theta}_i) - \sigma(t_{i-1}|\boldsymbol{\theta}_{i-1})$, $i = 1, 2, \ldots, N$, depending on whether the volatility at time t_i is estimated using information (parameters) available at time t_i or t_{i-1};

- the value at time t_i of the LMM-SABR call function for strike K and expiry T by $C_K^T(t_i)$;

- the value at time t_i of the Black call function for strike K and expiry T with Black implied volatility $\widehat{\sigma}_K^T(t_i)$ by $\widehat{C}_K^T(t_i|\widehat{\sigma}_K^T(t_i))$;

- the difference in Black implied volatilities and caplet (swaption) prices for maturity T and strike K between day $i - 1$ and day i by $\Delta\widehat{\sigma}_K^T(t_i) \equiv \widehat{\sigma}_K^T(t_i) - \widehat{\sigma}_K^T(t_{i-1})$ and $\Delta C_K^T(t_i) \equiv C_K^T(t_i) - C_K^T(t_{i-1}) = \Delta\widehat{C}_K^T(t_i|\widehat{\sigma}_K^T(t_i)) \equiv \widehat{C}_K^T(t_i|\widehat{\sigma}_K^T(t_i)) - \widehat{C}_K^T(t_{i-1}|\widehat{\sigma}_K^T(t_{i-1}))$, for $i = 1, 2, \ldots, N$, respectively.

Two more points: first, when there is the possibility of ambiguity, we call 'true' volatility the volatility that enters the (LMM)-SABR models, to distinguish it from the implied volatility; second, in this chapter we use carefully and punctiliously the words 'parameters' and 'state variables': 'parameters' only means β, ρ and ν – but not σ!

We have at our disposal for the analysis 818 daily records of the set $\{\boldsymbol{\theta}'_i\}$ and of $f(t_i)$. With this empirical information and with the definitions above we analysed the hedging performance of the SABR and the LMM-SABR models.

13.2.1 Estimation of the Unobservable Volatility

The swap rate and its volatility are the two state variables of the SABR model. However, only the first is directly observable from market values. In order to create a time series for the latent volatility state variable we proceeded in two different ways.

First, we simply recorded the SABR fitted values of the volatility for each trading day t_i, using the market prices of swaptions at time t_i, $C_K^T(t_i)$, and calibrating all the parameters and the unobservable volatility state variable (i.e., the set $\{\boldsymbol{\theta}'_i\}$) to these prices. Using the notation above, this is the time series $\{\sigma(t_i|\boldsymbol{\theta}_i)\}$.

Second, we estimated a value of the volatility in a manner more consistent with the assumption that the SABR model is a correct specification of the market (and its parameters, therefore, should be constant). To do this, we calibrated again the unknown volatility to the market prices, $C_K^T(t_i)$, of the swaptions at time t_i, but keeping this time the parameters, $\{\boldsymbol{\theta}_{i-1} = \beta_{i-1}, \nu_{i-1} \text{ and } \rho_{i-1}\}$, at the same values obtained from the fit to the market prices at time t_{i-1}. Using the notation above, the time series thus obtained is denoted by $\{\sigma(t_i|\boldsymbol{\theta}_{i-1})\}$. In theory, this is, of course, how one should calibrate the SABR model (and, for that matter, *any* model). We are therefore trying to answer the question: what fraction of the observed changes in market prices is explained by changes in the state variables (the 'good' changes) and by changes in the parameters (the 'bad' changes)?

Clearly, for a perfectly specified model the parameters should never change ($\{\boldsymbol{\theta}_i\} = \{\boldsymbol{\theta}_{i+1}\}$, $\forall i$), and the two time series would coincide ($\sigma(t_i|\boldsymbol{\theta}_i) = \sigma(t_i|\boldsymbol{\theta}_{i-1})$, $\forall i$). In reality, this will never be exactly the case. As we show below, differences in the two time series contain useful information about the hedging performance of the SABR model.

13.2.2 Tests of the Hedging Performance of the SABR Model

To test how well specified the SABR model is as far as delta hedging is concerned we proceed as follows.

1. **Set of Tests #1**. With the first set of tests we look at some key statistics of the marginal and joint distributions of the time series $\sigma(t_i|\boldsymbol{\theta}_i)$, $\sigma(t_i|\boldsymbol{\theta}_{i-1})$, $\Delta\sigma(t_i|\boldsymbol{\theta}_i')$, $\Delta\sigma(t_i|\boldsymbol{\theta}_{i-1}')$ and $\Delta f(t_i)$ and we test for their consistency with the SABR model. This has already been done in Chapter 9.

2. **Set of Tests #2**. With the second set of tests we look more directly at the hedging performance of the SABR model by comparing the realized and predicted changes in swaption prices, $\Delta C_K^T(t_i; \text{real})$ and $\Delta C_K^T(t_i; \text{pred})$ and at the realized and predicted changes in implied volatilities, $\Delta\widehat{\sigma}_K^T(t_i; \text{real})$ and $\Delta\widehat{\sigma}_K^T(t_i; \text{pred})$.

These first two sets of tests give us information about the quality of the SABR delta hedges and of the SABR vega hedges for swaptions of different strikes *but same maturity*. In order to explore the ability to hedge across swaptions of different expiries and swap tails, we must resort to testing a dynamic model like the LMM-SABR that links the different swaptions together. See below.

13.2.3 Tests of the Hedging Performance of the LMM-SABR Model

To assess the hedging performance of the LMM-SABR model across expiries we proceed as follows. Given a history of market SABR parameters for caplets, $\{\boldsymbol{\theta}_i\}$, we calibrate the volatility and volatility-of-volatility functions of the Rebonato (2007b) LMM-SABR model that we have described in Chapter 4 to the market prices of caplets. For each trading day this procedure gives us two time series of caplet parameters, $\{\boldsymbol{p}_i = a_i, b_i, c_i, d_i\}$ and $\{\boldsymbol{q}_i = \alpha_i, \beta_i, \gamma_i, \delta_i\}$. With these caplet-related parameters (and with reasonable assumptions about the correlations), we calculate the changes in the prices of various swaptions using the approximations reported in Chapter 6. See also Rebonato and White (2008) for further details. We then compare the predicted changes in swaption prices with the observed market changes.

For the sake of brevity, we do not go into detail about the choice of the correlation function. We simply note that (i) our procedure recovers exactly the SABR forward-rate/volatility; (ii) as noted in Rebonato (2006) the model prices of swaptions depend mildly on reasonable variations in the forward-rate/forward-rate correlation and more strongly on the shape of the instantaneous volatility function; (iii) the model prices of swaptions depend very weakly on reasonable variations in the volatility/volatility correlation block.

13.3   Hedging Results for the SABR Model

We found in Chapter 9 a surprisingly good agreement between the implied and the statistically estimated volatility, forward-rate/volatility correlation and volatility of volatility, pointing to a substantially correct specification of the model, but we noticed some small consistent discrepancies. We can explain these small but noticeable biases as follows. Let's begin from a qualitative discussion of the problem, which also defines clearly, at least in a stylized case, what we mean by a 'well-specified' model.

Let's assume that, as a first approximation, both the real market smile,[1] $\widehat{\sigma}^{\mathrm{mkt}}(x)$, and the SABR-produced smile, $\widehat{\sigma}^{\mathrm{SABR}}(x)$, are exactly given by a parabolic function of the strike, x:

$$\widehat{\sigma}^{\mathrm{mkt}}(x) = \zeta_0 + \zeta_1 x + \zeta_2 x^2 \tag{13.1}$$

$$\widehat{\sigma}^{\mathrm{SABR}}(x) = k_0 + k_1(x - \widetilde{x}_1) + k_2 (x - \widetilde{x}_2)^2 \tag{13.2}$$

with ζ_0, ζ_1 and ζ_2 market-determined parameters. (It is always possible to find an appropriate range of strikes over which this approximation is good.) To a very good degree of accuracy, the SABR quantities $\sigma(0)$, ρ and ν control the level (k_0), the slope (k_1) and the curvature (k_2) of the model smile, respectively – see Equation (15.12). The SABR model, however, also prescribes both the tilt point for the slope ($\widetilde{x}_1$) and the location of the minimum of the parabola ($\widetilde{x}_2$) – as shown again in Equation (15.12). Needless to say, one can always fit the parabolic market smile by choosing

$$k_0^{\mathrm{fit}} = \zeta_0 + (\zeta_1 + 2\zeta_2\widetilde{x}_2)\,\widetilde{x}_1 - \widetilde{x}_2^2\zeta_2 \tag{13.3}$$

$$k_1^{\mathrm{fit}} = \zeta_1 + 2\zeta_2\widetilde{x}_2 \tag{13.4}$$

$$k_2^{\mathrm{fit}} = \zeta_2 \tag{13.5}$$

However, there is in general no guarantee that, once this is done, the fitted quantities k_0^{fit}, k_1^{fit} and k_2^{fit} will retain the 'physical' interpretation of level of the volatility, of correlation between the volatility and the swap rate and of volatility of volatility. In particular, there is no guarantee that a naive best fit to market prices will locate the pivot point of the tilt and the inflection point of the curvature where the SABR model with the *statistically determined* ρ and ν would. But if they did, the model would indeed be 'well specified'.

Fortunately, the analysis above shows that the fitted model parameters turn out to be remarkably close to their statistically determined ('physical') values. It would be interesting to explore how much worse the fit would be if, instead of leaving it totally unconstrained, one introduced a Bayesian type of estimation, with the prior given by the empirically determined correlation and volatility of volatility and the likelihood function based on market information. We leave this topic for a separate investigation.

In order to see to what extent the small discrepancies observed above can impact in practice the hedging performance we move to the second set of tests.

---

[1] When we speak of 'smile' in this section we mean the whole set of implied volatilities, $\widehat{\sigma}(x)$.

Results for Set of Tests #2. For selected swaptions, we compared the actual changes, $\Delta C_K^T(t_i; \text{real})$, in swaption prices for a given strike, K, with the model-predicted changes in swaption prices, $\Delta C_K^T(t_i; \text{pred})$. The predicted changes in prices were calculated as follows:

$$\Delta C_K^T(t_i; \text{pred}) = \frac{\partial C_K^T}{\partial f} \Delta f(t_i) + \frac{\partial C_K^T}{\partial \sigma} \Delta \sigma(t_i | \boldsymbol{\theta}_{i-1}) \tag{13.6}$$

(The notation $\Delta \sigma(t_i | \boldsymbol{\theta}_{i-1})$ stresses that the volatility is refitted, but keeping the parameters at their t_{i-1} values.) We note that, by examining as we do below the performance of the test for different degrees of at-the-moneyness, we test how well one can offset using the model the volatility exposure at one strike with the volatility exposure at another strike for the same expiry (same-expiry vega hedging).

The regression of the predicted against observed changes in prices shows for all swaptions *and across all strikes* a very strong linear relationship, with slope virtually identical to 1, intercept almost exactly zero, and R^2 ranging from 0.952 to 0.996. See, e.g., Figure 13.1(a, b).

These findings should be compared with the poor performance of the Black model, discussed in Rebonato (2003). These tests indicate that changes in the state variables of the SABR model correctly account for the bulk of the observed changes in prices and therefore provide on average correct and unbiased 'hedge ratios'.

We want to focus more on the ability of the SABR model to suggest the correct same-expiry vega hedge. We do this because the good results of the test above have been obtained using changes in *prices*, which are naturally dominated to first order by changes in forward rates. If we look at implied volatilities instead, the first-order dependence on the forward rate disappears, and we can focus on vega hedging more clearly. Specifically, we would like to know whether the implied volatilities change in reality as a function of changes in forward rates and in 'true' volatility as the SABR model predicts. To estimate the model changes in implied volatility we used the expression

$$\Delta \widehat{\sigma}_K^T(t_i; \text{pred}) = \frac{\partial \widehat{\sigma}_K^T}{\partial f} \Delta f(t_i) + \frac{\partial \widehat{\sigma}_K^T}{\partial \sigma} \Delta \sigma(t_i | \boldsymbol{\theta}_{i-1}) \tag{13.7}$$

where the terms $\frac{\partial \widehat{\sigma}_K^T}{\partial f}$ and $\frac{\partial \widehat{\sigma}_K^T}{\partial f}$ were obtained from the Hagan formula, $\Delta f(t_i)$ was taken as market-given, $\Delta \sigma(t_i | \boldsymbol{\theta}_{i-1})$ was estimated as explained above, and the SABR parameters (β, ν and ρ) were kept at their t_{i-1} level. Figure 13.2(a–c) shows the excellent quality of a linear regression of predicted against observed implied volatilities: the slope of the regression is very close to 1 and the R^2 is very high for all swaptions (average 0.95, min 0.89, max 0.99).

Equation (13.7) shows that the model change in implied volatility comes from two contributions, but cannot tell us anything about their relative importance. To understand better what drives these correct predictions we look at the regression of the changes in realized implied volatilities versus the changes in predicted implied volatilities obtained using the changes in forward rates only. More precisely, we keep the volatility at its t_{i-1}

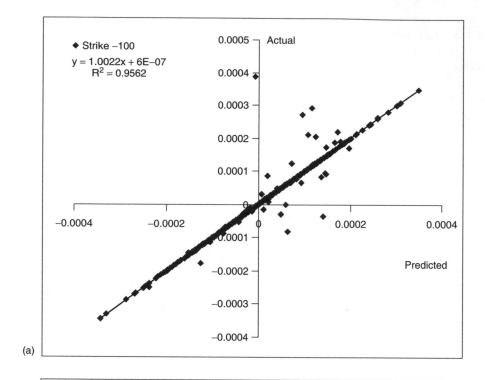

(a)

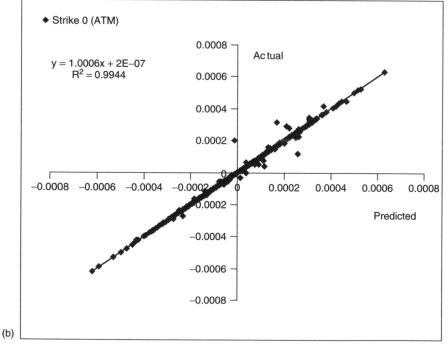

(b)

Figure 13.1   Predicted and observed changes in prices for the 10y × 10y swaption: (a) strike ATM −100 bp; (b) strike ATM.

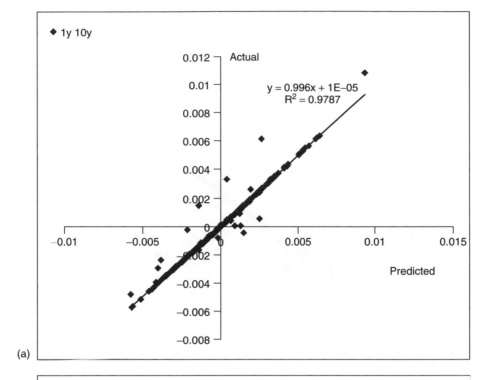

(a)

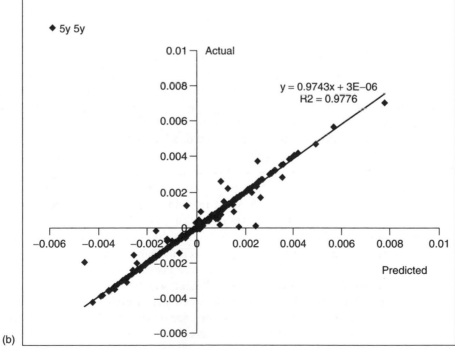

(b)

Figure 13.2   Actual and predicted changes in implied volatility: (a) $1y \times 10y$; (b) $5y \times 5y$; (c) $10y \times 10y$.

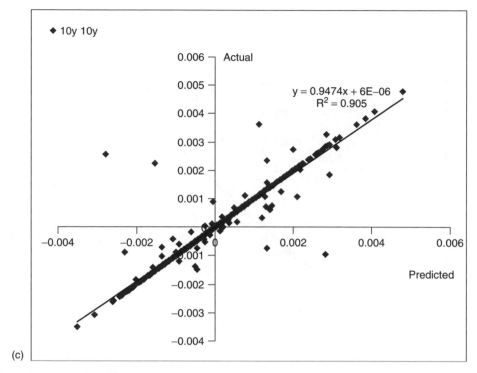

Figure 13.2   (*continued*)

level, we use the market change in forward rate as an input to the Hagan formula, and we convert the resultant change in price into a change in implied volatility. We find that the dependence between the forward-rate-predicted and experienced implied volatility has now all but disappeared. See Figure 13.3(a, b). To be clear: we are not saying here that a change in forward rate has no effect on the implied volatility. What we show is that if the change in forward rate is translated into a change in price and this into a change in implied volatility, then there is virtually no correlation between this quantity and market changes in implied volatility.

What is happening? True market changes in implied volatility are affected both by changes in 'true' volatility and in the forward rate. In order to see whether the SABR model predicts the component of this market change in line with reality we would like to have a 'controlled experiment': a number of days when the 'true' volatility did not change at all, but the forward rate did change. If we observed in reality many such days we could easily see the impact of changes in the forward rate also on the implied volatility. We approximate this controlled experiment in the following way.

Let's for the moment neglect the difference between state variables and parameters, and simply consider the Hagan formula as a function of four quantities, f, σ, ν and ρ.[2] To first order, and to the extent that the SABR model always perfectly fits the market, we can write

---

[2]The exponent β is always kept at 0.5.

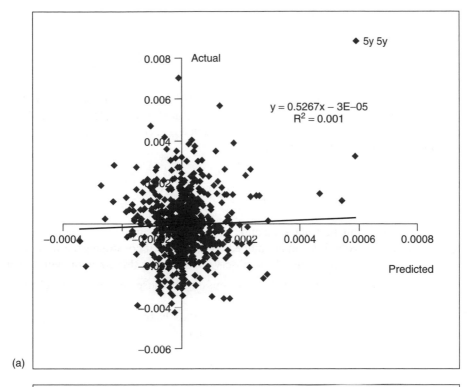

(a)

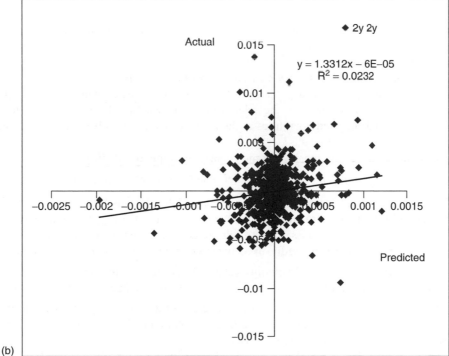

(b)

Figure 13.3   Regression of changes in predicted implied volatilities obtained using the change in forward rates only: (a) 5y × 5y; (b) 2y × 2y.

for the true realized change in implied volatility

$$\Delta \widehat{\sigma}_K^T(t_i; \text{real}) = \frac{\partial \widehat{\sigma}_K^T}{\partial f} \Delta f(t_i) + \frac{\partial \widehat{\sigma}_K^T}{\partial \sigma} \Delta \sigma_i + \frac{\partial \widehat{\sigma}_K^T}{\partial f} \Delta \nu_i + \frac{\partial \widehat{\sigma}_K^T}{\partial f} \Delta \rho_i \qquad (13.8)$$

We now define 'virtual' market changes in implied volatility. These 'virtual' market changes differ from true market changes because they are calculated from the Hagan formula using the true observed changes in forward rate and parameters, $\Delta f(t_i)$, $\Delta \nu(t_i)$ and $\Delta \rho(t_i)$, *but keeping the volatility at its t_{i-1} level*. Therefore:

$$\Delta \widehat{\sigma}_K^T(t_i; \text{virtual}) = \frac{\partial \widehat{\sigma}_K^T}{\partial f} \Delta f(t_i) + \frac{\partial \widehat{\sigma}_K^T}{\partial f} \Delta \nu_i + \frac{\partial \widehat{\sigma}_K^T}{\partial f} \Delta \rho_i \qquad (13.9)$$

This virtual change is our best approximation of what the change in the implied volatility would have been if the volatility had not moved: in this sense it constitutes our best proxy of the controlled experiment we would like to observe. Comparing this equation with Equation (13.7), note that the term $\frac{\partial \widehat{\sigma}_K^T}{\partial \sigma} \Delta \sigma(t_i | \boldsymbol{\theta}_{i-1})$ is missing because in the virtual change the volatility remains fixed.

Finally, the predicted changes in implied volatilities were calculated inputting in the Hagan formula the true change in forward rate $\Delta f(t_i)$:

$$\Delta \widehat{\sigma}_K^T(t_i; \text{pred}) = \frac{\partial \widehat{\sigma}_K^T}{\partial f} \Delta f(t_i) \qquad (13.10)$$

Note that, in calculating these predicted changes, we are not allowing the parameters to change.

With these definitions, we can finally estimate and compare 'virtual' and predicted market changes in implied volatilities *when only the forward rate changes*.

When prediction and virtual reality (our 'controlled experiment') are compared, Figure 13.4(a–d) now shows that the relationship between the changes in predicted and experienced (virtual) implied volatilities as the forward rate changes becomes much clearer. How do we interpret these results?

First of all what we find means that the changes in implied volatility caused by changes in forward rates, $\frac{\partial \widehat{\sigma}_K^T}{\partial f} \Delta f(t_i)$, are much smaller than the changes in implied volatilities coming from $\frac{\partial \widehat{\sigma}_K^T}{\partial \sigma} \Delta \sigma_i$. What we were seeing in Figure 13.3(a, b) was therefore a weak signal totally masked by a much stronger effect. Changes in true volatility, however, are not the only sources of 'noise' as far as forward-rate-induced changes in implied volatilities are concerned: in reality, the supposedly fixed parameters change as well. The second observation is that changes in implied volatility caused by changes in forward rates, $\frac{\partial \widehat{\sigma}_K^T}{\partial f} \Delta f(t_i)$, are sufficiently more significant than the 'noise' given by changes in parameters, i.e., by the terms $\frac{\partial \widehat{\sigma}_K^T}{\partial f} \Delta \nu_i$ and $\frac{\partial \widehat{\sigma}_K^T}{\partial f} \Delta \rho_i$ (which should be zero for a perfectly specified model) to still give a clearly detectable signal. These findings, as Figure 13.4(a–d) shows, are robust across expiries and levels of at-the-moneyness.

We have shown that the SABR model is close to being correctly specified and that it predicts on average a correct 'delta' and 'vega'. It offers the ability to offset effectively the

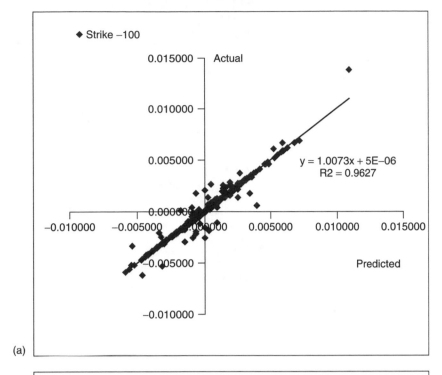

(a)

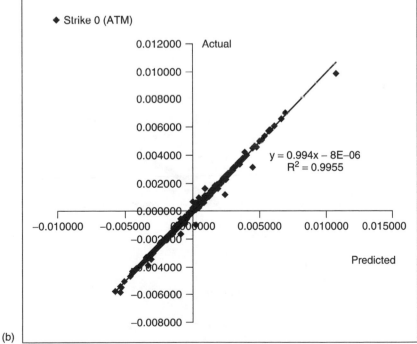

(b)

Figure 13.4   Comparison with (virtual) reality of model changes in implied volatility when only the forward rate changes: (a) 1y × 10y, Strike = ATM −100 bp; (b) 1y × 10y, Strike = ATM; (c) 10y × 10y, Strike = ATM −100 bp; (d) 10y × 10y, Strike = ATM.

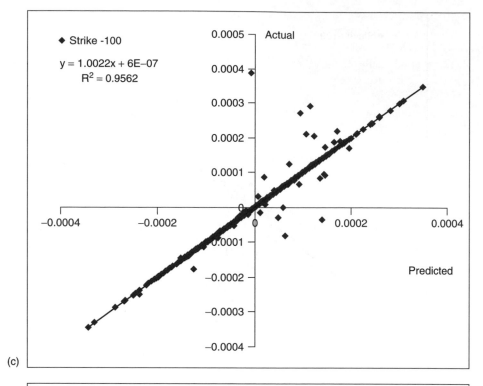

(c)

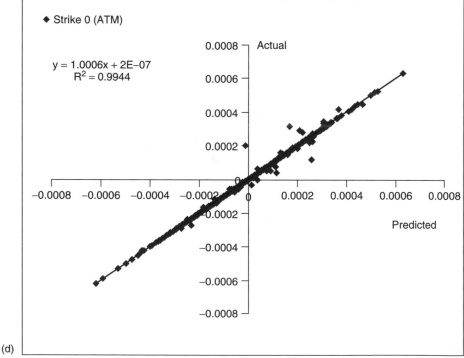

(d)

Figure 13.4   (*continued*)

volatility exposure arising for the same expiry across different strikes. These results give us confidence that the SABR model can be a good building block for our dynamic extension of the LMM-SABR model.

The very good results of the regression tests should not be interpreted as an indication that the model is 'close to perfect'. Ultimately, SABR is a purely diffusive model, and it cannot accommodate jumps either in forward rates or in volatilities. These are rare, but can be economically important. Their impact on a hedging strategy depends on the time to expiry and level of moneyness of the option when the jump occurs (essentially, on the gamma and 'vanna' of the option). This is probably why, despite the bias between statistically realized and model-implied volatility discussed in Chapter 9, selling volatility is not a 'free lunch'. So, for most days the SABR model appears well specified and the model parameters change very little. When the rare 'jumps' (unaccounted for by the model) occur, the SABR parameters have to be changed significantly. This is still a very significant improvement on the Black model or on the local-volatility models, which are clearly mis-specified even on 'normal' days.

13.4 Hedging Results for the LMM-SABR Model

Recall that now we try to predict the changes in swaption prices making use only of caplet information, i.e., *by calibrating the LMM-SABR model only to caplets*. Since caplets are a very special subset of swaptions, Test Set #3 is probably the toughest self-consistency test to which the model can be put. For instance, the model parameters used for the hedging tests could have been calibrated by a least-square fit to the whole swaption matrix. This would have guaranteed almost by construction better results for the test. Nonetheless, we prefer a demanding test in order to see to what extent the model can be 'stretched'.

Since the transformation from caplet to swaption volatilities depends on the *terminal* (as opposed to instantaneous) decorrelation among forward rates, and this mainly depends on the time dependence of the volatility functions (see Rebonato (2006) and the discussion of Figure 13.6 below), we are ultimately testing the functions $g(\cdot)$ and $h(\cdot)$, which are the crucial ingredients of the LMM-SABR extension by Rebonato (2007b).

Results for Set of Tests #3. The predicted and realized ATM volatilities of a 5y × 5y swaption are shown in Figure 13.5, which also displays the ATM volatility for two of the caplets to which the volatility curve had been fitted. The quality of the prediction is high, especially considering that the volatilities of the caplets that were used in obtaining the 5y × 5y swaption volatility are very different between themselves, and from the volatility of the target swaption (see Figures 13.5, 13.7 and 13.8). Yet the model, which only 'knows' about caplets, is able to predict an almost correct value for the ATM swaption volatility.

A regression of the model-predicted versus realized ATM volatilities over the whole period gives a correlation of 77%. This overall value masks two very different regimes: a period of 'normal' market conditions (approximately up to August 2007) and the exceptionally excited period that followed. The predictive power of the model is much better during the normal period (correlation of 85%). This is no surprise, and is no specific shortcoming of this particular model: no model with time-homogeneous or time-dependent (deterministic or stochastic) volatility functions can reproduce these features. As explained in Rebonato (2006) and in Section 4.8, the whole swaption matrix cannot be accounted for by any model (with deterministic or stochastic volatility) that does not 'know' that the current

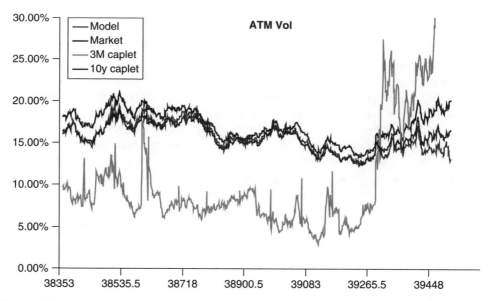

Figure 13.5 Predicted and realized ATM volatility 5y × 5y swaption, together with 3m and 10y caplets used as inputs.

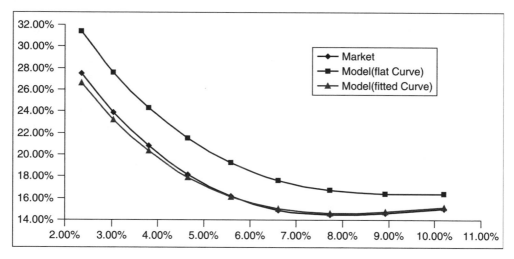

Figure 13.6 Prediction of the 5y × 5y swaption implied volatility curve for all strikes using only caplets as inputs.

excited period (which influences the prices of the short-dated options) will eventually subside, and the longer-dated options will therefore experience a volatility not dissimilar to the long-term volatility level.[3] To account for this feature a model must 'know' about the possibility of clusters of high volatility. Rebonato and White (2008) show that a convincing way to model this effect is by means of a two-state Markov-chain process for the volatility.

---

[3] Indeed Rebonato's (2006) paper was subtitled 'Why neither time homogeneity nor time dependence will do.'

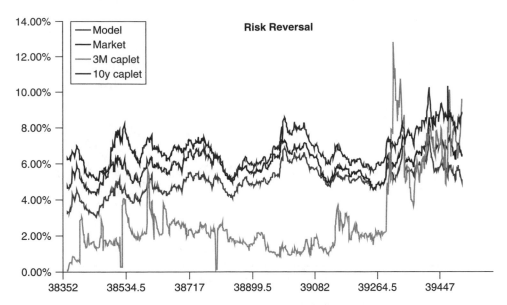

Figure 13.7 Prediction of the changes in risk reversal: 5y × 5y swaption.

There are, of course, other alternatives. Unfortunately, all these more complex models are computationally more expensive and more difficult to calibrate.

With the present version of the LMM-SABR model, during the 'normal' period the quality of the prediction of the whole smile (all strikes) for the 5y × 5y swaption *using only information from caplets* can be as high as shown in Figure 13.7. We stress that the volatility functions $g(\cdot)$ and $h(\cdot)$ were *not* fitted to this particular swaption.

We finally looked at the ability of the LMM-SABR model to predict changes in the risk reversal and strangle for the 5y × 5y swaption, again making use only of caplet information. See Figures 13.7 and 13.8. The quality of the prediction is again impressive, especially if one notes how different the strangles and risk reversals were in the period considered for the target swaption and for the caplets about which the model knows. (For instance, the strangle for the 10y caplet was sometimes 15 times as large as the strangle for the 3m caplet.) Even away from the at-the-money level, the quality of the translation from caplet behaviour to swaption behaviour effected by the LMM-SABR – and by the functions $g(\cdot)$ and $h(\cdot)$ in particular – is impressive.

13.5 Conclusions

We have examined the hedging performance of the SABR and of the LMM-SABR models by using the information from market data.

The results for the SABR model indicate that it is as close to a well-specified model as one can possibly expect for a purely diffusive pricing model that must retain analytical tractability. The predictive power of the model given the observed changes in the underlying state variables was found to be very high. An explanation was provided for the small systematic bias between the 'implied' and the statistically estimated values for the model parameters (correlation and volatility of volatility) observed in Chapter 9.

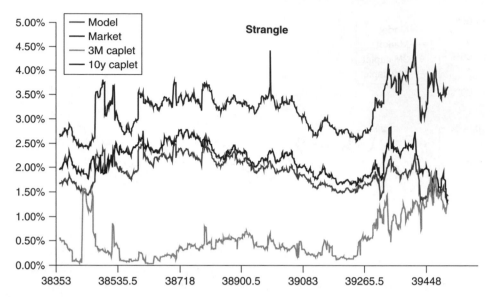

Figure 13.8   Prediction of the changes in strangle: 5y × 5y swaption.

For the LMM-SABR model we put it to a very tough test, i.e., we tried to predict changes in the swaption smile in the centre of the swaption matrix (the 5y × 5y swaption) after calibrating the model only to caplet prices. (Few traders would in practice try to hedge such a swaption with caplets.) Despite this, the results were good, at least during normal market conditions. The predicted levels of the ATM volatility, risk reversal and strangle were in fair-to-good agreement with the observed values, and the same applied to changes in the same quantities. During the period of exceptional turbulence of early 2008, the predictions of the model become understandably poorer, but no diffusive model with a single regime of volatility can be expected to handle such circumstances.

Given its ease of calibration, the availability of closed-form approximation for swaption prices, its ability to produce realistic future smiles and the overall good quality of its hedging performance even under a very severe test, the LMM-SABR model therefore appears to offer a simple and useful dynamic extension of the SABR model.

Chapter 14

Hedging the Correlation Structure

14.1 The Intuition Behind the Problem

Shocking the super-matrix

$$P = \begin{bmatrix} \rho & R \\ R^\dagger & r \end{bmatrix} \tag{14.1}$$

allows the capture and the hedging of much richer and subtler features of correlation risk than shocking the sub-matrix ρ in the context of the deterministic-volatility LMM. In order to capture the essence of the various dependencies, we use in this chapter the simplest type of correlation structure for the matrices ρ and r:

$$\rho_{ij} = \exp\left[-\beta \left|T_i - T_j\right|\right] \tag{14.2}$$

$$r_{ij} = \exp\left[-\gamma \left|T_i - T_j\right|\right] \tag{14.3}$$

$$R_{ij} = \text{sign}(R_{ii})\sqrt{|R_{ii}R_{jj}|}\exp\left[-\lambda_A \left(T_i - T_j\right)^+ - \lambda_B \left(T_j - T_i\right)^+\right] \tag{14.4}$$

The generalization to richer, and more satisfactory, forms of correlation, such as the Doust correlation described at length in Chapter 2 (see Section 2.6), is conceptually straightforward.

Let's start from the forward-rate/forward-rate block. Here the intuition from the deterministic-volatility case still applies, but we have to distinguish carefully between 'weighted-average-like' products (called 'swaption-like' products, or simply swaptions[1]

---

[1] A swap rate is (almost) given by a linear combination of the underlying forward rates – we say 'almost' because the weights display a weak dependence on the forward rates themselves. An option on a swap rate is therefore akin to an option on a weighted average of forward rates.

for brevity in the following) and spread-like products. For 'swaption-like' products, the lower the correlation among the forward rates, the lower the volatility of the weighted average (the 'swap rate' in the following). This makes perfect sense: if the correlation is low, when a particular forward rate moves, say, up, another forward rate can perfectly well be moving down, producing a small net effect on the 'swap rate' and muting the volatility of the latter. However, this effect is rather small for the range of correlations typically found among forward rates. Effective decorrelation is much more effectively obtained with a time-dependent volatility for forward rates. See the discussion in Chapter 2, and in Rebonato (2002). Anyhow, the sensitivity of a swaption price to an increase in overall correlation (a *decrease* in β) is clear: the level of the swap rate volatility should increase.

As for spread options, the opposite reasoning is at play: if the correlation is high, two forward rates must move almost in lock-step (the more so, the more their volatility is similar), their difference (the spread) moves very little, and therefore the spread volatility is low. So, an increase in overall correlation (a *decrease* in β) should bring about a decrease in the volatility of the spread. We noted in Chapter 10 (Section 10.4.1) that the effect of the instantaneous correlation is much bigger for spread options than for swaption-like options.

Let's now move to the block r. Consider the case when the correlation between forward rates is low (γ is high). Then, as the volatility of a forward rate increases, the volatility of another forward rate may very well be decreasing. Intuitively, this means that as a net result the volatility of the volatility of the swap rate may change relatively little. As the volatility of volatility of the swap rate is linked to the curvature of the swaption smile, a low correlation among volatilities (a high γ) means a low volatility of volatility for the swap rate and a low curvature for the swap-rate smile. If we look at Equation (6.29) in Chapter 6 (reported below for ease of reference), we can get direct confirmation of this intuition:

$$ V = \frac{1}{\Sigma_0 T} \sqrt{ 2 \sum_{i,j} \left(\rho_{ij} r_{ij} W_i^0 W_j^0 k_0^i k_0^j \int_0^T g^i g^j \widehat{h}_{ij}(t)^2 t\, dt \right) } \qquad (14.5) $$

If we rehearse the intuitive argument presented in Section 6.5, however, we can see that the volatility of volatility of the swap rate (and hence the curvature of the smile) will also depend on the correlation among forward rates.

The first-order analysis of the R block is similarly simple. First of all we can look at what happens when, *ceteris paribus*, the diagonal elements, R_{ii}, all increase in lock-step. This bit is easy: the swap rate becomes more negatively correlated with its own volatility, and the slope of the smile increases. More interesting is what happens when the diagonal elements, R_{ii}, remain the same and all the other correlations increase or decrease. Suppose that the non-diagonal elements go to zero. Then, when the ith forward rate moves up the jth volatility is just as likely to go up or down. As the volatility of volatility of the swap rate is to first order influenced by what the volatilities of the forward rates do, this particular deformation would produce, at the margin, an increase in the swap rate level and either an increase or a decrease in the swap rate volatility. So, the correlation between the swap rate and its own volatility should decrease as the correlation of the off-diagonal elements of R moves towards zero (i.e., as λ increases). The final result of all this is that the slope of the swaption smile should become higher when the elements of R become more negative.

So, to first order, our intuition suggests the following sensitivities:

1. the forward-rate/forward-rate correlation, ρ (the exponent β), affects the *level* of the swaption smile;

2. the forward-rate/volatility block, R (the exponent λ), affects the slope of the swaption smile;

3. the volatility/volatility correlation, r (the exponent γ), affects the curvature of the swaption smile.

By looking at the formulae for the volatility, the initial value of the swap rate and the correlation between the swap rate and its own volatility, however, one can see that as we go past first-order effects the parametrized correlation functions affect these quantities in a rather complex way. The next section will therefore show to what extent actual empirical analysis confirms the qualitative arguments presented above.

Methodologically, we have used in this section a very crude parametrization for the various correlation blocks, because we want to highlight the broad qualitative features. This analysis would not directly apply to CMS spread options, but, *mutatis mutandis*, the philosophy behind the hedging approach to correlation would not change: for effective hedging we want to express the sensitivity of both complex and hedging instruments to the same small number of correlation parameters, each endowed with a clear intuitive meaning. For real-life applications, the Doust model with the Rebonato and McKay (2008) parametrization offers, in our opinion, a good compromise between realism of description and parsimony.

The results below refer to four fundamental types of swaptions:

1. short expiries into short tails (1y × 2y)

2. short expiries into long tails (1y × 10y)

3. long expiries into short tails (10y × 2y)

4. long expiries into long tails (10y × 10y)

for strikes ranging from -150 bp to $+150$ bp around the at-the-money strike. We refer to these four swaptions in the following as our reference swaptions.

14.2 Hedging the Forward-Rate Block

For the four reference swaptions above we look at the changes in the Black implied volatilities as the correlation coefficient β is moved from 0 to 0.1 (decreasing correlation).

For all swaptions and for all strikes we observe a decrease in implied volatility. For a given reference swaption, the change in implied volatility across strikes is slow in the at-the-money region, and becomes more pronounced for the in- and out-of-the-money strikes. See Figures 14.1 to 14.3.

These variations are noticeable, but there are much larger differences across swaption types. As the de-correlation coefficient β is increased from 0 to 0.1, the long-tail swaptions display a decrease in implied volatility between 120 bp and 160 bp, while the short-tail swaptions only decrease by less than 20 bp. See Figures 14.2 and 14.3.

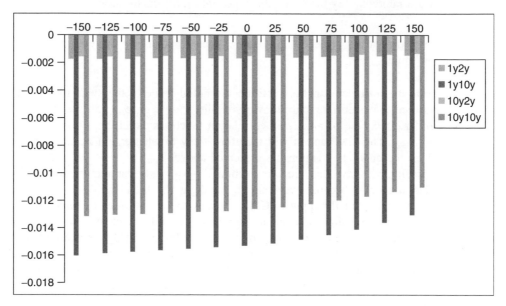

Figure 14.1   Changes in the Black implied volatilities as the correlation coefficient β is moved from 0 to 0.1.

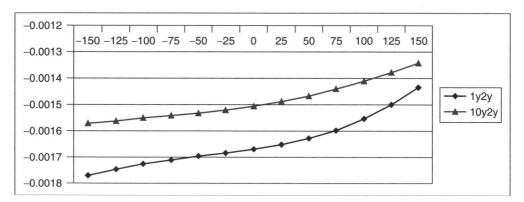

Figure 14.2   Changes in the Black implied volatilities as the correlation coefficient β is moved from 0 to 0.1 – expiries into short tails.

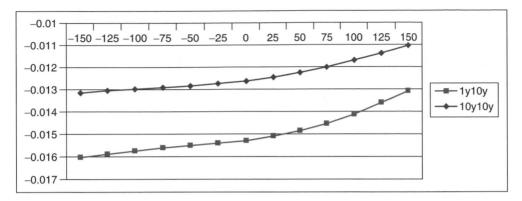

Figure 14.3   Changes in the Black implied volatilities as the correlation coefficient β is moved from 0 to 0.1 – expiries into long tails.

For the same change in β, the change in implied volatility as a function of the option expiry is much more muted. For the same length of the swap tail (2 years or 10 years in our study), the effect of the expiry is stronger for the shorter expiry.

Finally, we note that the magnitude of the decrease in implied volatility scales very well with the duration of the underlying swaps.

14.3   Hedging the Volatility-Rate Block

We proceed as above, but now we move the correlation parameter γ from 0 to 0.1 – i.e., we decrease the correlation among forward-rate volatilities.

The picture is now more complex. See Figures 14.4 to 14.6. Let's start from the similarities: the length of the underlying swap is still the dominant factor in determining the change in implied volatility for the four reference swaps, with the change in long tails still approximately scaling with the duration of the underlying swap.

The similarities, however, stop here. First of all, the magnitude of the effect (the change in implied volatilities) is somewhat smaller (assuming that one can compare the effect of a 0.1 change in β and in γ). Within this more limited range of variability, there are now very pronounced changes in implied volatilities as a function of strike. Overall, around the at-the-money level the effect is very muted. The long tails display the most dramatic behaviour, with the deeply in-the-money and out-of-the-money wings displaying the largest decreases.

The behaviour is therefore indeed of a change in the *curvature* of the smile of the sign predicted in the introductory considerations presented above, but our intuition failed to predict the whole story. We notice, in fact, that the point of inflection of the change in curvature (in strike space) is roughly constant across reference swaptions and is not at the money, but located at approximately 75 bp in the money. See Figures 14.5 and 14.6. The reason why the at-the-money change is so small is therefore that the change in γ gives rise to a small rigid shift (upwards) of the implied volatilities and a larger inflection with a pivot point at about 75 bp in the money.

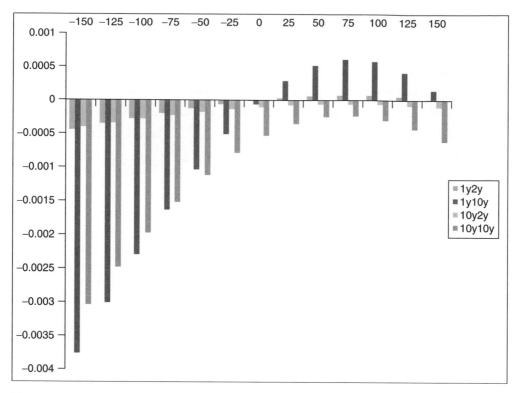

Figure 14.4   Changes in the Black implied volatilities as the correlation parameter γ is moved from 0 to 0.1.

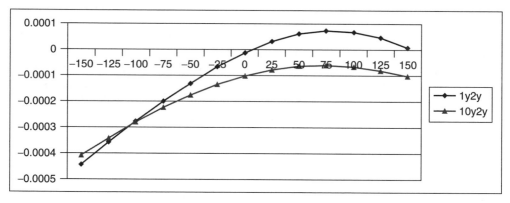

Figure 14.5   Changes in the Black implied volatilities as the correlation parameter γ is moved from 0 to 0.1 – expiries into short tails.

Hedging these subtle features is therefore rather complex, and even the sign of the change in implied volatility depends on a rather delicate balance of factors (shift and change in curvature). Luckily, for the same degree of decorrelation among volatilities as among forward rates (a 0.1 change in the decay constant), the effect is three to 10 times smaller than for a same-size change in β.

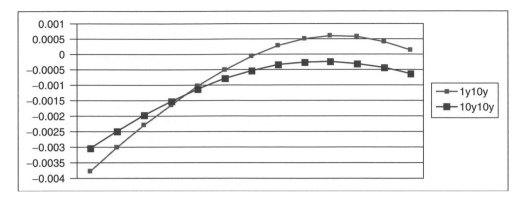

Figure 14.6 Changes in the Black implied volatilities as the correlation parameter γ is moved from 0 to 0.1 – expiries into long tails.

14.4 Hedging the Forward-Rate/Volatility Block

In this case there are few surprises. As λ_A and λ_B go from 0 to 0.1, the main effect is indeed a tilt in the smile. The dominant variable is again the length of the underlying swap, but the expiry now plays a bigger role than observed for changes in β and γ. See Figures 14.7 to 14.9. Interestingly enough, both for short and long tails short expiries display a more pronounced tilt (roughly twice as large as long expiries) – see Figures 14.8 and 14.9.

For out-of-the-money swaptions the magnitude of the change in swaption price for a 0.1 change in λ (which affects the **R** block) can be large (about 50 bp), making the magnitude of the effect intermediate between changes of the same magnitude in β and γ. Needless to say, it is difficult to say whether we are truly comparing like with like, i.e., whether a 0.1 change in, say, the β coefficient is truly as 'big' as a 0.1 change in γ or λ.

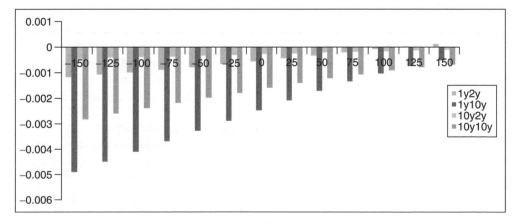

Figure 14.7 Changes in the Black implied volatilities as the correlation parameter λ is moved from 0 to 0.1.

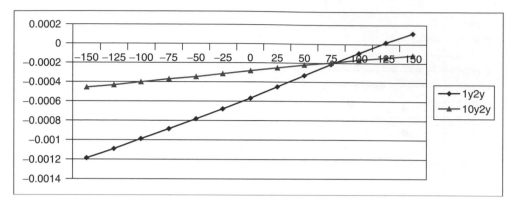

Figure 14.8   Changes in the Black implied volatilities as the correlation parameter λ is moved from 0 to 0.1 – expiries into short tails.

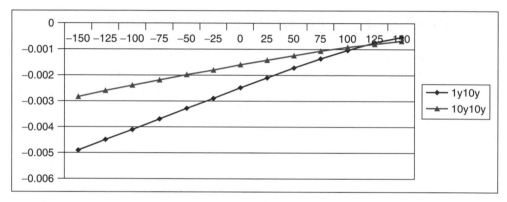

Figure 14.9   Changes in the Black implied volatilities as the correlation parameter λ is moved from 0 to 0.1 – expiries into long tails.

14.5   Final Considerations

The qualitative and quantitative descriptions of the sensitivity of swaptions to the various blocks of the correlation matrix have obvious relevance for hedging, as swaptions of various strikes are the plain-vanilla building blocks of any hedging strategy. They are also fundamental for scenario hedging, i.e., for hedging against those changes in parameters or state variables our model does not know about. Scenario hedging, i.e., hedging under conditions of market stress, is indeed the topic of the next chapter.

One instance of scenario hedging is hedging against so-called changes in risk-reversal risk, i.e., changes in the slope of the smile. Market experience has shown that these changes tend to occur in situations of market stress, and that, when this happens, they can be orders of magnitude larger than the change in risk reversals observed from one 'normal' trading day to the next.

The ability to scenario-hedge effectively against these market dislocations is therefore predicated upon the ability

1. to identify recurring modes of deformation of the smile surface associated with (different types of) market turmoil;

2. to identify which plain-vanilla instruments are more responsive to these modes of deformation (and hence lend themselves readily to acting as effective hedges);

3. to identify the underlying variables and parameters of a given model that can produce such changes in the plain-vanilla hedges;

4. to quantify the changes in the value of the hedges corresponding to these changes in the model variables and parameters;

5. to 'guesstimate' (at least approximately) how long it will take for the conditions of market turmoil to subside (days? weeks? months?).

In this chapter we have laid the groundwork for this enterprise, with particular emphasis on points 2, 3 and 4. The next chapter will show how to combine this information with the 'guesstimate' in point 5 in order to put in place what we call 'survival hedging'.

Chapter 15

Hedging in Conditions of Market Stress

When your only tool is a hammer, every problem begins to look like a nail.

Abraham Maslow, warning us not to use perfect replication as a hedging strategy when there is no good reason to do so.

15.1 Statement of the Problem

We explained in Chapter 4 (see Section 4.8) how a judiciously chosen, non-time-homogeneous volatility can effectively mimic the effects of a two-state Markov-chain model when markets are in an excited state.

In this chapter we want to make use of this insight in order to put in place what we call 'survival hedging', i.e., a set of transactions that can protect the value of a complex derivatives book in times of market turmoil. Using the terminology of Chapter 11, this is the most extreme case of out-of-model hedging (see Section 11.2). Yet, it is arguably the most important type of hedging. This is because, when market moves are 'normal', many reasonable hedging strategies perform adequately well, at least as long as some central features of the underlying process (e.g., its realized quadratic variation) are correctly captured. See the detailed discussion of this point in Chapter 3 of Rebonato (2004a). (The explanation for this feature, which is at the heart of the existence of a successful multi-trillion derivatives industry, is the 'robustness' of Black-like models – see Bouchaud and Potters (2000), Section 4.4, for a discussion.)

What the trader really needs is therefore some help on how to structure her portfolio under those market conditions that her model doesn't even know can exist – and cannot, therefore, offer hedges against. This is where Hamlet's warning to Horatio that opens Chapter 11 springs to mind.

The only hope of success in this enterprise is the discovery of some regularities in the changes in the shape of the smile surface at the onset of turbulence. Luckily, such regularities do exist, as shown in Figures 15.1 to 15.5. The first two figures clearly display the self-similarity of the swaption matrix over time during normal market periods

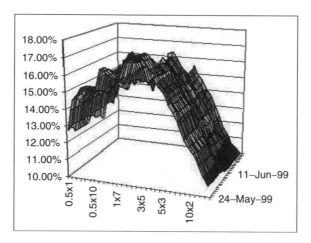

Figure 15.1   Swaption prices during the 24-May-99 to 29-June-99 period.

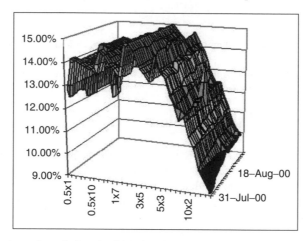

Figure 15.2   Swaption prices during the 31-Jul-2000 to 5-Sep-2000 period.

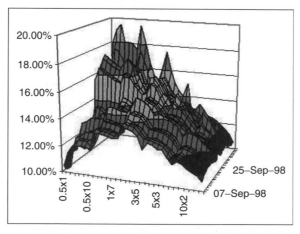

Figure 15.3   Swaption prices during the 7-Sept-98 to 13-Oct-98 period (LTCM period).

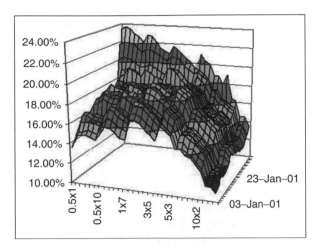

Figure 15.4 Swaption prices during the 3-Jan-2001 to 8-Feb-2001 period (Fed cuts).

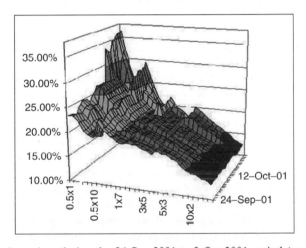

Figure 15.5 Swaption prices during the 24-Sep-2001 to 3-Oct-2001 period (post Sept 11).

(see Figures 15.1 and 15.2). Figures 15.3 to 15.5 show how, even in very different situations of market turmoil (the 1998 LTCM crisis, the unexpected rate cuts by the Fed in early 2001 and the aftermath of the 9/11 events), strong regularities become apparent in the deformation of the swaption matrix. We almost always notice, for instance, a greater increase in implied volatilities for swaptions of short-dated over long-dated expiries and, for the same swaption expiry, a greater increase in implied volatilities of short- over long-swap tails. Insofar as swaption volatilities are concerned, these are the 'fingerprints' of the onset of market turmoil. See Rebonato (2006), Rebonato and White (2008), Rebonato and Joshi (2002) for a fuller discussion.

15.2 The Volatility Function

For ease of reference let's briefly recall the essence of the approach described in Chapter 4 (see Section 4.8 and *passim*). As with the full Markov model described in White and

Rebonato (2008), we assume that there are two time-homogeneous volatility curves, *normal* and *excited*, given by

$$\sigma_{n,x}(t, T) = \left[a_{n,x} + b_{n,x}(T - t)\right] e^{-c_{n,x}(T-t)} + d_{n,x} \qquad (15.1)$$

To approximate starting in an excited state and decaying to an (absorbing) normal state, we specify the Markov approximation volatility as

$$\sigma(t, T; a_n, b_n, c_n, d_n, a_x, b_x, c_x, d_x, \lambda) = (1 - pe^{-\lambda t})\sigma(t, T; a_n, b_n, c_n, d_n)$$
$$+ pe^{-\lambda t}\sigma(t, T; a_x, b_x, c_x, d_x) \qquad (15.2)$$

See Chapter 4 for a detailed discussion. Here we simply recall that the parameter λ is related to how long we believe the volatility will remain in the excited state and that p gives the probability of being today in the excited state. For the rest of the chapter we will refer to the full parameter set $\{a_n, b_n, c_n, d_n, a_x, b_x, c_x, d_x, \lambda\}$ as $\boldsymbol{\theta}$ and to the 'normal' and 'excited' sets $\{a_n, b_n, c_n, d_n\}$ and $\{a_x, b_x, c_x, d_x\}$ as $\boldsymbol{\theta}^n$ and $\boldsymbol{\theta}^x$, respectively.

15.3   The Case Study

We want to analyse the survival-hedging performance under conditions of market stress. In order not to miss the wood for the trees we concentrate on one, relatively simple, instrument (a trigger swap) as our 'complex portfolio'. A trigger swap comes to life when a short-tenor reference rate (typically, a 3- or 6-month LIBOR rate) resets below or above a certain barrier level. Despite their simplicity, trigger swaps contain *in nuce* many interesting features shared by more complex products: they depend on the (terminal) decorrelation between rates of different maturity (the short-dated trigger rate and the longer-date swap rate of the swap that comes to life); the dependence on the volatility of the trigger rate is complex, because it depends on the location of the trigger rate with respect to the trigger level; they can display digital features. A full discussion of its properties is given in Rebonato (2002). Most importantly, the value of a Bermudan swaption can be closely approximated by the value of a multi-look trigger swaption, with judiciously placed trigger levels. So, survival hedging of a trigger swap can be a useful proxy (or at least a starting point) for survival hedging of a Bermudan book.

We will assume in the following that a historical time series of coefficients for the volatility function has previously been obtained. For simplicity we analyse in this chapter the case when we perform survival hedging only against the changes in at-the-money volatilities (linked to the function $g(\cdot)$). In order to put in place a survival hedge against changes in the shape of the smile as well, the same approach described below can easily be extended to include the function $h(\cdot)$.

We will also assume that we have classified all past trading days as normal or excited. This could be done formally, e.g., using Bayesian techniques such as the Baum–Welch algorithm and the Viterbi identification (see, e.g., Rabiner (1989) or Rebonato and Chen (2008) for an application); or it could be done more heuristically, looking at the changes in shape of the swaption matrix (the 'fingerprints' shown in Figures 15.1 to 15.5).

Once the classification has been done we will have at our disposal four subsets of the original time series of change in the coefficients of the volatility function, i.e., changes for normal-to-normal, for normal-to-excited, for excited-to-excited and for excited-to-normal transitions.

Finally, given the state classification above, we assume that we have established the coefficients of the Markov transition matrix, e.g., the probabilities of moving from one state to another, or of remaining in the same state. (See Hamilton (1994), Rebonato (2002) for a discussion of Markov-chain processes and of transition matrices.)

Consider then a portfolio consisting of one trigger swap and some yet-unspecified amounts, w_i, of N hedging instruments

$$\pi(\boldsymbol{\theta}, p) = T(\boldsymbol{\theta}, p) - \sum_{i=1}^{N} w_i S_i(\boldsymbol{\theta}, p) \tag{15.3}$$

where $T(\boldsymbol{\theta}, p)$ is the price of the trigger swap, and $S_i(\boldsymbol{\theta}, p)$ is the price of the ith hedging instrument. The hedging instruments will typically be caplets (to pick up the dependence of the value of the trigger swap on the short-tenor trigger rate) and swaptions (to pick up the dependence on the quasi-callability).

We want to choose the amounts w_i in such a way as to guarantee that the portfolio remains as close as possible to its value before and after the onset of market turbulence (and, of course, that it does so if no turbulence occurs). *We do not assume that we can predict when the turbulent period will arise*.

15.4 Hedging

The change in the portfolio value from t to $t+1$ is

$$\Delta \pi = \Delta T - \sum_{i=1}^{N} w_i \Delta S_i$$
$$= T(\boldsymbol{\theta}_{t+1}, p_{t+1}) - T(\boldsymbol{\theta}_t, p_t) - \sum_{i=1}^{N} w_i \left[S_i(\boldsymbol{\theta}_{t+1}, p_{t+1}) - S_i(\boldsymbol{\theta}_t, p_t) \right] \tag{15.4}$$

We want to look at this expression in four possible cases, i.e., when from the normal state we move to the excited or remain in the normal state, or when from the excited state we move to the normal or remain in the excited state.

15.4.1 The Normal-to-Normal State Transition

Since we are starting and ending in the normal state, $p_t = p_{t+1} = 0$. Therefore the portfolio only displays dependence on $\boldsymbol{\theta}^n$ (not on p_t), and we can write

$$T(\boldsymbol{\theta}_t, p_t) = T(\boldsymbol{\theta}_t), \qquad S_i(\boldsymbol{\theta}_t) = S_i(\boldsymbol{\theta}_t) \tag{15.5}$$

With this simplified notation, we have

$$\Delta \pi = T(\boldsymbol{\theta}_{t+1}^n) - T(\boldsymbol{\theta}_t^n) - \sum_{i=1}^{N} w_i \left[S_i(\boldsymbol{\theta}_{t+1}^n) - S_i(\boldsymbol{\theta}_t^n) \right] \tag{15.6}$$

since the portfolio only displays dependence on θ^n (not on p_t). Taylor-expanding the prices we have

$$T(\theta_{t+1}^n) = T(\theta_t^n) + \Delta\theta^{nn} \cdot \frac{\partial T}{\partial\theta^n} + \frac{1}{2}(\Delta\theta^{nn})^\dagger \frac{\partial^2 T}{\partial(\theta^n)^2}\Delta\theta^{nn} + \ldots \qquad (15.7)$$

where the notation $\Delta\theta^{nn} = \theta_{t+1}^n - \theta_t^n$ highlights that the changes in coefficients apply to the case when we start at time t in a normal state and arrive at time $t+1$ also in a normal state. A similar expression holds for the N hedging instruments. Keeping only the first-order terms we have

$$\Delta\pi = \Delta\theta^{nn} \cdot \left(\frac{\partial T}{\partial\theta^n} - \sum_{i=1}^N w_i \frac{\partial S_i}{\partial\theta^n}\right) \qquad (15.8)$$

If we define

$$A^{nn} = \frac{\partial S_i}{\partial\theta^n} \qquad (15.9)$$

and

$$b^{nn} = \frac{\partial T}{\partial\theta^n} \qquad (15.10)$$

we can rewrite Equation (15.8) more compactly in vector notation as

$$\Delta\pi = -\Delta\theta^{nn} \cdot (A^{nn}w - b^{nn}) \qquad (15.11)$$

For our particular choice of volatility function, if we just look at the case of persistence in the normal state, the vector θ^n is four-dimensional. In theory, if we had four hedging instruments, we could make $\Delta\pi = 0$ for any value of $\Delta\theta^{nn}$, simply by solving[1] $A^{nn}w = b^{nn}$. However, if we proceeded this way we would be likely to obtain the usual unpleasant feature of many solutions of linear problems, namely, the likely occurrence of very large positive and negative values for the weights (the more so, the closer to singular the matrix to invert). This would give us a mathematically perfect answer, but one unlikely to be executable in the market. This situation would be more likely to be encountered when we deal with the full transition from the normal state to an unknown state (see below), when the number of parameters (and therefore of hedging instruments to obtain a 'perfect solution') increases. What we would like to do instead is therefore to use fewer hedging instruments than degrees of freedom. If we proceed along this route, instead of constructing a deterministic portfolio we can only construct a minimum-variance portfolio in the spirit of what is done in portfolio theory – see also our approach in Section 11.4.3. As we shall see, this will serve our purposes very well.

To accomplish this we consider $\mathbb{E}[\Delta\pi^2]$, which can be calculated as

$$\mathbb{E}[\Delta\pi^2] = (A^{nn}w - b^{nn})^\dagger \Theta^{nn}(A^{nn}w - b^{nn}) \qquad (15.12)$$

---

[1]For non-square A one needs to use Singular Value Decomposition. As we argue below, even for square A this is better since there is no guarantee that A is not close-to-singular.

with

$$\Theta^{nn} = \mathbb{E}[\Delta\theta^{nn}(\Delta\theta^{nn})^\dagger] \tag{15.13}$$

where $x^\dagger$ denotes the transpose of vector x.

Where do we get Θ^{nn} from? It is just the empirical matrix taken from time series data of the changes in the coefficients for the normal-to-normal state transitions – it is in fact $\Omega^{nn} + \mu_{nn}^\dagger\mu_{nn}$, where Ω^{nn} is the covariance matrix of changes in the coefficients for the normal-to-normal days, and μ_{nn} is the vector of means.

As we said, we want to find a minimum-variance portfolio. To do so, we take the derivative of Equation (15.12) with respect to $\mathbf{w}$. Setting this to zero gives us

$$(A^{nn})^\dagger\Theta^{nn}A^{nn}\mathbf{w} = (A^{nn})^\dagger\Theta^{nn}\mathbf{b}^{nn} \tag{15.14}$$

which we can write as

$$A^*\mathbf{w} = \mathbf{b}^* \tag{15.15}$$

with

$$A^* \equiv (A^{nn})^\dagger\Theta^{nn}A^{nn} \tag{15.16}$$

and

$$\mathbf{b}^* \equiv (A^{nn})^\dagger\Theta^{nn}\mathbf{b}^{nn} \tag{15.17}$$

In theory Equation (15.15) can be solved exactly by direct matrix inversion as A^* is a square matrix. Once again, however, we strongly recommend looking for a solution allowing fewer hedging instruments than equations. Singular Value Decomposition (see Press *et al.* (1992)) offers a simple alternative. This will be particularly useful when A^* is close to being singular.

15.4.2 The Normal-to-Excited Transition

We want to follow the same strategy in the case of the normal-to-excited transition. Now the change in the price of the focus instrument (the trigger swap) is given by

$$\begin{aligned}\Delta T &= T(\theta_{t+1}, 1) - T(\theta_t, 0) \\ &\approx T(\theta_t^n, 1) - T(\theta_t^n, 0) + \Delta\theta^{nx}\frac{\partial T(\theta_t^n, 1)}{\partial\theta} \\ &\quad + \frac{1}{2}\Delta\theta^{nx\dagger}\frac{\partial^2 T(\theta_t^n, 1)}{\partial\theta^2}\Delta\theta^{nx} + \dots\end{aligned} \tag{15.18}$$

and similarly for the hedging instruments. Note that now the vector $\Delta\theta^{nx}$ is made up of those changes in coefficients that occur when there is a transition from the normal to the excited state and that the derivatives are taken with respect to the price in the excited state.

Why this is the case can be seen as follows. Consider the price of the trigger swap as a function of the normal coefficients, $\boldsymbol{\theta}^n$, of the excited coefficients, $\boldsymbol{\theta}^x$, and of the probability p (we neglect for the moment the dependence on λ, to which the same reasoning applies). Then we have

$$T = T\left(\boldsymbol{\theta}^n, \boldsymbol{\theta}^x, p\right) \tag{15.19}$$

In the transition from normal to excited state we have

$$\Delta T = T\left(\boldsymbol{\theta}^x, p = 1\right) - T\left(\boldsymbol{\theta}^n, p = 0\right) = T\left(\boldsymbol{\theta}^x, 1\right) - T\left(\boldsymbol{\theta}^n, 0\right) \tag{15.20}$$

Let's look at the term $T\left(\boldsymbol{\theta}^x, 1\right)$. To first order one can write

$$\boldsymbol{\theta}^x = \boldsymbol{\theta}^n + \Delta\boldsymbol{\theta}^{nx} \tag{15.21}$$

Expanding the function T in the excited state gives

$$
\begin{aligned}
T\left(\boldsymbol{\theta}^x, 1\right) &= T\left(\boldsymbol{\theta}^n + \Delta\boldsymbol{\theta}^{nx}, 1\right) \\
&= T\left(\boldsymbol{\theta}^n, 1\right) + \Delta\boldsymbol{\theta}^{nx} \frac{\partial T\left(\boldsymbol{\theta}^n, 1\right)}{\partial \boldsymbol{\theta}^n} + \ldots
\end{aligned} \tag{15.22}
$$

So, the derivative is taken in the *excited* state with respect to the coefficients in the *normal* state.

As for the term $T\left(\boldsymbol{\theta}^n, 1\right)$, one can formally write the identity $T\left(\boldsymbol{\theta}^n, 1\right) = T\left(\boldsymbol{\theta}^n, 0\right) + \left[T\left(\boldsymbol{\theta}^n, 1\right) - T\left(\boldsymbol{\theta}^n, 0\right)\right]$,[2] and therefore

$$
\begin{aligned}
\Delta T &= T\left(\boldsymbol{\theta}^x, 1\right) - T\left(\boldsymbol{\theta}^n, 0\right) \\
&= T\left(\boldsymbol{\theta}^n, 1\right) + \frac{\partial T\left(\boldsymbol{\theta}^n, 1\right)}{\partial \boldsymbol{\theta}^n} \Delta\boldsymbol{\theta}^{nx} - T\left(\boldsymbol{\theta}^n, 0\right) \\
&= T\left(\boldsymbol{\theta}^n, 0\right) + \left[T\left(\boldsymbol{\theta}^n, 1\right) - T\left(\boldsymbol{\theta}^n, 0\right)\right] + \frac{\partial T\left(\boldsymbol{\theta}^n, 1\right)}{\partial \boldsymbol{\theta}^n} \Delta\boldsymbol{\theta}^{nx} - T\left(\boldsymbol{\theta}^n, 0\right) \\
&= T\left(\boldsymbol{\theta}^n, 1\right) - T\left(\boldsymbol{\theta}^n, 0\right) + \frac{\partial T\left(\boldsymbol{\theta}^n, 1\right)}{\partial \boldsymbol{\theta}^n} \Delta\boldsymbol{\theta}^{nx} \tag{15.25}
\end{aligned}
$$

The same, of course, applies to the hedging instruments. We can therefore write

$$\boldsymbol{b}^{nx} \equiv \left(\frac{\partial T\left(\boldsymbol{\theta}_t^n, 1\right)}{\partial a_n}, \ldots, \frac{\partial T\left(\boldsymbol{\theta}_t^n, 1\right)}{\partial \lambda}, T(\boldsymbol{\theta}_t^n, 1) - T(\boldsymbol{\theta}_t^n, 0) \right) \tag{15.26}$$

---

[2]If one so wanted, one could formally interpret the identity $T\left(\theta^n, 1\right) = T\left(\theta^n, 0\right) + \left[T\left(\theta^n, 1\right) - T\left(\theta^n, 0\right)\right]$ as

$$T\left(\theta^n, 1\right) = T\left(\theta^n, 0\right) + \frac{\Delta T\left(\theta^n, 0\right)}{\Delta p} \Delta p \tag{15.23}$$

$$= T\left(\theta^n, 0\right) + \frac{T\left(\theta^n, 1\right) - T\left(\theta^n, 0\right)}{1 - 0}(1 - 0) \tag{15.24}$$

and

$$
A^{nx} \equiv \begin{pmatrix}
\frac{\partial S_1(\boldsymbol{\theta}_t^n, 1)}{\partial a_n} & \frac{\partial S_2(\boldsymbol{\theta}_t^n, 1)}{\partial a_n} & \cdots & \frac{\partial S_N(\boldsymbol{\theta}_t^n, 1)}{\partial a_n} \\
\vdots & \vdots & \ddots & \vdots \\
\frac{\partial S_1(\boldsymbol{\theta}_t^n, 1)}{\partial \lambda} & \frac{\partial S_2(\boldsymbol{\theta}_t^n, 1)}{\partial \lambda} & \cdots & \frac{\partial S_N(\boldsymbol{\theta}_t^n, 1)}{\partial \lambda} \\
S_1(\boldsymbol{\theta}_t^n, 1) - S_1(\boldsymbol{\theta}_t^n, 0) & \cdots & \cdots & S_N(\boldsymbol{\theta}_t^n, 1) - S_N(\boldsymbol{\theta}_t^n, 0)
\end{pmatrix} \tag{15.27}
$$

where a_n is the generic component of the normal vector $\boldsymbol{\theta}^n$.

If we redefine the column vector as

$$
\Delta \boldsymbol{\theta}^{nx} \equiv \begin{pmatrix} \Delta \boldsymbol{\theta}^{nx} \\ 1 \end{pmatrix}
$$

we can write

$$
\Delta \pi = -\Delta \boldsymbol{\theta}^{nx}.(A^{nx} \boldsymbol{w} - \boldsymbol{b}^{nx}) \tag{15.28}
$$

We have managed to recast the expression for the change in the portfolio during the normal-to-excited transitions exactly in the same form as in the normal-to-normal case. From this point on we can therefore follow exactly the same procedure to minimize the portfolio variance as we did above. When we do this, we find that we have to make use of the counterpart of $\boldsymbol{\Theta}^{nn}$, i.e., of the quantity $\boldsymbol{\Theta}^{nx}$:

$$
\boldsymbol{\Theta}^{nx} = \mathbb{E}[\Delta \boldsymbol{\theta}^{nx} (\Delta \boldsymbol{\theta}^{nx})^{\dagger}] \tag{15.29}
$$

with

$$
\boldsymbol{\Theta}^{nx} = \boldsymbol{\Omega}^{nx} + \boldsymbol{\mu}^{\dagger} \boldsymbol{\mu} \tag{15.30}
$$

The quantity $\boldsymbol{\Theta}^{nx}$ is therefore linked via Equation (15.30) to the empirical covariance matrix of the changes in the coefficients when there is a transition from the normal to the excited state. We clearly do not have many instances of this transition, and our uncertainty in the resulting covariance matrix (and in the vector of means $\boldsymbol{\mu}$) is therefore correspondingly large. This is where our knowledge of regularities in the changes in the swaption matrix comes in, and this knowledge can be used to 'regularize' our solution.

15.4.3 Normal-to-Unknown Transition

In reality we don't know for sure whether tomorrow we will be in a normal or in an excited state. Let $\mathbb{I}_{nn}$ be the indicator function equal to 1 when there is a normal-to-normal transition and 0 otherwise, and let $\mathbb{I}_{nx} = (1 - \mathbb{I}_{nn})$ be the indicator function for the normal-to-excited transition. It then follows that the change in our portfolio, $\Delta \pi$, is given by

$$
\Delta \pi = -\mathbb{I}_{nn} \Delta \boldsymbol{\theta}^{nn}.(A^{nn} \boldsymbol{w} - \boldsymbol{b}^{nn}) - \mathbb{I}_{nx} \Delta \boldsymbol{\theta}^{nx}.(A^{nx} \boldsymbol{w} - \boldsymbol{b}^{nx}) \tag{15.31}
$$

For our choice of volatility function, with 14 hedging instruments we could (in theory) make $\Delta \pi = 0$ for any values of $\mathbb{I}_{nn}$, $\Delta \boldsymbol{\theta}^{nn}$ and $\Delta \boldsymbol{\theta}^{nx}$. All the *caveats* about quasi-colinearity and 'bad' solutions now apply in spades. We would therefore like to use far fewer hedging instruments than 14, and so we proceed as above, and consider $\mathbb{E}[\Delta\pi^2]$:

$$\mathbb{E}[\Delta\pi^2] = p_{nn}(A^{nn}\boldsymbol{w} - \boldsymbol{b}^{nn})^{\dagger}\boldsymbol{\Theta}^{nn}(A^{nn}\boldsymbol{w} - \boldsymbol{b}^{nn})$$
$$+p_{nx}(A^{nx}\boldsymbol{w} - \boldsymbol{b}^{nx})^{\dagger}\boldsymbol{\Theta}^{nx}(A^{nx}\boldsymbol{w} - \boldsymbol{b}^{nx}) \tag{15.32}$$

where p_{nn} is the probability of staying in the normal state. Again taking the derivative with respect to $\boldsymbol{w}$, we have

$$A^{*}\boldsymbol{w} = \boldsymbol{b}^{*} \tag{15.33}$$

where now

$$A^{*} \equiv p_{nn}(A^{nn})^{\dagger}\boldsymbol{\Theta}^{nn}A^{nn} + p_{nx}(A^{nx})^{\dagger}\boldsymbol{\Theta}^{nx}A^{nx} \tag{15.34}$$

and

$$\boldsymbol{b}^{*} \equiv p_{nn}(A^{nn})^{\dagger}\boldsymbol{\Theta}^{nn}\boldsymbol{b}^{nn} + p_{nx}(A^{nx})^{\dagger}\boldsymbol{\Theta}^{nx}\boldsymbol{b}^{nx} \tag{15.35}$$

The quantity p_{nn} is the probability of remaining in the normal state, and is also estimated from the time series. To give an idea of the orders of magnitude, in the case we present below p_{nn} turned out to be 94.5%.

Note that we could have chosen to minimize $\mathbb{E}[|\Delta\pi|]$, or any other sensible expectation. However, by minimizing the chi-square, we put a lot of weight on preventing the large changes in portfolio value that would occur from a jump to the excited state. Thus even though p_{nx} is only 5.5%, the second term is very important.

15.4.4   Starting from the Excited State

Mutatis mutandis, hedging when we are currently in the excited state follows the same procedure.

15.5   Results

In order to test the quality of the survival hedging suggested above we attempted to preserve the value of a trigger swap under different market conditions: during normal times, during excited periods and during transitions from normal to excited states.

The underlying swap is a 10-year par swap, which will be cancelled if 6-month LIBOR resets in two years' time 1% below its time-0 forward level. The changes in the implied volatilities surface used as input to price the trigger swap and the various instruments used for the hedge were taken as actually encountered in reality (US$). We show below the results obtained using different 'patches' of actual changes in market implied volatilities over various 40-day periods. The weights of the hedging instruments were determined as described above and kept unchanged during the 40 days of the experiment.

15.5.1 Hedging Results for the Normal-to-Normal Transition

In the simplest test we looked at the performance of the survival hedging strategy during a normal-only period, started on 20th August 2005. The not-very-exciting results are shown in Figure 15.6. White and Rebonato (2008) chose to use only two hedging instruments: a two-year caplet (to capture the exposure to the 6-month index rate); and a 2 × 8-year swaption (to capture the exposure to the rate liable to be cancelled). The weights turned out to be 11.04 for the caplet and 0.50 for the swaption. Many other combinations would have given rise to reasonable and stable hedges. As the figure shows, the value of the unhedged trigger swap changes between 425 and 481 basis points (a variation in price of 13%). See the line labelled 'Trigger Swap Price'. The value of the hedged portfolio is displayed by the line 'Hedge with Offset'. One can see that its value changes over the same period by less than 2% (with most of the slippage occurring on a single day).

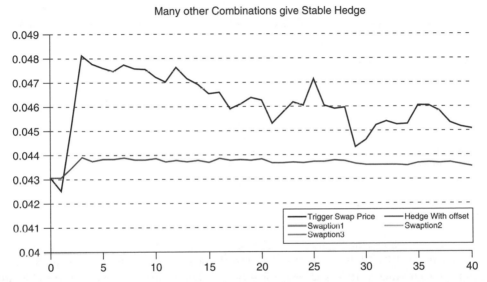

Figure 15.6 Hedge example: normal-to-normal state. Underlying 10y swap (at par), cancelled if 2y LIBOR (6m) is 1% below the current forward rate. Portfolio set up on 29-08-05 and held for 40 days (value is offset to equal trigger price on day 1). Natural hedge with 2y caplet and 2y × 8y (weights 11.04 and 0.50). Many other combinations give a stable hedge.

15.5.2 Hedging Results for the Normal-to-Excited Transition

Low Convexity

More interesting results are displayed in Figure 15.7. Here the same exercise was conducted during a period (the 40 days starting on 2nd July 1999) when there is a transition between a normal and an excited state. The weights for the caplet and the swaption are now 6.24 and 0.54, respectively. The change in value of the trigger swap is now much more dramatic (from 449 to 655 basis points), but the hedged portfolio remains remarkably stable, moving by just a few basis points around the initial value of 449 basis points. The results are clearly excellent, but we note that the turbulence occurs relatively early in the life of the trigger swap, and the convexity due to the trigger condition is therefore rather muted, making the test relatively easy. In order to put our methodology under more severe stress, we place the look condition of the trigger swap close to the onset of a large normal-to-excited transition. This is what we call a 'high convexity' test.

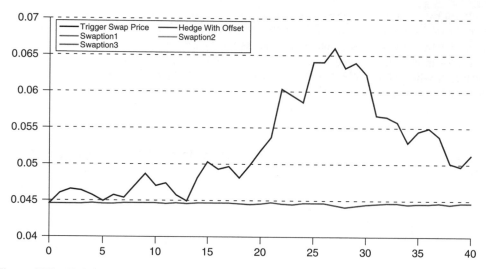

Figure 15.7   Hedge example: normal-to-excited state. Underlying 10y swap (at par), cancelled if 2y LIBOR (6m) is 1% below the current forward rate. Portfolio set up on 02-07-99 and held for 40 days (value is offset to equal trigger price on day 1). Natural hedge with 2y caplet and 2y × 8y (weights 6.24 and 0.56). Market starts in normal state but flips rapidly between states.

High Convexity: Correct Hedging

The results are shown in Figure 15.8. The underlying swap is a 10-year swap (at par), cancelled if 6m LIBOR is 1% below the current forward rate. The notional portfolio is set up on 10th August 1998 and held for 40 days. The caplet and swaption weights are now 20.4 and 0.454, respectively. Note that the value of the unhedged trigger swap changes dramatically from close to 0 to almost 200 basis points, and that a large part of the change is driven by the volatility curve change observed on 28th August 1998. Despite these dramatic changes the hedged portfolio keeps its value reasonably well, with a total slippage of about 30 basis points.

High Convexity: Wrong Hedging

Finally, we highlight the importance of including in the hedging strategy knowledge about the normal-to-excited transitions, even if these are relatively rare. To show this, we consider exactly the same deal and the same volatility history as above, but we only put in place the hedges that would apply to the normal-to-normal transition. This results in a lower higher weight for the caplet (from 20.4 to 3.51) and virtually no swaption hedge (the swaption weight goes from 0.454 to 0.014). This makes sense: if, close to the trigger condition, the trigger swap is worth as little as a few basis points, *and if there are no sudden moves to an*

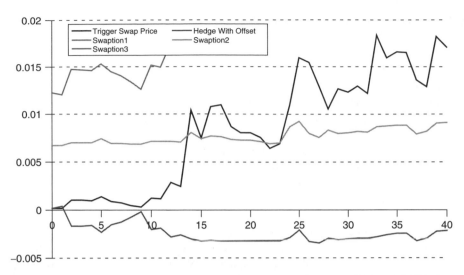

Figure 15.8   High-convexity case. The caplet and swaption weights are 20.4 and 0.454, i.e., now considering the swaption.

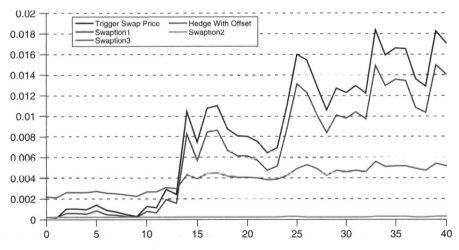

Figure 15.9   High convexity options. Underlying 10y swap (at par), cancelled if 6m LIBOR is 1% below the current forward rate. Portfolio set up on 10-08-98 and held for 40 days (value is offset to equal trigger price on day 1). Natural hedge with 6m caplet and 6m × 9.5y (weights 3.51 and 0.014). Here only the normal-to-normal hedge is applied, and it failed dramatically due to a large change in parameters (driven by curve change on 28-08-98).

excited state, there is very little chance for the trigger condition to do anything interesting. A sudden change in the market conditions does happen, however, during the period under analysis and now the simplistic hedge fails miserably. This is shown in Figure 15.9, which clearly displays that, when the transition occurs (28th August 1998), the hedged portfolio just does not have the right make-up to counteract the sudden change in value of the trigger swap, and its value simply drifts along with the value of the instrument it was supposed to hedge.

15.6   Are We Getting Something for Nothing?

In general 'survival hedges' are presented in terms of long out-of-the-money options. These hedging strategies are rarely put in place by traders because the insurance cost of the option (the 'negative carry' of its theta) is perceived to be too high. Here we do not seem to be paying any insurance premium, yet we achieve a portfolio that appears to be insulated from market turbulence. How are we getting something for nothing? Or, are we?

The solution of the conundrum is that with a bought-insurance hedging strategy the trader insures herself against losses if things 'go badly', but retains the upside potential if the market changes are such as to produce a windfall gain (after all, if a hedge fails, we could in theory even *make* money).

The survival hedging strategy we propose, on the other hand, attempts to anchor the value of the portfolio to zero, and therefore 'pays' for the downward protection by giving up the possible upside when the turmoil has set in and all the bets are off. The comparison between our strategy and the bought-insurance case is therefore not really fair. A more appropriate comparison would be with a collar option strategy (whereby the bought protection against the downside is financed by selling the possible gain in a 'favourable turmoil').

References

Andersen, L. and Andreasen, J. (1998) 'Volatility skews and extensions of the LIBOR market model', Working paper, General Re, New York.

Andersen, L. and Andreasen, J. (2000) 'Volatility skews and extensions of the Libor market model', *Applied Mathematical Finance*, **7**(1), 1–32.

Ash, R. B. (1965) *Information Theory*. Dover, New York.

Bartlett, B. (2006) 'Hedging under SABR Model', *Wilmott Magazine*, **July/August**, 2–4.

Baxter, M. and Rennie, A. (1996) *Financial Calculus: An Introduction to Derivatives Pricing*. Cambridge University Press, Cambridge.

Black, F. (1976) 'The pricing of commodity contracts', *Journal of Financial Economics*, **3**, 167–179.

Bouchaud, J. and Potters, M. (2000) *Theory of Financial Risks–From Statistical Physics to Risk Management*. Cambridge University Press, Cambridge.

Bouchaud, J.-P. and Potters, M. (2003) *Theory of Financial Risk and Derivative Pricing: From Statistical Physics to Risk Management*, 2nd edn. Cambridge University Press, Cambridge.

Brace, A., Gatarek, D. and Musiela, M. (1997) 'The market model of interest rate dynamics', *Mathematical Finance*, **7**, 127–147.

Burridge, P. (2007) Private communication.

Campbell, J. Y., Lo, A. W. and MacKinlay, A. C. (1996) *The Econometrics of Financial Markets*, Princeton University Press, Princeton, NJ.

Castagna, A., Mercurio, F. and Tarenghi, M. (2007) 'Smile consistent CMS adjustment in closed form: introducing the vanna–volga approach'.

Cover, T. M. and Thomas, J. A. (2006) *Elements of Information Theory*. Wiley InterScience, Chichester.

Deguillaume (2008) Master's thesis.

Derman, E. and Kani, I. (1994) 'The volatility smile and its implied tree', *Goldman Sachs, Quantitative Strategies Research Notes*.

Derman, E., Kani, I. and Zou, J. Z. (1996) 'The local volatility surface: unlocking the information in index option prices', *Financial Analysts Journal*, **52**(4), 25–36. doi:10.2469/faj.v52.n4.2008.

Doust, P. (1995) 'Relative pricing techniques in the swaps and options markets', *Journal of Financial Engineering*, **4**(1), 11–46.

Doust, P. (2007) 'Modelling discrete probabilities', Quantitative Analysis Group, RBS.

Doust, P. (2008) 'Two useful techniques for financial modelling problems', Submitted to *Applied Mathematical Finance*.

Duffie, D. (2001) *Dynamic Asset Pricing Theory*, 3rd edn. Princeton University Press, Princeton, NJ.

Dupire, B. (1994) 'Pricing with a smile', *RISK*, **7**, 18–20.

Dybvig, P. and Ross, S. (1992) *The New Palgrave Dictionary of Money and Finance Arbitrage*, Newman, P., Milgate, M. and Eatwell, J. (eds). Palgrave Macmillan, London.

Eberlein, E. and Ozkan, F. (2005) 'The Levy LIBOR model', *Finance and Stochastics*, **9**, 327–348.

Etheridge, A. (2002) *A Course in Financial Calculus*. Cambridge University Press, Cambridge.

Glasserman, P. and Kou, S. G. (2003) 'The term structure of simple forward rates with jump risk', *Mathematical Finance*, **13**.

Hagan, P. (2003) 'Convexity conundrums: pricing CMS swaps, caps, and floors', *Wilmott Magazine*, **March**, 38–44.

Hagan, P., Kumar, D., Lesniewski, A. and Woodward, D. (2002) 'Managing smile risk', *Wilmott Magazine*, **September**, 84–108.

Hamilton, J. D. (1994) *Time Series Analysis*. Princeton University Press, Princeton, NJ.

Harrison, J. M. and Kreps, D. M. (1979) 'Martingales and arbitrage in multiperiod securities markets', *Journal of Economic Theory*, **20**(3), 381–408. doi:10.1016/0022-0531(79)90043-7.

Henry-Labordere, P. (2007) 'Unifying the BGM and SABR models: a short ride in hyperbolic geometry', SSRN http://ssrn.com/abstract=877762.

Hughston, L. and Brody, D. C. (2000) 'Modern theory of interest rates–with extensions to foreign exchange, inflation and credit', Imperial College and King's College London, Lecture Notes.

Hughston, L. P. (2003) *Modern Risk Management: A History*. Chapter 7: The Past, Present, and Future of Term Structure Modelling. Risk Publications.

Hull, J. and White, A. (2000) 'Forward rate volatilities, swap rate volatilities, and the implementation of the LIBOR market model', *Journal of Fixed Income*.

Hunter, C. J., Jaeckel, P. and Joshi, M. S. (2001) 'Drift approximations in a forward-rate based LIBOR market model', published in *Risk Magazine* as 'Getting the drift'.

Hyvarinen, A., Karhunen, J. and Oja, E. (2001) *Independent Component Analysis*. John Wiley, Chichester.

Jaeckel, P. and Rebonato, R. (2002) 'The link between caplet and swaption volatilities in a BGM/J framework: approximate solutions and empirical evidence'.

Jamshidian, F. (1997) 'LIBOR and swap market models and measures', *Finance and Stochastics*, **1**, 293–330.

Joshi, M. S. and Rebonato, R. (2003) 'A stochastic volatility displaced-diffusion extension of the LIBOR market model', *Quantitative Finance*, **3**(6), 458–469.

Joshi, M. S. and Stacey, A. M. (2006) 'New and robust drift approximations for the Libor market model'.

Joshi, M. S. and Stacey, A. M. (2008) 'New and robust drift approximations for the LIBOR market model', *Quantitative Finance*, **8**(4), 427–434. doi:10.1080/14697680701458000.

Karatzas, I. and Shreve, S. E. (1991) *Brownian Motion and Stochastic Calculus*, 2nd edn. Springer-Verlag, New York.

Karatzas, I. and Shreve, S. E. (1998) *Methods of Mathematical Finance*. Springer-Verlag, New York.

Kluge, W. (2005) 'Time-inhomogeneous Levy processes in interest rate and credit models', Ph.D. thesis, University of Freiburg.

Lengwiler, Y. (2006) *Microfoundations of Financial Economics: An Introduction to General Equilibrium Asset Pricing*. Princeton University Press, Princeton, NJ.

MacKay, D. J. C. (2003) *Information Theory, Inference, and Learning Algorithms*. Cambridge University Press, Cambridge.

Madan, D. B. and Carr, P. P. (1998) 'The variance gamma process and option pricing', *European Finance Review*, **2**.

Madan, D. B. and Seneta, E. (1990) 'The variance gamma (V.G.) model for share market returns', *The Journal of Business*, **63**.

Mantegna, R. N. and Stanley, H. E. (1999) *An Introduction to Econophysics: Correlations and Complexity in Finance*. Cambridge University Press, Cambridge.

McKay, K. (2009) Ph.D. thesis, London School of Economics.

Merton, R. (1992) *Continuous-Time Finance*. Blackwell Publishers, Oxford.

Mikosch, T. (1998) *Elementary Stochastic Calculus, with Finance in View: 6 (Advanced Series on Statistical Science & Applied Probability)*. World Scientific, Singapore.

Neftci, S. N. (1996) *An Introduction to the Mathematics of Financial Derivatives*, 1st edn. Academic Press, New York.

Piterbarg, V. (2003) 'A stochastic volatility forward Libor model with a term structure of volatility smiles', SSRN http://ssrn.com/abstract=472061.

Piterbarg, V. (2005) 'Time to smile', *Risk*, 71–75.

Pogudin, A. (2008) 'Theoretical and practical aspects of hedging within SABR and LMM-SABR models', M.Sc. in Mathematical Finance, Oxford University.

Press, W., Teukolsky, S., Vetterling, W. and Flannery, B. (1992) *Numerical Recipes in C: The Art of Scientific Computing*, 2nd edn. Cambridge University Press, Cambridge.

Rabiner, L. (1989) 'A tutorial on hidden Markov models and selected applications in speech recognition', *Proc. IEEE*, **77**(2), 257–286.

Rachev, S. T., Hsu, J. S. J., Bagasheva, B. S. and Fabozzi, F. J. (2008) *Bayesian Methods in Finance*. John Wiley, Chichester.

Rebonato, R. (1999a) *Volatility and Correlation*. John Wiley, Chichester.

Rebonato, R. (1999b) 'On the simultaneous calibration of multifactor lognormal interest rate models to Black volatilities and to the correlation matrix', *Journal of Computational Finance*, **2**(4), 5–27. Working paper available at http://www.RiccardoRebonato.co.uk/.

Rebonato, R. (1999c) 'On the pricing implications of the joint lognormal assumption for the swaption and cap markets', *Journal of Computational Finance*, **2**(3), 30–52. Working paper available at http://www.RiccardoRebonato.co.uk/.

Rebonato, R. (2002) *Modern Pricing of Interest-Rate Derivatives: The LIBOR Market Model and Beyond*. Princeton University Press, Princeton, NJ.

Rebonato, R. (2003) 'Which process gives rise to the observed dependence of swaption implied volatilities on the underlying?', *International Journal of Theoretical and Applied Finance*, **6**(4), 419–442.

Rebonato, R. (2004a) *Volatility and Correlation: The Perfect Hedger and the Fox*, 2nd edn. John Wiley, Chichester.

Rebonato, R. (2004b) 'Interest-rate term-structure pricing models: a review', in *Proceedings of the Royal Society London*, Vol. **460**, pp. 1–62.

Rebonato, R. (2006) 'Forward-rate volatilities and the swaption matrix: why neither time-homogeneity nor time dependence will do', *International Journal of Theoretical and Applied Finance*, **9**(5), 323–356. doi:10.1142/S0219024906003767.

Rebonato, R. (2007a) *Plight of the Fortune Tellers*. Princeton University Press, Princeton, NJ.

Rebonato, R. (2007b) 'A time-homogeneous, SABR-consistent extension of the LMM', *RISK*.

Rebonato, R. and Chen, J. (2008) 'Evidence for state transition and altered serial correlation in US$ interest rates', accepted for publication in *Quantitative Finance* and available at http://www.riccardorebonato.co.uk/.

Rebonato, R. and Cooper, I. (1995) 'Limitations of simple two-factor interest-rate models', *Journal Financial Engineering*, **5**, 1–16.

Rebonato, R. and Cooper, I. (1998) 'Coupling backward induction with Monte Carlo simulations: a Fast Fourier Transform approach', *Applied Mathematical Finance*, **5**.

Rebonato, R. and Gaspari, V. (2006) 'Analysis of drawdowns and drawups in the US$ interest-rate market', *Quantitatice Finance*, **6**(4), 297–326. doi:10.1080/14697680600680555.

Rebonato, R. and Jaeckel, P. (2000) 'The most general methodology to create a valid correlation matrix for risk management and option pricing purposes', *Journal of Risk*, pp. 17–27.

Rebonato, R. and Joshi, M. (2002) 'A joint empirical and theoretical investigation of the modes of deformation of swaption matrices: implications for the stochastic-volatility LIBOR market model', *International Journal of Theoretical and Applied Finance*, **5**(7), 667–694.

Rebonato, R. and Kainth, D. (2004) 'A two-regime, stochastic-volatility extension of the LIBOR market model', *International Journal of Theoretical and Applied Finance*, **7**(5), 555–575.

Rebonato, R. and McKay, K. (2009) 'Estimation of volatility and correlation within the SABR framework', LSE working paper.

Rebonato, R. and White, R. (2008) 'Linking caplets and swaptions prices in the LMM-SABR model' accepted for publication in *Journal of Computational Finance*.

Rebonato, R., Pogudin, A. and White, R. (2008) 'Delta and vega hedging in the SABR and LMM-SABR models', *Risk*, December.

Redner, S. (1990) 'Random multiplicative processes: an elementary tutorial', *American Journal of Physics*, **58**(3), 267–273. doi:10.1119/1.16497.

Ross, S. A. (2004) *Neoclassical Finance*. Princeton University Press, Princeton, NJ.

Rutkowski, M. (1998) 'Dynamics of spot, forward and futures LIBOR rates', *International Journal of Theoretical and Applied Finance*, **1**(3), 425–445.

Schoenmakers, J. G. M. and Coffey, B. (2000) 'Stable implied calibration of a multi-factor LIBOR model via a semi-parametric correlation structure', Weierstrass-Institut fuer Angewandte Analysis und Stochastik, Working paper No. 61, Berlin.

Sornette, D. (2003) *Critical Phenomena in Natural Sciences: Chaos, Fractals, Selforganization and Disorder: Concepts and Tools*. Springer-Verlag, New York.

Sornette, D. (2006) *Critical Phenomena in Natural Sciences: Chaos, Fractals, Selforganization and Disorder: Concepts and Tools*, 2nd edn. Springer-Verlag, New York.

Taylor, S. J. (1986) *Modelling Financial Time Series*. John Wiley, Chichester.

Taylor, S. J. (2005) *Asset Price Dynamics, Volatility and Prediction*. Princeton University Press, Princeton, NJ.

White, R. and Rebonato, R. (2008) 'A swaption volatility model using Markov regime switching'.

Wigner, E. (1951) 'On a class of analytic functions from the quantum theory of collisions', *The Annals of Mathematics*, **53**(1), 36–67.

Index

Index compiled by Terry Halliday